Missing 411

THE DEVIL'S IN THE DETAIL

DAVID PAULIDES

Copyright © 2014 David Paulides
All rights reserved.

ISBN: 1495246426
ISBN 13: 9781495246425
Library of Congress Control Number: 2014901219
CreateSpace Independent Publishing Platform
North Charleston, South Carolina

Big Devil Lake • Devil's Doorway • Devil's Marsh • Seven Devils Mountains • Devil's Lake • He Devil Lake • Devil's Throne • Devil's Nest • Devil's Canyon • Kane Point • Purgatory Mountain • Devil's Den • Devil's Ridge • Devil's Backbone • He Devil • She Devil • Purgatory Lake • Seven Devils Lake • Devil's Tower • Devil's Postpile • Devil's Slide • Purgatory Flat • Purgatory Ridge • Devil Canyon • Devil Hill • Kill Devil Hills • Devil Track River • Devil's Corner • Devil's Chair • Devil's Washbowl • Devil's Rock • Devil's Kitchen • Devil's Hopyard • Devil's Island • Devil's Gap • Devil's Gorge • Devil's Plunge • Devil's Mouth • Devil's Wharf • Satan's Ridge • Hell Hole • Hell's Hollow Brook • Devil's Churn • Devil's Belt • Devil's Hole • Devil's Nose • Devil's Elbow • Devil's Creek • Devil's Point • Dirty Devil River • Devil's Paw • Devil's Creek Reservoir • Devil's Leap • Devil's Stairway • Damnation Creek • Lower Devil Lake • Upper Devil Lake • Devil's River • Monte Diablo • Devil's Step • Devil's Dance Floor • Devil's Window • Devil's Playground • Devil's Twist • Devil's Back Trail • Devil's Half Acre • Devil's Horseshoe • Devil's Limb • Devil's Wall • Devil's Bog Brook • Devil's Triangle • Devil's Post Pile • Devil's Garden • Diablo Valley • Diablo Mountains • Satan Pass • Hell's Half Acre • Seven Devils Spring • Lucifer Falls • Big Devil Swamp • Hells Half Mile • Devil's Corral • Devil's Dining Room • Devil's Fork • Devil's Knob • Devil's Orchard • Devil's Chair • Hell's Mesa • Devil's Chasm • Devil's Park • Devil's Washbasin • Devil's Throat • Devil's Bathtub • Devil's Bayou • Devil's Toenail • Devil's Den Hollow • Devil's Slide Rapids • Route 666 • Devil's Creek Spring • Devil's Run • Hellfire Run • Devil's Tea Table • Devil's Wedge • Devil's Potato Patch • Devil's Hammock • Devil's Garden Volcanic Field • Devil's Prong • Hell's Hollow • Devil's Hole Prairie • Hell Run • Diablo Range • Devil's Den Canyon • Devil's Pond • Devil's Bog • Kill Devil Hill • Devil's Dump Run • Devil's Orchard • Devil's Brach • Damnation Creek • Devil's Step • Satan Hill • Devil's Elbow Swamp • Devil's Clay Hole • Hell Hole Bayou • Devil's Bathtub Spring • Devil's Drain • Devil's Icebox • Devil's Wash Pan • Devil's Fork Creek • Devil's Cellar Hollow • Devil's Salt Cellar Ridge • Devil's Looking Glass • Devil's Spring Mesa • Devil's Wind Pipe • Hellgate Mountain • Devil's Brave Mesa • Hell Roaring Creek • Devil's Tooth • Devil's Graveyard • Devil's Hole Lakes • Hells Canyon Draw • Red Devil Mountain • Lucifer Lake • Devil's Pulpit • Devil's Stairs • Devil's Smoke Stack • Devil's Dome • Devil's Butte • Devil's Cascade • Devil's Marsh • Purgatory Flat • Devil's Pool • Devil's Wash Pan • Devil's Rose • Devil's Rock • Devil's Oven Lake • Devil's Crag • Devil's Playground • Hell Thicket Creek • Little Devil's Tower • Devil's Peak

Dedication

To All Search and Rescue Personnel

This book is dedicated to the men and women who have given their time, effort, and skill to finding missing people throughout the world. Many of you are volunteers who spend your personal time and money refining your skills and looking for the missing, sacrificing your time away from your families in the humanitarian effort of finding someone who is in desperate need of your assistance.

To the professional leadership offered by the first responders in all search and rescue efforts, this THANK YOU will never be enough. Every search and rescue team member has been dispatched in horrific weather, has missed holiday time with family and friends, and has generally pushed the level of human endurance. Much of society doesn't understand that the volunteer SAR member is the backbone of the search effort. We will forever be thankful for your generosity and love of humanity.

MISSING 411-THE DEVIL'S IN THE DETAILS

Introduction · *xi*

Chapter One: United States · *1*
   Alabama · *1*
   Arizona · *2*
   Arkansas · *11*
   California · *22*
   California-Central Sierra · *27*
   California-Central Coast · *32*
   California-San Francisco Bay Area · · · · · · · · · · · · · · · · · · *39*
   California-Southern · *42*
   Colorado · *46*
   Florida · *96*
   Hawaii · *104*
   Idaho · *106*
   Illinois · *119*
   Kansas · *121*
   Maine · *123*
   Maryland · *125*
   Massachusetts · *129*
   Michigan · *130*
   Minnesota · *140*
   Missouri · *143*
   Montana · *146*
   New Hampshire · *151*
   New Mexico · *154*
   New York · *163*
   North Carolina · *172*
   Oklahoma · *174*
   Oregon · *175*
   Pennsylvania · *178*
   South Carolina · *192*

Tennessee *195*
Texas *196*
Utah *198*
Virginia *201*
Washington *206*
Washington/Idaho Border *234*
West Virginia *239*
Wisconsin *241*
Wyoming *245*

Chapter Two: Canada *250*
  Alberta *250*
  British Columbia *252*
  Manitoba *259*
  Nova Scotia *260*
  Ontario *264*
  Quebec *265*
  Saskatchewan *267*

Chapter Three: Australia *270*
  New South Wales *270*
  Queensland *290*
  South Australia *294*
  Victoria *296*
  Western Australia *298*

Chapter Four: Borneo *300*

Chapter Five: Ecuador *303*

Chapter Six: United Kingdom *307*

Chapter Seven: New Zealand *311*

Chapter Eight: Switzerland *316*

Chapter Nine: Austria *320*

Conclusions · 323
   Cornerstone Cases · 323
   Weather Conditions · 326
   Criminal Allegations · 333
   Last in Line · 339
   Missing from inside the Home · 347
   Missing from inside a Vehicle · 348
   Locations Previously Searched · 349
   Scholars/Intellectuals · 352
   Disabled or Injured · 357
   Elevation Gain · 360
   Distance Traveled · 361
   Aircraft Associated with Missing Person Cases · · · · · · · · · 365
   List of Missing from this Book · 367
   National Parks · 396

Index · 401

INTRODUCTION

If you've read my Missing 411 books in the past, you know that it's the details inside the stories that make this series unusual. The stories about missing people are heartrending and bothersome, but without getting into the specific elements in each incident, a pattern would not emerge.

Isolated readers have commented that the stories seem to be repetitive. If I hadn't fed you a series of factual incidents explaining the repetitive nature of the cases, some would say I was fabricating the stories and the number of times the same case facts appear. Until you read hundreds of cases and understand the repetitive nature of the elements that exist, it would be very difficult to admit there is an underlying current to these incidents.

Without studying the multitude of cases, each individual event would merely be another missing person case. The FBI profiler does much of what we've done in reviewing criminal events to substantiate there is a serial element to any crime spree. Without that mass amount of data, without committing yourself to opening your mind to an unusual series of events, you won't see it. It's easy to deny anything. It takes an open mind, patience, and an aptitude for learning to uncover what might be occurring.

A few elements that we have tracked for the last four years are starting to emerge as a trend. We have been documenting individuals with a disability who disappear. The case may include autism, senility, an injured knee, or even diabetes. We opened this section to any condition that may require a pharmaceutical prescribed product or something that greatly inhibits lifestyle. On the opposite end of this scale, we added a section for scholars. We have been silently tracking this element in people who have disappeared who are highly intellectual. The number of very smart people who have vanished may surprise the reader. It may shock you when you learn the backgrounds of some of the individuals who have vanished and never been found.

Another refined element is claims of criminal conduct associated with a disappearance. You will be presented with a graph outlining the number of cases where family members, law enforcement, and involved parties have made allegations associated with the missing that some type of criminal conduct has taken place. The most common allegation by law enforcement is that the person had been abducted or kidnapped. I can tell you from personal experience, law enforcement is always reluctant to say a crime has occurred unless they have solid evidence. Police officers and deputy sheriffs don't like to be embarrassed, so if they are in doubt, they say very little.

Past readers of my books will instantly know that weather plays a major role in many of the cases we've chronicled. The usual involvement is that near the time the person disappears, the weather starts to turn bad, and rain and or snow inundates the area. There is a case in this book where the weather turns atrocious, and one of the biggest wind storms to ever hit a state engulfed a ranching area with the missing person in the middle of it. There seems to be a never-ending amount of cases where bad weather plays a major role on when and if the victim is found.

The idea that small children can disappear inside of homes is very troubling. Many parents have questioned how this can happen. We've presented cases where parents have set alarms on the doors. If they are opened, they know the child is going outside. In this specific case, the child and the dog got outside; the adult never heard anything, and the child was never found. How these events are happening without parental knowledge is a great question. There are more cases in this book that will baffle you and challenge your intellect to develop a logical answer.

If you are a parent and you've taken your kids to the mountains, you have no doubt walked the mountain trails with your children lagging behind. There was a *Huffington Post* book review written by Roger March titled: "*Missing 411-North America and Beyond*, Don't be Last in Line." Roger centered on the many cases where children disappear on a trail when they are last in line in the group. The same theory applies if you are walking ahead of a group on a trail—people are disappearing, and the results are unusual. In front of the line or far in back, danger exists, and there is a chart to exemplify it.

I have had dozens of people comment on the stories where children are found thousands of feet higher in elevation than where they had disappeared. We are not identifying older kids; these are toddlers. The most frequent comment from parents is that it's so obvious something else is happening. The child could never climb to those heights. I have included a chart that shows the ages, dates, and altitudes that these kids have achieved. This has bent our mind many times trying to understand what may be happening. There is a story in this book about a small girl who disappears from a rural location. The police chief gets worried and has the search team spread to outside the normal search areas. The girl is found on top of a mountain peak. Law enforcement makes the direct claim that the child was abducted and dumped there. The problem is, searchers were scouring the area when the child was found, and there doesn't seem to be any rational way for her to arrive at that location.

I get daily e-mails asking my personal opinion on what might be happening to the missing. I explain that I've received hundreds of e-mails from readers thanking me for not imparting my own beliefs about possible suspects and allowing readers to develop their own theories.

I will say that the field of suspects is narrowing.

One of the constant statements I make in interviews is that readers need to go outside of their normal comfort zone. If you've read a lot about Bigfoot, start reading about aliens. If you've studied reptoids, start reading about Lemurians. If you continue to stay on the same topics, you'll never see or hear the train coming down the tracks. As an example of this, Whitley Strieber read my books and invited me to appear on his radio show. He asked if I knew that one of the cases I documented in New York was mere miles from where he had one of his unusual encounters. I didn't know. I've also had e-mails from many listeners who claim I've nailed their beliefs through our research. They claim that I've proven their theory about what's happening, and they each point to different suspects on the list as the culprit. This is hard to accept, but I can't totally deny it, because I truly don't know. Whitley's claim is black-and-white. He wrote a book and documented the location, and it is mere miles from one of our victims who has never been found. I have always tried to stick with factual issues. If another researcher has solid evidence that something has happened in close proximity to what we've researched, we'll look at it.

There are many incidents in the world of strangeness that people have asked us to research. Many of the requests involve odd and unusual disappearances that have wild claims attached. We've looked at many of these and found that the vast majority of what you hear is absolute fabrication and opinion. In the incidents where there are few facts, we tend to stay away. I've actually gone to many law enforcement agencies and asked them to validate the claims circling in the media. The vast majority of the time, the detective laughs and offers to produce the report that proves it's a complete fabrication.

National Park Service

I have tried to steer clear of opinion about the law enforcement arm of the NPS and its handling of missing person cases. I believe the facts behind how the NPS deals with missing individuals are troublesome at best and criminally negligent at worst.

The NPS has a classification of "missing and presumed dead," which deals with cases where people have vanished and aren't in society. This is a method that the different arms of the Department of the Interior utilize to dispose of cases. In these cases, it doesn't count as a missing person statistic. They don't count the person as missing and don't place them on databases. Ultimately, this means that coroners and medical examiners who receive recovered remains can never place the bones with the body.

When we first started this project, we looked to the NPS for statistics about people missing inside their parks. The National Parks Service has a law enforcement arm that is trained at the best federal law enforcement training center in the world. These men and women are more highly trained then the majority of small-and medium-size police and sheriff's department officers. They are smart, well trained, and organized.

I originally asked NPS for a list of people missing from Yosemite National Park and a specific list from their entire NPS system.

Tracking missing people is not rocket science. It does not cost thousands of dollars and an expansive national computer system with special software. Each of the 392 parks and monuments under NPS only needs a clipboard and graph paper. Divide the paper into columns of location and date/time/case number/name/ disposition. Hang one clipboard in each of the 392 superintendents' offices. If someone goes missing, add them to your list. At the end of every month, the individual parks would send a monthly report to NPS headquarters. At headquarters you have a clerical staff that uses one inexpensive laptop with Excel software. Each month the clerk updates the missing person statistics. There is probably already a laptop at NPS that could be utilized for this application. I will purchase the clipboards and paper for each of the 183 locations if NPS would agree to this system. I know they won't.

I've had endless conversations about NPS and the Department of the Interior and their method of dealing with missing people. How in good conscience could they not track missing people? They have stated that they rely "on the institutional memory of our employees for questions like this." What if the employees with the knowledge retire? What if the employee with the knowledge transfers across country?

The NPS did respond when I asked for statistics and numbers of missing from Yosemite and all 392 locations. They stated they don't have this information, and it would cost me $34,000 for them to accumulate the list from Yosemite. What happened to their institutional memory? That seemed like a lot of money until they stated that it would cost me $1.4 million for a list from their entire system.

In late October 2013, we were investigating the disappearance of National Park Ranger Jeff Christensen from Rocky Mountain National Park. I filed a Freedom of Information Act (FOIA) request from the park service for documents and photos related to their investigation. On November 20, 2013, I received an e-mail from the National Park Service FOIA officer, Charis Wilson from Denver:

> Additionally the staff at ROMO are estimating that it will take 120 hours to search and review the files for the Jeff Christensen case, which you also requested, because they contain privacy related information that will need to be redacted before we can release the records. The rate per hour would be $60/hour. So

the current estimate to process the request comes to $7200 and does not include any copy costs. If you are still interested in obtaining these materials, please let me know that you are willing to pay the fees. Until we receive your confirmation we will not be able to process your request.

I've made dozens of FOIA requests from the park service over the years. The largest file we ever received was a box of documents sixteen inches high that weighed several pounds. This was regarding the disappearance of National Park Ranger Paul Fugate. It cost us forty dollars for all the documents.

I've showed Charis's e-mail about Jeff Christensen to several people. Nobody can believe that the park service actually is claiming it would take three weeks—120 hours—to review a case file. Remember, they are only looking for privacy-related information. This isn't a grammar check of the documents, and they aren't proofreading them for accuracy. How long can this take? This is yet another example of the park service treating the public like second-class citizens and restricting our access to key documents.

It's blatantly obvious that the Department of Interior is making a strategic decision not to track and maintain lists of missing people. If the park service had a series of disappearances in one location over a thirty-year period, this may indicate there is some type of underlying problem. But at this point, they can claim ignorance because they say they don't have the data. Because they can claim ignorance of the issue, they also can't be held legally liable over associated issues.

After four years and thousands of hours of research, we do have a database. An employee at Microsoft, Sue, was a fan of our work and spent hundreds of hours working the software and hardware issues to get our data loaded. I have made public statements to the NPS offering our services to them. The NPS has never responded. I realize that our data is just the "tip the iceberg" of all the missing in our national parks, but we are miles in front of their effort.

What has our data shown us? There are clusters of missing people across North America, clusters that nobody ever knew about. Many of these clusters are in national parks. The largest cluster of missing we've documented is in Yosemite National Park. These are not cookie-cutter missing cases; these are very unusual circumstances that replicate themselves across America.

Factors Involved in Disappearances
Berries

In *Missing 411-Eastern United States,* I included a chapter that dealt with berries and their association with missing people. Many berry pickers have vanished under strange circumstances, and there is also a correlation of several children being found in berry bushes or found holding berries. I won't attempt to explain the strangeness of the circumstances in these events. Please read the chapter before making a judgment.

In the book *The Good People: New Folklore Essays,* a few stories go directly to the correlation we developed. On page 364, stories from Newfoundland are found that bring together local beliefs and fairies. Here are a few of the stories:

> My grandmother told us "when you go berry picking on any other time in the woods, wear some kind of bandana on your head, because if you get lost the fairies will lead you astray, but they can't get you if you turn your bandana inside out."

> Although berry picking sounds safe enough, it does have its hazards. There were cliffs, foxholes, upturned roots, but by far the most dangerous were the fairies... Once they had you in their powers they could keep you in a trance for days. Sometimes you would wander aimlessly or sit on a rock by the stream. Even though no one can remember "being in the fairies," many can remember being one place one minute then someplace else the next and never being the wiser of how they got there.

**In many of the cases I've cited in each book, victims are found near creeks, rivers, and streams. Many of you have written to me stating that these areas have a lot of rocks and gravel, and it's hard to find footprints, and this may be the reason victims are left in that type of environment.

Page 346 had more stories: the following incident occurred on Fox Harbour.

> One year in August when the bake apples were ripe, she set out to go berry picking alone. When she failed to show up that evening they became worried and by nightfall a full search was carried out in the worst weather. It was raining torrents and the thunder and lightning persisted through the night. She was found in the morning in an area called the "Sound" in a condition, as Jim Spivey describes as "only in her bloomers." Her clothes were nowhere in sight. The woman later stated she was taken by fairies.

**I have repeatedly written about missing person incidents where people are found without the clothes they had left with. In many instances these individuals are found naked, sometimes in diapers, sometimes no shoes.

> A woman was once taken by the fairies and when they found her a week later, she was badly bruised but still alive. They saw that the fairies had taken her into the woods and kept her alive on berries. She couldn't remember anything that had happened to her.

Page 350

> They are fallen angels and live underground and are called "good people."

> About twenty five years ago a woman from Clarke's Beach went in over the "Earth Hill" as it was called to pick Blueberries and when six o'clock came she

wasn't home. It was dark by this time so a group of men went to look for her. It rained in torrents that night so the men returned without the missing woman. In the morning the search continued and this time they were successful in finding her. She was across a big river which would have to be crossed by a boat, and there was no boat in sight. They found her between two rocks. She was not wet and she said she was in a beautiful house all night with lots of food and lots of company. She said she was in the beautiful house with the fairies in the heart of the woods and had no explanation how she got across the river.

**This story brings many aspects of other cases I've covered into one story. Bad weather is a constant theme in many missing person cases. Berries are for some reason involved with disappearances in certain cases. In this instance the woman had her memory; in many cases victims have no recollection of what happened. How she crossed the river and how she stayed dry are key points to this story.
Page 351

One little boy was picking berries down to the marsh and he was gone an awful long time. They looked for him but couldn't find him. He was discovered hours later in the same place they had searched before. He couldn't remember anything and his berries…were all gone. They believe the fairies had taken him.

**This story is directly on target regarding dozens of stories I've cited. People who went missing in the forest were later found by search teams in the exact spot that had been searched previously. Sometimes the area had been searched multiple times. If the victims had a memory, they could explain how they arrived where they did. I realize this doesn't make logical sense, but this same scenario has replicated itself time after time. No, I do not believe that searchers have missed people the number of times that I've chronicled; no way!

Conscious-Unconscious

If missing people are found, they are most often recovered in a semiconscious or unconscious state. They are normally found lying facedown and many times limbs extended.

Clothing Removed

In cases where hypothermia could play no role, victims are found naked or with large amounts of clothing or shoes removed.

Fever

When a person disappears and search and rescue goes into the field to find them, they are thinking recovery. These people are not thinking that the event could be criminal or that there may be other factors at work. After the victim is found, they are normally taken to a physician. It is a rare event that reporters go to the extent of interviewing the doctor. In those rare times, we hear that the victim is in good health but has a slight fever. We find this to be an unusual event that needs to be documented.

Afternoon Disappearance

The vast majority of people have vanished in the afternoon to early evening. Refer to the time chart in the "Conclusions" section of the book.

Canines

In my first two Missing 411 books, I presented dozens of cases where children disappear with their dogs. Sometimes the canine reappears at the residence without the victim with the parent stating that the dog would never leave the child voluntarily. There are other times that the child is found miles from their home with the dog cuddling and keeping them warm.

The other unusual part of the canine association deals with Bloodhounds and other tracking dogs. In the events we chronicle, in nearly every one of the events, the dogs don't find the child and cannot locate a scent. Bloodhounds are given the victim's scent and sometimes walk in a circle and lay down. Sometimes they appear to be completely uninterested or scared. These are dogs that live for the event and are usually thrilled to search, but not in these cases. Readers have stated that maybe we should bring in the "Dog Whisperer."

Media Response

In *Missing 411-Western United States* and *Missing 411-North America and Beyond*, I presented a series of missing person cases starting in the Cascades of southern Oregon and continuing north through Washington to the Canadian Rockies. I have stated and will continue to claim that the numbers of missing in these areas are staggering. The Department of Interior (USFS and NPS) will continue to wipe their missing person slate clean by changing case statuses to "missing and presumed dead." Those cases won't show up on any database or statistical listing as an open missing person case.

It is obvious that members of the press have been reading my books. On June 8, 2013, on Oregonlive.com, an article titled "Lost in Oregon: Hiker's 2012 Disappearance Joins Hundreds of Unsolved Wilderness Cases" was published. The author chronicled the case of James Dutton, a victim I wrote about in my last book. The author did contact Oregon authorities about the number of missing in the state, and here were his findings: "A staggering 189 men and 51 women remain listed as missing since 1997 by the Oregon office of Emergency Management after trekking into Oregon's wildest places, said George Kleinbaum, search and rescue coordinator for the office."

Readers should take note that these numbers are only from 1997. I believe that there are probably five to eight times that many, and people are no longer tracking them.

The writer contacted Jake's mother and delved into the disappearance of Professor Daming Xu from University of Oregon. I also wrote about Daming, and both cases are truly baffling. Neither man was ever found. Jake's mother states: "There is a mystery here." Later she says: "Both Jake and the professor were experienced hikers on wilderness trails. Two grown men can't simply disappear from the mountains five years apart."

Jake and Daming are just two of dozens of people who have vanished under unusual circumstances in the Oregon Cascades. It's obvious that Jake's mother and the author of the article were stunned by the numbers and circumstances of the disappearances.

I don't live in a lofty perch, and I am not immune from the realities of why people aren't aware of these issues. On January 26, 2012, the *Knoxville Sun* ran an article titled "Great Smoky Mountain national park generates more revenue than any other national park." The article states: "A recently-released National Park Service study shows that the park's 9 million visitors in 2010 spent over $818 million dollars in gateway towns surrounding the park. In addition, 11,367 local jobs (full and part-time) were supported by park visitor spending." I've received hundreds of e-mails from readers telling me to "follow the money," and the answers will evolve. The same article lists the top five national parks for generating revenue for surrounding towns:

Great Smoky Mountains	$818 million
Grand Canyon	$415 million
Yosemite	$354 million
Yellowstone	$334 million
Blue Ridge Parkway	$299 million

**The largest cluster of missing people we've documented is in Yosemite.

Maybe the Department of the Interior (USFS, NPS, and Department of Fish and Wildlife) doesn't want the public to be aware of the dangers that exist in the woods, as this may affect tourism.

The Parental Affect

If you're not a parent, you may have difficulty understanding what a child can and cannot accomplish. The only times I've ever been challenged on some of the distances and elevations that children have allegedly achieved were by young, single people, many of whom never read the books. Parents with mature children have contacted me many times stating that there is no way a two-year old can climb a mountain and get to those heights.

You will read about me quoting a search and rescue handbook normally utilized to set search grids, *Lost Person Behavior* by Robert Koester. The author has studied missing person cases and has set search perimeters based on mountain versus flat-land disappearances. He also divides children into age segments and then provides guidelines about how far they would normally travel. He even gives guidelines for adults with dementia, climbers, cavers, the autistic, ATVs, and anglers. You will see me quoting this book in specific cases to highlight the ridiculous distances some children are alleged to have traveled.

Moving Forward

If this is your first Missing 411 book, I'd prefer you put this one aside and start with any of the other three. I'm not going to delve deeply into details to prep the reader for an understanding of this issue. I'm going hope you've had some basic background into how we got to this point.

<u>Important Abbreviations to Know:</u>
FBI-Federal Bureau of Investigation
RCMP-Royal Canadian Mounted Police
NPS-National Park Service
DOI-Department of the Interior
USFS-United States Forest Service
SAR-Search and Rescue
FLIR-Forward-Looking Infrared Radar
RMNP-Rocky Mountain National Park

CHAPTER ONE: UNITED STATES

Alabama

<u>Sex/Name</u>   <u>Date/Time Missing • Age • State</u>
F-Ann Bragg   12/02/51-10:00 a.m. • 76 • Birmingham, AL

Ann Bragg
Missing: 12/02/51-10:00 a.m., Double Oak Mountain, Birmingham, AL
Age at disappearance: 76 years

Articles vary regarding the location of this incident. Some indicate the location was ten miles southwest of Birmingham; others state it was two miles southeast of the city. I did locate a business district in the mountains to the southwest where the name matches.

Mrs. Ann Bragg lived in a rugged area of Double Oak Mountains. The region has cliffs, large boulders, and much wildlife. The Bragg family had three residences on the mountain, and each was approximately one-quarter mile apart. The family was close and regularly visited each other.

On December 2, 1951, Mrs. Ann Bragg left her residence and made the quarter-mile mountain hike to the home of her daughter. She stayed a short period of time, and at 10:00 a.m. she left for the return hike to her home. Ann never arrived at her residence.

There were stories that Ann had a memory that would fluctuate from time to time, and she would sometimes seem to lose that memory. But she had always made the trips between the homes without issue and never got herself into serious trouble.

The children searched the mountain and surrounding hills and called the local sheriff. Shelby County Sheriff A. E. Norwood led the rescue effort. He rallied over five hundred local residents to participate in the search, which lasted over a week. Heavy rains inundated the mountain during the search, which eventually led into freezing rains. The low-flying planes that were initially used in the search had to be cancelled. Canines brought to the scene never found her scent.

The sheriff stated that there was a possibility that Ann was a victim of foul play, but it was a difficult situation to understand since she was on a remote trail between two family homes, a trail she hiked regularly.

A December 30 article in the *Alabama Anniston Star* expressed the frustration of the extensive search and lack of evidence: "What happened to the mountain grandmother who seemingly vanished into thin air just four weeks ago today?"

Summary

The search for Ann was extensive and utilized woodsmen from the area who knew the territory. There were many boulders in the area, and the region around them was searched multiple times. Fortune tellers and preachers were consulted, and one stated that she would be found within the week; they were wrong. Witnesses from outlying communities reported seeing women that matched Anne's description, but nothing panned out.

At the end of the lengthy search and rescue effort, nothing of Ann was ever found.

Arizona

Sex/Name	Date/Time Missing • Age • State
M-Bud Fisher	11/18/32-p.m. • 4 • Gila Bend, AZ
M-Jack Hodges	12/29/56-a.m. • 7 • Seligman, AZ
M-David Miller	05/19/98-Unk • 22 • Red Rock Wilderness, AZ
M-Emmett Trapp	08/02/10-8:00 p.m. • 2 • Dewey, AZ

Bud Fisher
Missing: 11/18/32-p.m., Gila Bend, AZ
Age at disappearance: 4 years

Gila Bend is a desert city located approximately forty miles southwest from Phoenix. It sits directly west of the Sonoran Desert National Monument, which is managed by the National Park Service. The 2006 census listed the town's population as 2,055. Gila Bend sits in Maricopa County and was founded in 1872 and named for the Gila River.

On the afternoon of November 18, 1932, Mr. and Mrs. Jack Fisher and their son, Bud, were driving from their residence in San Antonio, Texas, to Los Angeles. They decided to stop and camp for the night just outside of Gila Bend.

The family was at their campsite for just a short period of time when Bud vanished. The parents searched and yelled for the boy but failed to locate him. The Maricopa County sheriff's office was notified. Sheriff J. McFadden took charge of the rescue effort and immediately listed the aid of all Gila Bend residents. The sheriff also called upon a friend with an airplane to take to the skies and search. The following three days, the effort escalated with almost a thousand people. Several Bloodhound teams from the state prison in Florence were on the scene the second day, and none could find a track or pick up a scent. The airplane crisscrossed the sky and found nothing to indicate the lad was anywhere in the area.

By the end of the second day, no clues could be found of where the boy may be. Sheriff McFadden called on Apache Indian scout Mack Burns. The tracker followed a meager trail for miles, more miles than anyone could believe. Many of the locations didn't have foot tracks, just small indentations in the sand. They did locate a small shoe, but it was never publicly stated if it was Bud's.

The morning of November 22, Mack was back on the trail and making slow progress. A group of deputies went ahead of the tracker and started walking more miles into open desert. A November 22, 1932, article in the *Salt Lake Tribune* had this statement about what searchers found along with the headline "Missing Child Found Asleep,": "Tired, hungry and thirsty, but otherwise apparently none the worse for three days of desert wandering, 4-year-old Bud Fisher, missing since Friday was found asleep this afternoon in a dry sandy wash 15 miles from here [Gila Bend]."

I have continually explained that the missing people we profile are found many times in and around creek and river banks. This is one of the specific places where it can be very difficult to find and identify tracks. It's also one of those locations that have many rocks and boulders. There was no mention of the boy suffering from dehydration, even though he was lost in the desert without water for three days. When Bud was located, he was not wearing shoes. One article stated that he had discarded them because he had worn the soles through. There were never any articles stating the condition of his feet.

If Bud was found fifteen miles from Gila Bend, it's a certainty that he didn't walk a straight line—he wandered, thus making the trip much greater in distance. In Robert Koester's book, *Lost Person Behavior*, he states that a four-to six-year-old child traveling on flat ground will be found within a radius of 4.1 miles or less 95 percent of the time. It's a flat guarantee that Bud traveled almost four times the distance Koester claims in his book, and he did this without shoes?

Bud was found in the afternoon, and he was found asleep. Too many times to count, lost children are located in a semiconscious or unconscious state, almost as though they are in an altered state of consciousness. I understand that some children take afternoon naps, but it's not a normal place or a standard time for kids to be sleeping while they are lost. If you've read my other books, the facts surrounding this disappearance come together to mimic many stories of children who have suddenly vanished and are later found in locations that are too far outside the range of normal search parameters for them to be considered "standard" disappearance cases.

Jack Hodges
Missing: 12/29/56-a.m., Seligman, AZ
Age at disappearance: 7 years

On December 29, 1956, in the morning hours, Mr. and Mrs. Lloyd Hodges of Seligman were with their son, Jack, and his dog visiting a nearby ranch. Sometime in the morning hours (never described in any article), Jack and his dog disappeared. Cowboys, parents, and friends all started to search for the boy. Just as the search was getting organized, Jack's dog returned without him. At the end of that first night, searchers in Jeeps, ground teams, and the United States Air Force—with two planes and a helicopter from Luke Air Force Base—were looking for the boy. Several teams of Bloodhounds from the state prison in Florence had started their efforts to locate a scent and were not having any luck.

I encourage readers to look at Google Earth and view the area around Seligman. There are not large trees with significant coverage. There are scrub bushes and small brush. Airplanes should've seen the boy if he was crossing large, open spaces. Bloodhounds should've picked up a scent.

Temperatures at night had gotten down to fourteen degrees, and searchers were very concerned about Jack's welfare.

Two days after the boy vanished, two cowboys were twenty miles from Seligman Ranch when they made the following observation as is described in the January 4, 1957, article in the *Big Spring Herald*: "Two cowboys, Oscar Pannich and Alvin Wagner spotted him on the slopes of Mount Floyd, some 20 miles north of Seligman in a barren area that extends to the southern reaches of the Grand Canyon." Later in the same article there was clarity on the distance the boy traveled: "Searchers estimated the warmly-clad youngster must have walked some 50 miles, mostly in circles."

Jack was flown to Williams and hospitalized in good condition. He stayed one night for observation and was released.

Summary

It's hard to imagine any adult traveling fifty miles in two days. Traveling across rough mountains and hills with temperatures dropping to fourteen degrees and surviving this ordeal in good condition is hard to believe. In Robert Koester's book, *Lost Person Behavior*, he states that a child seven to nine years of age will be found 95 percent of the time seven miles or less from the point last seen in mountain terrain. Searchers state that Jack traveled more than seven times that distance!

We forget that Jack went missing in the middle of the desert. He walked fifty miles and wasn't dehydrated? I find that impossible!

There was no water in the area where the search took place. There was some snow on the mountain, but it wasn't melting; it was too cold. For readers who don't know, if you eat snow, this will drop your core body temperature, causing hypothermia and dehydration. The idea that Jack ate snow and returned in the condition he did does not make sense.

I will continue to present these cases to exemplify a point. We can't ignore what seems illogical. We can't attempt to reconcile in our minds what seems uncomfortable to believe.

David Barclay Miller
Missing: 05/19/98-Unk, Red Rock Secret Mountain Wilderness, AZ
Age at disappearance: 22 years

While I was doing the research for this story, I was immediately drawn to David Miller. You will read about a young man who lived life honestly, tried to do the right things, was a leader, and had a spiritual side.

David was raised in Bethesda, Maryland, and led a very privileged lifestyle, of which he never took advantage. He was drawn to the outdoors at a young age and continued to pursue that love through his life and career.

One of the many reasons this young man lived life fully was that he had two siblings who were disabled from a debilitating and rare bone disease. His perspective of their lives gave him an appreciation for what he had. A December 26, 1999, article in the *Washington Post* had an interview with a coach who worked with David, and he explained the special attitude he possessed: "'I've coached for 20 years and I've never seen a kid like him who would give everything he had,' recounted Al Hightower, former athletic director at Potomoc, where Miller graduated in 1993. 'Where the motivation came from, it's certainly a gift.'" David was the kid who was always picked as the team captain and had notoriety for never giving up—leadership qualities!

David went to Bates College in Maine and studied religion. He wrote his college thesis on the Sun Dance of the Lakota Sioux tribe and even went to New Mexico to understand their culture.

The Southwest seemed to appeal to David, and he applied for the United States Forest Service and got that dream job as a wilderness ranger in April 1998. His first assignment was in the Coconino National Forest in Arizona. Rangers work long days and hours, and David got his first three days off the weekend of May 19.

David Miller took a backpack and supplies and drove to the Beaver Creek Ranger Station and signed in at the Vultee Arch Trailhead. He was traveling alone and was last seen May 19 at the ranger station. When he didn't return to work the following week, a search was initiated for the ranger.

Searchers knew David had signed in for a two-and-a-half day hike. This gave the supervisors an idea on how far to set search perimeters.

The Yavapai County sheriff was given the responsibility of running the search operation. They put multiple dog teams, ground teams, and helicopters into the 47,194-acre wilderness. It is an area with gorgeous red rock spires, lots of animal life, and high rims that can be cool and moist compared to much of Arizona's landscape. Many consider this location to be one of the area's most difficult wilderness zones to enter. One of the main trails through the region is the Devil's Bridge Trail.

None of the different types of search teams were finding any of David's tracks or equipment. On May 26, 1998, the formal search for David Miller was terminated. In the book *Mysterious Sedona* by Tom Dongo, he had this comment on page 30 about the outcome of the search: "Not a single trace of David Miller was ever found. True, he may have fallen into one of the areas with small and large side canyons. It may be years until some trace of him is discovered, but why didn't the dog teams find him?"

Summary

I filed a Freedom of Information Act request against the Department of the Interior (DOI) at the United States Forest Service (USFS). David was a DOI employee and went missing in a wilderness zone. The USFS stated they had no relevant files on David Miller. How is that possible? I also filed special paperwork with the Yavapai County sheriff's office and asked for his file to be released. They refused.

There are several aspects of this case that disturb me. If David had gone into a small crack or canyon to explore, chances are he would've left his big backpack and sleeping bag in a safe location. If the equipment was left behind, Bloodhounds should've found it. The search for the ranger lasted only four to five days. This is hard to understand. I've written about other rangers who have vanished, and their searches sometimes lasted many, many weeks. Why wouldn't the USFS mount and continue with a prolonged search for one of their own? Why wouldn't they have any paperwork on this?

There is something very unusual and uncomfortable that resonates inside me about David. He was a very unique man and the only ranger I've ever read about or personally met who had a degree in religion. While I can't group David with others who've had a disability, he did have an unusual DNA background. With two siblings possessing a disabling bone disease, it was unusual he never acquired it. His demeanor, spiritual side, athletic prowess, and never-give-up attitude indicates to me that David should've been one of the people who walk out of that wilderness.

There still has never been anything recovered indicating where David vanished in the Red Rock Secret Mountain Wilderness.

Emmett Trapp
Missing 08/02/10-8:00 p.m., 1800 Block of Lavender Sage Road, Dewey, AZ
Age at disappearance: 2 years

If you are an owner of *Missing 411-North America and Beyond*, pull the book out and read the story on page 417 about Tristen "Buddy" Myers from Roseboro, North Carolina. Tristen's disappearance from his aunt's home has almost the exact elements as the disappearance of Emmett Trapp.

The Trapp family lived on the 1800 block of Lavender Sage Road in Dewey, Arizona, approximately eighty miles north of Phoenix. This is a very rural area. The Trapps lived at the end of a dirt road that sits next to a small set of mountains with open space behind the residence.

On August 2, 2010, Emmett's mom put him and his three other siblings to bed. She checked on Emmett and found him asleep, and she lay down for a short nap. She woke just before 8:00 p.m. and found that Emmett and the family dog were gone. She searched the house and yard several times and found nothing. She called Emmett's dad at work and then the Yavapai County sheriff.

A deputy arrived in ten minutes and immediately started to search the yard and residence. The deputy organized searchers and found people were yelling for Emmett. During this initial stage, the family dog came back to the residence from the desert. The sheriff's office called for a helicopter with FLIR and multiple Bloodhounds. The first twenty-four hours of the search frustrated law enforcement. An August 5, 2010, article on CNN.com and KPHO had the following statement: "'A little 2-year old is gonna cry out, is going to be uncomfortable, is going to be hungry,' Dwight D'Evelyn of the Yavapai County Sheriff's department told KPHO. 'We haven't heard that yet. There's been no trail that leads anywhere that we've been able to track, so yeah, it's odd.'"

This area of the Arizona desert doesn't have huge trees or boulders to hide beneath. It does have small bushes that a boy could crawl into, but his heat signature would show on FLIR. They were finding nothing. Multiple Bloodhounds were covering the area around the residence and not finding any scent.

There was a second CNN.com article about Emmett on August 5. This article stated that searchers had found Emmett's body at 11:30 a.m. on August 4. Here is a statement from the article about the find: "The body of Emmett Trapp was found by search and rescue personnel at 11:30 a.m. about one mile from his home, lying in a muddy pit once used to collect products from a former mining site." An article in the *New York Times* on August 5 stated that an individual, not part of the formal search, had found Emmett in the pit, which was outside the formal search perimeter, just over one mile from his residence. Emmett was not wearing shoes, just a diaper and a dinosaur-print pajama top.

A sheriff's department spokesman stated that after thirty-nine hours in the elements, Emmett died of exposure. The second CNN article of August 5 stated the following about Emmett's journey: "Newnum [Sergeant, Yavapai County] said the door to the house was unlocked at the time of Emmett's disappearance, and it appears the boy walked as many as four miles, crossing hilly rough terrain before he was found."

Summary

After reading thousands of missing person cases, we are bound to find a few that are identical. The elements that exist in the Emmett Trapp case and the Tristen Myers case are too similar to ignore. There are actually several cases like this that are quite similar.

As a dad who raised two kids, I can't imagine a child at two years old leaving his or her residence at near dark and walking into a lonely desert with the dog, no way. The deputy stated that Bloodhounds were not finding a scent, and they could not locate tracks. He also stated that the boy should be making sounds and complaining; they heard none of this. Where was Emmett for thirty-nine hours?

There were several comments on local Arizona newspapers asking why the sheriff's department never released autopsy results and asking how they had missed the boy during the search. If you are a reader of my books, you'd understand why the searchers missed Emmett. I don't think he was there.

Chapter Update

As this book was being submitted for editing and publication, there is another hiker who disappeared and hasn't been found. Thomas Lang was dropped off by his father at the Manzanita campground in Oak Creek Canyon in Sedona on December 18, 2013. The twenty-two-year-old had planned a five-day trip while he was fasting. He carried water, camping gear, and his guitar, but no food. An extensive search has not found any evidence of where he might be.

Arkansas

Sex/Name	Date Missing • Age • State
F-Maretha Yarborough	03/26/30-Noon • 3 • Waldron, AR
F-Barbara Sue Jones	11/25/53-Unk • 22 mos. • Marianna, AR
F-Joan Treece	04/14/54-1:00 p.m. • 3 • Mountain Home, AR
M-Timothy Box	09/28/87-4:00 p.m. • 2 • Mountain View, AR
F-Haley Zega	04/29/01-11:30 a.m. • 6 • Newton County, AR
M-Justin Sides	04/30/03-3:45 p.m. • 3 • Wynne, AR
M-Landen Trammell	09/11/12-8:00 a.m. • 3 • Onia, AR

Maretha Yarborough
Missing: 03/26/30-Noon, Waldron, AR
Age at disappearance: 3 years

If readers of my past books remember the name "Waldron," there is a reason. There are several people who have disappeared in a cluster surrounding this region. In *Missing 411-North America and Beyond*, I wrote about the disappearance of three-year-old Pearl Turner from just outside Waldron. She disappeared on October 19, 1923, at noon. There was a massive search, and she was never found. The similarities in the Yarborough and Turner cases are enlightening.

Waldron is a very small city sitting close to the Oklahoma border. The area has hundreds of small bodies of water and a few mountain ranges. On March 26, 1930, at approximately noon, Maretha (spelled different ways in various articles) was playing in a barn close to her home with her three brothers. The brothers walked off and headed toward home with the young girl trailing behind. Once the boys started to look for her for lunch, she couldn't be found. The family searched the farm and couldn't locate her. Searchers from the community started to converge on the Yarborough property. A March 27, 1930, article in the *Hope Star* had this statement regarding the feelings of searchers: "Whether she was lost or kidnapped remains a mystery."

Various articles state that between two hundred fifty and three hundred searchers looked for the girl the first afternoon. That day, the rescue effort couldn't locate any evidence of the girl being in the area. Slowly searchers started to venture farther and farther from the property.

On March 27, 1930, at noon, two searchers were eight miles from Maretha's home and on the summit of Pilot Mountain when they found the girl wearing just a dress. She was alive and in very good condition. No other details were available. She was without shoes.

Summary

Search and rescue manuals state that a three-year-old lost in a mountain environment will be found 95 percent of the time at a distance of 2.8 miles or less. Maretha was found on top of a mountain eight miles away. The vast majority of children will walk downhill when lost, not uphill.

It's obvious from the statement of the searchers that kidnapping was at one time considered a possibility. The Yarborough family was extremely lucky to find Maretha.

Barbara Sue Jones
Missing: 11/25/53-Unk, Marianna, AR
Age at disappearance: 22 months

This disappearance comes with some strong words from searchers about their efforts. With this being my fourth book about missing people, I can tell you that Arkansas has quite a few unusual disappearances involving both adults and children.

Barbara Sue lived seventeen miles southeast of Marianna on a rural farm surrounded by swamps and marshes. The property was located near the Mississippi border and very close to the Mississippi and White Rivers and the White River National Wildlife Refuge. There are hundreds of small bodies of water just west of the property, and this area near the Jones property was known for its superb duck hunting.

On November 17, 1953, Mr. and Mrs. Jimmy Jones and their seven children moved to their rural farm. Sometime during the day of November 25, the day before Thanksgiving, Barbara Sue was playing in her yard when she disappeared. The family conducted a brief search and then called the authorities.

The Lee County sheriff's office took charge of the rescue effort with Sheriff C. S. Langston as the commander. Almost immediately a call to the National Guard for additional assistance was made. Four hundred police officers, National Guardsmen, and volunteers searched the area surrounding the Jones farm while wading through bogs and swamps looking for the small toddler.

Three days after Barbara Sue vanished, one of the sheriff's commanders gave his feelings about their efforts up to that point in a November 28, 1953, article in the *Camden News*: "Chief Deputy Sheriff H. Smith said the search failed to uncover any trace of the child and it seemed useless to go over the territory again. He said it would have been impossible for the child to have wandered out of the area covered in the search." The search had covered all of the water surrounding the farm, and the sheriff believed there was no way the child could've gotten through the bogs at her age and size. The search continued for another two days, and the sheriff made a statement to the *Camden News* on November 30, 1953: "'I've never been up against a case like this,' said Langston. He said that he had no reason to suspect foul play but that a routine investigation of this angle is being conducted." As a former law enforcement officer, there is never anything "routine" in an investigation of a missing person. If there was never any suspicion of foul play, the sheriff wouldn't have started an investigation. I'm sure that the sheriff was baffled because the property around the bogs and marshes was soft and mushy, excellent terrain to find footprints. The search teams were finding nothing.

After ten days of formal and informal searches, the effort to find Barbara Sue was terminated.

Just after the search was stopped, a work crew was on a piece of land four miles from the Joneses' property near an abandoned logging road when they found a diaper. On December 4, 1953, Mr. Jones went to the scene and confirmed that the diaper was the same type worn by his daughter. A secondary intensive search was again started at this new location. Hours later, Mr. Jones and two other searchers found Barbara Sue's body in a wooded section.

The autopsy on the girl's body indicated that she died of starvation and exposure four to five days after she disappeared.

Summary

There were some inconsistencies in the articles I reviewed for this story. Many articles stated that Barbara Sue was twenty-two months; others stated twenty-three months old. Many articles stated this event happened ten miles south of Marianna; others stated seventeen miles southeast.

There were never any statements from the sheriff after the body was found. There can be no mistake that the Chief Deputy Sheriff had stated that it was impossible for the girl to get outside the search area. How did she manage to get four miles from her residence? Where was she for four to five days? It seems strange that the coroner stated the girl died of starvation. I've spoken to many medical examiners who have said that most people can live ten days without food; they just need water. Barbara Sue was surrounded by water.

For readers of my past books, you'll know that there are several cases where children have disappeared from a residence after they had recently moved in. You'll also recognize that we've repeatedly stated in past books that water plays a role in the disappearances.

Joan Marie Treece
Missing: 04/14/54-1:00 p.m., Mountain Home, AR
Age at disappearance: 3 years

This incident occurred on the outskirts of Mountain Home adjacent to Lake Norfork in northwestern Arkansas. This is located 140 miles northeast of a cluster of missing people in Mena and just east of two disappearances chronicled in *Missing 411-Eastern United States*. The lake is a large, meandering body of water that stretches into Missouri, just five miles north.

On April 14, 1954, three-year-old Joan Treece was staying with her uncle while her mom looked at property nearby. She was playing in the yard when she inexplicably disappeared at approximately 1:00 p.m. The yard and surrounding area was searched, and then a call was made for additional assistance.

Almost immediately after Joan vanished, heavy rain hit the area around the lake and made searching difficult. The teams stayed in the field until 2:30 a.m. without finding a clue of where the girl may be. An April 16, 1954, article in the *Joplin Globe* expressed the feelings of the sheriff about the circumstances: "For a while Sheriff King expressed fear that the little girl might have been the victim of foul play." You can tell that law enforcement was in fear that first night.

Twenty hours after Joan vanished, she was located by a searcher two miles from her uncle's home in a cedar brake. She was wet and muddy but in otherwise good condition. Bloodhounds had worked that trail since the prior day and did not find Joan.

Joan did not make any statements that appeared in news articles I reviewed. There were no details about what she was or wasn't wearing when found.

Joan's case mimics many in Arkansas and the surrounding areas. Bad weather, the comment by the sheriff about foul play, and the inability of Bloodhounds to pick up a scent are all consistent circumstances of the cases we review. If you are a longtime reader of my stories, you are starting to realize that children at the homes of friends and relatives are more susceptible to these types of disappearances.

Timothy Box
Missing: 09/28/87-4:00 p.m., Mountain View, AR
Age at disappearance: 2 years

Mountain View, Arkansas, is situated approximately sixty miles north of Little Rock in a heavily wooded and rural environment. The actual location of this incident is two miles east of the city at the foot of Iron Mountain. I have written about another disappearance just south of the city on the outskirts of Heber Springs.

Timothy was the son of Kenneth and Virginia Box. The parents were both deaf and could not speak. In June 1986, the parents realized that Timothy was going to have a difficult time developing his speech, so they placed him with his grandparents outside of Mountain View.

On September 28, 1987, at 4:00 p.m., Timothy was outside his grandparents' home playing with their two dogs and a cat. The grandparents came outside, saw the boy, and went back inside for a few moments. They returned outside and found Timothy and the animals gone. Calls were made for the pets and Timothy; there was no answer. The local fire department and law enforcement were called and asked to help search for the boy.

Just as searchers were arriving, the grandparents found their cat in the woods on a tree looking out into the woods, as though it was waiting for the dogs and Timothy to come home.

Helicopters, Bloodhounds, equestrians, and two hundred ground searchers were brought in during the three-day effort to find the boy. An October 1, 1987, article in the *Courier News* had the following description of the search effort: "'We've had hundreds of people walking through the entire area, but we've seen absolutely nothing of the boy,' Sheriff Dave Barnum said, adding that the search easily covered a four-five mile radius." Weather also hampered search efforts to some degree. It had rained during the time that Timothy was missing.

The rescue effort included one hundred high school students, fire departments, USFS, law enforcement, and volunteers from the community. After three days, law enforcement started to make statements about foul play and unusual circumstances. These statements were very vague, and they refused to clarify.

On October 1, searchers were near a creek and briar patch and found Timothy alive. He was transported by helicopter to Children's Hospital of Arkansas where Dr. Mike Hudson evaluated the boy. The physician and the searchers wanted to question Timothy about his excursion, but he didn't say anything. An October 3 article in the *Ocala Star Banner* had this statement from the doctor: "We don't know exactly what happened out there, that's why we want to observe him for a couple of days." The doctor stated he was surprised that Timothy wasn't dehydrated and remarked on how good of condition he was in. Timothy did have extensive scratches over his body, and it had appeared that he had eaten berries. You can tell from the physician's statement that authorities were concerned about what had happened to the boy while he was away.

There was never any mention of what happened to the family dogs or what the boy was or wasn't wearing when he was found.

Summary

There are many facts of this disappearance that have elements of what I've described in past cases: berries, boy was found in an area previously searched, he disappeared with family dogs, it was raining in the area during the search, and authorities spoke about foul play.

It's always unusual when there is a follow-up story about a missing person case. Someone found it strange that Timothy wasn't talking about what happened during his excursion, and a reporter made contact with his relatives months after the incident. The interview statements are described in a December 27, 1987, article in the *Ukiah Daily*: "His family says the boy, who celebrated his third birthday November 17, is doing fine but rarely talks about his adventure in late September except to say he 'went around and around.' He also won't go outside by himself. 'He always wants me or someone else to come out with him,' Timothy's grandfather, George Box said recently."

I'm not sure what Timothy experienced during his disappearance, but whatever happened scared that little boy.

F-Haley Zega
Missing: 04/29/01-11:30 a.m., Newton County, AR
Age at disappearance: 6 years

Some of you may remember the name and location of this event as it was highlighted in a *Dateline NBC* segment. There are some very unusual claims made by this victim that could be related to a historical event in that same area.

On April 29, 2001, Haley Zega was with her grandparents, Jay and Joyce Hale. The group had decided to travel to the Upper

Buffalo Wilderness Area thirty miles southeast of Harrison. If an area has the classification of a "wilderness area," this means there can be no bicycles or motor-driven vehicles of any type inside the area. This region is very remote and wild.

At approximately 11:30 a.m., Haley asked her grandparents if they could hike to a nearby waterfall. They said no, and she got very upset. The adults continued to slowly walk down the trail, and Haley fell farther behind. After a short period of time, the grandparents lost sight of the girl and turned back to find her. Jay and Joyce searched for ninety minutes and continually yelled for the girl. They heard nothing and could not locate Haley. The pair now turned back toward the parking lot to seek additional assistance.

The Newton County sheriff responded along with the park service, fire departments, National Guard, and a slew of two hundred volunteers. Helicopters with FLIR took to the sky, and other volunteers were on horseback and mules. There were up to eight teams of Bloodhounds attempting to track the girl. One team of dogs tracked a scent to near a roadway and stopped. This action was interpreted by searchers to mean Haley may have been picked up by a vehicle. At the end of two full days of searching, nothing was found.

Fifty-one hours after Haley had vanished, Lytle James and William Villines (not part of the formal search) were riding mules and looking for the girl. The pair was two miles from where Haley was last seen when they observed her sitting next to a brook with her feet hanging in the water. Lytle said the girl appeared tired or groggy and had scratches on her face, legs, and arms but appeared otherwise in good condition. She was brought back to the searchers and later transferred to a medical center for observation.

After Haley recovered her strength, she was questioned about her journey. She told her parents that the first night she slept on top of a bluff. This was puzzling because two helicopters with FLIR were hovering above that location and never saw her. The second night she said that she slept in a cave. She also stated that she had tried to climb steep, boulder-strewn hills and fell back into the water a few times. The girl then explained that she had assistance along the way from another girl. Here is a partial transcript from her *Dateline NBC* interview with Rob Stafford.

Haley: The first moment I was lost I met her and then after I was found she went away.

Stafford: She was an imaginary friend who Haley says showed up just when she needed help the most.

Haley: Her name was Alicia. She was four years old.

Stafford: What's she look like?

Haley: She had black hair and brown eyes.

Stafford: What did you talk about?

Haley: We sang songs and told jokes.

Stafford: What else did Alicia do?

Haley: She helped me get down a hill.

Stafford: A steep hill? How did she do that?

Haley: She got in front of me and made sure I didn't fall.

Stafford goes on to state that this may be a little girl's imagination, or was it something else? He says that there is a strange twist to the story. As it turns out, twenty-three years prior to this event, another little girl disappeared in this same spot and was found dead. Stafford states that this girl was almost four years old and her middle name was not Alicia, but Alana.

Summary

I've put this story in the book for multiple reasons. I do believe that something unusual happened to Haley when she was alone in the woods. The fact that another girl disappeared in the same spot does not surprise me. I have been tracking incidents where the person who is the last in line on a trail vanishes, as was the case in this story.

Many of the searchers on this rescue publicly questioned how a six-year-old girl could've maneuvered around the dangerous terrain where she vanished. There are many steep valleys and cliffs throughout the region.

Many of the people I have written about were in the presence of relatives when they vanished. Haley was with her grandparents when she went missing.

The two searchers who located Haley refused the reward and asked that it be donated to charity, which it was.

M-Justin Sides
Missing: 04/30/03-3:45 p.m. • 3 • Wynne, AR
Age at disappearance: 3 years

This is another story that I probably could've written one time, changed the dates, names, and location, and it would've worked. The number of times this exact scenario has played itself out is mind-boggling.

Wynne, Arkansas, is approximately eighty miles northeast of Little Rock and twenty miles west of the Tennessee border. The city sits near the Village Creek State Park and hundreds of small bodies of water.

On April 30, 2003, at approximately 3:45 p.m., Justin was playing in the yard of his family's rural home with his two dogs. The family stated that Justin and the dogs seemed to suddenly go missing, and a search started. Once they couldn't locate the group, the local sheriff was called. Hours after Justin disappeared, the family dogs returned to the residence without him.

The search effort quickly climbed to two hundred professional and volunteer searchers, multiple canine teams, and airplanes. There was a comment about the weather in the May 2, 2003, *Blytheville Courier*: "The search Thursday was hampered by foul weather. A severe thunderstorm pelted the area about noon, and much of the search was suspended for a time. After the rain passed, searchers with dogs got back on the trail." Searchers also used the words "the search dogs appeared confused" in describing the effectiveness of the canines.

On May 1 at about 2:45 p.m., a single searcher was driving an ATV through the woods, yelling the boy's name. He was approximately one and a half miles from Justin's residence when he saw him stand up. Here is a statement from the searcher from the same article quoted earlier: "'He was just standing there like "What am I doing here?"' South said. You could tell by all of the scratches on his legs that he had been through a lot of brush, but overall he looked pretty good." Justin was taken to a hospital and found to be in good condition but slightly dehydrated.

Summary
Here are the factors in this incident that replicate themselves in other stories:

- Child disappears with dog.
- Child disappears from rural residence.
- Bad weather hits the area of the search.
- Bloodhounds can't find the boy.
- When the child is found, he or she has scratches on his or her body and are in a semiconscious or unconscious state.

Landen Trammell
Missing: 09/11/12-8:00 a.m., Onia, AR
Age at disappearance: 3 years

This case is very close in geographical proximity to the disappearance of Timothy Box in Mountain View. The location of this incident is just twelve miles south in Onia, another very rural community.

On September 11, 2012, Landen was being watched by his grandfather. The following is a September 12, 2012, article in the *Huffington Post* that quotes other news sources about the specifics of the disappearance: "KTHV reports the boy was being watched by his grandfather at the time of his disappearance. The man said he thought his grandson was asleep on the couch but discovered that he was missing when he went to check on him." It wasn't until relatively lately that we started to understand how many children have vanished from inside homes under conditions that surprised the caregiver. There is a section in the back of this book that has a list of children who disappeared under conditions that mimic Landen's case.

The Stone County sheriff was called, and they orchestrated a major response from a variety of search organizations. Over three hundred professional law enforcement and forestry services personnel responded.

The first day of the search could not produce a clue of where the boy might have been. Bloodhounds couldn't pick up a scent, and a law enforcement helicopter equipped with FLIR could not find his heat signature. Searchers on foot and equestrians found nothing to point in any direction.

The second day of the search had the USFS respond in force. One of the forestry workers, Bradley Taylor, was approximately three miles from the Trammell residence and found the boy playing in mud at the edge of a stock pond, which contained just inches of water. Taylor stated that the boy appeared to be making mud pies. Landen was found after spending thirty hours away from his house. He was transported to the Stone County Medical Center and found to be in good condition with cuts and bruises.

How this little boy got out of his house without his grandfather knowing and how he made it three miles through the woods without being found by canines and FLIR is truly an unreal story.

California
Northern California Mountains

Sex/Name	Date Missing • Age • State
M-Asa Lee Lakey	04/20/30-Unk • 6 • Mount Burney, CA
M-John Nezza	07/17/65-Unk • 80 • Mount Shasta, CA
M-Danny Hohenstein	12/01/92-5:00 p.m. • 6 • Paradise Pines, CA

Asa Lee Lakey
Missing: 04/20/30-Unk, Mount Burney, CA
Age at disappearance: 6 years

The disappearance of Asa Lee Lakey immediately struck a familiar note with me. I have written about the area where the small boy disappeared in two past books. Only males have disappeared in this area, and here is the list:

Book-Name	Date Missing • Age • City
West-Billy Coleman	01/01/40 • 14 • Viola
NA-Lee Littlejohn	12/23/77 • 18 mos. • Redding
West-Austin Sparks	01/04/04 • 15 • Montgomery Creek
NA-Patrick Amen	12/23/77 • 40 • Manton

Book abbreviations:
West= *Missing 411-Western United States*
NA= *Missing 411-North America and Beyond*

All of the above disappearances occurred within a forty-mile radius of each other. Asa's incident would be the case farthest north and would also constitute the oldest case.

The Lakey family took an Easter weekend outing and drove with the group to an area just outside of Burney. The car was pulled to the side of the road, and Asa exited and walked into the woods to explore. The boy didn't come out. The parents yelled for the six-year-old and went into the woods to look. They saw nothing and never got a response from their son.

The Lakeys notified the local sheriff, and a search was initiated for their son. Airplanes from Mather Field in Sacramento were summoned as well as professional trackers, Bloodhounds, and volunteers. Law enforcement initially believed the search would be quick, as there was no reason for the boy to go deep into the woods with the sound of vehicular traffic on the roadway.

On the second day, one of the Bloodhounds appeared to pick up a scent and tracked it uphill and away from the car. This action didn't make sense to searchers. Rescuers were very concerned about the boy's welfare, as temperatures had been dropping very low at night, and many were worried about possible hypothermia.

At the beginning of the third day of searching, two men were on the slopes of Mount Burney and made an amazing find as is described in the April 23, 1930, *Pittsburgh Press*: "Sheltered by a crude lean-to of his own making and hugging the earth for warmth, the six-year old boy was found alive and well." Searchers stated that just before finding the boy, they had found a small piece of cloth torn off by a bush, and this had convinced them they were on the correct path.

The path that Asa took to get to his location is almost unbelievable. The *Pittsburgh Post-Gazette* of April 24, 1930, had a description: "The child had wandered 13 miles and across a 3,000-foot mountain ridge." Readers need to keep in mind that this feat was accomplished in less than three days.

Summary

In Robert Koester's book, *Lost Person Behavior*, he states that a six-year-old child in a mountain setting will be found 95 percent of the time within 6.6 miles or less. Asa didn't just bust the bank in miles, but he also went over the top of a high ridge.

Bloodhounds didn't find the boy.

John Nezza
Missing: 07/17/65-Unk, Mount Shasta, CA
Age at disappearance: 80 years

I usually don't include missing mountain climbers in my books unless there are extenuating circumstances. I think the disappearance of Mr. Nezza would be considered unusual.

I have written about one other climber on Mount Shasta that vanished. In *Missing 411-Western United States* I explained the disappearance of Carl Landers from the mountain on May 25, 1999. The head of the search and rescue teams looking for Carl was completely befuddled by the disappearance, as he explained there was no place to hide. He either had to go up, in, or have evaporated, because the sixty-nine-year-old marathon runner couldn't be found.

John Nezza was not your average eighty-year-old man. He was in great shape and had summited Mount Shasta forty times. You read that correctly—forty summits under his belt. I doubt there was a more experienced climber of the mountain then or now.

On the morning of July 17, 1965, Mr. Nezza left his cabin at the Sierra Alpine Lodge and headed for the mountain. A July 25, 1965, article in the *Hayward Daily Review* had the following information: "Nezza was last reported in the Lake Helen area about three or four miles from the lodge." What is fascinating about this location is this is the area where Carl Landers vanished and was also never found.

Helicopters, airplanes, and dozens of searchers covered Mount Shasta in an effort to locate John. A multiday search covering the entire mountain, from top to bottom, found nothing.

Summary

There are some interesting parallels between the Lander and Nezza case. There was approximately thirty-four years between incidents, time enough for rescuers and law enforcement to forget the Nezza case. Both men were in extraordinary shape for their age. Both were alone in the same area when they vanished; how very strange! Both searches were extensive and complete, and no equipment or either man's body was ever found.

Danny Hohenstein
Missing: 12/01/92-5:00 p.m., Paradise Pines, CA
Age at disappearance: 6 years

I sincerely hope that someone with political power is reading these stories, as this is another of dozens that mimic each other in facts. It's amazing that these cases have been ignored and shoved to the side, as they tell a story of replicating specific elements.

Danny Hohenstein lived in the foothills of the Sierra Nevada Mountains in Northern California. I have spent days in this region and can attest to the beauty it can represent. It can also get very wild quite quickly. Paradise Pines is a small subdivision approximately eighty miles north of Sacramento at an elevation of 2,200 feet. This enclave sits just one half mile west of Magalia Reservoir and just east of Butte Creek.

The afternoon of December 1, 1992, had Danny Hohenstein and his mother, Jacklyn Carter, going to Paradise Pines so Jacklyn could clean the home of a friend. It was in the late afternoon when Jacklyn entered the house as Danny played with a local cocker spaniel that he knew well, Lady. Jacklyn wasn't in the house long when she returned to the street and found Lady and Danny gone. She called for her son but did not receive a response. The Butte County sheriff's office was called.

Butte County put on a major search effort. Helicopters, canines, and over one thousand professional and volunteer searchers combed the region around the house. The effort to find Danny was hampered by freezing rain that hammered the area while searchers were in the field.

Just to the east of the residence and down a steep ravine was Butte Creek, and much of the focus was in that area. On December 4, searchers found Lady in the ravine, alive. Lady was found less than a mile from where Danny was last seen. This was the last and only clue as to Danny's possible location.

Once Lady was found, Butte County combed through everything at the ravine and in the surrounding area. Deputies got more frustrated as time went by. They knew the area that Danny disappeared was a tight-knit community where everyone knew the cars driving the road, and the crime of abduction was never considered. After five full days of searching, the effort was terminated.

A June 6, 1993, article in the *Orange County Register* had this quote from a Butte County sergeant: "'We don't have any concrete evidence to indicate that's what happened [satanic cult],' said sheriff's sergeant Tony Burdine. 'We are not sure who did take Danny or why. This case gets more frustrating all the time. It is a nightmare.'" This gives you some insight into the thoughts of the sheriff: Danny had been abducted. Search and Rescue Captain Dave Lee made a comment that in his twenty-four years of experience, this was his most frustrating case because of a complete lack of any clues.

Investigators and search and rescue personnel initially believed that Danny had wandered into the ravine near where Lady was found. After combing the ravine with hundreds of searchers, their belief was there was no way he was there.

Nothing happened on this case for six years, then came the bombshell. A group of hikers were in the ravine near the house where Danny had disappeared. They found a skull, four bones, and tattered clothing—they had found Danny Hohenstein. In a location that had been searched too many times to count, there were the boy's remains. The bones were sent to a forensic anthropologist, and he tentatively identified the remains as Danny. He stated that he did not see any obvious signs of trauma and could not confirm the cause of death. The remains were sent to the FBI for further analysis.

In a strange twist to this case, the FBI held the remains an inordinate amount of time and would not release them till 2000. This is the second time I have documented the FBI holding remains for a lengthy period—they also did this in the case of Robert Springfield when he vanished and his remains were found in Montana. The Springfields eventually had to sue the FBI to get the remains; refer to *Missing 411-Western United States* for details. It would be fascinating what the FBI laboratories are finding in relationship to these bodies. I have filed Freedom of Information Act requests in the past against the FBI attempting to get lab results on deceased individuals. They claim they cannot release the information because it's an invasion of the person's privacy. I remind them that the person is deceased; they don't respond.

Summary

I believe that something unusual occurred to Danny. It would appear that what happened to him has happened to possibly hundreds of others, all of the cases mimicking each other in basic elements. No, I don't believe that searchers missed Danny in the canyon, nor do I believe that the Bloodhounds searching the canyon missed his scent. I also don't believe that the coroner and the forensic anthropologist were inept in their ability to find a cause of death.

There is a sinister element to these disappearances.

California-Central Sierra

Sex/Name	Date Missing • Age • State
M-George Penca	06/17/11-2:40 p.m. • 30 • Yosemite NP, CA
M-Robert Willis	10/31/08-Unk • 38 • Dinkey Creek, CA
F-Dr. Katherine Wong	02/19/99-2:00 p.m. • 47 • Bear Valley, CA

George Penca
Missing: 06/17/11-2:40 p.m., Yosemite NP, CA
Age at disappearance: 30 years

28 | Missing 411-The Devil's in the Detail

I sent the National Park Service (NPS) a Freedom of Information Act request on this case asking for all reports, photos, and search and rescue summaries. They refused to supply 250 pages of documents they stated they had, claiming that this was an open law enforcement case. Remember, I have received dozens of open missing person case files from the NPS. They were gracious enough to send me the missing persons "wanted poster" on Mr. Penca. It is completely unclear why the park failed to send search reports, photos, or interviews of witnesses. Yosemite continues to live outside the rules.

Yosemite National Park

MISSING PERSON

GEORGE PENCA
30 years old, 5'10", 240 pounds
Dark brown hair about 4 inches long, blue eyes, stocky build, speaks English. Last seen wearing gray sweatpants with white stripe, a black t-shirt that says "D & B" or a black tank top, gray/blue running shoes, had a blue cloth bag.

Photos taken Friday 6/17/11

Last seen at the top of Upper Yosemite Falls on Friday 06/17/11, at 2:40 pm

If you were near the top of Upper Yosemite Falls, the Upper Falls Trail, or any trail between the Valley and Tioga Road on Friday or Saturday 06/17 or 6/18 please call the Yosemite National Park Search and Rescue Office at (209) 372-0311 or (209)372-0252 whether you have seen George or not. Your information will help us focus the search area. If you have trouble getting through you can call (209) 379-1992 at any hour.

George Penca traveled with his church group from Southern California to Yosemite National Park. The group made a decision on the morning of June 17, 2011, that they would make the hike to Upper Yosemite Falls via the Upper Falls Trail. At approximately 2:30 p.m., the group decided to start back to the car from the top of the falls. George was near the back of the group, lagging behind. The group got to the parking lot, but George never arrived. The group notified NPS, and a search was initiated.

George was never found.

How a man can disappear on one of the busiest trails inside Yosemite is a complete mystery.

Robert Willis
Missing: 10/31/08-Unk, Dinkey Creek, CA
Age at disappearance: 38 years

Robert Willis was a very experienced hunter and a devoted family man. He left his residence in Caruthers for the short drive to up into the Sierras to his destination of Dinkey Creek, just south of Shaver Lake. The creek runs at six thousand feet, and the mountains surrounding the valley are above nine thousand feet. There is a significant amount of exposed granite to the northwest, and his destination is surrounded by five large bodies of water. Robert knew this was going to be a two-day trip as he needed to return for his son's football game.

Mr. Willis left his home on October 30, 2008, and was supposed to return on October 31. He was reported missing, according to search and rescue reports, on November 3 at 5:45 a.m. The Willis family responded into the woods and located Robert's 2000 Nissan Frontier pickup. It did appear that Robert had taken all of the equipment he would've needed.

The Fresno County sheriff's office led the rescue effort. They brought in two helicopters, an airplane, Bloodhounds, the USFS, National Park Service, and SAR teams from throughout the area.

Searchers knew that Robert liked to hunt Hall's Meadow, and that is where the search was centered. The longer the search effort continued, the worse the weather got. On November 13 the effort to locate Robert was halted because of heavy snow and freezing temperatures. There have been additional searches; they found nothing.

Summary

The area where Robert vanished is in the area between Yosemite and Sequoia-Kings Canyon National Park, a region where there are many missing people.

Dr. Katherine Wong
Missing: 02/19/99-2:00 p.m., Bear Valley, CA
Age at disappearance: 47 years

As someone who lived in California my entire life until 2012, I had never heard of the disappearance of Dr. Katherine Wong. When I started the research on this case, I was immediately disturbed as the facts started to roll out. There was no doubt to law enforcement and the press that something very unusual happened to the pediatrician.

On February 19, 1999, Dr. Katherine Wong and her husband, John, left their residence in Milpitas, California, for the four-hour drive to the Bear Valley Ski Resort thirty miles south of Lake Tahoe. This is one of the closer snow ski locations for San Francisco Bay Area residents.

The Wongs skied together that day. At one point, they decided to go down the mountain on different runs. Once John reached the bottom, he waited for his wife. She never arrived. The ski patrol was notified and then the Alpine County sheriff's office. By the end of the day, nothing was found of Katherine.

The alpine search and rescue team worked the rescue effort for two days. Helicopters flew the sky, canines were on the ground, and there were also dozens of ground searchers. After two days of intensive searching, nothing was found. Heavy snow and freezing conditions were now moving into the resort area, and the search was terminated.

In mid-May 1999, search teams went back into the area after much of the snow had melted. They again found nothing. A May 25, 1999, article in the *Union Democrat* conveyed the feelings of law enforcement: "A missing San Jose pediatrician once thought to have suffered an accident on a ski trip, may have vanished voluntarily or met with foul play, investigators now say." Later in the same article was this: "'We're going to keep looking, but experts say that there's very little chance she's up there,' Milpitas Police Sergeant Steve Pangelinan said. 'We're going to spend time looking into other possibilities...that she either met with foul play or left voluntarily."

On June 8, 1999, the Bear Valley SAR team again went back to the resort and continued searching for Dr. Wong. A June 9, 1999, article in the *Union Democrat* had this description of what they found: "Members of the Bear Valley Search and Rescue Team found scattered remains and articles of clothing and ski equipment believed to be that belonging to a missing woman about a half mile south of the Bear Valley Ski area, outside of marked boundaries. It was unclear how Dr. Wong ended up outside the ski area. 'There is very little to identify, she could have been killed by a coyote or bear,' said Sheriff Skip Veatch."

Bear Valley ski resort has a base elevation of 6,500 feet and reaches heights of 8,500 feet. Fifteen hundred people daily ski the slopes. Dr. Wong disappeared at the height of winter, the middle of February. There was up to twenty feet of snow on the ground at different locations of the resort when the doctor vanished. Is someone trying to convince us that bears were not hibernating when the incident occurred?

Summary

Investigators found Dr. Wong's driver's license, clothing, and scattered bone fragments. Various articles stated that law enforcement was handling this as a crime scene.

This scene is very reminiscent of other body recovery locations I have described in past cases. Refer to *Missing 411-Western United States* and the disappearances of Charles McCullar and Robert Winters. Both men disappeared in different locations at different times in the middle of winter, and very small bones and bone fragments were later found. The agencies investigating each incident described it as "baffling" as to what might have occurred.

You can tell by statements from law enforcement that they were stymied as to what happened to Dr. Wong.

Think of the ski run as a trail. I have explained many times that the last person down the trail is the most likely to disappear. Dr. Wong was the lone skier on her run when she vanished. It is very perplexing that the ski patrol and SAR workers were unable to locate her when she vanished. When people disappear in deep snow, tracks are quite evident. Where were the doctor's tracks leaving the groomed runs? I have no doubt that if there were tracks leaving the resort's runs, SAR would've followed them. This fact only makes the mystery deeper.

I could never determine if the sheriff conducted DNA testing of the bones or just relied on her clothing and driver's license for positive identification.

California-Central Coast

Sex/Name	Date Missing • Age • State
F-Anna Christian Waters	01/16/73-2:15 p.m. • 5 • CA

Anna Christian Waters
Missing: 01/16/73-2:15 p.m., Half Moon Bay, CA
Age at disappearance: 5 years

In the realm of researching missing people, there are few upbeat stories and many that are taxing to the soul. This is my second round of studying the case of Anna Christian Waters. My first effort was two years ago when I traveled to Half Moon Bay, pulled newspaper archives from the county library, and then drove the road where the disappearance occurred. I spent several days in the area of her residence, hiking local trails and reviewing documents, trying to understand what happened to this beautiful young girl.

Anna's mother, Michaele Benedict, wrote a very touching book about Anna's disappearance, *Searching for Anna*. Michaele clarifies many significant points about what happened that were not correctly reported in the local newspapers. I purchased the book, read it twice, and prepared my notes for writing. Somehow, somewhere, the book, notes, and archives vanished, the only time this has ever happened to me. I made a second trip back to Half Moon Bay and purchased the book again. After reading it a fourth time, I am more convinced than ever that Anna's story deserves to be here.

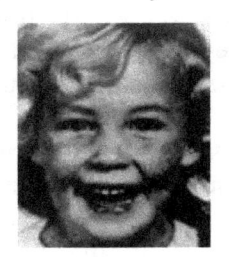

Half Moon Bay is a small coastal city forty miles south of San Francisco situated on State Highway 1. The city's claim to fame is an annual pumpkin festival where farmers from around the nation bring their pumpkins to be weighed—some roll in at over one thousand pounds! On the north end of the city is a gorgeous harbor, and just northwest of the mooring is the location of the world-famous Mavericks Big Wave surf contest. Farther north of the harbor is a famous location known to drivers throughout the Bay Area as "Devil's Slide." The treacherous piece of roadway is routinely closed when rocks fall down the hillside and block the roadway.

The location of this story is approximately four miles south of Half Moon Bay on Purisima Creek Road. This street extends east from Highway 1 up an idyllic valley and terminates at the eastern end at a trailhead for the Purisima Creek Redwoods Open Space District. This area is restricted to hiking and, I believe, horseback riding. I have spent many hours in this area and have seen the climate change drastically from foggy and wet to hot and dry. Many of the areas are dark, wet, and rarely see human traffic. This is also the area where I wrote about the disappearance of Douglas May and the subsequent finding of his body in the same open space district (*Missing 411-North America and Beyond*). Just northeast of the open-space region is Crystal Springs Reservoir and the surrounding property owned by the city and county of San Francisco. This is one of the most well-protected pieces of land in Central California. No public access is allowed except under isolated circumstances; they have guided tours, although these are rare. This property is pristine and very wild.

The small valley where Anna vanished has changed drastically in the last forty-plus years. Many of the residents are now extremely wealthy Silicon Valley executives and entertainers. The small shacks that existed in the 1970s have been replaced by large mansions and tall fences.

In Michaele's book, she describes Purisima Creek as a location that contains trout and, in her words, "is an herbalist's delight." The creek banks contain redwood sorrel, blackberries, red alder, and much more. She states that the Pacific Ocean was located four miles west of their home at the time of the disappearance.

In researching this case, I was also investigating the backgrounds of the parents, a normal procedure in all disappearances. The information I found on Michaele Benedict was stunning. Michaele is an excellent writer, and you can tell from her story she has a high intellect. In the mid-1960s, she worked for the *Knoxville News Sentinel* where she started as a copy girl and finished as a reporter. Yes, this is the same *Knoxville News Sentinel* I wrote about in regard to the Dennis Martin disappearance in 1969. Michaele wrote briefly about the Great Smoky Mountains and working in Knoxville, an interesting coincidence. After leaving Tennessee, she went to work for a United Nations delegation in New York as a writer in some capacity. She had two children at this point and had just met a young doctor, later to become Anna's father, George Waters.

California-Central Coast | 35

George was attending medical school in New York and later got a job at San Francisco General Hospital. Michaele and George eventually married and moved to California.

Anna was born on September 25, 1967, at the University of San Francisco Medical Center, one of the top medical institutions in the nation. George didn't appear to be interested in being a dad to Anna and distanced himself from Anna, Michaele, and her two other children. It was when the group was living in San Francisco that Michaele met Joe Ford, and a close friendship started. The four eventually moved away from George and settled on Purisima Creek Road in San Mateo County, California. After they settled into the ranch on Purisima Creek, Joe and Michaele married. Anna attended Hatch Elementary School, and Michaele was a teacher's aide two days a week.

Up until January 1973, life on Purisima Creek appeared to be quite idyllic for Michaele and her family. One of the few notations in Michaele's book about a disruption in life happened the night of January 14, 1973. Anna came into Joe and Michaele's room crying because she had had a bad nightmare. She stated that a giant spider was chasing her and asked if she could sleep with them, and she did.

The morning of January 16, 1973, started in a strange way. It was raining very hard, and Purisima Creek was flowing exceptionally high. At 10:00 a.m. a rooster attacked a local neighbor as she was walking into her pasture. This was no demure attack; it attacked so violently that a local blacksmith in the area had to kill it. At 12:20 p.m. Anna's school bus pulled up the road, and Anna exited and came into their house. She went into her room and changed into play clothes. Michaele told her to put on her red raincoat because of the weather. Anna went into their backyard adjacent to the creek and played with their dog and her toys. There were friends coming and going from the residence, and Michaele remembers hearing noise coming from the backyard, kid-type noise. Sometime between 1:30 and 2:00 p.m., Anna came back into the house and dropped her red raincoat inside. Sometime between 2:15 and 2:20, Michaele remembers it getting very quiet (her words), and she went into the backyard to look for Anna. She wasn't there. She yelled for the five-year-old; no answer. She went into their residence, into the front yard, and eventually down the street; no Anna. She eventually saw Joe, and they both looked. It quickly became obvious that Anna was not in the area.

At approximately 3:00 p.m., the San Mateo County sheriff's office was called, and at 3:15 p.m. the first deputy arrived. The deputy sounded his siren in an attempt to get Anna to come close; it didn't work. Just east of Michaele's residence and upstream from their residence, Charlene Machado was feeding her horses in a corral near the creek when she heard the following, as is described on page 31, paragraph 2 of *Searching for Anna*: "Heard the siren then noticed a crackling sound along the creek in a place where there were no animals. Her first thought was that someone was stealing something."

More deputies arrived at Purisima Creek Road, and soon helicopters were searching fields and the creek area. As the sun started to set, the deputies advised the family that they were going to leave and be back in the morning. (As a side note, I don't believe that this search practice would be the standard today. I believe most searchers would stay and call Anna's name through the night.)

At 8:30 a.m. on January 17, Bloodhounds arrived and started their search. One canine went to the rear yard, walked around the area, and then walked upstream slightly and stopped. The handler told Michaele that this was an inconclusive response. Multiple teams of divers responded throughout the creek and searched in fast-moving water in multiple locations, finding nothing. As the days moved forward, the water level dropped and the divers continued their search. It appears from the effort that law enforcement believed that Anna was in the creek. She was wearing oversized rubber/vinyl boots. If she was in the creek, the boots should've come off and been found; they were never located.

One of the archived articles I found was a January 25, 1973, issue of the *Half Moon Bay Review*. It stated: "Captain Herbert Elvander said the child's pet dog kept running back and forth between the house and creek after Mrs. Ford noticed her daughter missing from the backyard." If this was true, I understand why the focus was downstream from the creek. As anyone who has read my other books knows, downstream does not always hold the answers.

The search was eventually terminated without finding one piece of evidence of where Anna may be located. It was at this point that law enforcement started to consider other possibilities. There was much written about Anna's father and his strange relationships with others in San Francisco. I won't go into detail on any of that, as law enforcement and private investigators determined that none of it was related to Anna vanishing.

One of the most fascinating documents related to Anna's disappearance was a comprehensive report written by detectives in the San Mateo sheriff's department. This document was replicated in Michaele's book starting on page 87.

Item #2 in the report dealt with the Bloodhound that went to Anna's backyard. The report stated, "The owner of the dog nonetheless felt the dog had gotten a scent. Curiously, the dog double backed (upstream) before quitting." This item also stated that there were small footprints beside the creek that were similar to Anna's. This wasn't a surprise, as it was her backyard.

Item #6 addressed the dirt road paralleling Purisima Creek. It stated that this road was impassible at the time Anna had vanished because of recent weather, making an abduction by vehicle nearly impossible.

Item #7 was regarding the wording that Purisima Creek and the surrounding area were "wild." It clarified that there was a hunting club and a four-wheel-drive road not far from where Anna disappeared.

Item #8 was very revealing. I found it interesting that the deputies chose to address it. There was a general consensus that responding deputies had canvassed the neighborhood and spoken to the sixteen residents that were closest to Anna's home. A survey found that these neighbors had never been questioned even though there was "somewhat unusual phenomena at the time." I think the "unusual phenomena" refers to the rooster and the sounds heard near the creek.

Item #9 states that because of dams, logjams, and barbed wire fences, it is impossible for a body to make it from Michaele's residence to the ocean, even under the flood conditions that were present on January 16.

Part II of the sheriff's office report clarifies that they never found any piece of Anna's clothing. Part III is conclusions and has one fascinating fact. The neighborhood where Anna lived had a group of watchdogs that were very loud. The owners and the canines moved from the area one week prior to her disappearance, quite a coincidence.

The San Mateo County sheriff's office eventually made a statement that they believed there was a probability of abduction.

Anna has never been found.

Readers of my past books know there are certain elements that appear in cases that make them inclusive in the books. The elements that are present in Anna's case that point to inclusion:

- No trace of Anna was ever found.
- Anna's dog was with her in the backyard at the time of disappearance.
- It was raining the day she disappeared.
- Anna was wearing a red raincoat just prior to vanishing.
- Water was near the location of her disappearance, the creek and the Pacific Ocean.
- Berry bushes and sorrel were in the creek area.
- The yard was described as "quiet" by Michaele just as she realized she hadn't seen Anna.
- Bloodhounds never were able to track any scent for a significant distance.
- Sheriff believes abduction is a probability.

Unusual Aspects:

- Watchdogs in the neighborhood left one week prior to the disappearance.
- Neighbor hears strange noises around the creek upstream just after the disappearance.
- A rooster attacks a neighbor the morning of the disappearance.
- A strange coincidence is that Michaele worked for the *Knoxville News Sentinel* in the mid-1960s as a reporter.

Summary

In no way do I believe that any family member or any neighbor played any role in Anna's disappearance. There are too many factors involved in her vanishing that match cases I have written about in the past. The elements I have described seem to point upstream. The Bloodhound showed interest upstream, and a neighbor heard strange sounds near the creek bank upstream, an area that probably never got the same attention as downstream. Search and rescue books would indicate that she probably fell into the creek, and if she did not—if she wandered—it would be downhill. Readers of this series know that in a significant number of cases I outline, children go uphill, sometimes for thousands of feet. In this area, safety from the public and safety from recognition could be had by going upstream and uphill into the confines of the open-space district.

California-San Francisco Bay Area

Sex/Name	Date Missing • Age • State
F-Patricia Connolly	01/29/42-Unk • 2 • Menlo Park, CA
F-Red Cramer	08/27/45-7:00 p.m. • 30 mos. • Los Gatos, CA

Patricia Connolly
Missing: 01/29/42-Unk, Menlo Park, CA
Age at disappearance: 2 years

I know this area very well, as I was raised just miles south and worked for my dad in this neighborhood. This region of the San Francisco Bay Area has changed drastically since this event happened. The disappearance occurred in a residence on the fringe of Stanford University adjacent to San Francisquito Creek. As I relate this story, you need to get to a computer and observe the area where this happened and where it ends—it's unreal. California Highway 280 did not exist in 1942, and the area was fairly rugged and rural. This area is now the home of the rich and famous of Silicon Valley.

Patricia Connolly was two and a half years old when she lived at 12½ Bishop Lane in Menlo Park. The residence is on the north side of San Francisquito Creek with the Stanford University golf course on the other. On January 29, 1942, on a stormy night with freezing temperatures, the creek was running high. Somehow, late that night Patricia and her dog vanished from the residence, and the sheriff was called. A February 3, 1942, article in the *San Mateo Times* had the following: "Sheriff James McGrath said the child's footsteps were traced to the edge of San Francisquito Creek near the Stanford University Campus. Dragging the swift stream has failed to locate her body. Patricia's pet dog was found wandering in the vicinity shortly after she was reported missing." Understand, it's storming, the creek is running very high, and deputies find Patricia's tracks and her dog at the creek side. Law enforcement now does the normal thing: drags the creek for days, looking for the body. From Patricia's residence to the shores of San Francisco Bay, it is approximately 6.6 miles, all downhill.

The search for Patricia Connolly continued for almost one week until deputies terminated their efforts under the belief that her body was washed to the bay.

On February 26, 1942, twenty-eight days after Patricia disappeared, Palo Alto resident H. D. Haggitt was hiking in a ravine three air miles west of her residence when he made a discovery as is described in this April 27, 1942, article in the *San Jose News*: "Hiking through a gully where the remains were found, made the gruesome find which ended the search which in its early stages included use of Bloodhounds and was aided by scores of volunteers." The same article describes the location of the find as the "Varsity Park picnic grounds on Portola Road behind Stanford University." The article doesn't explain the difficulty in getting from the Bishop Lane residence to the Portola Road location. I can comfortably say that it is a near impossibility for Patricia to voluntarily disappear from her residence on a freezing and rainy night, wander down near her creek, and manage to stay inside the creek bank as she went uphill for over three miles. She would've had to cross the creek to get to the Portola Road location and then manage to get over a 650-foot-tall mountain range with an extremely steep eastern slope.

The same *San Jose News* article quoted earlier stated that Patricia died of exhaustion, meaning the coroner could not determine the cause of death.

Summary

This is another case where a small child disappears from his or her residence during the night. Law enforcement attempts to rationalize the disappearance by claiming the child fell into a rain-swollen creek. In reality, Patricia's body went in the exact opposite direction, uphill over three miles into the foothills. The more important question is, how many two-and-a-half-year-old children would wander into a dark, raining, freezing night?

I could not find one article that showed any concern for where Patricia disappeared and where she was found. I put this case into the same classification as the disappearance of Ryan Hoeffliger (January 1984, Hayden Lake, ID) and Ann Marie Burr (August 1961, Tacoma, WA). Each of these cases happened on the fringe of rural locations. The incidents happened in 1942 (CA), 1961 (WA), and 1984 (ID), nineteen years between the first two incidents and twenty-three years between the final two, just enough time to ensure that nobody would connect the dots. I have no doubt that another incident has happened since 1984; I just need to find it. Three different western states and three extraordinary stories.

Red Cramer
Missing: 08/27/45-7:00 p.m., Los Gatos, CA
Age at disappearance: 30 months

If there was ever a case that hit close to my home, this is it. I lived in Los Gatos for over twelve years and in fact lived on the road where Red disappeared. I know this area extremely well. I almost fell out of my chair when I read about this incident, as it clearly fits the profile of what we've researched.

Los Gatos sits at the far southern end of the San Francisco Bay Area. Many would consider the small city a suburb of San Jose. It's a location where many of the high-tech executives live and their children attend school. This is the last city in the southern area before the Santa Cruz Mountains start and extend to the Pacific Ocean.

On August 27, 1945, at 7:00 p.m., two-year-old Red Cramer was playing in the yard of her family's small ranch on Shannon Road when she suddenly vanished. The road extends from the valley and goes through the mountains to the southern end of San Jose. The parents notified the constable of Los Gatos, E. O. Wood, and he in turn notified Santa Clara County Chief Deputy Sheriff Jack Gibbons. The two law enforcement veterans enlisted fifty searchers to assist in looking for Red.

The search got started very quickly. Constable Wood obtained the canine services of Bill Thompson of Sunnyvale, and he brought Bloodhounds to the scene. Thompson claimed he found a faint scent trail but lost it quickly.

On August 28, Constable Wood got further assistance from Moffitt Field. A blimp was put into the sky above Los Gatos in an effort to find the girl. The blimp and the Bloodhounds found nothing.

At approximately 12:30 p.m., a searcher was outside the search grid when they made an amazing find as is described in the August 28, 1945, edition of the *San Jose Mercury*: "The baby was found up a canyon five miles from her home when one of the foot searchers, who complemented a sheriff's posse, volunteer firemen and a corps of Bloodhounds, saw the sun shining on her red blonde hair. It took almost 45 minutes for the rescuers to bring the child down the canyon." Imagine: the child is found uphill and five miles from her family's home, and it takes forty-five minutes for rescuers to walk down.

Summary

The mountains in the area where Red was found are steep and dry. I've talked about this case with many who know the area, and nobody can believe the facts surrounding it. According to Robert Koester's book, *Lost Person Behavior*, children in the age range of one to three who disappear in a mountain environment will be found 95 percent of the time at a distance of 2.3 miles or less. Red was found uphill five miles from her home. Could your two-year-old have accomplished this feat?

California-Southern

Sex/Name	Date/Time Missing • Age • State
M-Tomas Cabrera	05/31/85-a.m. • 3 • Tecate, Mexico
M-Alyof Krost	10/01/13-5:45 p.m. • 62 • Lake Arrowhead, CA

Tomas Cabrera
Missing: 05/31/85-a.m., Tecate, Mexico
Age at disappearance: 3 years

This is one of the most unusual cases I've ever documented when you look at the distance that this child allegedly covered. It is definitely in the realm of the unbelievable.

On May 31, 1985, and in the morning hours, Tomas Cabrera was with his father as his dad was working in a field on the outskirts of Tecate, Mexico. Vicente Rea Cabrera was Tomas's father and had been watching the boy. He stated that he last saw Tomas as he placed him sitting on a rock overlooking the field. He stated that he returned in just a few minutes, and his son was gone. He searched the area calling Tomas's name but didn't get a response and couldn't locate his son. Vicente notified the workers around him, and they asked local policia for assistance.

Tecate is located on the United States border approximately twenty-five miles east of San Diego and Tijuana.

Tecate police notified the United States Border Patrol and requested they keep an eye on the border should Tomas just happen to get into that area.

Thirty hours after Tomas vanished, border patrol agents scouring the area for the boy made a lucky discovery as is described in the June 5, 1985, article in the *Free Lance Star*: "Agent Mike Gregg found Tomas in a desert area known as Tierra Del Sol, a quarter mile north of the Mexican border and 70 miles east of San Diego, about 30 hours after he was reported missing, Stille said." Later in that same article, the agent in charge of the area made a statement about the distance traveled: "Stille estimated that Tomas walked through nearly 15 miles of desert." You might want to read that statement again. In the same article was a description of Tomas when he was found: "Tomas was curled up beneath a bush, naked, exhausted and shivering, he said."

Tomas was transported to a United States hospital. Border restrictions were dropped, and his parents were brought to the hospital to be with their son.

Summary

In Robert Koester's book, *Lost Person Behavior*, he states that a three-year-old boy will be found 95 percent of the time after traveling two miles or less. Tomas supposedly crossed fifteen miles of desert in the hot months of June.

Tomas had scratches on his face and body and was slightly dehydrated but in good condition.

Border agents stated that it was their belief that the small boy must've found a hole in the border wall and found his way into the United States. It was also their understanding that the boy traveled the fifteen miles. There were no claims of foul play.

Tomas disappeared sitting on a boulder—coincidence? Boulders have been implicated in many disappearances. The boy was found naked and under brush, another commonality with many cases I've chronicled.

Alyof Krost
Missing: 10/1/13-5:45 p.m., Lake Arrowhead, CA
Age at disappearance: 62 years

During the last year we started to pay closer attention to the educational background of the individuals who have disappeared. Alyof Krost is one of those humans on the brilliant side of the educational equation. Professor Krost was an instructor of physics at the Otto Von Guericke University in Magdeburg, Germany.

Krost was with a group of other Germans who traveled to the United States to attend a science conference at the University of California, Los Angeles conference center at Lake Arrowhead. He had attended this annual conference many times.

The area around the conference center had fields with large boulders and acres of small scrub bushes and rolling hills. On September 30 Professor Krost joined a group of tourists for a hike through the area. Everyone in the group returned safely. On October 1 there was another hike, led by two guides on the Pinnacle Trail. There were twenty tourists, a guide leading the group, and a guide at the back of the group. Sometime during the hike, Krost got tired and noticed that the guide at the rear wasn't feeling well. Both men decided to take a break and allow the main group to hike ahead. Krost stated he felt better and resumed hiking toward the main group. The rear guide waited several more minutes until he felt better and then started hiking the trail. The guide reached the lodge with the other tourists and realized that Krost hadn't. The two guides walked back down the trail, searching for the man, and couldn't locate him. The San Bernardino County sheriff was called.

During the first several days of searching, the wind around Lake Arrowhead was horrible, which forced many of the planes and helicopters that were available to be grounded. Winds as high as sixty miles per hour were clocked in the valley.

Search and rescue teams from throughout the state responded with Bloodhounds and ATVs all working the area in a three-and-a-half mile radius. The searchers were finding nothing. Helicopters with FLIR eventually covered the area and found nothing of value. Searchers stayed on this case for almost two weeks and still could not locate anything indicating that Krost was in the region.

Summary

There are a few elements of this disappearance that concern me. When Professor Krost stopped on the trail because he was tired, the rear guide also had to stop. I have stated in past books that the person in the back of the line tends to disappear more than anyone else in a hiking group. In this case the person at the back of the line was the guide, and he needed to stop. If Krost hadn't stopped and continued with the group, would the guide have been the one to vanish? Krost continued to hike, leaving the guide behind resting. Krost was now the last hiker when he vanished. Did something happen to Krost and the guide that caused them both to stop and need to rest?

Bloodhounds searching for Krost never found a scent. Weather kept planes and helicopters grounded for a few days. Krost was the last in line when he vanished.

If you've read my other books, it's an unusual event when a reporter mentions someone's nationality. The times that nationality is mentioned, in an abnormal number of occasions, it seems that the background is German.

You will read in this book about our renewed focus on a person's intellect. Remember Professor Krost's expertise: physics.

Forty miles northwest from Lake Arrowhead is the Devil's Punchbowl, a location where off-duty Los Angeles County Deputy Sheriff Jonathan Aujay was hiking alone on June 11, 1998, and disappeared. The deputy was never found (See *Missing 411-Western United States*).

Colorado

Sex/Name	Date Missing • Age • State
M-H. F. Targett	6/21/21-a.m. • 55 • RMNP, CO
M-Gregory Aubuchon	07/20/21-Unk • 18 • RMNP, CO
F-Margaret Turner	10/09/24-a.m. • 20 mos. • Durango, CO
M-Alfred Hotchkiss	10/01/29-a.m. • 2 • Ridgeway, CO
M-Vernon Daniel	12/15/29-2:00 p.m. • 2 • Bayfield, CO
M-Benjamin Saul	08/10/31-6:00 p.m. • 3 • Jarre Canyon, CO
M-Steve Benson	03/15/36-10:30 a.m. • 3 • Two Buttes, CO
M-Floyd Chandler	10/11/37-4:30 p.m. • 41 • Stove Prairie, CO
M-Hoyt F. White	09/05/40-Unk • 33 • RMNP, CO
M-Thomas Evans	06/16/46-a.m. • 20 • RMNP, CO
M-Harley Booth	07/03/46-Unk • 30 • Devil's Gulch, RMNP, CO
F-Sandy Barcus	07/21/56-Noon • 2 • Nederland, CO
M-Bobby Bizup	08/15/58-6:00 p.m. • 10 • RMNP, CO
F-Judy Boltjes	05/02/59-2:00 p.m. • 6 • Deckers, CO
M-Gregory Aubuchon	07/20/71-Unk • 18 • RMNP, CO
M-Christopher Vigil	04/30/78-6:30 p.m. • 9 • Greyrock Mountain, CO
M-Dr. Maurice Dametz	04/29-81-3:45 p.m. • 84 • Pike National Forest, CO
M-Christopher Harvey	07/11/84-3:30 p.m. • 14 • Pagosa Springs, CO
M-Keith Reinhard	08/07/88-4:00 p.m. • 49 • Silver Plume, CO

Colorado | 47

F-Sarah Wolenetz   07/11/92-3:00 p.m. • 11 • RMNP, CO
M-Jeff Christensen   07/29/05-Unk • 31 • RMNP, CO
M-Mitchell Dale Stehling   06/09/13-4:08 p.m. • 51 • Mesa Verde NP
M-Gene George   09/21/13-Unk • 64 • Mount Harvard, CO

Introduction

This is one of the largest chapters in the book. I never intended to focus on Colorado; the disappearances just continued to roll in.

One of the surprising aspects of research is what you find when you start to dig deep. A shocking find was the third piece of the missing boy equation in far northern Colorado. The case of Christopher Vigil is missing boy number three in a triangle that includes Jaryd Atadero and Alfred Beilhartz (*Missing 411-Western United States*). Jaryd was found deceased under unusual circumstances; Christopher and Alfred have never been found.

Another unusual find is at the far southern end of the state along the Animas River. Five children have disappeared within a ten-mile radius of the river between Ouray and Durango from 1924–2003. I credit another researcher (Scott Nelson) with forwarding me the information on the river. In 1765 Spanish Explorer Juan Maria De Rivera originally named the river Rio De Las Animas, the river of lost souls. The explorer supposedly named the river this because so many of his soldiers disappeared in its vicinity.

H. F. Targett
Missing: 6/21/21-a.m., Chasm Lake, RMNP, CO
Age at disappearance: 55 years

Mr. Targett was staying at the Long's Peak Inn on the east side of the peak. He had traveled to the park from Los Angeles with the intent of scaling the mountain.

On June 21, 1921, Mr. Targett left the inn very early in the morning with the intent of summiting and being back in the afternoon. He never arrived. The National Park Service immediately started a full-scale search for the climber. There was a one-week effort to locate Targett, and there was nothing found that could place him on the mountain. Searchers essentially could not find tracks, discarded clothing or equipment, nothing.

On September 20, 1940, nineteen years after Targett disappeared, there was a stunning discovery in an unlikely location as is described in the September 21, 1940, article in the *Galveston Daily*: "Percy Dawson of Austin, Texas, and Miss Edith Perron, a Chicago radio official, found the skull as they crawled on hands and knees through a dense growth of shrubbery in the Chasm Lake area." Four of the teeth were compared to Targett's, and it confirmed to be him. There were no other bones found in the area.

Officials stated that the skull was partially crushed. There was no explanation as to why no other bones were found or why the skull would be in this unlikely position, deep within foliage in an area with almost no other ground cover. The location of the find was approximately one mile from Chasm Lake and near the foot of Long's Peak. There was also no explanation why the people who found the skull were on their hands and knees in the middle of shrubbery.

Readers, take note of the location of this find. Many of the people found in the disappearances I chronicle are located in thickets and bushes. The location around Chasm Lake is a region where many unusual events occur. The name of the lake has some interesting possible meanings.

Margaret Turner
Missing: 10/09/24-a.m., Durango, CO
Age at disappearance: 20 months

This case could be the centerpiece for the Missing 411 series. The difference in this incident, compared to many others, is that law enforcement officers verbalized what many others have refused to do. The sheriff made statements to the press about the impossibility of the situation and claimed from the beginning this was a criminal abduction.

In the morning hours of October 9, 1924, Margaret Turner was at her residence in a rural area outside of Durango with her mother. It's unknown how the small girl got out of her mother's sight, but she disappeared, and her mother started to search her yard. After a short while, it was apparent that Margaret wasn't in the area, and the La Plata County sheriff's office was called. Deputies arrived and called for additional assistance from the community. Volunteers from the city were put into groups and given areas to look for the toddler.

On the afternoon of October 10, a group of searchers were far outside the bounds of where anyone thought Margaret would be found. Five miles west of town, across several major roadways and on top of a barren peak, the girl was found alive. The sentiments of law enforcement are stated in this *Milwaukee Journal* article of October 14, 1924: "Being barely able to walk, however, Sheriff Rowe said, it would have been impossible for the baby to have scaled the heights where she was found or to survive the cold of Thursday night without shelter afforded somewhere else. The spot where the baby was found is in high country, sparsely overgrown with scrub oak." Later in the same article is more information: "Authorities believe that whoever placed the child on top of the peak did so some time during the day Friday, as death from exposure would have been certain if it laid there all of Thursday night. The child was probably kept in a shelter Thursday night and the kidnapper removed it to the mountain Friday." I could not agree more.

Summary

The disappearance and recovery of Margaret Turner is so similar to many of the cases I've written about that it can't be denied. In this case, Sheriff Rowe was willing to publicly state the obvious and not claim the child walked the path herself. The real question in my mind is twofold. One, why would anyone choose a mountain peak that does not have any trees, only small scrub bushes? Whoever put the girl there risked being seen by searchers in the area; why not pick a location farther from the city? The fact is that a group of high school boys were given the day off to look for Margaret, and they were the ones to make the find. The last question: Where was the child held during the night?

There was never any mention of child abuse.

I truly believe that this case is very important. Many children we've documented are found in areas high above from where they disappeared. It appears to be an accepted fact that the girl wasn't on the peak all night, or she'd have been suffering from severe exposure or worse. It would seem nearly impossible for anyone to place her on the top of the peak during the day without being seen. Why would anyone hike with a child to the top of the peak when they could stop on any nearby road and place her on the shoulder?

This case will never be solved utilizing conventional theories.

Alfred Hotchkiss
Missing: 10/01/29-a.m., Ridgeway, CO
Age at disappearance: 2 years

Ridgeway is approximately eighty miles south of Grand Junction and seventy miles northwest of Pagosa Springs. Pay special attention to the details of this case and compare them to the facts surrounding the disappearance of Vernon Daniel.

On October 1, 1929, Alfred was at his rural ranch home outside the city. Mrs. Archie Hotchkiss last saw her son in the morning hours near the barn. She looked for the boy and then called the sheriff and neighbors for assistance. The search gained momentum as the days went by and soon escalated to unreal numbers as is explained in this October 9, 1929, article in the *Pittsburgh Press*: "The wooded mountain slopes near here were searched by more than 1,000 men and women today for 2-year old Alfred Hotchkiss, who disappeared a week ago. Yesterday it was estimated 4,000 persons took part in the hunt. Today, after irrigation ditches had been drained and remote sections searched, officers said they were of the opinion the baby had been kidnapped."

The question of what happened to Alfred was of concern to the community, and many thought maybe an eagle or mountain lion had taken the lad. The problem with the animal abduction scenario was that there was no evidence that either creature was in the area. After ten days of searching, the effort was terminated, and law enforcement was now more adamant than ever that the boy was kidnapped. The issue with the kidnapping scenario was that the Hotchkiss property was very visible in every direction; thus they could see anyone approaching, and they hadn't when Alfred vanished.

Almost one month after the boy disappeared, a cowboy made an astonishing find as is described in this October 28, 1929, article in the *Salt Lake Tribune*: "Missing nearly a month, the body of 2-year old Alfred Hotchkiss was found today in a willow swamp in a wild mountain region about 12 miles from the home of his parents. A cowboy in search of stray cattle found the body." Later in the same article is this explanation: "Authorities believe the baby died of starvation and exposure after wandering for what was estimated to be a day and a night after leaving his home." Authorities are claiming that a two-year-old boy covered twelve mountain miles in two days.

Summary

I don't think any parent believes that a two-year-old could cover the miles in the mountain country where Alfred lived. I doubt any two-year-old could cover twelve miles on flat ground.

Reminder: now read the details of the Vernon Daniel case and review the facts, date, location, age, etc.

Vernon Daniel
Missing: 12/15/1929-2:00 p.m., Bayfield, CO
Age at disappearance: 2 years

You are going to read about a few cases in the area of this incident. Bayfield is located approximately fifteen miles east of Durango and forty miles west of Pagosa Springs in the far southern portion of Colorado.

On December 15, 1929, at 2:00 p.m., Mr. and Mrs. Jewel Daniel and their son, Vernon, were visiting the Oscar Groves Ranch on the far northern outskirts of Bayfield. Somehow Vernon got out of his mother's sight while they were near the barn and vanished.

The ranch hands got the word to Durango, and six hundred people arrived to assist in finding the boy. The volunteers formed groups and scoured the mountains and land around the ranch, going nonstop through the night. Everyone was concerned for the boy's welfare because of the extremely cold weather in the area.

On the morning of December 16, a few searchers were in an area that nobody thought would be productive. A December 18 article in the *Billings Gazette* had this description of the area where Vernon was located: "Monday, Vernon was found unconscious beneath a tree. He had managed to make his way up and down the steep slopes, over rocks and fallen boughs, so the searchers missed him." He had traveled three miles over extremely rough terrain to eventually be found under a tree. He was taken to a doctor and found to be in serious condition. He did survive.

The location of this disappearance is important when you consider other incidents in the area. I believe that the family was very fortunate to get Vernon back.

M-Benjamin Saul
Missing: 08/10/31-6:00 p.m., Jarre Canyon, CO
Age at disappearance: 3 years

This case is intriguing for many reasons, primarily its location. The parents' residence cabin was off Jarre Canyon Road, approximately one mile west of Rampart Range Road.

Going back to review cases in this area is scary. In *Missing 411-Western United States,* I wrote about the disappearance of Teresa Schmidt, age fifty-three. She was attending a medical conference with her husband at a dude ranch fourteen miles southwest of the location where Benjamin Saul disappeared. Theresa went missing September 6, 2002, and has never been found. Eight miles south from the Saul disappearance was the case of Maurice Dametz, which is chronicled in this chapter. Maurice was an elderly man who vanished while searching for gemstones. He was never found. All of these disappearances are near a specific location, which was identified in an article associated with Benjamin's disappearance, an August 11, 1931, article in the *Pittsburgh Press*: "The whole of Jarre Canyon which is in the shadow of Devil's Head Peak, rising some 10,000 feet above the level of the sea, is rock strewn and precipitous." Many of the missing people I've written about have disappeared in an area that have "devil" names associated with geographic locations and are covered with boulders.

On August 10, 1931, near dinnertime, Benjamin Saul was outside his parents' cabin when the boy disappeared. The parents yelled and called for the boy without getting a response. The family wasted little time and contacted the local forest ranger and sheriff. Law enforcement contacted additional volunteers. Searchers on horseback and several teams of Bloodhounds converged on the Saul cabin. A pilot from Denver flew the sky for a day looking for the boy. For the following thirty-seven hours, searchers combed the entire valley at a radius of five miles and found nothing showing that Benjamin was in the area. They did see a mountain lion and various other wildlife, but no boy. Bloodhounds were not locating a scent.

It was thirty-eight hours after Benjamin had vanished, and a group of tourists were staying at the Roundup Ranch, not far from the Saul cabin. The group got an early start and was going down a trail adjacent to the highway. The tourists saw a small boy near an old crashed vehicle and approached him. It was Benjamin. The boy was found less than a mile from his cabin. He was weak, hungry, and thirsty. He was reunited with his family and taken to Deckers and on to a hospital in Colorado Springs. He had lost his right shoe and sock, and his clothing was torn.

In the past I've written about missing children sometimes being found with a fever. Benjamin was stated to have a fever but no other serious conditions.

Some articles about this incident stated that he had seen puppies and kitties, while other articles stated he had not seen any wildlife. This case continues a trend where children are found, but not found by search teams. Benjamin was located in an area where many hiked and rode horses every day: a location where it would be almost impossible not to see the boy. It's very hard to imagine how the boy didn't hear searchers the prior day while they were in the area he was found.

Based on the other disappearances in this area, the Saul family was very fortunate to get Benjamin back.

Steve Benson
Missing: 03/15/36-10:30 a.m., Two Buttes, CO
Age at disappearance: 3 years

We've chronicled many types of weather conditions that have facilitated the disappearance of a child; the following type of weather is a first. Two Buttes is located at the far southeastern portion of Colorado and near the borders of Oklahoma and Kansas. There are no large trees in this area, just many thousands of acres of farms and grasslands.

On March 15, 1936, at approximately 10:30 a.m., three-year-old Steve Benson was playing in the yard of his family's farm. Steve somehow and for some unknown reason wandered away from the residence, and his parents started to search for the boy. After a short period of time, the family called the neighbors and the sheriff for assistance.

Searchers covered an area five miles from the farm in an effort to locate the boy. Two hundred CCC youths assisted in the search along with hundreds of local farmers. The local high schools were closed, and those youths were utilized in the search.

As late afternoon came to Two Buttes, the weather started to turn for the worst. The region was hit by a "Black Blizzard": a dust storm of epic proportions hit the town and essentially turned the area dark. Searchers were distraught because they did not believe anyone could live through the storm without shelter. A March 16, 1936, article in the *Daily Ardmoreite* provided the following information about finding Steve: "Three-year-old Steve Benson walked into a farm house alive today after spending the night lost in one of the worst 'black blizzards' dust storms ever to strike this area. More than 500 persons were searching for the boy, expecting to find him smothered or frozen to death when he reached the farm home of Dewey Fetters, six miles from where he disappeared." Temperatures in the area of Two Buttes had dropped below freezing during the night and with the wind chill, it was much colder.

There was another March 16, 1936, article in the *Greeley Tribune* that explained Steve's condition when he was found: "Doctors examined him and said his condition was 'exceptionally good' considering that he had been in the open for hours in a dust storm that reduced visibility to zero."

When Steve was interviewed, he made an interesting statement about where he had been and what he had done when he was gone. He told his parents that he had fallen asleep. He stated he didn't remember much else. When he was in his parents' arms, he immediately went to sleep and didn't say anything. Steve was found just wearing his overalls; he had lost his shoes.

Searchers were shocked about where Steve was found. The same *Greeley Tribune* article quoted above had the following about the feelings of searchers: "'We had not hunted as far as the Fettter home because we believed it was impossible for the boy to have wandered that far in the dust,' said Night Marshal W.C. Schweitzer of Two Buttes."

Summary

Doctors were amazed that Steve was found in such good health after being out in horrific weather. It's truly amazing that the boy survived the dust storm and the freezing temperatures. Why didn't Steve receive frostbite to his feet and toes?

Searchers were stunned that Steve was found six miles from his home. How the boy was able to avoid searchers in an area where prior to the storm you could see for miles is amazing.

M-Floyd Chandler
Missing: 10/11/37-4:30 p.m., Stove Prairie, CO
Age at disappearance: 41 years

In *Missing 411-Western United States,* I chronicled the disappearance of Alfred Beilartz from Rocky Mountain National Park and Jaryd Atadero from north of that location along the Cache La Poudre River. In this book I am adding Chris Vigil, who went missing on Grey Mountain fifteen miles north of Floyd Chandler. Mr. Chandler disappeared inside the triangle of the three other disappearances. This is a tight cluster of three boys and one man.

Floyd Chandler was a wealthy rancher, landowner, and hunting guide. He was described as one of the most knowledgeable guides and hunters in the Fort Collins area. On October 11, 1937, Mr. Chandler had gone to scout deer for the upcoming season with his longtime friend and neighbor, O. R. Eberhart. They arrived at the camp and separated, with each scouting separate areas. Mr. Chandler was supposed to arrive back at camp by dark, but he didn't. About the time that Mr. Chandler was supposed to arrive, it started to rain and continued through most of the night and early morning. Mr. Eberhart searched for his friend for two days before enlisting the assistance of law enforcement. The October 16, 1937, *Greeley Daily Tribune* had a detailed explanation of where Mr. Chandler had disappeared: "The cabin known as 'Jay Bosworth's Upper Camp,' is eight and one half miles straight west of the Stove Prairie Schoolhouse. Stove Prairie Schoolhouse is seven miles south of Stover Prairie Landing. Stove Prairie Landing is 27 miles west of Fort Collins on Poudre Canyon Highway."

Planes, Bloodhounds, and huge numbers of ground teams worked the mountains in a method defined by the sheriff in an attempt to locate Chandler. An October 14 article in the *Greeley Tribune* had this description of the search: "Long lines of searchers walking fairly close together were attempting to cover an area seven miles square, Jackson said: 'This would be 49 square miles.' Every precipice down which Chandler may have fallen was examined closely." This was considered one of the biggest searches ever in this part of the state.

Law enforcement teams were baffled because they weren't finding the normal tracks and evidence that Chandler was anywhere in the area. After almost three weeks of committed effort, on November 3 the search was terminated.

On December 6, 1938, the *Greeley Tribune* had the following headlines: "Crumpled Body of Johnstown Man Is Under Cliff, Found 3 Miles from where Rancher Disappeared 14 Months Ago." Mr. Chandler had been found. Yes, Mr. Chandler was found just three miles from where he disappeared, well inside the search area. This same article described the area, and you can tell that Sheriff Gooch was suspicious: "Gooch stated that officers are giving careful scrutiny to the conditions and place of finding Chandler's hunting rifle. It had apparently fallen over the thirty foot cliff at the same time he did. The barrel was stuck in the soil at the base of the cliff, the sight was bent and the gun was otherwise undamaged. It was badly corroded. Officers were investigating the circumstances for the outside possibility that if there was foul play, the murderer might have thrown it over the cliff to simulate a natural fall. Chandler's body had rolled several feet beyond the gun and lodged against a tree." You can tell by the tone that the circumstances at the scene had disturbed the sheriff. I would say that finding the rifle stuck in the ground was highly unusual and almost simulates an effort to throw it.

Mr. Chandler's body did go through a coroner's inquest. He was found to have a head injury as is described in the December 7, 1938, *Greeley Tribune*: "The doctors reported that the skull fracture had been caused by a large blunt instrument which could have been caused by falling on a rock." The doctors stated that death was instantaneous.

Mrs. Chandler didn't believe the coroner's conclusions because her husband's background and his knowledge of the outdoors. She hired a private investigator who worked the case for several weeks, but he did not produce anything of value that made it to the newspapers.

Summary

Floyd Chandler was found fourteen months after he disappeared by a trapper who had a cabin in the area. The trapper stated that he walked over a log and found the body. He told the paper that the body had not decomposed much. The December 6, 1938, article in the *Greeley Tribune* had this description of his find: "William G. Ferris. A 43 year old trapper who has a cabin about three miles from the spot, stumbled onto the body a mile above the confluence of the Little South Poudre and the main Poudre River." The body was found in an area that had previously been searched. The coroner's inquest found that Mr. Chandler had died accidentally from a fall. I don't think Mrs. Chandler agreed with the findings.

Hoyt F. White
Missing: 09/05/40-Unk, RMNP, CO
Age at disappearance: 33 years

Hoyt White was a very experienced climber, having made the summit of several peaks in Rocky Mountain National Park. He wasn't just a great climber. Mr. White was a brilliant Kansas attorney who worked for the Yates Center Law Institute in Woodson County.

On August 31, 1950, Mr. White left Kansas and drove to Estes Park, Colorado, to stay at the summer cabin of his aunt. He had been to this location several times and had told his aunt that he truly enjoyed climbing the peaks in the park. Family members never heard from Hoyt after he arrived, and they called park officials to check on his status.

National Park employees found the car of Mr. White on September 16 parked near the Twin Sisters Peak trail area. A large group of park officials started the search for the climber and notified his family about what they had found. Family and friends of Hoyt immediately left Kansas to assist in the search.

The search for the attorney grew to nearly two hundred people who were covering every side of Twin Peaks. There were almost 125 CCC workers committed to the mountain as well as local volunteers and park employees.

On September 19 a CCC employee was on the mountain and found Mr. White as is described in the *Iola Register* from September 20, 1940: "Whitaker, one of 125 CCC enrollees who had deployed over the sides of the 11,425 foot peak in search of White, found the body lodged under a log about 125 feet from the base of a cliff." Later in the same article was further clarity as to why the body wasn't found earlier: "Herschler said that searchers passed within 25 feet of the body earlier but the log concealed it. White probably was killed instantly in the accidental tumble from the rock ledge, the ranger said. The attorney's skull was crushed and most of his clothing torn away." Most of his clothing torn away from a fall— hmm. Considering that White was wearing a significant amount of clothing, this is hard to understand. As readers of past books will remember, many people are found under logs, a location where FLIR cannot find you. Knowing that this mountain does not have significant ground cover, this must've been one of the few locations where there even was a log. Officials state that Hoyt fell seventy-five feet and then rolled 125 feet to his location under a log. That's a long roll after a fairly short alleged fall.

Searchers did find Hoyt's diary and discovered that his last entry was September 5. Park officials made a statement that they thought Hoyt was trying to take a shortcut and went off-trail a great distance to get to the place where he was found. Searchers missed Hoyt's body multiple times because it was under the log.

It would appear that when you go off-trail in Rocky Mountain National Park, bad things happen.

Thomas H. Evans
Missing: 06/16/46-a.m., Flat Top Mountain, RMNP, CO
Age at disappearance: 20 years

During the week of June 10, 1946, a group of United States Air Force soldiers stationed at Lowry Field in Denver had won the praise of their commander for keeping an exceptionally clean facility. The two hundred soldiers were taken to Rocky Mountain National Park for a vacation day.

On June 16 the soldiers were loaded into buses and taken to the picnic grounds at the base of Flat Top Mountain. One of the soldiers in the group was Thomas Evans, a twenty-year-old private from Akron, Ohio.

You'd think that someone would've known that Evans had left the group or was planning to embark on a hike to a high peak, but nobody saw him leave. A June 21, 1946, article in the *Times Herald* had the following about how the search started: "The search was started Monday when roll call at the air field near Denver disclosed that Evans was missing. Fellow soldiers said he had not returned with the rest of the outfit Sunday night." In the same article, it states that mountain experts claim that Flat Top Mountain is one of the most dangerous in the Rockies.

The search started on June 17 with twenty military police officers with mountain climbing experience and nine combat mountain experts from Camp Carson. The national park also committed manpower to the effort to find Thomas. All of the soldiers involved in the search were given a week's worth of rations and orders to find the private. Airplanes were also assigned to fly the mountains looking for the lost man. Weather challenged the searchers, and it even snowed during late June.

The search lasted three weeks without anyone finding any evidence of where the young soldier may be. Almost immediately after the search ended, on July 7, 1946, a Massachusetts tourist, G. Burton Davy of Boston, was four miles west of Bear Lake Lodge, an area near where Thomas's group was based, when he saw something unusual. He was in a region between Flat Top Mountain and Bear Lake when he saw a small waterfall being stopped by something. Davy went to investigate and found Thomas's body. Articles state that the body was wedged in a ledge from an apparent fall. Rocky Mountain National Park Superintendent George H. Miller made statements to the media that Thomas had died from a twelve-foot fall and was found just fifty feet from a trail used daily by soldiers involved in the search. It was the feeling of park officials that Thomas was attempting a shortcut.

This area of the park has had many unusual disappearances and deaths. It's amazing the number of times that park officials can't find bodies and everyday hikers do. I truly don't believe that park officials and searchers are this inept. It almost appears as though the body simply isn't there when the area is searched.

M-Harley Booth
Missing: 07/03/46-Unk, Devils Gulch, RMNP, CO
Age at disappearance: 30 years

Devils Gulch is located in the far northeast area of the park. This region is not traveled as much as many areas in this region. I'm not sure how it obtained its name.

Harley Booth was a student at Colorado A&M in their forestry department. On July 3, 1946, he had traveled with the students on a class excursion. Somehow Harley got separated from the group, and they couldn't find him. The class contacted the local sheriff's office and park rangers.

Harley was not your normal student. He was tough and had significant life experience. He had recently completed his five-year commitment in the US Army Air Corps and had enrolled in school to get his degree.

After two days of not finding a trace of the student, Larimer County Sheriff Ray Barger enlisted the service of the Civil Air

Patrol. They put two planes into the air, flying the area surrounding the disappearance.

Ground teams and air support continued for nine days until there was a break in the case. The July 12, 1946, *Moberly Monitor* had the following details from Sheriff Barger: "He said the body was found in an isolated gulley west of Drake, Colorado. Barger said the body was found by forest rangers and members of the Poudre Canyon Civilian Public Service Camp. They relieved a party of college students who began their search Wednesday." More specific details of the location of the body were found in the *San Antonio Light* on July 14, 1946: "The body of Harley Booth, 30, Colorado A&M student from Pleasant Hill, MO, was found yesterday at the foot of a 150-foot cliff in the Devils Gulch area of Rocky Mountain National Park. Deputy Sheriff Art Denig said Booth apparently fell. He disappeared a week ago." I think its interesting wording by the deputy, "he apparently fell."

Summary

There were very few details that could be found about this incident. You will read about other Colorado A&M students who have disappeared. This is the second disappearance in the park that I've chronicled where the word "devil" is in the name. In *Missing 411-Western United States,* I wrote about Alfred Beilhartz, who disappeared and was last seen in "Devil's Nest." He was never found.

Sandy Barcus
Missing 07/21/56-Noon
Location: Jasper Lake, CO
Age 2 years

The Barcus family drove to an area west of Eldora, Colorado, to look at cabin sites. They then drove farther west and found a location to have a picnic. They stopped in an area with dozens and dozens of small lakes at an elevation near eleven thousand feet in the Arapahoe National Forest, south of Rocky Mountain National Park. The family arrived at the picnic site, and Sandy was asleep in the backseat. They left her in the truck and set up as she slept. Somehow, she got out of the truck and out of the family's view. They returned and found Sandy gone. They searched and yelled for the girl in the area and did not receive a response. They called law enforcement. A July 23, 1956, article in the *Aiken Standard* had the following information: "She spent the night in the freezing high country with only a light summer dress to keep her warm. She left her shoes in the family car when she toddled off to explore the Jasper Lake area."

The closest lake west of Jasper is Devil's Thumb Lake. Jasper Creek flows out of Jasper Lake and meanders down a valley and flows into Middle Boulder Creek at approximately 9,600 feet. Nearly three hundred volunteer searchers, two Civil Air Patrol planes, and three hundred airmen from Lowry Air Force Base spent twenty-one to twenty-five hours (varies depending on the source) looking for shoeless Sandy. It rained nonstop during the effort to find the young girl.

On July 22, a Boy Scout troop and its scoutmaster were in the small community of Eldora. They were near Middle Boulder Creek and viewed a small girl standing next to the creek on the opposite side. Scoutmaster Glen Powers crossed the creek and picked up the girl (still wearing her red dress) and attempted to question her. The only thing that Sandy said was "Looking for my mommy." It's interesting to note that the majority of the searchers were five miles east of the Scouts' location when they found her.

A July 23, 1956, article in the *Billings Gazette* had the following about the location where Sandy was found: "Deputy Sheriff Dale Guetz estimated the girl had walked six or seven miles from where her family had left her asleep in a truck at a picnic grounds."

Sandy was transported to a hospital in Boulder, where she was found to be in good condition considering she had multiple scratches and slightly swollen feet.

Summary

The area where Sandy left the truck and the location where she was eventually located in twenty-one to twenty-five hours (depending on the article you read), it makes no sense that a two-and-a-half-year-old girl could manage that journey unassisted. There is a large amount of exposed granite, thick woods, and fast-flowing creeks. There are no paths or trails along this route, and it would not be an easy journey for an experienced adult hiker. The reason there were no experienced searchers in the area that Sandy was found was that nobody believed she could make that journey. In Robert J. Koester's book, *Lost Person Behavior*, he states that a one- to three-year-old child will be found within 2.8 miles or less from the point last seen 95 percent of the time. Sandy disappeared at eleven thousand feet in elevation and was found at nine thousand feet, a drop of two thousand feet. Koester states that someone in Sandy's age bracket, if going downhill, will be found 95 percent of the time after going down 1,216 feet. Sandy was found far outside the search and rescue guidelines.

I want every parent to think about his or her child when that baby was two years old. Could he or she have made a seven-mile trek in blistery cold rain, hacking their way through wild wilderness with no paths or trails, and do that in twenty-five hours?

M-Bobby Bizup
Missing: 08/15/58-6:00 p.m., RMNP, CO
Age at disappearance: 10 years

If there ever has been a missing case that had religion associated with military, it is the Bobby Bizup disappearance. When I first stumbled onto this event, I was shocked at the details and surprised that there wasn't more follow-up after the boy was found.

Bobby was nearly deaf. He wore a hearing aid, which gave him some ability to hear, but not much. His father was a master sergeant at Lowry Air Force Base.

On the eastern perimeter of Rocky Mountain National Park is Allenspark, a small community on Highway 7. One of the landmarks in this area is the Saint Catherine of Siena Chapel, which sits adjacent to the roadway. It is a gorgeous chapel made of rock that has a small body of water surrounding half of it. The chapel sits at the entrance of the St. Malo Catholic retreat, whose property abuts the national park at the base of Mount Meeker. The elevation of St. Malo is approximately 8,500 feet.

"Photo of Saint Malo grounds with Mount Meeker in the background."

On June 14, 1993, Pope John Paul II was in Denver for World Youth Day. The church stated that he was on a day off when he took a helicopter from Denver to Estes Park and then down to St. Malo to spend an afternoon going to the chapel, walking the trails behind the camp, and sitting and reading poetry next to the creek. The Pope put on a pair of new white sneakers with yellow laces and walked the trail. He stated that he had climbed mountains as a youth, and he truly enjoyed the excursion. Reports stated that the pope hiked for two hours on the trail and got to an elevation of ten thousand feet.

In the late 1950s and early 1960s, St. Malo hosted summer camps for boys. In 1986 the Catholic Church built a large building reminiscent of a small multistory hotel that hosted up to six thousand people per year. On November 14, 2011, a fire broke out in the residential center that destroyed a large portion of the forty-nine-room building. As of the date of this book, the building has not been rebuilt.

On August 15, 1958, ten-year-old Bobby Bizup was attending St. Malo's boys' summer camp. It was near 6:00 p.m. when Bobby was behind the resort on Cabin Creek, fishing. He was approached by a camp counselor and told that he needed to come in and get ready for dinner. The counselor turned and headed back to the resort, thinking that Bobby was behind him, but he wasn't. When the counselor arrived at the camp and realized that Bobby wasn't behind him, he got other counselors, and a search started. The formal search for the boy started at 6:30 p.m.

From the start of the search, counselors were compromised in their efforts to find Bobby based on his disability and inability to hear very well. It was difficult for counselors and searchers to understand how the boy could've been confused on where he was going, as the creek went downhill directly to the camp. The opposite direction was labor intensive; as it went uphill to Mount Meeker, anyone would know that the camp wasn't that way. In the book *Death, Despair, and Second Chances*, author Joseph Evans explained what happened early in the search: "Through Tuesday, August 19, over 300 searchers were involved with this massive search. Many were from Lowry Air Force Base, where Bobby's father was a Master Sergeant. The weather was wet and drizzly. In the initial period of the search, roadblocks were set up to check vehicles and seek information. Several people thought they saw Bobby at different locations around the Tahosa Valley. Bloodhounds gave strong indications the boy had moved north toward Estes Park." An August 21, 1958, article in the *St. Joseph News-Press* had the following headlines: "Missing Boy Believed to be Hiding." Later in that same article, the feelings of the camp management were expressed: "He is partially deaf and has a speech defect. 'I think he just took off,' said the reverend Richard Hiester, camp director. 'We definitely think he's somewhere near the camp,' Father Hiester said."

On August 25 the formal search for Bobby Bizup was called off by the National Park Service searchers and local deputies. The August 26, 1958, article in the *Billings Gazette* had a statement from Bobby's parents: "'We don't know what happened to our boy, but we don't think we'll ever see him again.' The missing boy is the only child of Bizup, who is stationed at Lowry Air Force Base near Denver, and Mrs. Bizup, his mother, has been seriously ill since he disappeared on August 15."

Several camp counselors continued to search the area where Bobby vanished even after the formal search was terminated. The boundary for the national park is just a few hundred yards behind St. Malo's facilities, and he may have been fishing in the national park when he was approached by the counselor.

On July 3, 1959, three counselors who had worked at St. Malo the previous year were still searching in their off-duty hours for Bobby. Neil Hewitt, Jerry Cusack, and Mike Courtney were in no-man's-land, 2,500 feet straight up the side of Mount Meeker, three miles west of the camp, when they broke out of the forest and hit timberline. At the junction of timberline and Cabin Creek, they found remains that were later identified as Bobby Bizup. A July 9, 1959, article in the *Greeley Tribune* detailed the find: "The identification was made from a few scraps of clothing, a few bones and a fragment of a hearing aid. The remains were made last Friday by three counselors."

The last sentence in the segment on Bobby Bizup in the book *Death, Despair, and Second Chances* states something that past readers have read before: "The ravine he was found in had been searched three times by different groups, indicating he may have wandered a great deal."

Summary

If there was ever a case that exemplifies a profile of what I've chronicled in the past, it is Bobby Bizup. Bloodhounds track the boy north—wrong. The director of the camp believes the boy is hiding from searchers—wrong. The weather doesn't cooperate with the effort to find the boy; it is wet and drizzling. Bobby has a severe disability; he is essentially deaf. He disappears next to a body of water, the creek. Bobby was found 2,500 feet above where he was last seen and in an area of Mount Meeker where you could see the camp from the location.

The location where Bobby was found is not a leisurely hike. This is a strenuous effort up a steep side of a high mountain.

A friend and I recently took the hike behind St. Malo and followed the creek toward Mount Meeker. This is a gorgeous trip as it parallels the creek up in elevation. I must say that it was a bit discomforting, as there were no trails or roads crossing this area of the park other than what we were on between the retreat and Mount

Meeker. When we were on the trail, we didn't see any people or wildlife, which was odd. The absence of wildlife seemed unusual with nobody in the area, and it appeared the trail was not used. After the pope visited this site, the church put a series of religious insignias and photos on the first portion of the trail, almost indicating it was a blessed and sacred site. The farther we hiked toward Mount Meeker, the more we both believed that it was impossible for Bobby to not know he was moving away from the retreat. There could be no mistake about the direction he was heading.

There is one last item that I find odd about this incident. Joseph Bizup made a statement in the August 26, 1958, *Billings Gazette* that he didn't think that he'd ever see his son again. I realize that people make unusual statements under extreme stress, but I have never heard a parent give up hope of finding a child so early in an effort. The grief that Joseph and his wife must've had is mind-boggling.

Judy Boltjes
Missing: 05/02/59-2:00 p.m., Deckers, CO
Age at disappearance: 6 years

This case joins the disappearances of Theresa Schmidt (*Missing 411-Western United States*), Maurice Dametz, and Benjamin Saul, who have all disappeared in a tight cluster near the Rampart Range Mountains and in the shadow of Devil's Head Mountain/Lookout.
Dates of disappearances in this cluster:

Benjamin Saul	8/10/31	(28 years till the Boltjes incident)
Judy Boltjes	5/02/59	(22 years till the Dametz disappearance)
Maurice Dametz	4/29/81	(21 years till Schmidt disappears)
Theresa Schmidt	9/06/02	

I've stated many times that cluster disappearances are separated by decades. If the disappearances were closer in time, law enforcement would see the patterns and understand something unusual is occurring. The only inconsistent pattern to this rule is in national parks. Disappearances in those areas are occurring at a more rapid pace, and the park service is claiming they aren't tracking the disappearances.

On May 2, 1959, in the afternoon hours, Judy Boltjes, her stepfather, Kenneth, and her four-year-old brother went for a hike in the Rampart Range west of Sedalia. Sometime during that hike, Judy told her dad that she wanted to walk the trail back to her mother and eleven-year-old sister. Ken said it was fine, and Judy started down the trail alone. Judy never made it back to the family picnic site where her mom was waiting. After Ken and Judy's brother made it back, they realized Judy had disappeared. They searched the trail and then looked for assistance.

By the end of the day on May 2, almost one hundred searchers and two teams of canines were looking for the girl. They went back to the trail where the girl was last seen, and the dogs couldn't pick up a scent. The teams searched late into the night and were ready to start early the next morning.

Early in the morning of May 3, campers on the South Platte River made an unbelievable discovery as is described in the May 4, 1959, article in the *Milwaukee Sentinel*: "A half naked 6 year old girl with a weak heart wandered into a public campground 20 miles west of here Sunday after being lost for 17 hours in the Rampart Mountains." It was disclosed that Judy had rheumatic fever and subsequently had a very weak heart. Many of the articles stated that the area where she disappeared was very rugged. The May 4, 1959, *Sarasota Herald Tribune* had more information on Judy's trip: "Judy Boltjes, suffering from rheumatic fever, was about 12 miles from the spot where she was last seen Sunday afternoon."

Summary

Judy disappears in a cluster setting where two people have never been found. The girl has a bad heart, rheumatic fever, and covers twelve miles of rugged terrain in seventeen hours. According to SAR manuals, a healthy six-year-old in a mountain setting will be found within 2.3 miles or less from the point last seen. If you are scratching your head wondering how this can happen, you are not alone.

Remember, Judy supposedly did this just wearing pants—no shoes, no shirt, and no coat. She had scratches over her body but was described in good condition.

Gregory Aubuchon
Missing: 07/20/21-Unk, RMNP, CO
Age at disappearance: 18 years

In the past three books we have chronicled a series of unusual disappearances from national parks. This is yet another case that defies logic and boggles the mind.

Gregory Aubuchon was with his family vacationing in Rocky Mountain National park on July 20, 1921. The family had been camping at the Glacier Basin Campground in the park for five days. He told his family that day that he wanted to climb Longs Peak the following day. His dad told him that the family had planned to leave that day, as they were headed for Cheyenne, Wyoming. When Mr. and Mrs. F. P. Aubuchon awoke the morning of July 21, Gregory was gone. The parents searched the area and could not find their son and notified park officials. A search was immediately initiated on the slopes of Longs Peak.

The search for Gregory was intense and continued night and day on the slopes of Longs and in the surrounding forest. Searchers found nothing to indicate the boy was anywhere on the mountain. After five days of covering the slopes and the surrounding forest, the formal search for Gregory was abandoned. The family had a good relationship with the superintendent of the park, L. C. Way, who committed to continue searching with his resources when the time permitted, The Aubuchons left the park and eventually made it to their home in Indiana.

It wasn't until late September 1921 that there was any new information on Gregory's disappearance. A September 24, 1921, article in the *Hoosier Democrat* explained what was found: "The mystery surrounding the disappearance here on July 20 of Gregory Aubuchon, 18 year old son of Mr. and Mrs. F.P. Aubuchon of Michigantown, Indiana, auto tourists in the Estes Park region last summer, has been solved. Young Aubuchon's blackened body, reduced almost to a pulp, was found Friday noon at the bottom of a 2,200 foot precipice on the north side of Longs Peak overlooking the beautiful Chasm Lake."

Pay close attention to where Gregory was found: you will hear this name several times in this chapter, Chasm Lake. Over two months after Gregory had disappeared, his body is found in an area where hundreds of people pass on a weekly basis. There is a reason the noted article started with "the mystery surrounding the disappearance." The park officials believed that Gregory left the family tent in the middle of the night to hike the mountain, yet his parents never heard him leave the campsite. The same article that was quoted above stated that Gregory's clothes were "nearly torn" from his body. Several articles I researched stated that he fell 2,800 feet; others stated 2,200 feet. In the book, *Death, Despair, and Second Chances* by Joseph Evans, it states the following about the exact location of the body: "On September 16, 1921, Aubuchon's body was found on Mills Glacier by Rangers Higby and McDaniel. The reports stated that the body had been found, 'about under the Notch,' but it was undetermined if he was climbing up or down. He did not sign the register, so most likely he was ascending when he fell."

The reason this case is in the book is multifold. Gregory disappeared in the middle of the night; some believe he was intent on climbing Longs. He had been camped at that location for five days; why not climb it in the previous days, before his family was going to leave? Where was his body for two months? There was a very intensive search for Gregory on Longs for weeks before his body was found; where was it?

As you read the stories in this chapter, pay close attention to "Chasm Lake." This area around Longs Peak has had several very unusual disappearances and falls. I have climbed a lot in my life, and I respect and admire the mountains for what they bring to people's lives. I don't believe that everything that happens on the mountains can be explained through conventional answers. If you have read my books, people have completely and literally disappeared on mountainsides above the timberline where there was no place to go (Carl Landers, *Missing 411-Western United States*). When Chasm Lake continues to factor into disappearance after disappearance, someone needs to take heed. When journalists state "mystery surrounding the disappearance," maybe someone should pay attention. Maybe the park service should start tracking this.

M-Christopher Vigil
Missing: 04/30/78-6:30 p.m., Greyrock Mountain, CO
Age at disappearance: 9 years

This is another of the many cases that greatly affected me. All of the missing cases are tragic, but Chris's disappearance seemed abnormal and wrought with unimaginable obstacles from the very beginning.

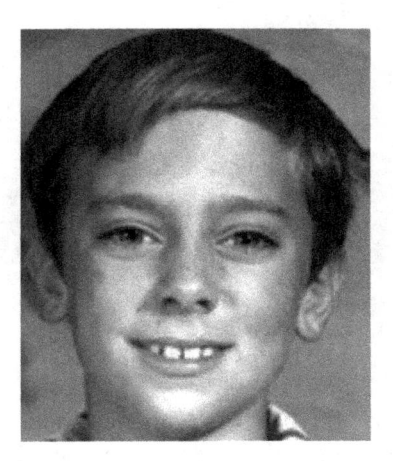

Greyrock Mountain isn't imposing. When you're in the parking lot in the Cache La Poudre River Valley, you can't even see it. The trail starts after you cross the river and then abruptly climbs two thousand feet in a little over three miles. This trail is not for people who aren't used to climbing at over seven thousand feet in elevation. After you reach the top of the trail, you are rewarded with a stellar view of a giant, solid rock: the mountain. This sight reminded me a lot of Goat Rock and the location where Theresa Schmidt vanished and was never found (*Missing 411-Western United States*).

On April 30, 1978, at 2:00 p.m., Marian Vigil decided to take her two sons from their residence in La Porte to Greyrock Mountain for an afternoon hike. La Porte is one of the closest cities to the mountain, and the trip was quick. At 2:30 Marian took her four-year-old son, Eric and her nine-year-old son, Chris across Highway 4, and then they crossed the Poudre River, making their way to the trail.

The group was just one-quarter mile into their hike when Chris told his mom that he was going to jump ahead and meet them at the top. This probably wasn't an unusual request since Chris ran two miles every day at a local track, putting him in excellent shape.

"Greyrock Mountain"

Chris made his way up the switchbacks and at some point met a single man hiking the trail, Allen Schoupan. He and Allen struck up a conversation and then somehow got separated. Chris continued up the trail. He came upon two girls and asked if they had seen the man. The girls stated they had, and he was up ahead. Chris took off ahead of the two and started yelling Allen's name.

Allen Schoupan was a man in his late fifties. He later stated that he last saw Chris at 4:30 p.m. at the junction of Greyrock Meadows and Greyrock Trail. He reported that the boy got out of his view and he could hear him on the east side of the mountain in the drainage, but he couldn't see him.

The girls that Chris had passed on the trail ate their lunch and had started back down when they reported they were passed by Mr. Schoupan. They stated that he appeared to be in a rush and looked worried. They reached the bottom of the mountain where Schoupan met with Marian and assisted in reporting Chris as missing.

Marian and Eric had terminated their climb when they determined the trail was too difficult and were waiting at their car for Chris. Marian called the Larimer County sheriff. By 6:38 p.m. the on-scene deputy had called for helicopter support, and at that time the first obstacle hit searchers.

At the approximate time the helicopter was arriving on scene, heavy rain, wind, and fog had inundated the Greyrock area, and the chopper had to be sent back. The visibility in the area was almost zero, a horrible turn of events. Ground teams came into the area, but the weather was so bad that they couldn't make it up the mountain with zero visibility.

May 1 was a Monday, and the weather was still horrific. Rain, sleet, and fog were still keeping the mountain shrouded, and no air support could be utilized. The Larimer County Horse Posse, canines, and 170 professional searchers faced huge obstacles as they trampled their way up the mountain trail to the base of the rock. I've made this hike in pristine conditions, and it was difficult. After the hike to the base of the rock, you are spent. I wonder how much energy the searchers had after their climb.

Starting Tuesday there were twelve inches of snow on the ground, and it was still accumulating. One hundred and fifty searchers made the trek up the mountain, and there was partial clearing that allowed two helicopters to fly into the area. Searchers on the ground and in the air were finding no evidence of tracks or discarded clothing—essentially nothing to show Chris was on the mountain.

The weather continued to deteriorate up until there were forty-five inches of snow on the ground on Saturday. There were so many injuries to searchers on Thursday and early Friday that Larimer County called off all rescue efforts until weather and ground conditions improved.

On May 12 Larimer County made a request to the governor's office for the use of the National Guard. The governor determined it would cost the state $50,000 to activate the guard, and the request was denied. It was stated that the National Guard is not used in many ground situations, and thus they wouldn't approve the cost. I can tell you for a fact, National Guard units across the United States are regularly used in search and rescue. This was a bad decision by the governor.

On May 13 Allen Schoupan was asked to come back to the search location and reenact what had happened when he saw Chris. Allen did this and then stayed and helped with the search efforts.

On May 15 all formal search efforts to locate Chris were suspended.

The girls who were on the mountain and saw Chris the day he vanished were questioned again by deputies. They stated that they had heard a "strange" type of shout when they were on the top of the mountain. Here is the quote from the Larimer County sheriff's report: "Intuitively, she sensed that something was wrong and wanted to investigate but did not do so as she feared for her well being." The girls stayed up on top of the mountain just long enough to eat and then went back down.

On July 19 Chris's father, Leroy, contacted Larimer County detectives and complained that he was disgusted with the manner they were handling his son's disappearance. There were no other details in the case file.

Thirty-four years after Chris Vigil vanished, Larimer detectives made contact with Marian and took DNA swabs to enter into a national database of missing people. To this date, Chris has never been found.

Summary

There have been several theories about this case. Search teams at the time believed that the weather changed so rapidly that Chris had about ninety minutes before hypothermia set in, and he'd then seek shelter. They used this theory to explain the fact they found no tracks. Ten thousand search hours were devoted to this effort. You can guarantee that every conceivable location that Chris could've hid was checked multiple times.

When I first found this case, I wasn't surprised. Chris's disappearance is the third missing boy I've found in northern Colorado with his incident being the one farthest east. The three cases make a concise triangle. From the Alfred Beilhartz case in Rocky Mountain National Park (missing July 2, 1938, four years old, never found) to the Jaryd Atadero disappearance (missing October 2, 1999, Poudre River Canyon) twenty-seven miles west of Greyrock. The Beilhartz and Atadero cases happened fourteen miles apart. A tooth, skull cap, and small bones from Jaryd were found four years after he disappeared. The incident also happened in Larimer County, and the sheriff stated that he couldn't positively state what had happened to the boy.

The Atadero and Vigil cases have the Poudre River in common. Jaryd was walking directly next to the water before he vanished. Chris and his family crossed the river before they started to hike. Both hikes were started by driving Highway 14 to the trailhead. Both boys were hiking ahead of their groups when they disappeared. Two of the three boys I've described have never been found.

The official Larimer County Sheriffs Department report on this incident was obtained and utilized in preparation for the writing of this segment.

Dr. Maurice "Doc" Dametz
Missing: 04/29/81-3:45 p.m., Pike National Forest, CO
Age at disappearance: 84 years

When I first stumbled onto this case, there were a few elements that immediately struck me as unusual. The number-one item: this occurred in the "Devil's Head" area of the Pike National Forest. The word "devil" comes up many times in descriptions of the areas where people disappear under the criteria of this study. The other item that struck me: Maurice "Doc" Dametz was a lifelong minister and had a PhD in theology.

A Google search of Maurice Dametz shows that he has written many religious papers about Christian life. At Denver University Maurice wrote his thesis paper on the "Focal Point of Christian History."

On April 29, 1981, Doc and his good friend, David McSherry, went to an area sixteen miles south of Highway 67 on Rampart Range Road to dig for rocks. At the time of the incident, this area was called the Virgin Bath Picnic Area. David and Doc had gone to this area more than fifty times to dig for minerals, and each knew the area very well. The two men arrived near 10:00 a.m. and decided to split up, both going to the west side of the roadway. David stated that he knew that Doc was digging at two spots, each about fifty yards apart.

At approximately 3:45 p.m., David called out for Doc and didn't receive an answer. He walked to the area he thought he'd be and couldn't locate him. David now walked back to their car and honked the horn: no response. There was a group of three passing motorcyclists that David flagged down and asked to help with the search. The group searched for two hours and found nothing. At this point another motorist volunteered to drive off and call the sheriff. The deputy was summoned at 7:30 p.m. and arrived at 8:44 p.m. The Douglas County sheriff was placed in charge of the search effort. He then called the Arapahoe Search and Rescue Team. Searchers started to arrive throughout the night, and Bloodhounds got to the scene at 11:45 p.m.

Searchers were challenged, as this area has steep hills with lush, tall pines and deep forests that are very wild.

David told the sheriff that Doc took medication for a blood condition and that he had bad knees, which made it difficult for him to move around. David couldn't understand how Doc had gotten from the area because he wasn't extremely mobile. The idea that he was lost made no sense—he'd been here over fifty times.

A one-week search of the Virgin Bath region found nothing to indicate that Doc had ever been in the area.

On July 18, 1981, Mrs. Maurice G. Dametz wrote a letter to Colorado Governor Richard Lamm (see insert). What struck me about this letter was her statement that "Maurice might have met with foul play or have been carried out of the area." Knowing that her husband had bad knees, she knew he wasn't walking out. Mr. Dametz was five foot eleven and 150 pounds, not a small man.

Governor Lamm did respond to Mrs. Dametz. He was very sympathetic to her cause but did not offer any additional services to locate Doc.

Mr. Dametz disappeared fifteen miles northeast from the Cheesman Reservoir and the general area where fifty-three-year old Teresa Schmidt vanished on September 6, 2002, and was never found (see *Missing 411-Western United States*).

6489 Ute Highway
Longmont, Co 80501
July 18, 1981

Governor Richard Lamm
136 State Capitol Building
Denver, Colorado 80203

Dear Governor Lamm:

On April 29, 1981, my husband, Reverend Maurice G. Dametz, age 84, and a close friend of ours, were rock hunting in the Devil's Head area of Pike Natbnal Forest when they became separated and my husband apparently became lost. There was an extensive five day search conducted which resulted in no clues as to his whereabouts, and as of this date, he is still missing with no new information. Many notices of his disappearance with pictures, description and reward offer for information leading to finding him were posted throughout the region, but they have brought no results whatsoever.

Relatives, friends, his hunting partner, my daughter and I have been in contact with the Sheriff Department of Douglas County, and we have talked with Stan Bush and Tom Fiore, search leaders. We feel the Sheriff Department does not have the time or the resources to do a more intensive investigation than they have already done.

Since the search was very thorough, we must consider that while separated from his partner, Maurice might have met with foul play or have been carried out of the area. Therefore, I am writing to you asking you to appoint some government agency or department to do something on our behalf. We feel that perhaps there is some agency or department that we are unaware of that could make a more extensive investigation.

Any assistance you will be able to give us will be deeply appreciated by myself, my family, and our many, many friends.

Anxiously awaiting your reply, I am

Sincerely yours,

Mrs. Maurice G. Dametz
Mrs. Maurice G. Dametz

Readers need to keep perspective on something. An eighty-four-year-old man doesn't get up and run off into the countryside. Search and rescue teams should be finding these individuals. Don't become callous to these incidents; these are fathers, brothers, and relatives who are loved by many. Mr. Dametz had a church filled with hundreds who loved him, and he is someone who started many couples' lives by being the minister in their marriage ceremony. Something is not right about this scenario.

The fact that Bloodhounds, hundreds of searchers, and professional teams couldn't locate Mr. Dametz makes me wonder what the possibilities could be on how he vanished.

Summary

I've been to this area and hiked the region where Doc vanished. It is very thick with big trees and little ground cover, and the inclines are steep. I did find a few small open-pit type mines where others have dug for minerals. I cannot understand how a man with bad knees could get out of this area.

Christopher Harvey
Missing: 07/11/84-3:30 p.m., Pagosa Springs, CO
Age at disappearance: 14 years

I quickly discovered that the disappearance of Christopher Harvey was in no way going to be your standard missing person case. The number of obstacles and confusing facts associated with this story are troubling.

On July 11, 1984, Chris and his family were at their vacation home in Hinsdale County, Colorado. The family had traveled from their primary residence in Andrews, Texas. Their mountain home was at the base of the San Juan National Forest, seventeen miles north of Pagosa Springs. At approximately 3:00 p.m., Chris took the family dog and went to a neighbor's house to talk to him about attending a possible band camp at the end of summer. Chris and his dog left his friend's house at about 3:30 and went into oblivion.

This area is at the far northern end of Hinsdale County and is the last community before reaching deep and thick forests. It is so far north, Hinsdale County had contracted with Archuleta County for patrol functions in the area where Chris vanished. The Harveys made the call to the Archuleta County sheriff's office at 11:00 p.m. to report their son missing. According to the Harveys, Archuleta County didn't start to search for Chris until noon the following day, and then the search was terminated the following day at 4:00 p.m. I've never heard of any county performing such a short search. It appears that Archuleta County then handed the case to Hinsdale and told them to search. The timing of this handoff is not understood.

Hinsdale County called for helicopter support from the armed forces and got it. Soldiers from Fort Carson responded and participated in the effort along with other search and rescue teams from throughout southern Colorado. A tracking dog was brought into the area, but the sheriff stated that the dog's effort was "frustrated" by fresh rainfall. The Civil Air Patrol committed four planes to the search.

It's very unclear exactly when Hinsdale County took the search over from Archuleta County, and they aren't saying why or when they did. A *Denver Post* article about the search had this statement from the Hinsdale County sheriff: "Smith added that miscommunication with his neighboring county had delayed the start of Hinsdale County's search"—an interesting statement that doesn't explain why or when the search changed hands, or the politics behind the move.

On the eleventh day after Chris had disappeared, Hinsdale County Sheriff Burt Smith made the statement that there was a 95 percent chance that the boy was not in the county. The *Victoria Advocate* ran a story on October 12, 1984, with the sentiments of Mrs. Harvey: "'One of the things that has been a problem for law enforcement is that there has been no clues,' she said, noting that he disappeared with only the clothes he was wearing. The family doesn't know if he was abducted, ran away or met another fate. 'I can tell you 100 different theories.'" All search efforts were terminated on July 22.

I did find articles that stated that Chris's dog returned to the residence, but none gave a date.

Summary

This is one of very, very few instances where I truly believe that something that I don't understand is taking place regarding this case.

Colorado has a law very similar to the Freedom of Information Act; files are to be released to the public except under a few circumstances.

On March 6, 2013, I sent an e-mail to the Hinsdale County sheriff requesting a copy of the report. He responded stating that he would get it. I heard nothing for a month, so I called the sheriff's administrative assistant and asked if she knew the status of my request. She stated that they were having a difficult time finding the file but that she'd send the undersheriff to the storage area in the substation to attempt to locate it. This back-and-forth exchange went on for months. First they didn't have the manpower to copy it; then they had fires in the county and didn't have the time to copy it. After more than four months of patiently waiting, I volunteered to drive the five hours to their facility and copy the file in their presence. It was at about this time something changed. The sheriff and his administrative assistant both agreed to get the file and copy it for me (once they found it, of course).

During one of my last e-mail exchanges with the sheriff, I was suddenly e-mailed by a contract attorney for Hinsdale County who practices in Denver. He told me to stop communicating with the sheriff and not to speak or communicate with him any further. I couldn't believe what I was hearing. The attorney told me that the case was being reviewed and worked by a cold case team and that no release would be made. He reiterated that I was not to contact the sheriff. The attorney told me that he had spoken to a member of the Colorado Bureau of Investigation and had been advised to not release the case. I told him that they wouldn't do that; only the attorney general would recommend something so extreme, and that was only if there were suspects. I asked for the bureau employee's name; he refused to disclose it.

The sheriff in Hinsdale County and I had had very cordial communications. I never sensed any tension in the e-mails, and they were always moving toward me getting the file. The sheriff never made one innuendo that I wasn't going to get Chris's file. The statement of the attorney saying that I wasn't to speak to the sheriff any longer is puzzling. Does he not want me to tell the sheriff what he is telling me? What if the attorney is telling me a lie just to get me off the case?

Several individuals I know have made many enlightening statements about why the attorney has entered the case. Here is a list of the possibilities:

1. The sheriff's office lost or destroyed the case file. I did contact Archuleta County asking for their reports on the incident. They stated they didn't have any reports, even though they were the ones who took the initial report and searched for Chris two days. Where are these reports? Officials in Hinsdale County stated that they thought their case file was in storage at another facility. They made many excuses about why the file wasn't copied.
2. Another possibility is that this is a cover-up. The case is listed on databases as a "nonfamily abduction," a stranger abduction. Did the county develop a suspect that had close ties to someone in Hinsdale government, and they are trying to keep this from the public?
3. Maybe they are embarrassed at a complete lack of follow-up on this case.
4. There is something strange and unusual in the case file that the sheriff does not want publicized.
5. The sheriff wants to incubate himself from the public and have the attorney be the brunt of any fallout so he can later claim ignorance.
6. This case is classified as a nonfamily abduction. If the facts are as the family states and there is no evidence of anything, how can the sheriff justify the classification?

It's very hard to imagine that Hinsdale County has a "cold case team" working this incident when they didn't have enough personnel to go offsite and locate the file. The tone of the e-mails with the sheriff indicated he hardly had the personnel to handle emergency calls in the county. If this is true, how could he form a "team" to work a case that's thirty years old and no leads? How long could this team work on a case like Chris's? Understand, Hinsdale County has several old and unsolved homicides and major crimes, and they are committing a cold case team to this incident—do you think this is believable?

M-Keith Reinhard
Missing: 08/07/88-4:00 p.m., Silver Plume, CO
Age at disappearance: 49 years

    This is another story that's as much about a small community as it is about Keith Reinhard. Keith was a sportswriter for the *Chicago Daily Herald*. He was successful and had a good life. He had been married for two years to Carolyn, and they lived in a suburb of Chicago.
    Keith had a lifelong friend in a man named Ted Parker. Ted owned a building in Silver Plume, Colorado. This was a location in the middle of the Rockies, which Keith had visited several times in the past. In June 1988, Keith told his wife that he was taking a sabbatical from his writing job and moving to Silver Plume to write a novel and take a stab at running a small antiques business. Carolyn didn't like the idea of a separation, but she wanted to give her husband the space.
    Keith moved into an interesting and unusual situation. He was renting a storefront from his friend, Ted, located on Main Street in Silver Plume, a community of 140 people at an elevation of 9,114 feet. The town sits on the north end of Highway 70 west of Denver. Keith learned that the space he was renting was formerly operated as a bookstore by a man named Tom Young. Tom had disappeared months earlier, and a missing person report was on file with the Clear Creek County sheriff.
    Keith's landlord, Ted Parker, was running KP's Café in a building called KP Hall. The building used to be the home of the Knights of Pithius. Ted had worked hard to renovate the ancient structure. It sat against the mountains on the north side of the city. Silver Plume is not a busy city, and you can quickly miss it as you travel the

highway. The town has a few viable businesses, but it can easily remind you of a town in disrepair attempting to make a comeback.

Keith soon learned that his small antiques business wasn't making much money and the dream of bringing his wife out to live here was slipping away. Carolyn and Keith wrote and talked, and she scheduled a trip out to see him on August 11.

As the weeks pushed on, Keith took an interest in the disappearance of Tom Young. He started to ask questions of locals and his landlord friend. Keith was starting to pen a story about Tom's disappearance, and it appeared this may be his project.

On August 7, 1988, at approximately noon, Keith was walking in town and saw local resident Larry Dougherty. He asked Larry if he was interested in going with him later in the afternoon for a hike. Larry declined. Keith later had a discussion with another local, Perry Davis. He told him he was going to hike Mount Pendleton and asked if he'd join him. Perry stated he didn't want to go. It was later learned that Keith told Ted the same thing as he did Perry: no thanks was the response. Keith had asked three people to join him on his hike, three people politely declined.

Keith had attempted to summit Mount Pendleton in the past. Each time he had been rebuffed by altitude and fatigue. On August 7 at 4:00 p.m., several people saw Keith walking toward the base of the mountain, traveling under Highway 70 toward the trailhead. He wasn't carrying a backpack or heavy clothing and appeared almost out for a casual walk. The hike up the mountain and back took a minimum of six hours. The idea of leaving at 4:00 p.m. seemed irrational. When Keith didn't return, the Clear Creek County sheriff was called.

In preparation for this story, another researcher and I went to Georgetown and met with Captain Bruce Snelling from the Clear Creek County sheriff's department. Bruce gave us full access to the Reinhard and Young cases. He answered every question and allowed us to make full copies of both case files.

If the story isn't unusual enough at this point, one week prior to Keith disappearing, elk hunters found the body of Tom Young. He was found leaning against a tree with his dog on his lap. Tom and his dog had been killed by a bullet to the head. It was the opinion at the time that Tom had killed his dog and then himself. A pistol was found at the scene, along with a box of bullets and a small backpack.

Captain Snelling admitted that the pistol had not gone through ballistics testing. When he attempted to retrieve the gun from evidence and have the testing completed, he found that someone in the department had already destroyed it.

At this point you have Tom Young, who was renting a room from Ted Parker, dead, supposedly by suicide. You have Keith, renting the same room and asking questions about Tom's death, showing up missing.

There was a big push to find Keith. Twenty-eight different search and rescue organizations along with canines and air support responded and combed the area around Silver Plume.

While the search was ongoing, a psychic named Judy from Illinois called the Clear Creek County sheriff's department and offered her opinion on where Keith was located. The following quote comes directly from page 5 of the deputy's primary report on Keith: "She further described Pavilion Point past and present rather accurately, so accurate in fact that a lot of search time both from air and by ground teams were spent in that area. It was also one of only two areas where dogs got any scent." Judy appeared to have quite an unusual ability. After a significant amount of effort, Keith wasn't found at Pavilion Point.

The search continued with several helicopters and some airplanes assisting. On August 12, Civil Air Patrol pilot Terry Leadens was flying his Cessna 182R with observer Dan Drobney. They were given an area three and a half miles south of Silver Plume and asked to circle the region and look for evidence. There were severe downdrafts that day, and something unusual happened to the plane. In a report titled *Accidents in Mountain Rescue Operations* by Charlie Shimanski, he explains what happened: "A passenger reported that the pilot said, 'I don't like the feel of this.' A paramedic said the passenger also related that they had hit a downdraft." A helicopter pilot flying in the area said the winds were not conducive for fixed-wing flights, especially in the trenches. The broken trees indicated a decent angle of forty-five degrees. The distance from the first tree strike to the main wreckage was forty-two feet. The aircraft came to a rest on its nose. The terrain elevation was about 10,600 feet.

Pilot Terry Leadens died, and passenger Dan Drobney had serious injuries. Dan was airlifted by a military crew from Fort Carson. He survived.

The report indicates the search for Keith Reinhard was terminated on August 13. Some SAR reports indicate that limited operations continued to August 15.

There have been many rumors over the years about what happened to Keith. Some believe he is living someplace else. Other people believe that something cruel and unusual happened to the man. I sincerely doubt that Keith planned a disappearance. People who work hard to conceal where they are going usually will not invite others to walk with them the day they want to disappear. I do find it highly unusual that Keith would leave so late in the day to climb a mountain. I can understand him taking a late afternoon hike, but not going to the top of Mount Pendleton.

The Clear Creek County sheriff has an enormous case file on this incident. They are as puzzled as you are.

Keith has never been found.

Sarah Wolenetz
Missing: 07/11/92-3:00 p.m., Bear Lake, RMNP, CO
Age at disappearance: 11 years

This disappearance happened at Bear Lake inside Rocky Mountain National Park, approximately four miles northwest of Chasm Lake. The elevation in the area is 9,800 feet with dozens of small lakes and ponds in the surrounding area.

Sarah was with her Fort Collins church group of nine people. They had decided to take a weekend hike from Bear Lake on the Fern Lake Trail and then meet at the Flattop Mountain Trail and then return to Bear Lake. The group was making the trek in an effort to raise money for missionary work their church was sponsoring. Just after starting the hike, Sarah got a sore heel, and with the approval of her father, the group decided to leave her behind with a pile of coats, water, and food. They told her to stay there and they'd return after their hike.

The group returned at 3:00 p.m. to the location where Sarah had been left and couldn't locate her. They searched for a short period of time and called for park rangers. Officials arrived at the scene and soon summoned Bloodhounds. As officials were starting their search, they discovered something unusual as is described in the July 13, 1992, issue of *The Coloradoan*: "Authorities found an arrow that the 11-year old made directing the group to a point overlooking Bear Lake. Mack said they suspect she made the arrow to let others know she'd be in a different place than what had originally been arranged." Searchers did follow the arrow's direction but found nothing of value. The search for Sarah extended long into the night with dogs and searchers not finding the young girl.

The morning following Sarah's disappearance, searchers got an early start and the results are explained in the same article referenced above: "At 5am Sunday her body was found at the base of a cliff near the northwest side of Bear Lake." How searchers missed this the first day is unbelievable. There's a trail that completely encircles the lake, and there is another trail above the lake to the north, but there is no trail on the northwest side of the lake. The trail on the north looks directly to the area where the body was found. Why Sarah would be in the area she was found is unknown. Sarah also knew her mom was down the trail waiting at the parking lot; she knew that safety and comfort was there. For exact clarity on where Sarah was found and the beliefs of her father, we refer to the July 14, 1992, article in *The Coloradoan*: "'At the place we provided for her, she was completely screened off the trail and had extra coats and food,' her father said. There was no indication of cliffs anywhere near her." You can hear the anxiety in her father's words that where they left her, there was no hazard.

Summary

In my years of researching missing people, I have never heard of a child leaving an arrow on the ground indicating the direction they were traveling. To make this more to the point, I have never heard of an adult leaving an arrow on the ground. Sarah walked in the exact opposite direction of where her mother was located and into a more rural location, deeper into the woods.

There was never any description of the condition of the young girl's body or her clothing.

M-Jeff Christensen
Missing: 07/29/05-Unk, RMNP, CO
Age at disappearance: 31 years

There have been few unusual disappearances of national park rangers; this classifies as being near the top. The incident happened near the thirteen thousand foot elevation and in an area where there is little to no ground cover with lots of rocks and several small bodies of water.

If you could mold the national profile of what you'd want in a national park service ranger, you'd have Jeff Christensen. During the off seasons for the last seven years, Jeff was an emergency medical technician and ski patrolman in Winter Park. The blond-haired, thirty-one-year-old physical specimen was residing in Fraser, Colorado, when he reported to work at Rocky Mountain National Park in the morning hours of July 29, 2005. The Minnesota native loved the outdoors and enjoyed the freedom of hiking and patrolling the backcountry. On this day he was going out alone to patrol the Lawn Lake Trailhead. He would be armed with his service pistol, and he'd have a walkie-talkie.

At approximately 1:30 p.m., a group of visitors were near the summit of Mount Chiquita and reported talking with Jeff. The conversation was short, and each moved on. This was the last time anyone saw the ranger alive.

The National Park Service obviously wasn't keeping track of their employees very well. The first time anyone realized that something might be wrong with Jeff was when he didn't report to work the following morning. It's apparent that there was nobody checking at the end of the day that all backcountry rangers made it in safely. Once they realized he didn't check in for work, they contacted his residence and realized he never made it home. Later in the day on July 30, the park service finally realized that one of its cherished rangers was lost somewhere in the backcountry.

The park service kicked a major search into gear. Five helicopters were deployed into the area where Jeff was last seen along with two hundred ground searchers and five Bloodhound teams. The search continued for five days without any leads and the dogs not picking up a scent. On Wednesday something very unusual happened inside a national park: gunshots were heard along with radio static. An August 4, 2005, article on *Thedenverchannel.com* had the following details: "Late Wednesday, park rangers responded to a report of gunshots heard in the area and fired several weapons into the air as a standard response. Another ranger in a different location reported hearing a response shot a few minutes later. Rangers also reported they heard a two-way radio being keyed." The park service made another statement that Jeff was a capable mountaineer who had the ability to cover long distances in short periods of time.

On August 6 and just under three-quarters of one air mile from where Jeff was last seen, a group of three hikers was in the area of Spectacle Lake, just below the east face of Mount Ypsilon, and found the body of Jeff Christensen. The hikers were in no way associated with the search effort. An Associated Press article of August 7 had the following statement about where Jeff was found: "On Saturday, when the hiker discovered Christensen's body, searchers were focusing on an area where rangers and park visitors on Wednesday heard gunshots and radio clicks that might have come from the missing ranger." There was never an explanation of where the park service was searching. A further description of where Jeff was located was in the *Dailycamera.com* on September 21, 2006: "On August 6 Christensen's body was found, not by searchers but by three hikers in a large basin below Mt. Chiquita. He had died of a fatal head injury, probably from a fall, on the day he went missing, but clearly had been alive after his accident. He had bandaged his head and hiked away from the accident site [which has never been found]. His radio was in working condition and he was in a location from which he could have radioed for help, but he mysteriously did not."

Summary

The Larimer County coroner estimated Jeff's time of death as somewhere between 6:00 p.m. and midnight on July 29.

I did request the coroner's report from Larimer County and received it ten days later:

Neck-No major Injury
Chest-No Injury
No injury to ribs or sternum.
No injury to posterior torso.
No gross deformities.
No internal injuries or evidence of blunt force.

Jeff did have head injuries and died of skull fractures and an epidermal hematoma.

When I originally started to research this case, I filed a Freedom of Information Act request with Charis Wilson, the Denver Regional National Park Service administrator for organizing these filings. Over the last several years, I have filed dozens of these requests with Charis. I understand that she is merely the messenger and not the author of the response. Several weeks after requesting the Christensen file, I received this from Charis:

> The staff at ROMO are estimating that it will take approximately 120 hours to search and review the files for the Jeff Christensen case, which you also requested, because they contain privacy related information that will need to be redacted before we can release the records. The rate per hour would be $60/hour. So the current estimate to process that request comes to $7200 and does not include any copy costs. If you are

still interested in obtaining these materials, please let me know that you are willing to pay these fees. Until we receive your confirmation we will not be able to process your request.

In the past four years, I have received two files from the National Park Service that came to me in boxes. These cases were also about missing rangers, Randy Morgensen and Paul Fugate. Fugate has never been found and is still an open case, yet the park service chose to release it, contrary to its position on other "open" cases that the agency has refused to supply. These files cost us less than forty dollars each to receive. Each of these incidents received national press and is still widely reported. The Christensen case is closed, and few details about what really happened have ever been widely reported. It's apparent that the park service does not want the intimate details of its incident reported, based on the price that was quoted.

There is something seriously wrong with this incident. How could Jeff be found less than one air mile from where he was last seen and be found in a "large basin" and not be seen by ground teams and helicopters? Jeff was alive for some period of time—why didn't he utilize his radio and call for assistance, or fire his weapon to alert people to his injury? I never did find out where the park service was searching for the gunshots and radio traffic they heard. Hearing gunshots and radio clicks in a national park is very, very odd and unusual, and happening in conjunction with the disappearance of a ranger makes it extremely odd. I also never found out if Jeff's gun had been fired.

I did request the National Park Service report from its Critical Incident Management Team. It has been ten weeks, and I still have not received it as of the publishing of this book.

It's troubling that the National Park Service doesn't have policies in place to ensure that someone is checking on rangers and ensuring they make it back from patrols every day. It's also confusing that the investigation couldn't determine where Jeff's accident occurred, or if something much more unusual happened related to the gunshots and the radio traffic.

Colorado | 91

Mitchell Dale Stehling
Missing: 06/09/13-4:08 p.m. • Mesa Verde NP
Age at disappearance: 51 years

The story about the disappearance of Dale Stehling is as unusual as the location where it happened. Mesa Verde National Park is located at the far southwestern corner of Colorado in the Four Corners region. The park was the home to the Pueblo Indians, who lived there from 600 AD to 1300. The park protects five thousand archeological sites and six hundred cliff dwellings. President Theodore Roosevelt dedicated the park on June 29, 1906.

The cliff dwellings are some of the most impressive buildings in the world. The Cliff Palace and Long House dwellings have 150 rooms. A significant number of Native Americans called Mesa Verde home. One of the long-held mysteries of this area is that archeologists and historians don't have any idea why the Indians left the area and vacated their buildings.

Mesa Verde
National Park Service
U.S. Department of Interior
Colorado

Mesa Verde National Park requests your assistance in locating this person.

Subject: **DALE STEHLING**

PHYSICAL DESCRIPTION
- Age: 51
- Height: 6 feet
- Weight: 230 pounds
- Hair: Brown
- Eyes: Brown

Dale Stehling was last seen Sunday, June 9, 2013 on the Petroglyph Trail near Park Headquarters. He was wearing a khaki colored "Mesa Verde Museum Association" baseball cap, brown sunglasses with round lenses, brown tee-shirt, tan/khaki shorts, calf height white socks, and Red Wing brand Men's Oxford walking shoes. The only items in his possession were a cell phone, cigarettes, and wallet.

If you have any information regarding this individual
Please Contact NPS Dispatch (970) 529-4622

Denean Stehling is a pediatric care nurse, and Dale was a retired butcher with a bad back. They had planned an adults-only trip to tour the national parks of the United States. The couple had been married for thirty-two years and had four children and six grandchildren. They left their home in Goliad, Texas, and were driving in their motor home through the Four Corners area on day number four of their trip when their vehicle needed servicing. This area was not a planned stop, but maintenance forced the inevitable, a trip to Mesa Verde National Park.

On June 9, 2013, at approximately 4:00 p.m., Dale and Denean were at the Spruce Tree Trailhead when Dale stated he wanted to climb the trail a quarter mile to see the dwelling. Denean stated that she would wait for him because the one-hundred-degree heat was making it difficult to hike. Dale left without water but was carrying a cell phone that was supposedly turned off. When Dale didn't return from his hike, Denean reported her husband as a missing person to National Park officials. The park started its search at 7:20 p.m.

On Monday, June 10, the search for Dale continued with more searchers, a helicopter, equestrians, and canines. It's a rare day when a reporter covering the national park system becomes part of the story. Jodi Peterson is a writer for the *High Country News* and was in Mesa Verde for an interview with the park superintendent about the diversity in national parks. She didn't initially realize that a massive life-and-death search was occurring. Jodi did meet with the park superintendent, Cliff Spencer and was given details regarding Dale's disappearance. After the meeting she decided to take a hike, as is explained in the June 19, 2013, edition of the *High Country News*: "Late that afternoon, despite the 102 degree heat, I decided to hike the 3 mile long Petroglyph Trail, which splits off from the Spruce Tree House Trail and leads upward along the east wall of Spruce Canyon. Steep and rugged, it sidles along ledges and alcoves, squeezes between tall rocks, and ascends rough stairsteps hewn from sandstone blocks. Just after I passed the panel of petroglyphs for which the trail is named, I heard a man's voice from somewhere up ahead. 'I need some help,' he called, sounding gravelly, weary. I couldn't pinpoint the location and I thought whoever I'd heard was probably talking to some companions. I kept walking." Jodi walked up and out of the canyon and didn't see anyone. Jodi thought that she might have heard the missing man calling for help and decided to head for park service headquarters. Jodi eventually reached the chief park ranger. In the same *High Country News* article was this: "The chief ranger was excited too. Cautious relief washed over his face. 'We thought we heard a call for help in that area yesterday,' said one of the other rangers in his office." Jodi told her story to the leader of one of the search teams, and they took resources back into the area to search.

The search for Dale continued at full scale for a week. The effort was reduced at day eight and continued to be reduced. A July 5, 2013, article in the *Victoria Advocate* had two different interesting statements. The first was something that Denean stated to the reporter: "When I look back, there were a lot of signs that we shouldn't have taken this trip." There were no other details given. The other interesting fact came from the park service following up on Dale's phone: "The ranger told Denean that a partial ping from her husband's cell phone was retrieved. About 7:00 p.m., his phone attempted to make a call to its voicemail. Since then, his phone has gone directly into voicemail and no other GPS pings shown." From past cases I've researched regarding cell phones, when a phone directly dialed its voicemail under conditions such as Dale's, it was related to a fall. The person in that event was located at the bottom of a cliff. Later in the same article were the results of the park service's search and rescue attempt of Dale: "There were no clues. No signs of life. No signs of death. No footprints to follow." I'm not sure about the statement "No signs of life": What about the statements asking for help heard by two separate people on two different days?

Summary

When two different people hear statements from a man asking for help in the same area, how can he not be found? Why couldn't Bloodhounds brought into the area pick up a scent? After Dale was missing a month, searchers were still in the area on a part-time basis looking for him. Why didn't cadaver canines pick up the odor of rotting flesh? It is guaranteed that his body would be far into decomposition after a month, and the cadaver dogs should've reacted.

This is a classic disappearance where nothing is found, there is no evidence, canines can't locate a scent, weather is at its extreme, and there is high mystery about a voice nobody can find.

The disappearance of Hildegard Hendrickson from Wenatchee, Washington, happened June 8, 2013. The disappearance of Dale Stehling occurred June 9, 2013. Both people have never been found.

Gene George
Missing: 09/21/13-Unk, Mount Harvard, CO
Age at disappearance: 64 years

This incident occurred directly in the area of Mount Harvard in Chaffee County. The real story behind this incident involved the city of Buena Vista and what has transpired around it in the last three years.

I'll start with the background of Gene George. Gene was a maritime attorney who specialized in maritime personal injury and marine insurance. In 2012 he was named by the Cleveland Admiralty as the maritime lawyer of the year. In 1973 he graduated from law school from the University of Michigan. He worked for a law firm in Cleveland but lived in Bay Village, Ohio. He was single.

Gene traveled from Ohio to Colorado and eventually made his way to a motel in Buena Vista. Buena Vista translates to "Good Views," and that's exactly what you'll find in this small mountain community located almost in the geographical center of Colorado. It is surrounded by giant mountains and has a comfortable summer climate.

The calamity surrounding Buena Vista started on June 22, 2011. In *Missing 411-North America and Beyond,* I wrote about the disappearance of Dr. Michael Von Gortler and his daughter, who were climbing Mount Missouri. He was a physician in Boulder and had a summer home in Buena Vista. His daughter was a student at University of Colorado at Boulder. The pair had spent time at Michael's summer home and then left for the mountain from that residence. The two disappeared on the mountain. The facts surrounding their disappearance on a perfect summer day with no inclement weather is baffling.

On September 18, 2013, Gene George was in his motel room in Buena Vista and called his girlfriend, telling her that he was going to hike to the base of Mount Harvard. He never told her that he was going to attempt to summit. This was the last time Gene contacted his friend.

On September 22, the motel called the sheriff to report that Gene hadn't checked out of his room. All of his belongings were there, and it appeared they hadn't been touched in a few days. On that afternoon, Chaffee County sheriff's deputies started their search. They did get lucky by finding Gene's car at the trailhead to Cottonwood Creek near Mount Harvard. They put 280 searchers, twenty canine units, and flew thirty hours in a helicopter looking for Gene over four days. Dogs never found a scent, and they never located any supplies indicating he was on the mountain or in the area. The deputies did locate one hiker who believed he had seen Gene on the summit of Mount Columbia on September 21. This didn't make any sense since he hadn't communicated to anyone he'd be in that location. He also never stated he'd summit any mountain.

The Von Gortlers disappeared on June 22, 2011, on Mount Missouri. Mount Missouri is the first mountain to the northwest from Mount Harvard. The distance between the two mountains is just three miles.

As the search for Gene was still ongoing, a disaster of huge proportions occurred on Mount Princeton, fourteen miles south of Mount Harvard, also in Chaffee County. A family from Buena Vista had taken two cousins with them to a location near the base of Mount Princeton, Agnes Caille Falls. It was early in the morning on October 8 when the family was walking just below the mountain when one of the biggest rockslides in the area's history came crushing down and killed five of the six people in the group. Some of the boulders were over one hundred tons in size. This was a well-established family from the city with kids attending the high school and parents as coaches. It was a devastating blow to the community.

The Chaffee County sheriff had already started to reduce the size of the search for Gene, but the rockslide reduced the effort even more.

I've often sat and imagined what the odds were that any family would be in that exact position to be victimized by the rockslide.

Just as the book was going to press, a hiker was one quarter mile from the main trail that Gene was on and found his wallet and other items laying on the snow. SAR team members went into the area and found what they believed to be Gene's body. This is truly an unreal find considering that Colorado has had 150% of the normal snowfall and Gene disappeared prior to heavy winter snow. The sheriff has not released autopsy results.

Florida

Sex/Name	Date/Time Missing • Age • State
M-C. G. Lee (Son of)	11/29/23-Unk • 4 • Clearwater, FL
M-Al Snider	03/05/48-5:00 p.m. • 28 • Sandy Key, FL
M-C. H. Trotter	03/05/48-5:00 p.m. • 48 • Sandy Key, FL
M-Don Frasier	03/05/48-5:00 p.m. • Unk • Sandy Key, FL
M-Jimmy Howard	02/25/51-11:30 a.m. • 2 • FL
M-Ben McDaniel	08/18/10-7:30 p.m. • 30 • Vortex Springs, FL

C.G. Lee (Son of)
Missing: 11/29/23-Unk, Clearwater, FL
Age at disappearance: 4 years

The Lees left their home in Tarpon Springs and traveled to Pasco County for a Thanksgiving weekend of hunting. The details of the disappearance are unexplained in any of the articles I've reviewed, but their son vanished on November 29, 1923, and a massive search was started. I should state here that back in the early 1900s, it was the practice of newspapers to never reveal the names of small children. The name of this child could not be found.

I could explain what happened during the search, but a December 1, 1923, article in the *Evening Independent* had a lengthy examination of events leading to a happy Thanksgiving: "County Commissioner Ed Beckett attended the commissioner's meeting at the courthouse yesterday, related some of his experiences while assisting in the search for the lost boy. He said the entire countryside had been aroused and every available man went out in the woods looking for the boy. Commissioner Beckett described how he found the footprints of the child at least 10 or 12 miles from the location of the camp where he strayed from. Going through the swamp with a flashlight in the back of the old Whidden place, the little boy's tracks were discovered in the white sand where a fallen tree had burned. They were lost in heavy palmettos and Mr. Beckett was obliged to leave the searching party when it began to rain, about 2 o'clock yesterday morning."

At approximately 1:30 p.m. on November 30, the boy was found sleeping in the middle of the swamp. The exact location of the discovery was never documented.

Summary

In Robert Koester's book, *Lost Person Behavior*, he states that a four-year-old boy would be found 95 percent of the time 6.6 miles from the point he was last seen. This boy had traveled at least ten miles and possibly twelve or more. This wasn't walking through your neighborhood on a sidewalk; this was through swamps, sand, and around dangerous animals. This is hard to believe.

Mimicking other disappearances, the boy was found asleep. The distance the boy traveled was far outside the bounds of anything considered normal. Searchers located the boy in a swamp.

Al Snider   Age at disappearance: 28 years
C. H. Trotter   Age at disappearance: 48 years
Don Frasier   Age at disappearance: Unknown
Missing: 03/05/48-5:00 p.m., Sandy Key, FL

Readers, be ready for a profound paradigm change. The past three books have dealt with disappearances on land; now we are moving to water. I have been reminded numerous times that as long as the disappearance matches the profile we've established, we must include it. This case matches the profile in many ways. Don't be disturbed that we are including this case until you've read the facts. If we were to exclude this case because it wasn't identical to the other six hundred-plus cases, we wouldn't be doing true research. We'd merely be looking for cases that met a specific niche.

Al Snider was one of the best jockeys in the world. In the days previous to his disappearance, he had rode Citation and won the Flamingo Stakes at Hialeah Park. On March 4, 1948, he was offered a full-time contract by the prestigious Calumet Farms to ride their ponies. Snider was destined to ride Citation at the Kentucky Derby, a dream ride.

On March 5, 1948, in the afternoon hours, Snider, Trotter (a horse trainer), Frasier (a Canadian manufacturer), and some others were on the *Evelyn K*, a sixty-five-foot yacht owned by John B. Campbell, the secretary of New York Racing. The skipper pulled into Sandy Key, and the three men got into a fifteen-foot wooden skiff to catch redfish. An April 30, 1948, article in the *Sun Sentinel* interviewed witnesses to the disappearance and explained how fast a storm came up: "One minute, Snider and his friends could be seen sitting on the skiff in calm channel waters. The next minute, under gusting winds and rolling waters, they were gone." People aboard the *Evelyn K* were watching the skiff and saw it disappear behind the palms, the last time the men were seen. Later in the same article was this: "Newspaper accounts say the storm was accompanied by 45 mph winds, winds which toppled a 70-foot elevator tower on Miami Beach and snapped telephone lines. 'It was a very unusual storm,' Trotter recalled [Trotter's son]. 'It became so dark, and it seemed to last about an hour. There was lightning, heavy winds.'"

The crew of the *Evelyn K* went straight into the area looking for the skiff and spent considerable time searching. They couldn't locate it.

The Coast Guard was immediately advised, and soon after a major search was started. The *Evelyn K* made it back to port without any damage. In a strange coincidence, Gregory Peck's yacht (*The Tonga*) was also in the area and made it back to port without any damage.

The Coast Guard contacted other armed forces and asked for assistance. Soon there were over thirty planes, boats, blimps, and helicopters looking for the lost men. One week after the disappearance, the skiff was found ten miles south of Everglades City overturned in Rabbit Key. The life preservers and everything in the skiff was gone. There was a small rope dangling from the front. There were no oars or equipment, nothing.

On March 16 there was another major incident taking place in conjunction with the search. A March 17, 1948, article in the *St.*

Petersburg Times had this description: "Tragedy nearly struck twice when a large Army helicopter aiding in the search crashed in the thick mangrove swamps on a small island in Chatham River. The craft's three occupants escaped unhurt, however. The helicopter had been flying low over a roofless shack on a small island when a downdraft plunged it into the ground." As you read this book, make a mental note of the number of times aircraft crash in conjunction with these search and rescues. It seems there is an abnormal amount of crashes. In case you wondered where the army was searching for the men, it was inside Everglades National Park.

In the three weeks of the search, there were a number of items found that were initially thought to be associated with the men. Footprints were found on a remote island, and Bloodhounds were put on them. They found nothing. There was a hat found that was supposedly worn by Canadian manufacturer Don Frasier. The hat was found floating in a remote canal. The army sent a series of troops into the area on four-day assignments. They found nothing. In another strange coincidence, there was an arrow found made of sticks in the sand. Troops were sent into that area and also found nothing. There was even a bottle found floating weeks after the incident that seemed it might have come from the men. There was writing scratched into the bottle; this lead led nowhere.

Decades later, no evidence of where the men went was ever located. Articles continually reminded readers that the area where the men had vanished was very shallow water. They could easily have gotten out of the boat, walked to land, and weathered the storm. Other articles say that Al Snider and Trotter were cautious and honorable men who would've pulled up anchor and gone back to the *Evelyn K* at the first sign of bad weather.

Summary

The factors in this disappearance that match what I've written about in the past are stunning. Bad weather inundates the area for an hour, causes massive confusion, and the disappearance is set in motion. Bloodhounds, search and rescue planes, and ground teams find nothing. Decades after the disappearance, not even a piece of the men's clothing has ever been found. I think the helicopter crash is an unusual coincidence that happens too frequently in these cases.

When Al was invited to attend the fishing adventure on the yacht, he immediately called his best friend, Eddie Arcaro in California, and invited him. Arcaro had a ride set in California and couldn't get away. In one of the most unusual coincidences I have ever written about, Al's best friend, Eddie Arcaro, was signed by Calumet Farms and rode Citation to the Triple Crown. In an absolute display of how honorable Arcaro was, he gave half his earnings for winning the Triple Crown to Al's daughter, Nancy.

Jimmy Howard
Missing: 02/25/51-11:30 a.m., 63 miles west of Miami, FL
Age at disappearance: 2 years

Jimmy lived with his parents, and they were vacationing in an extremely rural environment off the Tamiami Trail near Ochopee, Florida. On February 25, 1951, at approximately 11:30 a.m., Jimmy was sleeping inside his house trailer that was parked on a lonely road while his mom and dad searched for firewood in the woods. The parents returned from their short excursion and found the boy had disappeared.

The Howards searched the area around the trailer, yelling and looking for the boy without seeing anything or getting a response. The Collier County sheriff was called. A February 26 article in the *Lowell Sun* described the feelings and search efforts of the sheriff: "Footprints believed to be Jimmy's were found between the trailer and a nearby swamp, but 60 men walked an arm's length apart across a three mile area last night without turning a trace of the youngster. 'We are all baffled by it,' Sheriff L. J. Thoru of Collier County said. 'He was so little he couldn't have gone far.'" The sheriff put five airplanes into the area around the search location. The planes could not locate the boy.

On February 26, almost twenty-four hours after Jimmy disappeared, searchers were two and a half miles from the place that the boy was last seen and found him alive in tall saw grass. In an area that was infested with alligators, poisonous snakes, and bears,

Jimmy had evaded injury and was found alive. He was transported to a hospital where the physician stated he was in good condition.

Summary

Jimmy was found inside the search perimeter in an area that had been already covered. He was asleep inside a trailer and somehow got out and walked into danger without his parents hearing or seeing him.

There are too many of these identical disappearances for it to be pure chance.

M-Ben McDaniel
Missing: 08/18/10-7:30 p.m., Vortex Springs, FL
Age at disappearance: 30 years

For readers of my past books and individuals who think they've identified the suspect in these cases, time for another paradigm shift. This is the first case where I've researched an incident that happened underwater. The area of this disappearance is much like many of the areas I've identified in the past: there are hundreds of small bodies of water in the immediate region. Vortex Springs is forty miles east of Pensacola and ten miles south of the Alabama border. This is a private facility that is protected by fence, lock, and key. It is a private fresh water spring that is very complex, with many great arms to dive.

I do have some experience with scuba and cave diving. Ben McDaniel had been diving since he was fourteen years old; I was certified when I was twelve. I've dove at many worldwide locations and understand the extreme dangers that accompany cave diving.

On August 18, 2010, at 7:30 p.m., experienced diver Ben McDaniel entered the water at Vortex Spring alone and disappeared into its depths. He was observed entering the cave by two divers who were exiting.

Ben was not a small person. At six feet two inches, he was a big man. An April 15, 2011, article on the *TampaBay.com* website had the following statement: "He switched on his lights as he began his descent into Vortex Spring. Two divers saw him coming, lights aglow, his white helmet surging toward the mouth of the cave, toward a sign that said STOP, toward another bearing a picture of the Grim Reaper and the words: GO NOT FARTHER. THERE'S NOTHING IN THIS CAVE WORTH DIVING FOR. And then he was gone."

Two days after Ben entered the spring, an employee found his truck and equipment outside the perimeter and called the sheriff. Deputies searched his vehicle and found his wallet, money, and dive logbook. The sheriff stated that Ben had been mapping the cave bottom and had planned to make a deep dive.

The reason this case is in the book is because it is a huge mystery. The sheriff enlisted the aid of some of the most experienced and rational cave divers in the world. One of those divers, Eric Sorensen, owned a local cave exploration company and had gone deeper into Vortex Spring than anyone.

Early in the search, divers found two tanks filled with air belonging to Ben, which had been placed for decompression. The cave starts fifty feet from the surface, where you then enter a tunnel that gets progressively narrower. At three hundred feet into the tunnel, a diver would reach a locked gate. Divers need to get the key to go farther from the owners of the site. Rescuers searched all of the common public areas quickly and found nothing to indicate that Ben was anywhere easily searched. Divers pushed farther and deeper into remote areas of the cave, as much as 1,500 feet of horizontal travel. There was never any indication in anything I reviewed that

Ben had the key to enter the restricted zone. It would appear from search efforts, though, that someone believed he did.

The tanks belonging to Ben indicated he was going to stay down longer than our bodies would allow without staying at a shallow depth. Additional tanks at a shallow depth allow the body to release noxious gases that could kill divers if the diver decided to come straight up without stopping and decompressing. It shows that Ben had preplanned this trip.

Eric Sorensen is a much smaller man than Ben, and this allowed him to enter areas of the cave that Ben couldn't access. Eric and a team of sixteen divers spent thirty-six days looking for the man. There was a $10,000 reward for finding a body, and this further encouraged experienced divers to get into the cave and access special areas they knew.

Eric utilized smaller tanks that he held under his arms to allow him to get into very small openings. He claimed that in all of the areas he entered there were no scratches on the walls, no sediment disturbed, and no evidence that anyone had been there.

During the 1980s, thirteen people had died in Vortex Springs. New owners took over and hoped to make diving safer. In April 2012, another cave diver at the springs died. Many believed the person was trying to get the reward for finding Ben, but this was never confirmed.

Summary

Cave diving is one of the most dangerous sports in the world. One of the first rules about this sport is never dive alone. Why Ben entered the springs by himself, I have no idea.

I do believe that Vortex Springs has been thoroughly searched ten to twenty times. There were reports just after Ben vanished that cadaver dogs brought to the area indicated they had smelled gases related to a corpse. There has never been an indication that cadaver dogs have since gone back and smelled anything.

This incident was so strange that the Discovery Channel highlighted it on their series, "Disappeared."

Vortex Springs has been searched and dove by scuba enthusiasts hundreds of times since Ben vanished. They have never found any of the equipment he was wearing or carrying. They have never found any indications he tried to squeeze into areas that might have been tight for the big man.

Why have I included this case into a dialogue of missing people? When you get into the unexplained, you better keep an open mind, or you'll be the victim of your own biases. Think of the bottom of this cave as a normal search zone that was divided into grids. Experts had gone into the area and cleared it. Nothing was there. Multiple teams went into the areas and determined Ben was not there. When you look at the area around Vortex Springs on Google Earth, it appears much like swamp zones where other people have vanished. It has hundreds of bodies of small and large ponds.

Ben was alone, like the vast majority of the missing we have highlighted in the past. There were no witnesses to the man vanishing. Searchers failed to find his body. Secondary canine and cadaver searches failed to indicate a possible body in the water.

I believe that something very unusual and unexpected happened to Ben, not dissimilar to the cases I have documented in the past.

Hawaii
**A Special Report

In early 2013 a friend took their family to Maui for a week's vacation. During that trip, they scheduled a van island tour. The night after the tour, I was called and told that I had to interview the Native Hawaiian driver of their van. He had told stories of Hawaiian life, customs, and ancient history that they had never heard before, my friend said that they'd be valuable in my next book. Once my friend returned back to the mainland, we met and discussed the tour. It wasn't long before the guide was on the phone, and I was booking a flight to Maui.

Roy Aricayos is a Native Hawaiian who specializes in their history and background. In June 2013 Roy was gracious enough to agree to meet with me and my friend and discuss his knowledge of Hawaiian disappearances. It should be noted that Roy never was told my name, what books I've written, or what I wanted to discuss.

This was a "cold call" meeting. He did know that I was a writer and wanted to discuss specific aspects of Hawaiian life.

Roy was like many of the older Maui people; he was born to live on a plantation. His dad was making just one dollar a day and lived in a plantation-owned building that had a roof, electricity, and water. He had eleven brothers and sisters who lived in cramped quarters in a sugar hill plantation near the Lahaina Mountains. There were two hundred people in his camp, and many would have starved if they didn't work hard. He stated that the workers were allowed to have few personal belongings. The only assurances the plantation gave families were basic living. Eventually, Portuguese people were brought to the islands for their leadership skills and soon took those jobs from the natives.

One of the Hawaiian customs that was hard for a mainlander to understand was that many Hawaiians did not bury their deceased. It was believed that they should get back to the water, and that's where the dead went.

There were little people living in the Hawaiian mountains who were called Hune. They weren't seen often, and people tried to avoid them. Most of them were only two feet tall. There were also giants who lived on Maui. The island's last king, King Kamehameha (July 1782–May 8, 1819) was seven feet tall. In 1990–1992, when the Ritz Carlton Hotel was being built in Kapalua, Roy states that they found an extremely tall native princess in the excavation process. She was reportedly buried near the front of the hotel, and this was kept quiet.

I asked Roy to explain what he knew about the disappearances of Hawaiians. He told me about a group called "Night Marchers." They are a group of warriors who come out during the full moon. They rarely come out during daylight hours. He states that they are the old guard of the royal family. If they lost a battle, they would kill themselves en masse; they are then held in a sort of purgatory and tasked with guarding the trails of the island. Roy explained that islanders will see torches coming down the mountain to the beaches. If you are caught on the beach as they enter, you must lay on your stomach and strip naked, if possible. If you happen to look at them, you will either be taken, or you'll die. You get naked before they reach the beach to show your humility. Historically, it has been known that children who see them on the beach will follow the warriors and be lost forever. Land in ancient Hawaii was divided by streams, and it is those streams that the warriors need to descend to the beach.

Molokai supposedly has more activity with Night Marchers than any other island. Roy stated that on full moon nights, the "gate" is opened from sunset till 3:00 a.m. It is during this time that the marchers will be seen.

We had a brief conversation that Roy initiated about portals. He stated that Maui had two, and there was one in Hana and one at the Black Rock in Kaanapali by the Sheraton Hotel. In ancient times the Hawaiians built their cemeteries over known portals.

Summary

The information that Roy gave me that hit a chord was about people who went missing in the presence of the Night Marchers. He told me about how people must lay on their stomach on the ground, naked. This is exactly how many of the missing people are found in my books. His statement that if the witness looks up, they die or are taken, also fits with how many of the missing are found. There is no way Roy knew of any of the incidents in the Missing 411 books, or even that I wrote books about the missing. It was a very interesting meeting.

Idaho

Sex/Name	Date Missing • Age • State
M-Lawrence Marsh (Son of)	06/15/1907-6:00 p.m. • 19 mos. • ID
M-Dailey Hamerly	05/25/33-2:00 p.m. • 2 • Moscow, ID
M-James Madison	09/11/52-6:00 p.m. • 67 • Nez Perce National Forest, ID
F-Shirley Hunt	06/27/58-11:15 a.m. • 8 • Weippe, ID
F-Susan Adams	09/30/90-Unk • 42 • Selway Bitterroot, ID
M-Joshua Stauffer	05/07/99-4:00 p.m. • 3 • Downey ID
F-Amelia Linkert	09/23/13-Unk • 69 • Craters of the Moon NP
F-Jo Elliott Blakeslee	09/23/13-Unk • 63 • Craters of the Moon NP

Lawrence Marsh (Son of)
Missing: 06/15/1907-6:00 p.m., 13 miles northwest of Caldwell, ID
Age at disappearance: 19 months

Caldwell sits twelve miles west of Boise and ten miles east of the Oregon border. The location of this incident is thirteen miles northwest of Caldwell, very near the Snake and Payette Rivers. This area is desolate and similar to a high desert area.

On June 15, 1907, at approximately 6:00 p.m., Mr. and Mrs. Lawrence Marsh realized that their nineteen-month-old son was missing from their rural home. They quickly searched the area and called for the boy without getting a response. The family made the trip to neighbors' and asked for assistance in finding their boy.

It wasn't long before a formal request was made to the area penitentiary for Bloodhounds. There were several dogs sent, and articles indicated they found nothing.

A June 21, 1907, article in the *Spokesman Review* had the following information on the search and rescue: "Harold Hawthorne finally found the little one 8 miles east of its home. He was searching in that direction with a party, but first turned back declaring that the child could not have traveled so far, but he pushed on until he finally found the baby's tracks." Hawthorne did find the child alive.

Articles describe the baby's condition as good but with scratches on his face and legs.

Summary

It's very hard to understand why Bloodhounds failed to find the scent of the child. Much of this area is open sage brush country with very few locations where a baby could hide.

The statement of the searcher and his reluctance to push farther away is indicative of most people who would be looking for a nineteen-month-old baby. Robert Koester's book, *Lost Person Behavior,* is a book used to set search guidelines on SAR missions. The book states that a child one to three years old traveling on flat ground will be found 95 percent of the time within 2.0 miles or less. This tot was found in four times that distance. Is this believable?

M-Dailey Hamerly
Missing: 05/25/33-2:00 p.m., Moscow, ID
Age at disappearance: 2 years

This incident happened in close proximity to a cluster of missing people just on the Washington side of the border. Moscow is located between Lewiston and Coeur d' Alene and approximately twenty-five miles north of Hells Gate State Park.

On May 25, 1933, at approximately 2:00 p.m., Mrs. Cecil Hamerly was returning to her seven children at their residence after briefly visiting a neighbor and Mr. Hamerly was cutting firewood just slightly away from the house. After Mrs. Hamerly arrived home, she realized that Dailey had disappeared. The parents and the kids looked for the boy but couldn't locate him. The family contacted the sheriff to respond to their home eight miles east of Moscow. The local sheriff arrived and immediately called for additional searchers.

The on-scene deputy had found the boy's tracks crossing a field and entering a thick forest area. The tracks were lost in the woods.

Two hundred searchers arrived late in the afternoon and encountered heavy rain and strong winds. Searchers stayed through the night and kept yelling and looking for the boy with their pine torches and flashlights. The night searchers saw nothing and didn't get a response.

The next morning fifty men from the National Guard arrived to help in the search along with multiple Bloodhound teams from Spokane, Washington. Law enforcement was very concerned about the boy's welfare because of freezing temperatures and another violent thunderstorm and rain that hit the area during the night.

At approximately 2:30 p.m., two searchers were in the same plowed field the boy initially crossed. The men were one-quarter mile from the residence and found the child in a furrow. He was alive and in very good condition.

A May 27 article in the *Lewiston Morning Tribune* had this description of the boy and his condition: "Despite the fact he was in the timber all night, according to the belief of persons who had stalked the field where he was found, a physician this afternoon said the boy had suffered no ill effects, despite the below freezing temperatures last night. The belief is that the boy had never gotten more than a half mile from home. The absence of all signs of having suffered from the cold convinced searchers the boy had spent the night under cover."

You might want to read this paragraph again.

The night prior to the boy being found, the area around the Hamerly residence had been inundated with freezing rain from a major thunderstorm. It's unrealistic to believe that a two-year-old boy wouldn't suffer from exposure after being out in these elements. Dailey suffered no ill effects. The searchers believed that the boy must not have been out in the weather that night, somehow.

Why didn't Dailey respond to the two hundred searchers in the area yelling his name during the night? Was he even in the area during the night?

Why didn't multiple Bloodhounds find the boy?

James Madison
Missing 9/11/52-6:00 p.m., Nez Perce National Forest, ID
Age at disappearance: 67 years

There are a few cases where I've written about hunters who disappeared under extremely strange circumstances. James Madison was a lifetime hunter and outdoorsman and was one of the few individuals who nobody would have thought could get lost.

James was camping with his good friend Claude Buffalo in an area fourteen miles east of the Red River Ranger Station in the Nez Perce National Forest. This was a remote location. The men wanted to get an early jump on hunting season. The season would start on September 15.

At approximately 6:00 p.m. on September 11, Jim and Claude established their camp. They planned to hike the following three days and find the perfect spot to drop their game. James knew they needed water, and he headed for the creek with a bucket and his rifle. After almost thirty minutes, Claude became concerned for his friend and started looking for him. He called Jim's name throughout the night and heard nothing. The following morning Claude drove to the ranger station and reported Jim missing.

The rangers brought local sheriff's deputies, and they brought Bloodhounds. The searchers found nothing and were getting frustrated. A September 16 headline in the *Lewiston Morning Tribune* stated it all: "Hounds Stymied in Woods Hunt." The dogs weren't finding a scent trail, and they weren't finding tracks. The search continued.

On September 23 four airmen from the local military transport school took to the air looking for James. The air force was in the sky for two days and saw nothing of value.

On September 24, late in the afternoon, four hikers found something in a remote section of the Salmon River, miles from where everyone thought James would be: a body, facedown, twenty feet from shore in eighteen inches of water. A September 26 article in the *Lewiston Morning Tribune* had the following description of the body: "Robertson said death apparently was caused by exhaustion rather than drowning. Madison was clad in underwear and a T-shirt. He was barefooted and the soles of his feet were worn to the bone." The article further states that he was found fifteen miles from his camp, and it was believed that he walked ten days before reaching the site at the river. The coroner stated that James had been in the water for three to four days.

In total, almost 150 people searched for James. Bloodhounds picked up one scent and tracked it for miles to another hunter. James's track was never found by the dogs. He was found in an area nobody had believed he would be.

Summary

In the thousands of cases I've reviewed, I've never read where someone removed their boots and then wore their feet to the bone. I won't state the obvious here. The weather was moderate at the time of the disappearance, and nobody could explain where James's clothes went.

There is another case where a boy disappeared when his father and he were in the forest cutting wood. The boy was with his brother, went to get the water, and started to walk back but spilled the load. His brother continued back to his dad, and the boy went back for more water. After he got the water, he stated (after he was found) that he didn't recognize where he was and got lost. Could this be a possible explanation for what happened to James Madison? There doesn't seem to be any logical explanation for many of the things that James experienced. This area of Idaho has many strange disappearances.

F-Shirley Hunt
Missing: 06/27/58-11:15 a.m., Weippe, ID
Age at disappearance: 8 years

This incident happened at a ranch five miles from Weippe, Idaho, very near Lolo Creek. This is one of the key stories in the book because of one important statement made by the victim. If you go back and read the title of this book, it's the details that will explain and define the missing issue.

On June 27, 1958, at 11:15 a.m., Shirley Hunt was playing in the yard of her parents' rural ranch. It is unknown how this happened, but Shirley disappeared from the yard, and the parents made a cursory search. Once they were unable to find the girl, a call was made to Weippe for additional assistance.

Seventy-five community members from Weippe arrived at the Hunt homestead and started to split into search teams. Just as the groups were leaving, rain started to inundate the area and continued through the afternoon.

Searchers made little progress. They weren't hearing the girl and weren't getting a response from their calls. At 6:00 p.m., one mile from the Hunt residence, searchers Leo Cochrell and Anton Larson of Weippe found Shirley. A June 28 article in the *Lewiston Morning Tribune* had the following information on the condition of the eight-year-old: "Shirley was barely able to talk when found. She said she had 'Just started walking.'" Search members believed that the girl had walked in circles for hours before she was found. But read that statement again: "Just started walking." I think is an important revelation. Had Shirley *just* started to walk when she was found?

Two men from a local mill had been in an airplane over the search area during the entire afternoon and never saw the girl. They had headed back and were out of the area when she was found. Is this coincidental?

Shirley was located just a mile from her residence. This area had been completely covered by the searchers during the day, and nothing was located. Many of the children I have written about in the past are found in a semiconscious state and do not say anything. I believe that the description by searchers that Shirley could "barely talk" and that she was "just starting to walk" is important.

Susan Seymour Adams
Missing: 09/30/90-Unk, Selway-Bitterroot Wilderness, ID
Age at disappearance: 42 years

Susan Seymour Adams was raised in Austin, Texas. Her mother was an employee at Nambe Mills, a retailer with many stores. Once Susan disappeared, Nambe Mills held benefits to raise money for her search. The effort got national attention; you may have seen the associated publicity.

Susan and her husband, Tom, had taken a guided horseback trip into the Selway-Bitterroot Wilderness for hunting. The hunter's camp was established twenty air miles west of Hamilton near Battle Lake. On September 30, 1990, Susan took her bird-watching book and camera and took a short hike out of camp, saying she'd be back soon. Susan didn't come back. Hunters, hikers, and volunteers searched for eight days and found nothing. At the end of the eighth day, rain and snow hit the area, and search efforts were terminated. Snow continued for many days and covered any evidence that would've led to her discovery. There was a secondary search that started in early October. This effort had to stop after two days because of heavy rain. There was a third search in July 1991, and again nothing was found.

Approximately one year after Susan had vanished, this article appeared in the September 22, 1991, *Santa Fe New Mexican*: "On September 30, 1990, Susan Seymour Adams walked out of a hunting camp in the Selway-Bitterroot Wilderness area and disappeared. Intensive searches were conducted following her disappearance, but were hampered by the remoteness of the area, the rugged terrain and snow. Additional efforts in July 1991 after the snow melted were also unsuccessful. Based upon the local sheriff's office investigations and the professionals, an Idaho district judge on July 19, 1991, declared Susan dead of injuries and/or exposure as of September 30, 1990."

You will not read about Susan on any database, and she's not listed as a missing person. She has officially been declared dead without her body ever being found.

Susan is also another of a long line of people who have disappeared with a camera in their hand. There are several people who have taken a short hike and seemed to evaporate away. Remember, she wasn't going to hike far; she hadn't taken extra supplies, and nobody found a trace.

M-Joshua Stauffer
Missing: 05/07/99-4:00 p.m., Downey ID
Age at disappearance: 3 years

Rodney and Melanie Stauffer took their son, three-year-old Joshua, with them to visit his grandparents on the outskirts of Downey, Idaho, twenty miles south of Pocatello and twenty miles north of the Utah border.

Sometimes in these stories, it's not perfectly clear how fast children vanish. In this May 14, 1999, article in the *Deseret News* is an explanation how fast Joshua went missing: "One minute he'd been in the yard playing. The next minute he was gone. The search had started immediately." Imagine this was your child, and he vanished that quickly. You would be yelling and screaming and expecting an answer. It was May 7, 1999, at about 4:00 p.m. when Joshua disappeared from his grandparents' rural yard. The parents couldn't locate the boy, and they weren't hearing anything in response to their calls.

The Bannock County sheriff was called. He made a request for Bloodhounds, airplanes, equestrians, and foot searchers. There was a limited response at the beginning of the effort, probably because people thought the boy would be found quickly. At the end of the first night, the group had swelled to over two hundred. Searchers were getting concerned for the boy's welfare because temperatures were dropping below freezing.

At the beginning of the second day, the sheriff was getting very concerned at the lack of clues and the lack of reaction from Bloodhounds to any scent. Local law enforcement called the FBI and asked for help.

Planes and helicopters with FLIR were not seeing anything from the air, and ground teams were covering lots of area but not finding clues of value.

On May 8, 1999, searchers were continuing to move farther from the grandparents' home and started toward a large hill. A May 10, 1999, article in the *Lewiston Morning Tribune* had this description of what was found: "Rescue teams followed footsteps that eventually led them to the boy a full five miles from the Williams home. Bannock County Sheriff Lorin Nielsen said finding Stauffer was a miracle. It is unusual for a child that age to walk so far, though the exercise may have kept him alive, he said." A searcher approaching the hill thought he saw something near the top that was red. Joshua was wearing a red shirt. The team had climbed the hill and found the boy lying near the top, curled up under a juniper tree.

Joshua was flown by helicopter to Bannock Regional hospital, where it was determined he was dehydrated and had a slight case of exposure.

Summary

Joshua was found far outside the range of where 95 percent of all three-year-olds travel in hilly or mountain terrain. He was also found uphill on top of a mountain, a very unusual location for a small boy who had traveled that lengthy distance.

It seems that the more cases we find, the more common it becomes that children disappear from relatives' homes over their own.

Joshua recovered and was eventually released from the hospital.

Amelia "Amy" Linkert   Age at disappearance: 69 years
Jo Elliott Blakeslee   Age at disappearance: 63 years
Missing: 09/23/13-Unk, Craters of the Moon National Monument

This is one of the most unusual disappearances I've ever researched. The victims of this tragedy and the circumstances of their deaths do not come together in any logical order. It would appear that these two ladies shouldn't have been where they were.

I didn't know much about this monument before I started this story. An archive search for information on Craters of the Moon found a March 20, 1939, article in the *Lewiston Morning Tribune* that made a few fascinating points: "Few have ever heard of the midget tribe, that many believe inhabit the three 'Lost Valleys' of the crater region." Later in the same article was more clarity: "Probably one of the most interesting takes is that of the tribe of dwarfs, thought by the Indians to have inhabited the vast lava rock regions. The midget tribe was accused of having caused the death of many a brave warrior, who wandered into the lavas in search of game, never to return." Each time I research a new location, I try to find some of the local stories that you may not see posted in the local parks' headquarters.

Amy Linkert retired from Lowell Middle School in Idaho where she was a longtime teacher. She purchased a trailer and wanted to travel the country visiting parks. Jo Elliott was a graduate of the University of Washington Medical School. She had retired from the US Navy Reserve as a commander, and her medical career included private practice in Washington and Idaho. She most recently was a physician at the Snake River Correctional Institute in Ontario, Oregon. Both women were extremely religious and attended church regularly.

On September 19 the women parked their trailer at the KOA campground in Arco and drove to Craters of the Moon National Monument and the Tree Molds Trailhead. The pair had told friends that they would be back in Boise on September 21. When Jo didn't report to her job at the correctional facility, they reported her as missing on September 23. The formal search for the women started on September 24. Searchers found the women's truck parked at the trailhead with their two Labradoodle dogs in the back and their purses and cell phones were in the front seat.

There was an initial big push to search for the women. On September 25 they found a body. It was initially reported that it was Jo Elliott Blakeslee and then days later, the ID was changed to Amy Linkert. There was never any clarity as to why there was an initial misidentification. There was a comment in a September 26 article on KTVB.com: "Dan Buckley, the monument's superintendent, says that the Idaho Army National Guard and Butte County Sheriff's Office located the body by helicopter around two miles southwest of Tree Molds Trail Head parking lot in a very rugged and inaccessible area of the lava field." You read that correctly—"in a very rugged and inaccessible area." If it was inaccessible, how did she get there? It should be stated that these women were not athletic distance hikers. Their own families made statements to the press that the pair would never leave their dogs more than an hour in the truck, and they wouldn't hike far. Park officials and the sheriff were at a loss to answer why Amy would've left the trail.

The search continued for Jo. Helicopters, eight canine teams, the Civil Air Patrol, and ground teams were all working in a grid-type pattern looking for the woman. On October 1, there was a curveball thrown at the search. The national park was shut down because of budgetary issues. It wasn't long until there were emergency funds made available, and ten searchers went back into the grid.

The trailhead for Tree Molds isn't far from Devil's Orchard Nature Trail. This entire area is an unbelievable array of some of the most rugged and dangerous areas to hike off-trail of anywhere in the national park and national monument system. If you looked at the countryside, the thought of leaving the trail would never enter my mind. It's too rough, too sharp, and overall too dangerous.

Also around the October 1 time frame, inclement weather hit the area and continued to slow search efforts. The bad weather continued for several days and grounded helicopters. It was also during this time that Jo's uncle made statements that he didn't know if the women had been abducted or were victims of some other crime.

By October 12, cave specialists had been inside the park and were searching lava tubes. The sheriff stated there had been three to four thousand hours dedicated to the search and ten thousand miles of hiking had taken place.

Helicopters went back into the air when weather permitted. They were searching in a slowly growing circle from the location where Amy had been located, believing that Jo would be somewhere in that immediate area.

On October 23, twenty-eight days after Amy was located, searchers found Jo's body. A helicopter was working the area of the lava fields and made the discovery from the air. An October 23, 2013, article on KIVI.com had this explanation: "A helicopter search of the lava fields north and west of the Tree Molds Trail early Tuesday evening yielded the location of Dr. Jodean 'Jo' Elliott Blakeslee. Her body was located approximately one mile from the location where searchers earlier found the body of her hiking partner Amelia 'Amy' Linkert."

The finding of Jo's body raises more questions than it answers major concerns. This finding means that air searchers continued for twenty-eight days and, working inside out from the location of Amy's body, never found Jo. With numerous different helicopter crews and pilots assisting in the search, it is extremely difficult to understand how the body wasn't found sooner, if Jo was there. Several of the helicopters had FLIR—this highlights body heat on the ground. Apparently FLIR never reacted to Jo's body.

The families of the women made several statements to the press that they could not understand why or how the women would've entered the lava fields. They felt that both would have stayed fairly close to the truck to take care of their dogs. The location of Jo's body was described by park superintendent Dan Buckley in an October 25 article on Magicvalley.com: "'She was in a nasty piece of lava,' Buckley said. 'It's dangerous and treacherous out there.'"

Eight separate canine teams failed to locate either of the bodies. If we follow standard logic, Jo's body was in that field for at least twenty-eight days. Cadaver dogs trained to smell dead bodies never found her.

Summary

It's now March 2014, and the coroner is still investigating the cause of death to Dr. Blakeslee. Toxicology results take no more than six weeks, and autopsies are usually completed immediately after a body is located. I filed a FOIA against the park service immediately after both bodies were found, and I still have not received a copy of the report. The park service is claiming they can't complete the report until they have a cause of death from the coroner. The park service did say that they could not see any injury on either woman that would've caused them to be incapacitated.

I think it's quite a coincidence that several cases I have highlighted in this book involve an excessive delay by coroners in coming to a finding of death. This is not normal and could be considered very unusual.

Readers, look at the profile photos of Jo and Amy and then look at the photo of Hildegard Hendrickson from Washington. Hildegard disappeared from Wenatchee, Washington, on June 8, 2013, and has never been found. Each of the women had short hair and large builds. In past books I have written that it appears that many of the women who vanish have very short hair and, from the back, could possibly pass as a male.

Illinois

Sex/Name	Date Missing • Age • State
M-Henry Nutter	07/06/1919-Unk • 6 • Fox Lake, IL

Henry Nutter
Missing: 07/06/1919-Unk, Fox Lake, IL
Age at disappearance: 6 years

Fox Lake is located in the far northern section of Illinois, just two miles south of the Wisconsin border. There are hundreds of small bodies of water in this region.

This story has several elements that will sound familiar to readers of past books. I wrote a chapter in a book about berry pickers who have disappeared, and this incident involved a picker, both in the disappearance and the recovery.

On July 3, 1919, the parents of Henry Nutter had left the boy with a friend, Ernest Brassaw, who lived near Fox Lake. The parents were taking a trip to Chicago, and the boy was staying with a family who had children near his age.

A July 23, 1919, article in the *Kansas City Star* had a segment on how Henry Nutter disappeared: "It was Sunday July 6, when Henry with a number of playmates went berry picking. Leaving him by a berry bush, his companions went in search of drinking water. When they returned, he was gone. Posses searched the woods to no avail." Law enforcement officers called in Bloodhounds, and they tracked the boy's scent deep into the woods until they reached a massive swamp, where the dogs stopped.

The days of searching went on for more than a week. Families continued to look for the boy, and there was never any evidence produced as to where he might be. Ten days passed without finding Henry.

On the eleventh day of Henry's disappearance, two men uninvolved in the search were near Grand Lake berry picking when they heard a very odd sound. A July 18, 1919, article in the *Milwaukee Journal* described the sound: "Both thought the child's call a bird song. Roy Johnson and George Erickson, who made the rescue heard the faint cry and were undecided at first whether to investigate. 'But I never heard a bird call quite like that,' one suggested. 'I want to see what it looks like.' The pair worked their way through the underbrush. The call came again, more distinct but still like a bird's note. They then saw the child. Naked, Henry was half lying, half sitting under a tree. He watched the two men approach but made no move toward them." Later in the same article was this: "When he was lifted he was unable to utter a coherent word. His eyes stared vacantly and for a time he was obviously demented."

Henry was emaciated, had bug bites over his body, and was found without any clothing or shoes. He was taken to a hospital, where he later told physicians that he hadn't eaten or drank water during this entire time. In the same *Milwaukee Journal* article as quoted earlier was this about what the boy remembered: "The child has no clear recollection of his eleven days wandering." Physicians believed the boy hadn't drank or eaten anything.

Summary

I have always remembered the rule of threes in survival: You can live three minutes without air. You can live three days without water. In a harsh environment, you can usually live three hours without shelter. You can live three weeks without food. (Refer to Livescience.com for details on the rule of threes.)

Let's remember Henry's incident. He is claiming that he lived eleven days without water—not credible. He also stated that he hadn't eaten anything, even though he was in an area with plentiful berries.

The boy couldn't remember details of his eleven days. He was found naked. Bloodhounds tracked the boy to a large swamp and then stopped. These are all classic indicators that have been covered in dozens of stories.

Kansas

Sex/Name	Date Missing • Age • State
M-Marvin Koepke	12/10/1922-5:00 p.m. • 4 • Junction City, KS

Marvin Koepke
Missing: 12/10/1922-5:00 p.m. • Junction City, KS
Age at disappearance: 4 years

The location of this disappearance was the outskirts of Junction City, Kansas. The Smoky Hill River flows along the east side of the city, and Milford Lake is to the northwest. The city is almost surrounded by several lakes and dams of various sizes.

Mr. and Mrs. George Koepke owned a small ranch on the outskirts of the city. On December 10, 1922, at 5:00 p.m., George was in the barn fixing an automobile while his wife was milking cows. Marvin and his sister (Myrtle, age twelve) were with other children from the area playing outside. Two dogs belonging to Marvin's family chased a rabbit across a road with Marvin and the other kids running after them. Marvin stated that he wanted the rabbit and continued running toward the forest. A December 15, 1922, article in the *San Antonio Light* stated the following: "The children tried to frighten Marvin. 'There are Boogers in the hills,' one of them said. 'You had better not go out there.' But Marvin replied there were no Boogers in the day time and solemnly walked away from them. The children were diverted by their play and Marvin wasn't missed until an hour later."

Over the next twenty-four hours, cavalrymen, Boy Scouts, city folks, and law enforcement all came to the Koepke farm to assist in locating the small boy. Over two thousand people participated in looking for Marvin over four days. Two private planes worked the search area in a checkerboard pattern, not finding a trace. A December 12, 1922, article in the *Emporia Gazette* expressed the belief of searchers: "Those leading the searching parties today held two theories. One that the boy had been run down by a motorcar and his body carried away, or that he had been drowned in the creek that flows past the Koepke home." Another article expressed another view of the search, as was documented in a December 12 article in the *Owosso Argus-Press*: "The men, who returned Monday night from a 26 hour search, asserted it was their belief that the boy was not in the wide area searched. Bloodhounds lost the scent a short distance from the Koepke residence and that led to the belief in some quarters that the boy might have been kidnapped." The area of the search was unusually cold and prompted searchers to express concern that the boy may not live through the frigid temperatures.

On December 14, four days after Marvin had vanished, a farmer three miles from the Koepke residence was walking his land and found the boy's body. He was lying on his back with no signs of violence. There were no news articles indicating what he was or wasn't wearing. It was the ruling of physicians that they believed that Marvin died late in the night the first day he went missing. This means he was supposedly lying in that same position in the pasture the entire time.

A December 14, 1922, article in the *Hutchinson News* described searchers' feelings about the discovery: "Searchers declared they had been over the entire pasture Monday and Tuesday and were at a loss to know how the body could have been overlooked at that time as it was visible today at a distance of at least fifty feet. The spot where the body was found is at least two miles from the route taken by Bloodhounds who were on the trail in the road near the Koepke home."

Summary

This is another in a very long line of cases where searchers can't explain how they missed the body during their search. The articles also expressed the surprise from the dog handlers that the body was found two miles from where the canines last had a scent. These are two major factors readers need to key in on: Bloodhounds don't just stop tracking; the scent must've evaporated. Bloodhounds love to do their work; they thrive on it. Two thousand searchers and two airplanes don't miss a body lying in the middle of a pasture for three days. Searchers are not inept!

Maine

Sex/Name	Date/Time Missing • Age • State
F-Lillian Carney	08/08/1897-Noon • 6 • Masardis, ME
F-Geraldine Largay	07/23/13-Unk • 66 • Sugarloaf Mountain

Lillian Carney
Missing: 08/08/1897-Noon, Masardis, ME
Age at disappearance: 6 years

In *Missing 411-Eastern United States,* I wrote an entire chapter about unusual disappearances of berry pickers. You can add this case to that list.

Masardis is located in the far northeastern section of Maine. It is fifteen miles west of the Canadian border and ten miles west of Aroostook State Park. The area is surrounded by lakes, rivers, ponds, and swamps.

On Sunday, August 8, 1897, Mr. and Mrs. Charles Carney took their six-year-old daughter, Lillian, with them while they went blueberry picking. The family was at the location for only a short time when Lillian vanished. The family looked for the girl for approximately an hour and then went for assistance in finding the girl.

The first night there was a limited response from the residents of Masardis. On Monday morning two hundred volunteers came to the location. People were walking the area calling for the girl and not getting a response. On Tuesday three hundred residents arrived. Many members of the community closed their businesses in a show of community support and solidarity.

At 10:00 a.m. on Tuesday, Mr. Burt Pollard was two to three miles from the area where the girl had vanished and found Lillian. The girl didn't say a lot, but she made one interesting statement that appeared in the August 12, 1897, article in the *Lewiston Evening Journal*: "She said the sun shined all the time in the woods." The weather there at that time was partly cloudy.

People who do know northern Maine know that it rains frequently even in the summer months. Lillian was six years old and knew the difference between the sun and the moon. Her statement is interesting and may shed some light as to why she was missing for forty-six hours.

I believe that the Carneys were very fortunate to get Lillian back alive.

Geraldine Largay
Missing: 07/23/13-Unk, Sugarloaf Mountain, Appalachian Trail
Age at disappearance: 66 years

George and Geraldine Largay were from Brentwood, Tennessee. The pair had been married for thirty-two years. Geraldine was a retired nurse and an extremely experienced hiker who had always wanted to trek the Appalachian Trail. George would be the "supporting cast" and ensure that Geraldine had the proper food and supplies. He would meet her at certain points along the hike as he'd be driving their car. Geraldine carried a cell phone and would keep George updated on her progress.

The hike started in April in West Virginia. She was traveling north with the eventual goal of reaching Baxter Park at Mount Katahdin in Maine. This trip would've been 1,150 miles.

Geraldine had traveled 950 miles and had continually met with her husband along the way when she was last seen in Maine. On July 22, 2013, she sent George a text message stating that she was eight miles from her next stop where they would meet. She never arrived for the July 23 meeting. George called the Maine Warden Service on July 24 and reported his wife as missing. An October 22, 2013, article in the *Kennebec Journal* had this information about the day Geraldine was last seen on the trail, July 22: "It rained heavily the day Largay, 66, of Tennessee was last seen."

The warden service put canines, airplanes, and ground crews into the area where Geraldine was last known to be. A 4.2-square-mile area near Lone Mountain and Mount Abrahm were covered extensively by hundreds of searchers. The three-week rescue effort found absolutely nothing. Cadaver dogs were brought into the area near the end of the search, and they also found nothing. An August 16, 2013, article in the *Morning Sentinel* reported the feelings of the searchers: "Lt. Kevin Adam of the Maine Warden Service called the search for Largay mystifying, saying almost all hikers who disappear from the trail are found within a day." Several attempts to ping Geraldine's cell phone showed the phone was not functioning. She has never been found.

Summary

The Appalachian Trail has been associated with many disappearances and strange cases over the years. I have written about many of these incidents in past books. Geraldine was not a rookie to hiking. She knew the hazards and the trail route very well. This is not a case of someone getting casually lost. If she were disoriented, she would've responded to the hundreds of searchers in the area. If her body was anywhere within the region she was thought to be, canines or cadaver dogs would've picked up a scent.

I believe the onset of heavy rains and her subsequent disappearance are too coincidental to ignore and fit the pattern of inclement weather and missing people I have chronicled.

It should be stated that Geraldine went missing on July 23, 2013, and Jerry Duran went missing at Hardware Ranch, Utah, on July 24, 2013. As I've stated many times, there is a hopscotch effect in these cases. A case will occur in one area of the United States, and the next one is in another area of the continent.

Maryland

Sex/Name	Date/Time Missing • Age • State
F-Myrtle Gray	07/30/53-Noon • 3 • Churchton, MD
F-Susan Jackson	07/07/54-5:00 p.m. • 3 • Rockville, MD

Myrtle Gray
Missing: 07/30/53-Noon, Churchton, MD
Age at disappearance: 3 years

This is an unusual story for a variety of reasons. Articles on this incident state that the missing girl lived in close proximity of Fort Meade. The victim's brother was with her when she disappeared, and he has a disability that inhibits his ability to speak. This incident occurred very near Chesapeake Bay. There is more you are about to learn.

The disappearance happened in Churchton, Maryland, approximately ten miles south of Annapolis and adjacent to Chesapeake Bay.

On July 30, 1953, at approximately noon, Myrtle and Charles Gray were playing behind their home in the woods. Their twenty-two-year-old mother was home in bed sick. The children's grandmother, Mrs. Catherine Blount, was watching the kids as the mom rested. Six-year-old Charles came back from the woods without his sister, and Catherine got nervous. Charles had a disability, so he couldn't explain what happened to Myrtle. Catherine searched the woods and the home and then called the neighbor for assistance, who then called the sheriff.

Law enforcement arrived and called for volunteers and soldiers from Fort Meade. Within hours there were five hundred people combing the swampy woods behind their home. The army actually sent one of their planes into the sky to see what they could find.

The search continued for three days without one sighting or any evidence of Myrtle being in the area. At the three-day point, a lone searcher made an amazing find as is described in the *Afro American* of October 3, 1953: "Refusing to utter a word, her survival remained a mystery after a 72-hour search which began Thursday and ended within a half mile of State Highway 256." Myrtle was found alive.

All of the quotes about this incident have come from the same article.

Myrtle was taken to the hospital and found to have scratches on her face, hands, and body. Police did question the mother, and she stated that she had no idea how Myrtle got lost. In the same article was this statement from law enforcement: "At Anne Arundel General officials stated that the child was found 'well fed and dry.' Apparently they concluded the girl had been cared for by some unidentified person or persons." The article also stated that the area in which the girl vanished was "snake infested," yet she didn't get bit.

Searchers stated that Myrtle appeared frightened when she was found. Law enforcement was questioned by the press about how a three-year-old girl could survive three days under the conditions that were present. Here is their response: "Both police and parents on Monday were at a loss to explain how she survived the three-day ordeal."

Officials and parents continued to try to get Myrtle to talk about her three days; she continually refused to say anything.

Summary

The law enforcement group investigating this incident made statements about outside involvement in the disappearance. They would normally not say anything to the press. They did this time. People recognized that Myrtle could not have been in such good condition without outside support. The question is who would take the girl, then put her in the immediate area of the search so that she'd be found? Who would risk being identified and possibly observed doing this?

This is another in a long line of cases where it's obvious that a child had assistance while he or she was missing. It's also another case where the child was placed in an area to be found. One of the more astounding coincidences in this case—Myrtle's brother couldn't explain what happened because of a disability, and the victim won't say anything. Why wouldn't Myrtle talk?

Why do most of the people who disappear and are chronicled in our books either refuse to talk about the incident or can't remember what happened? Maybe all of the victims who fall into this category really don't *want* to talk and so claim they don't remember.

Susan Jackson
Missing: 07/07/54-5:00 p.m., Rockville, MD
Age at disappearance: 3 years

This is one of the very few cases involving a disappearance of a person of color. Susan was a black female living with her disabled father ten miles outside of Rockville on Berryville Road. The road parallels much of Seneca Creek and is in an area of many ponds, swamps, and small bodies of water.

In the late afternoon of July 7, 1954, Susan was home when somehow she disappeared. It was believed that she may have been playing in the backyard near the woods, but nothing was confirmed. When her grandfather couldn't find her, he notified cousins in the neighborhood and asked them to help search. Soon there were law enforcement and fire agencies helping in the search for Susan.

Eighteen hours after the girl had vanished, Morman Pyles of the Chevy Chase fire department was a mile and a half from her residence and one mile from Seneca Creek when he found the girl in a clump of bushes. She was alive. Susan was brought back to law enforcement and her family, where they made an interesting observation as is noted in the July 10, 1954, *Baltimore Afro-American*: "Although she had been missing during a violent rainstorm and was found in a water-soaked area, the tot's clothing was dry, rescuers reported." The same article had this about her reaction: "Little Susan had nothing to say at all of the attention and emotion being demonstrated over her. She looked wide eyed, but her lips were expressionless."

Law enforcement was obviously puzzled over Susan's lack of being wet and how she was able to be in the area of her home and not be initially found. Toward the end, police stated that they believed she had wandered from the home. In the same article quoted above are the feelings of some family members: "Other members of the family, however, speculated that the child had been taken away from the home." Law enforcement stated that they would continue to investigate the incident and determine if there was any foul play.

Summary

I believe that this is one of the very important cases that we need to understand and keep in the front of our mind. It wasn't pure accident that Susan was dry. The article stated that she disappeared in a "violent rainstorm" and was located in an area with much water, yet she came out of it dry. Where did she get shelter?

It seems a bit coincidental that the two cases in this section are both females and disappeared almost one year exactly apart.

Massachusetts

Sex/Name	Date/Time Missing • Age • State
F-Irma Santos	2/02/47-2:00 p.m. • 5 • Carver, MA

Irma Santos
Missing: 2/02/47-2:00 p.m., Carver, MA
Age at disappearance: 5 years

Carver is a small city located in southern Massachusetts near the coast. The region has hundreds and hundreds of small bodies of water and swamps.

On February 2, 1947, Irma was with her seven-year-old brother, Robert, and three-year-old brother, Roger, with their parents visiting their grandparents. The children went into the yard near the house, and Irma somehow disappeared. The boys went into the residence and told their parents they couldn't find their sister. The family made a cursory search and then called authorities.

The community responded quickly and in force. Almost two hundred people volunteered and spent over two days looking for the young girl.

The search was methodical and covered the entire area around the residence up to two miles away. Fifty hours after Irma vanished, there was a statement from the Carver police chief in the *Lewiston Daily News* of February 4, 1947: "Chief Smith reported earlier today that he was 'beginning to see evidence of foul play' after a fruitless search with a police Bloodhound and draining a cranberry bog." This statement shows excessive frustration by law enforcement and the belief they had covered all possible areas.

Fifty-four hours after Irma had vanished, her two uncles were one half mile from the grandparents' residence and found the girl in the woods at the base of a tree. A February 5, 1947, article in the *Lowell Sun* had this description: "The child was found asleep when found. Her clothes were tattered and covered with brambles and her shoes were missing." Irma was transported to the hospital and found to have frostbite in both feet and to be suffering from shock and exposure. Statements were made in several articles indicating that Irma never said anything and never smiled while in the hospital.

Summary

I've written many stories about missing children and adults who are missing their shoes when they are found. Many are found unconscious or in a semiconscious state. These same people are also found near bodies of water.

Law enforcement believed for some time that the girl had drowned in a cranberry bog, and then they believed that she may have been a victim of foul play. It was apparent that searchers could not believe that they hadn't found Irma. I'm sure it was shocking to everyone involved when the girl was found just a half mile from the house.

It should also be noted that Irma vanished while visiting her grandparents. It seems that kids vanish an inordinate amount of time while visiting relatives, especially grandparents.

Michigan

Sex/Name	Date/Time Missing • Age • State
F-Amber Rose Smith	10/08/13-1:30 p.m. • 30 mos. • Paris, MI
M-Cullen Finnerty	05/26/13-9:27 p.m. • 30 • Webber Township, MI

Amber Rose Smith
Missing: 10/18/13-1:30 p.m., Paris, MI
Age at disappearance: 30 months

When I originally read this case, there seemed to be many factors that we would normally identify for an incident to be included in the study. When I realized it occurred in Paris, Michigan, I almost fell out of my chair. Just twelve miles northwest of Paris is Baldwin, the location of the disappearance of Cullen Finnerty on May 26, 2013. Cullen's case is one of the most unusual I have ever researched. To have another case just miles away and five months later—the coincidence is not beyond me.

The Smith family lived in a very rural residence of Newaygo County in the 8000 block of East 13 Mile Road in Paris. Looking at this residence on Google Earth, it looks like it's in a thickly wooded area. The house is supposedly on the fringe of the Manisteee National Forest.

In the early afternoon of October 8, 2013, Dale Smith was in the front yard of his residence with his daughter, Amber, and the family's two dogs. He entered the residence to use the restroom and returned to the front yard in just a few minutes. Dale found the area vacant: no Amber and no dogs.

Dale spent thirty minutes yelling for Amber and searching the yard. After several minutes the dogs returned from the woods without Amber. It was at this point that Dale called the Newaygo County sheriff. One question I want all readers to ask themselves: How did this girl get away from the residence so quickly that she would not hear her dad yelling for her?

The responding deputy questioned Dale and found that Amber was a child with challenges. He was told that she had severe mental and physical disabilities.

Once the deputies were on the scene, they made a call for additional emergency responders and volunteers to assist in the search. Within hours over three hundred people were searching the woods for the young girl.

Volunteer and professional searchers utilized Bloodhounds, helicopters, ATVs, and hundreds of people on foot. Their primary search area was a four-square-mile area near the residence. At the end of the first night of searching, nothing had been found to indicate that Amber was in the area.

Early morning October 9 found more searchers at the scene, all going back into the woods in grid patterns to look for the young girl. Temperatures had been cold the prior night, and deputies were concerned about the child's welfare.

At 1:40 p.m., a group of searchers found Amber approximately one and three-quarters miles from her residence standing on a road looking at them. She was calm but did not speak a word. She had scratches on her body and face and was transported to the hospital for observation. I could not find any notes indicating what she was wearing.

An October 9, 2013, article on MLive.com had the following statement from Newaygo County Undersheriff Brian Boyd: "It's hard to imagine how a 2½ year old can survive that distance through the woods with that kind of temperature." The following is another quote from the same article: "Authorities said it's hard to believe Amber Rose Smith, 2, was standing and alert when searchers found her safe Wednesday after she spent 24 hours in the woods alone." An article published October 10, 2013, on Fox 17 Online stated the following: "'There's some that aren't convinced that she walked that entire distance, that maybe she was dropped off. Those are things we might want to determine,' stated Brian Boyd, Newaygo County Undersheriff."

I applaud the deputies who recognized the near impossibility that a thirty-month-old severely mentally and physically disabled girl could travel miles through the woods and be standing alert and healthy after near-freezing temperatures and a lengthy trip on foot.

Amber was released from the hospital and found to be in good condition.

Summary

This area of Michigan is one of the most active areas in North America in regard to unusual disappearances. I have documented cases from the late 1800s up until today that defy conventional explanations (see *Missing 411-Eastern United States* for details on these incidents).

This area is covered with lakes, rivers, swamps, and creeks. There are thousands of square miles of forest in this region where you'd rarely see anyone.

Cullen John Finnerty
Missing: 05/26/13-9:27 p.m., Webber Township, MI
Age at disappearance: 30 years
**Spotlight Case

When I first heard about Cullen's disappearance and where it had taken place, I immediately was paying attention. In *Missing 411-Eastern United States,* I had written about the 1868 disappearance of three-year-old Katie Flynn from Walhalla. She disappeared from her father's lumber camp. After an extraordinary effort and search, she was found with something that was difficult to describe. Katie lived thanks to the efforts of her father and the other hunters. Walhalla is approximately five miles east of Webber Township.

In April 1949, Jacqueline Simons went missing from her grandparents' rural home in Colfax. This small city is thirty miles southeast of where Cullen went missing. Jacqueline's story is featured in *Missing 411-North America and Beyond.*

There is a reason we study history. Without digging deep into the archives, we may have never known that this specific location of Michigan has a highly unusual past.

This is the story of Cullen John Finnerty. There is really nothing normal about Cullen or the circumstances behind his disappearance and death.

Cullen was a big man and showed he wasn't afraid of anything. At 6'2" and 240 pounds, he was an imposing figure. He had a great high school life and athletic career, and it appeared he would be getting a scholarship to play Division I college football. One by one the offers didn't come through, and Cullen was left with the University of Toledo. He redshirted (didn't dress for any games) his freshman year. He transferred to Grand Valley State in 2002.

Cullen was one of the widest, broadest, and strangest quarterbacks his college coaches had ever seen. The majority of quarterbacks spend their career learning to avoid the rush and the huge offensive linemen—not Cullen. He let his own players know that he wanted to be hit and would hit in return. This mind-set initially frustrated his coaches, but they eventually learned to live with his style.

Cullen proved he was a great quarterback by winning championships his junior and senior year at Grand Valley. During his career he passed for just under eleven thousand yards and ran for two thousand yards. He had a 28-0 record during those two years. If there were any thoughts that Cullen wasn't tough, he played an entire playoff series with a broken collarbone. Anyone who has broken his or her collarbone knows this is excruciatingly painful. The man was known to never miss a practice. He was intense and loved the game.

When Cullen was about to leave Grand Valley State, it was said around campus the school had had the most successful program in Division II college history while he played on their team. Quite a tribute.

In 2007 Cullen was signed as an undrafted free agent by the Baltimore Ravens football team. He later played for a brief period with the Denver Broncos. He later went to play professional football in Europe and then came back to the States for a stint in arena league football.

As his football years started to wane, Cullen met a former all-state volleyball player from Grand Rapids, Jennifer. In 2010 the couple married and later had two children, Caden and Makinley. The couple was raising their family in Howell, Michigan.

On Memorial Day weekend in 2013, Jennifer's family planned to go the area near Webber Township for a three-day getaway. The Finnertys decided to join them. The weekend was going great, and the family was enjoying the lush landscape around the Baldwin River.

The Finnertys were staying at a rented cabin on Whalen Lake Drive in Webber Township. In the early-evening hours of May 26, Cullen told family members he wanted to go fishing one more time on the pontoon boat. He put on his waders and jacket and had family members drop him off at 8:45 p.m. in the area of Fortieth Street and the Baldwin River. He took his fishing pole and entered his boat at Location #1 (Baldwin River at W. Fortieth Street). The trip was to be at least thirty minutes but no more than forty-five minutes.

The Baldwin River flows south from the location where Cullen was dropped. At 9:27 p.m., Jennifer received a frantic call from Cullen. According to the Lake County sheriff's report, he stated "he was being followed by two, one of whom was about 20 feet behind him. He told her that he said something to the man, who didn't reply. He said he was getting out of the river, taking off his clothes [he had on waders] and then he hung up the phone." I think it's important to note that Cullen said he was taking off his *clothes*, not his waders. Nobody knows why he would've even been taking off the waders if he were in a state of rush or panic with somebody chasing him. Jennifer told the sheriff that her husband "sounded paranoid and scared."

A report that we received from the sheriff's department, which is titled "Cullen Finnerty Search Summary Report," stated that there were other calls at 9:34 and 9:36 p.m., in which he stated that he was being followed by two individuals who "made him nervous." He was then quoted as saying "gotta go, gotta go." It was said that Cullen sounded out of breath and anxious. The 9:36 p.m. call was from Matthew Brink to Cullen. Matthew asked him where he was at. Cullen told him, "I'm not sure, it's getting a little rough, I think a couple of guys are following me."

Just before Cullen terminated the 9:27 p.m. call, he gave Jennifer his cell phone coordinates from his iPhone 5. The location was off

S. James Road near Coho Lane (Location #2). This area is very thick and lush around the river.

Jennifer and her family went to the location where it had been agreed that they would meet Cullen. He was not there. At 10:37 p.m. Deputy Kreiner was dispatched to the area of the Baldwin River and James Road to take a missing persons report on Cullen. The deputy met with family members, accumulated information, and started to react to the circumstances.

The Lake County deputy made an important and critical decision regarding Cullen. He contacted Cullen's wireless provider and requested that they ping his cell phone from their tower. This is a process where the provider can determine the phone's GPS coordinates from triangulating the location from multiple towers.

The wireless provider gave the deputies four different locations that pinged up to 4.37 miles apart. I've never heard of a ground-based search for someone who was on foot where the pings were so far apart.

One location was almost straight east from the spot where Cullen had been dropped on the north side of Highway 10 and East Gladys Street (Location #3). There were three other locations where pings were made. One was just north of Bray Lake (Location #4) and two just south. We now have a triangle of the locations related to Cullen.

Triangle Locations:
Location #2-Farthest south where Cullen gave GPS coordinates on the river
Distance from Location #2 to Location #3: 5 miles
Location #3-Farthest east, north of Highway 10 near Gladys Street
Location #4-North of Bray Lake
Distance from Location #3 to Location #4: 4.37 miles
Distance from Location #4 to Location #2: 2.52 miles

It took me two hours to properly investigate and understand the distances and locations that were given. It is impossible to go on ground from point to point inside the triangle without crossing a paved road. These are not open plains or deserts; these are thick, lush, and difficult-to-travel plots of land that are sometimes swampy and wet.

The search for Cullen was started immediately. The results of the phone pings puzzled searchers.

On May 27, 2013, at twelve minutes past midnight, Jennifer called Lake County dispatch, advising them that she had located Cullen's boat floating along the river near Fortieth Street. One oar was missing. The family searched the area, calling Cullen's name.

At 1:56 a.m., deputies went to the cabin on Whalen Lake Drive and again met with Jennifer. A discussion centered on medication Cullen was taking, and according to the report, the deputy implied that this might be a "paranoia episode." Jennifer tried calling Cullen's phone again; it rang several times and then went into voicemail.

The start of May 27 was not good for searchers. Skies were cloudy and rainy, and there was a lot of area to cover. Thirteen sheriff's deputies, twenty-two reserve officers, and almost one hundred local volunteers were covering a large area. Cadaver dogs and other canines and a helicopter were covering other areas. Nobody had any success finding Cullen.

During the two days of the search, there was much talk in the community about what may have happened to Cullen. A June 8, 2013, article in the *New York Times* titled "Questions Linger About Death of Former Quarterback" had statements about the incident: "'Some people talked about him getting abducted,' Martin, Finnerty's college coach, said, as he waved his hand dismissively. 'There would have been a standoff. There would have been a quick resolution if that happened.'" Instead, the search dragged on. Two separate local residents e-mailed the undersheriff with a clue. Finnerty, they wrote, "had been spooked by Bigfoot." In the same article was an interview with Dave Kibbey, who owns a parcel of property across the street from the campground where Cullen docked the boat. Kibbey states that the night that Cullen vanished "they heard yelling around dusk. The owls were out that night." Kibbey thought it was part of the holiday weekend partying. Kibbey stated there was no way that he believed that Cullen was lost. He stated that he would've run into someone somewhere.

As the search continued to press on, Grand Valley State sent a busload of coaches and players to assist in the search effort. There were now hundreds of people available and on location and able to search. Searchers did get frustrated, as the sheriff was trying to keep some people out of possible crime areas and didn't want areas trampled. Many of the searchers weren't happy about the way they were being utilized.

On May 28 at 7:49 p.m., Cullen was found. His body was located almost exactly in the geographical center between locations #2 and #4, on the northeast corner of Little Star Lake and at the southwest corner of Merrillville Road and W. Fortieth Street. His body was less than a half mile from the roadway.

I received Cullen's entire case file, including crime scene photos. Out of respect for the family, I won't reproduce the photos here. Some are extremely graphic. Contrary to what some articles stated, Cullen was found facedown with his legs extended. He was in an area with very light foliage. He appeared to be wearing all of his clothing. His face was straight down into the ground, and his right arm was tucked under his chest. His feet were pointed outward. There was very little debris on the bottom of his felt waders. His left hand appeared to be clutching some debris, possibly leaves. His left upper arm was extended out from the body, and the arm was bent at the elbow (ninety degrees) with the hand even with his left ear.

Cullen was wearing waders with suspenders that crossed on his back in an "X" design. One suspender (crossing over his left shoulder) was twisted multiple times. When the body was turned over, this same twist existed on the front. As someone who has worn waders hundreds of times, I can attest that this is uncomfortable. It would be surprising if Cullen had started his trip with this condition existing.

He was bleeding from the nose area, yet there was no obvious injury to any part of his body. The area under his body did not appear to be scuffed or vegetation uprooted. If he had been moving and fell, there might be some damage to the growth in that area. No damage to the small vegetation was observed.

There was a multitude of crime scene photos taken of the body and the surrounding areas. There was one photo taken of Cullen's right leg, but the photo was centered on the ground just to the right. I sent this photo to an optical physicist for his opinion on what was being photographed. That report is pending.

Cullen was sent to the Kent County pathologist for an autopsy. What followed was one of the most inconclusive autopsy reports imaginable. Dr. Stephen Cole stated that there were no obvious signs of death, either through toxicology or by autopsy. He did make some assertions about possibilities. Nothing was confirmed. A Boston University medical team stated "a definitive cause of death could not be determined." There was no trauma to the body. He didn't have a heart attack, and they didn't find anything that caused the death.

I don't want to make light of Cullen's death. I think it's extremely unusual and complicated by the fact that no conclusive cause of death can be found. Cullen had other unusual parts to his life. There was a time when he believed the FBI was following him. He became paranoid and drove 150 miles in an attempt to get away and find safety at a relative's. This story was placed in many articles. I wouldn't have placed it here, except some would say that I was covering up relevant facts. I don't think it is a relevant fact.

How Cullen got from the location where his boat was found to the place where his body was located is the million-dollar question. As I stated earlier, it is impossible to move point to point in the triangle and not cross a roadway. Cullen was smart enough to know that if you're on a roadway, you can always find a residence. Many people in the area commented that they didn't understand how he could've gotten lost. There was nothing in the toxicology results that would indicate a problem with his ability to rationalize or utilize a high level of mechanical skill. His cell phone was found in a front pocket, indicating the pings must've come from the phone when it was with Cullen.

As you read through this book, start to make a mental note of the number of times that a medical examiner either hasn't determined a cause of death or is unable to find one. There are cases in Australia, Idaho, and now Michigan. I find this highly unusual.

It's a rare event when we have a victim calling people as an incident is unfolding. The pings of his cell phone show something very, very unusual was occurring. I still don't have any idea how he could've covered the distances indicated by his cell phone pings. If Cullen wasn't afraid to stare down a three-hundred-pound lineman, what caused to him to become so afraid that, as some past readers have told me, "Cullen was scared to death."

Minnesota

Sex/Name
M-Hickle Ware

Date/Time Missing • Age • State
06/11/38-p.m. • 4 • Pine River, MN

Hickle Harley Ware
Missing: 06/11/38, Pine River, MN
Age at disappearance: 4 years

This disappearance occurred eleven miles southwest of Pine River and fifteen miles northwest of Brainerd. I know this area well, as I've spent many summer days at Minnesota Hockey Camp in Nisswa, an outstanding training center for developing hockey players. On the days away from camp, I made many trips to the Leech Lake Indian Reservation and the region near Bena. I have heard many fascinating stories from elders about life in this area.

During my initial research into missing people, I came across the story of Kory Kelly, a thirty-eight-year-old hunter who disappeared in the Red Lakes Wilderness eighty miles north of Pine River. I can adamantly state that the areas where Hickle and Kory disappeared are almost identical. I chronicled Kory's disappearance in *Missing 411-Eastern United States*. I still classify that case as one of the most unusual I've ever researched.

This area of northern Minnesota is loaded with wildlife and filled with areas where man has probably never walked. The swamps are huge and filled with mosquitoes, bugs, and dangerous conditions. In preparing the Hickle case, I read many accounts where searchers worked in teams going through spots that were almost impenetrable.

On June 11, 1938, Hickle was told to go with his two older brothers (ages nine and twelve) into the fields to gather the cows. The family owned a small ranch, and they needed the cows in the corrals. Mrs. Ware gave the boys a bag lunch, and they made their way through the swamps and fields to a point one half mile from the residence. It was midafternoon and the boys had finished their lunch when Hickle's older brothers told him to stay at his location and they'd take the group of cows back to the house. Hickle knew the area well, as he had been there many times, and he made the walk back to his residence alone. Once the boys arrived at their corral, they returned. The brothers immediately returned to Hickle's location and couldn't locate him. They searched, yelled, and looked for their brother for an hour and then ran home. The parents went to the scene and searched and also found nothing. It was at this point that the family went into the city and gathered three hundred residents to assist in the search.

I should state here that this research was confusing. Several articles from other states identified the missing boy as "Dick Harvey Ware," but the newspapers of Pine River called him "Hickle Harley Ware." In the hopes that the local newspaper got the name correct, I went with its rendition.

Late in the first night of the search, Mrs. Ware and a group of searchers believed they heard a loud cry come from deep in the swampy woods. She ran into the water and was about to cross in the dark when she was pulled back. There was only one loud cry heard, and it never happened again. The following two days, nothing of evidentiary value was found.

Bloodhounds, military officers, and nine airplanes from the 109th Observation Squad from Camp Riley were ordered by the governor to enter the search. The weather was so bad with thick clouds and heavy rain that the planes couldn't enter the area the first four days.

Law enforcement interviewed Hickle's older brothers multiple times and confirmed for the media that their story held up. Hickle was known by his brothers and family as a tough four-year-old who had grown up in the woods and swamps. He was known to regularly chew wintergreen and drink water from the lakes. He was a mountain kid living in the swamps.

Hickle also had an unusual habit that caused his parents not to be as alarmed at the beginning as maybe they should've been. A

June 16, 1938, article in the *Pine River Journal* had this: "Then too, the fact that the boy had a hobby of disappearing for short periods of time, often to be found asleep somewhere near the buildings, tended to lessen the graveness of his disappearance."

The search for Hickle continually gained momentum until it reached numbers between fifteen hundred and two thousand. After several days of searching, the weather cleared enough for multiple planes to enter the area and make grid patterns over the search area. The planes made low-speed passes over the lakes at treetop height for nine hours. The pilots and spotters reported to search leaders that there was no way that Hickle was anywhere in the area or in the lakes, as they could see to the bottom of the water.

After seven days the search for the four-year-old was terminated. The rescue effort appeared to end for an unusual reason: the community apparently ran out of money to feed searchers. Multiple news articles made appeals to locals for money and supplies until they apparently ran out of money, something I've never seen in a search.

I scoured news articles for updates on the Hickle case. I found one. Thirty days after the boy vanished, there was an editorial in a Minnesota paper about the dangers of the swamps and the specific danger to berry pickers as they entered their seasonal harvest. The writer specifically noted Hickle's disappearance and how searchers were unable to find any trace of the boy.

There was only one possible clue found by the thousands of searchers looking for the four-year-old. Two miles from the Hickle residence on an abandoned logging road, a small child's barefoot track was found in the mud. Searchers believed that it had to be recent, or the heavy rains happening at the onset of the search would've washed it away. Nothing else was ever found.

Summary

I believe the pilots when they stated that Hickle wasn't in the area they searched. I also believe that Hickle didn't voluntarily leave the area, as he was a mature four-year-old who knew his way home. Based on northern Minnesota's history of highly unusual disappearances, this case fits the profile.

I find Hickle's habit of disappearing for short periods of time and then reappearing, sleeping near property buildings, interesting. I've explained throughout the Missing 411 books that many of the missing people are found sleeping or semiconscious. Is it possible that Hickle had experienced bouts of being missing on multiple occasions and then was found in various locations of the property, asleep?

In *Missing 411-Eastern United States,* I explained how there were eight people missing from 1920–1929 who fit our profile. The decade from 1930–1939 the number jumped to thirty-four, and it appears that this number is still climbing. The numbers of missing for the following two decades also rose significantly. What happened that triggered a four-fold increase of missing people from decade to decade, and what continued to occur that kept those numbers rising?

Missouri

Sex/Name	Date/Time Missing • Age • State
M-John Kennon	08/31/35-5:00 p.m. • 2 • Mexico, MO
M-Billy Hoag	05/10/67-4:30 p.m. • 11 • Hannibal, MO
M-Joey Hoag	05/10/67-4:30 p.m. • 13 • Hannibal, MO
M-Craig Dowell	05/10/67-4:30 p.m. • 14 • Hannibal, MO

John Wesley Kennon
Missing: 08/31/35-5:00 p.m., Mexico, MO
Age at disappearance: 2½ years

Mexico, Missouri, is eighty miles northwest of Saint Louis and is in an area with hundreds of small bodies of water. It is just forty-three miles southwest of Hannibal.

On August 31, 1935, at 5:00 p.m., John and a seven- and ten-year-old boy were playing a half mile from John's farmhouse residence. The boys were playing a game of hide and seek when the older boys hid from John. Once they came out of their hiding places, they looked at the last spot they left the boy; he was gone. The boys contacted their parents, and a search was started immediately.

The search started with limited participants, then it quickly jumped to 150 volunteers combing the rugged countryside. Just hours into the rescue effort, rain started to fall and continued for the next two days. Many of the searchers were working an area near Whetstone Creek and not having any luck. Other searchers had seen timber wolves in the area and were nervous about John being found alive. Many were surprised that the boy wasn't found quickly, since he was not wearing shoes and just wearing a romper. A day into the search, thirty-five members of a National Guard unit came into the rescue effort.

Sixty-five hours after John had vanished and just after two inches of rain inundated the search area, John's uncle was searching an area when the boy almost walked into his arms. He was described as being in remarkably good condition with scratches but no hypothermia. He recognized his uncle and went to him. The boy was taken to his farm, where he fell asleep immediately.

Rescuers were shocked that the boy didn't ask for food or water and just went to sleep. He had scratches on many areas of his body but was otherwise in good condition. He was later taken to a hospital when it was determined that the boy had a fever of 101 degrees. He lived.

Billy Hoag   Age at disappearance: 11 years
Joey Hoag   Age at disappearance: 13 years
Craig Dowell   Age at disappearance: 14 years
Missing 5/09/67-4:30 p.m.
Murphy Cave, Hannibal, MO

This is an unusual incident for my books, but this is needed to keep your paradigm fluid about disappearances and open to new ideas and locations.

On May 9, 1967, there was new construction taking place on the south side of Hannibal in conjunction with a new roadway on Highway 79. There were new openings to Murphy Cave being exposed in that same area. After school let out, the boys went home and gathered equipment they thought they'd need for cave exploring. The boys never told their parents that they were going back to the cave, but they had told them that they had located a new opening. Lynn Strube and John James (fourteen and thirteen years old, respectively) had accompanied the trio to the mouth of the cave that day and then left. When the boys didn't come home, a missing persons report was filed with the Hannibal police. This report started one of the largest underground searches in United States history.

At 7:00 p.m. on the first night, the Mark Twain Rescue Squad was at Murphy's Cave searching. They put a dachshund from the Hoag neighborhood into the area and never got a response. They put a police dog into the area in an attempt to pick up a scent, and it found none.

There was a 150-man military police battalion team that assisted along with National Guard teams in exploring several caves in the area along with spelunking teams from several states. They spent weeks searching the maze of caves and never found footprints or any evidence the boys were in the system. Rescuers explained several times that Murphy's Cave was a maze and posed significant challenges. Law enforcement questioned the Hoag boy's father, Mike Hoag about the incident. He stated that he had whipped the boys several times about going into the caves and thought the message had been sent that they had to stay away.

The search became so complex that the state of Missouri dug up a portion of Highway 79, purportedly looking for a new tunnel entrance that had been concealed when the highway was built. It was never found. A closed-circuit television system was put into the smallest openings in an effort to see if the boys had gotten inside; they found nothing.

After a month of searching Murphy's Cave by several of the top cave experts in the world, they proclaimed that they had found no evidence that the boys were inside. Many of these experts held private meetings, in which they expressed their depression that they weren't successful in finding the boys.

This case is considered one of the most perplexing underground disappearances of all time.

Montana

Sex/Name	Date Missing • Age • State
M-Arnie Olson	08/11/47-5:00 p.m. • 4 • Mount Skalkaho, MT
M-Jerry Monkman	04/25/53-5:00 p.m. • 11 • Choteau, MT
M-Timothy Shear	11/23/75-p.m. • 22 • Little Bell Mountains, MT

Arnie Olson
Missing: 08/11/47-5:00 p.m., Sapphire Mountains, Mount Skalkaho, MT
Age at disappearance: 4 years

I've written about disappearances in the Sapphire Mountains in past books. These are some of the most rugged regions in North America. There are many small lakes, rivers, and streams as well.

On August 11, 1947, Mr. and Mrs. Elmer Olson and their four children had arrived and were establishing their small wood-cutting camp in an area near the Salkaho Divide. Arnie was playing with his two siblings. It was approximately 5:00 p.m. when the parents suddenly realized he had vanished with the family's Australian shepherd, Pal. The family searched until dark and then went to call the Granite County sheriff. An August 13, 1947, article in the *Montana Standard* described the area of the search: "The camp, around which the search is concentrated, is near 7,258 foot high Skalkaho summit in some of western Montana's most rugged and heavily timbered country." I did some research on this mountain and found it to be 8,400 feet in elevation. Other articles described the area as near Mud Lake, which would make the stated elevation appropriate but nowhere near the summit.

Over five hundred searchers responded to look for Arnie. Men dragged Mud Lake looking for his body. Businessmen from the Bitterroot area closed their businesses and dedicated their time to looking for the boy.

There was no evidence found of Arnie until late Wednesday afternoon, when two smoke jumpers heard the loud whine of a dog. They searched until well into darkness and were unable to find anything. The men stated that they only heard silence as they pressed through darkness, hearing nothing after the initial sound. Thursday morning the men again went into an area near the summit of Mount Hughes near Fuse Creek where they had heard the whine. An August 15, 1947, article in the *Daily Interlaker* described what and where the searchers found Arnie: "An Australian Shepherd dog, 'Pal' remained with the boy and his barking led searchers to the body near the top of Mount Hughes, where coroner R.R. Wilson of Phillipsburg reported he died of exposure." Other articles stated that Arnie had fallen from a small ledge but was still found near the summit. The trip from the Olson camp to the location of Arnie's body is rugged, steep, and unbelievable for a small four-year-old boy. He would've had to travel downhill for two hundred feet and then up the extremely steep mountainside of Mount Hughes to the 8,200-foot summit.

Many articles stated that the searchers were compromised in their efforts by a steady stream of wind and rain during each day that Arnie was missing. There were no statements about what the boy was or was not wearing. Articles stated that Arnie had walked four miles and climbed over one thousand feet during his trek.

Summary

It makes no sense that Arnie would've walked up the extremely steep side of Mount Hughes, especially since his family's camp would've been downhill behind him and in view. The other option is that he walked many more miles around the base of the mountain and then uphill following Fuse Creek. Either of these options is unreal.

One article stated that the sheriff was traveling to the scene with the coroner to investigate the case. It did not go into detail about why the sheriff was going to the scene or what was obviously suspicious.

Jerry Monkman
Missing: 04/25/53-5:00 p.m., Choteau, MT
Age at Disappearance: 11 years

In the thousands of missing persons reports I've reviewed, the disappearance of Jerry Monkman classifies as one of the top five

I've ever read for the sheer distance a child has traveled. There are many parts of this story that fit the criteria to be included in the study, but the distance the boy traveled boggles the mind.

Jerry was one of a group of Boy Scouts that went to the foothills of the Rocky Mountains on a weekend getaway. The group was twenty-five miles west of Choteau, Montana, and on the edge of the Teton Canyon on April 25, 1953. I think it's important to understand the physical frame that Jerry possessed, as is described in this April 27, 1953, article in the *Herald Journal*: "A frail 11-year old Boy Scout became lost from fellow hikers in the rugged Teton Mountains last night and lawmen and volunteers using planes and a Bloodhound engaged in a dramatic search today." The key word in the article: "frail." The Scouts and the three adult leaders searched through the night and were unable to find him.

The entire city of Choteau, all sixteen hundred residents, came to the search site and participated in the effort to find Jerry. A Bloodhound from Hamilton, Montana, was flown to the scene and did track an alleged scent, as is described by Teton County Undersheriff Walt Magee in this April 27, 1953, article in the *Spokesman Review*: "Magee said the Bloodhound had led the searchers 12 miles north and east from the Boy Scout campsite into a swampy area." The article didn't clarify what happened after the dog reached the swamp; I can only imagine that the area was searched. This area was reached just twelve hours after Jerry vanished, a phenomenal distance for anyone to travel in the time span. In the same article that explained what the Bloodhounds found, it also stated that it had rained the day the dogs were in the field, and this inhibited their ability to track any scent.

Jerry had suffered from asthma for several years, and law enforcement was concerned about finding the boy as soon as possible. Airplanes continued to circle the skies around the Boy Scout camp, and searchers were finding nothing of value.

At approximately 8:00 a.m. on April 27, an astonishing find was made as is explained in the April 28, 1953, *Spokane Daily Chronicle*: "As most of Choteau's 1600 residents joined in a search, he was found 38 hours later—not by the search parties but by 8-year old David J. Waldner of the Rockport Hutterite colony. Riding horseback, David came upon Jerry as he stumbled across a field near the colony. At that point he had trudged nearly 30 miles north and west from the Boy Scout Camp and was roughly the same distance from Choteau." Jerry was described to be in good shape and suffered only from a minor case of shock and exposure.

When the boy was asked about his thirty-eight-hour journey, he stated that he slept under trees and wasn't bothered by any wild animals.

Summary

I think it's important to review this case closely. The Bloodhound tracked a scent twelve miles north and east from the Boy Scout camp and lost it in a swamp. Readers of my past books know that many missing children are found in swamps. Where the Bloodhound tracked the scent is very suspicious to me. When Jerry was interviewed, he never made any statement about a swamp.

The Bloodhound tracked north and east, and Jerry went north and west and was eventually found thirty miles away thirty-eight hours after he disappeared. Jerry stated that he slept under trees, indicating that he did sleep for part of this journey. If Jerry slept for eight hours, that means he was on his feet for thirty hours and negotiated thirty miles in thirty hours. I seriously doubt the boy was moving nonstop for that entire thirty-hour time span. Jerry was negotiating his way over very rough mountains, not a flat, level plane. In Robert Koester's book, *Lost Person Behavior*, he states that a child ten to twelve years old will be found 95 percent of the time within 5.6 miles or less in a mountain area.

Jerry was described by searchers and Boy Scout leaders as "frail." It was stated that Jerry had asthma, a breathing disorder that could have a major impact on someone taking a long-distance hike at altitude. I hike regularly at eight thousand to ten thousand feet and run four to five miles daily. I seriously doubt I could cover thirty trail miles in thirty hours in the Tetons. One more fact of concern: Jerry wasn't on a trail; he was bushwhacking across country, an even more arduous journey.

Do you believe Jerry made that journey unassisted?

Timothy Shear
Missing: 11/23/75-p.m., Little Bell Mountains, MT
Age at disappearance: 22 years

The Little Bell Mountains are located almost in the geographical center of Montana, approximately one hundred miles north of Bozeman. The mountains reach elevations nearing nine thousand feet and are located in the Lewis and Clarke National Forest. These are rugged and wild mountains and known for the excellent hunting.

On November 23, 1975, United States postal worker Timothy Shear went hunting in the area near the boundary lines of Meagher and Judith Basin Counties. Timothy didn't come out of the mountains, and his friends notified law enforcement. The first two days focused on Meagher County, and it then switched to Judith Basin County because a hunter was found who claimed to have spoken with Timothy on November 23.

Searchers did find some interesting pieces of possible evidence. They first located an orange hunting vest hanging in a tree, the same type Timothy wore. What is interesting about this is that it matches what was found during the search for Jimmy Rambone in Quebec. He disappeared, and searchers found his orange vest hanging in a tree, but Jimmy was never found (*Missing 411-North America and Beyond*). Searchers also located a lean-to shelter that appeared to be recently made. In several of the searches for missing people, ground teams have located these in the areas where the person vanished.

Bloodhounds and helicopters from Malmstrom Air Force Base were used in an attempt to locate Tim. Two days after Tim vanished, a severe snowstorm hit the area and dropped two feet of snow, inhibiting search efforts.

Air and ground searchers failed to find any tracks or campfires that may have been made by Timothy. Bloodhounds failed to pick up Tim's scent at any location.

The best I could determine was that Timothy Shear was never found.

New Hampshire

Sex/Name	Date Missing • Age • State
M-Robert Cass	10/14/1925-1:00 p.m. • 3 • Ashland, NH
M-Stephen Rowan Griffin	10/09/10-Unk•2• Richmond, NH

Robert Cass
Missing: 10/14/1925-1:00 p.m., Ashland, NH
Age at disappearance: 3 years

Robert "Bobby" Cass and his pet dog, Fluffy were with Bobby's grandfather while he was chopping wood near the top of Bridgewater Mountain. It was October 14, 1925, at approximately 1:00 p.m. when Bobby and Fluffy wandered away and out of view of his grandfather. Grandpa searched for the pair, couldn't locate them, and called for assistance.

Searchers worked through the night when heavy rain started to fall. This region is very thick with lush timber and made searching slow and cumbersome.

While searchers were out looking for the boy, Fluffy returned to his residence, one half mile from the location where they had been chopping wood. Bobby's parents attempted to get Fluffy to accompany them back into the woods, but the dog refused to go.

Searchers went through the night calling Bobby's name and scouring all sides of the mountain. The October 15, 1925, article that appeared in the *Boston Daily Globe* described what the searchers found early the following morning: "Between 300-400 men had searched all night within two hundred yards of the spot where the boy was lying. 3-year old Bobby Cass was lost on Bridgewater Mountain last night, was found at 6:16 this morning, lying on a 30-foot ledge over Devil's Den." There was no mention of what Bobby was wearing or if he made any statements. He was found two miles from the place he disappeared and in an area that had been searched many times.

This is another of the many cases we've chronicled where people disappear or they are found in an area that has an unusual name such as "Devil's Den." The other factors that exist in this case that are in many of the cases we document: the child disappears with a canine, bad weather hits the area at the time searchers are moving through the vicinity, and the child is found in an area that had been searched.

Stephen Rowan Griffin
Missing: October 9, 2010, Richmond, NH
Age at disappearance: 2 years

Katie Griffin had sent us a note stating that she had heard about our research and felt that the disappearance of her son fit our profile. She explained that on October 9 2010, her husband and son went to their grandparent's home for a family party. The location of the event was 236 Route 32 in Richmond, New Hampshire. This location is just 6.8 miles southwest from the location of the disappearance of three-year old Louis Denton on October 7, 1947, See Missing 411 Eastern United States. This location is also 33 miles directly east of Bennington, Vermont and one of the largest clusters of disappearances in North America. This residence is less then one mile north of the Massachusetts border.

Mr. Griffin took his two-year old son Stephen Rowan Griffin and his two brothers to the party. At approximately 3p.m., there was a large group of family members in the woods behind the home when someone saw Stephen chasing the family's cat. In a very short period of time, Stephen was missing. The group searched and yelled for the boy and then notified law enforcement.

The New Hampshire Fish and Game responded and started to search for the child. Within hours, other volunteers in the community brought their ATV's and started to prowl the area. Searchers were calling Stephen's name and his nickname, "Ro." There were no responses.

Early on Sunday morning, a group of volunteer searchers made an astounding discovery as is described in the October 10 article in the *Boston News*, "WMUR-TV says Stephen Rowan Griffin of Richmond was found Sunday morning clinging to a tree in a swamp 11 hours after he disappeared. He was last seen chasing a cat while at his grandmother's house, about three miles from where he was found. Local and state troopers and game officers were involved in the search. Stephen was found by a group of adults and family members who often hunt and ride all-terrain vehicles in the area. They went to an area where the child's sneakers were found, called his name and he called back." The article states that they first found his sneakers and later found Stephen.

In my communication with Katie Griffen, she told me that her son had also lost his sweatshirt. When he was later questioned about where it went, he stated it was up in a tree. He also stated that he had seen cows while he was missing even though there was no cows anywhere near the location where he was found. The sweatshirt was never found. Another article released on October 11, 2010 on *emsworld.com* stated, "The group had to wade into the swamp to reach Rowan." I asked Katie the following: the article stated that the searchers had to get wet to go into the swamp to get to the location where your son was found. The million-dollar question, how did your son get to that location in the swamp without getting wet? This is her exact response: "And that's the answer I cannot give. But I'm blessed to have my very opinionated, rambunctious 5 year old still with me." She did state that when she first saw her son, he had a blank stare on his face and appeared to be in shock.

Katie did clarify that Ro (Stephen) had somehow manipulated his way uphill from the party when most of the searchers were looking downhill. He then managed to get through cliffs, through a swamp and was found hugging a tree in the middle of that swamp. There was no adequate reason why he was hugging the tree other then he was scarred.

It does seem slightly coincidental that the other case we have documented in this area (Louis Dunton) also happened in October, it was a boy and he was three years old. Coincidence?

In our studies of the missing, there have been many children that have vanished and were found in locations that didn't seem possible. The disappearance of Stephen "Ro" Griffin is a classic case where even his parents can't explain how the boy got into the location where he was located.

New Mexico

Sex/Name	Date Missing • Age • State
M-Timoteo Griego	06/20/38-p.m. • 4 • Leyba, NM
M-Celestino Trujillo Jr.	04/09/47-11:30 a.m. • 3 • Ledoux, NM
M-Patrick Sanchez	04/11/71-2:30 p.m. • 4 • Chilili, NM
M-Kenny Robinson	04/11/71-2:30 p.m. • 5 • Chilili, NM
M-Michael Henley Jr.	04/21/88-p.m. • 9 • Zuni Mountains, NM
F-Megumi Yamamoto	06/09/09-4:00 p.m. • 26 • Mount Baldy, NM

Timoteo Griego
Missing: 06/20/38, Leyba, NM
Age at disappearance: 4 years

Leyba is a very small community south of Santa Fe and eight miles west of Villanueva State Park. It sits in a desolate setting adjacent to an open mesa and wild lands.

On June 20, 1938, in the afternoon hours, Timoteo was in the garden of his grandparents' ranch. He was supposed to be digging up weeds. The grandfather, Esquipula Solano, saw that the boy was cutting down corn instead and yelled at him. The boy turned and walked from the garden. After a short period of time, the grandparents looked for the four-year-old and couldn't find him. The local sheriff was called to assist in locating the lad.

San Miguel County Sheriff Ceferino Quintana arrived and led the search from the beginning. When the search team started to look for tracks and other evidence pointing to where the boy may have gone; they found nothing.

Timoteo disappeared in a desert landscape that backs up to a mesa with trees. June is one of the hot months for this region, and there was no water source where he was believed to be headed.

The sheriff had utilized over four hundred searchers, which included forest rangers, his deputies, law enforcement from Santa Fe, and a posse of CCC enrollees. A June 23, 1938, article in the *Clovis News* described what was found at the end of three days of searching: "'It seems almost impossible that the child is alive,' Sheriff Quintana said. 'But we found fresh footprints this morning about three miles from where we found the child's clothing last night. The barefoot prints indicate without a doubt that Timoteo was alive last night or early today. In the time the boy has wandered about, judging from the many tracks we found,' the sheriff continued, 'He must've walked 30 or 40 miles.' The small prints made since he took off his clothing shows he covered an area of about 10 miles. 'How he lived as long as he has,' Sheriff Quintana said, 'I do not know. We haven't found a trace of water in the area and there is little the child could have eaten.' The child's clothes, the sheriff said, were found neatly folded beneath a tree."

Very late in the day of June 23, 1938, nineteen-year-old Elvirez Castellano was searching for his cousin on the mesa and found him alive, three miles from the point where his clothing had been found. The boy was naked, heavily scratched, and sunburned but alive. A June 24, 1938, article in the *San Antonio Light* explained what a physician discovered when Timoteo was examined: "He was rushed to a hospital at the little mining town of Terrero, where Dr. Warren G. Smith said he was suffering from hunger, exposure and fright. In occasional spells of semi-delirium, the physician said he expressed a strong desire to return to the mesa." Later in the article was this last line: "Searchers said his tracks indicated he had walked nearly 40 miles." Readers need to remember what the doctor stated the boy was suffering from.

Summary

There are so many facets of this story that are difficult to believe, I'm not sure where to start. How about going back to the feelings of the sheriff: "It seems almost impossible that the child is alive." The boy not only lived—he wasn't suffering from dehydration. The average temperature for this region in June is eighty-five degrees with lows going down to forty-nine degrees. The physician never noted that Timoteo was dehydrated. How is this possible after being alone for four days in this environment?

Searchers found the boy naked without shoes and located his clothing folded under a tree. Many of the victims I've written about lose their shoes and clothing. A four-year-old folding his clothes when he was supposedly fighting the elements seems odd.

Finally, I have never heard of a four-year-old traveling forty miles in four days through a harsh environment. The boy supposedly traveled ten miles a day and didn't become dehydrated after four consecutive days of this activity. It also seems odd that searchers found no tracks leaving the area of the grandparents' home and then suddenly find footprints three miles away.

There was never any mention regarding what happened to the boy's shoes.

The statement the physician made about Timoteo wanting to get back to the mesa where he was found is quite puzzling. Most young children are scared and want to be in a protective environment with their parents. What happened on the mesa that prompted the boy to want to return?

Celestino Trujillo Jr.
Missing: 4/09/47-11:30 a.m., Ledoux, NM
Age at disappearance: 3 years

The exact location of this disappearance was in the Monte Aplanado region near the small town of Ledoux in the foothills of the Sangre de Cristo Mountains, an area I have written about in the past. The elevation in this area is approximately eight thousand feet with dozens of small bodies of water just north and west. The residence where this incident happened was quite near what is now Morphy Lake State Park. This area has big trees and heavy timber.

Celestino Trujillo Jr. went to his uncle's home on April 9, 1947, with his father to cut and collect firewood. At approximately 11:30 a.m., the boy asked his dad if he could walk down to a nearby pen and look at his uncle's goats, and his dad said that was fine. Celestino Sr. watched as his son walked toward the pen and then resumed cutting wood. Thirty minutes later, Celestino Sr. went into the house for lunch and didn't see his son at the pen or in the residence. The adults now searched the yard and could not locate the boy. Las Vegas and Santa Rosa police and the New Mexico state troopers all responded to the rural residence.

The troopers called for Bloodhounds from the state penitentiary, and the police officers got additional assistance and started ground searches. Almost from the beginning, the search had challenges. An October 6, 1993, article in the *Rocky Mountain News* reviewed the search for the boy: "A search ensued. Authorities combed the woods, and schools were let out so students could help, but no trace of the boy was found. Bloodhounds came in the second day but could find no trail after coming to a dirt road near the pens."

Readers need to know that this is a very rural location without significant traffic, hardly any traffic. Everyone in this area knows one another; the roads to residences are rarely traveled, and you can see others coming from a long distance.

The second day that Celestino was missing, snow started to fall. Law enforcement told the family that they would find him now because they would see his tracks in the snow…except they didn't find any tracks. The Bloodhounds did not find his scent. Search teams did drain several bodies of water and found nothing of value.

There was an April 15, 1947, article in the *Las Vegas Daily* (NM), and it explained the ongoing theory about what happened to Celestino: "Organized search for the boy who had been missing from his home near Ledoux since last Wednesday was abandoned yesterday under the belief that he could not have survived in the snowy mountain region. An early theory that the child was kidnapped is now thought unlikely."

Celestino's parents were again interviewed in 1993 and affirmed their belief that their boy had been kidnapped. They didn't explain how a kidnapping might have occurred, but they did find it strange that Bloodhounds and professional trackers were unable to find anything leading to the boy.

Summary

Celestino Sr. and his wife, Andrea, moved to Greeley, Colorado, several years ago. They, like all parents of missing kids, want to believe their child is still alive and the opportunity exists to meet again.

There are too many factors with this story that match many other disappearances of missing children, children who have never been found:

- A child disappears from a rural location at a friend or relative's residence.
- There are many water sources in the area.
- Bloodhounds can't find a scent.
- Trackers cannot find any evidence of the child in the area.
- The weather turns bad immediately after the disappearance (snow in this case).
- A kidnapping theory is initially thought possible, then withdrawn by law enforcement.
- The mountains in this disappearance have a history of unusual missing person cases.
- The date of this incident is during a period of years of mass disappearances of young children across the United States.

Patrick Sanchez   Age at disappearance: 4 years
Kenny Robinson   Age at disappearance: 5 years
Missing: 04/11/71-2:30 p.m., Chilili, NM

It's a strange occurrence when two people disappear simultaneously from anywhere. It's an even stranger day when two small boys get out of sight of their parents and cannot be found. This is the story of two little boys who vanished in the mountains near Albuquerque.

The disappearance of Patrick Sanchez and Kenny Robinson occurred on an Easter Sunday in 1971. The two boys went with their parents to an area on the eastern side of the Manzano Mountains, fourteen miles southeast of Albuquerque and five miles north of Chilili.

The families arrived in the area on the east side of the Manzano Mountains, and Patrick and Kenny just took off running into the mountains. The parents stated that they quickly lost sight of the pair and then started to search. Once it was determined that the boys weren't responding to the parents' calls and they weren't coming back to the cars, they called the sheriff.

Hundreds of searchers poured into the area to assist in finding the boys. The boys are cousins, and it was felt that they would stay together. Seven hours after the pair vanished, searchers found Kenny Robinson, asleep under a tree. Searchers could not locate

Patrick. They did try to interview Kenny, but he wasn't of any assistance.

The following two days found two sets of Bloodhounds, helicopters, planes, and over one thousands searchers were looking for Patrick. Forty hours after Patrick vanished, two United States Air Force sergeants found the boy sitting under a tree. An April 13, 1971, article in the *Albuquerque Tribune* had the following information about the distance Patrick traveled: "He must have walked twenty miles in those two days, said Lt. Odell." Other articles stated that he was found ten air miles from where he was last seen. Wow, a four-year-old boy allegedly walks twenty miles in forty hours—believable? Don't misunderstand what I am stating, I am not implying that search and rescue personnel are lying; I am questioning the ability of a four-year-old. According to Robert Koester's book, *Lost Person Behavior*, a four-year-old will be found in a mountain area within 3.7 miles or less 95 percent of the time.

You would think that if a four-year-old traveled twenty miles in forty hours, he would be fatigued, exhausted, dehydrated, etc. I refer to an April 14, 1971, article in the *Charleston Gazette* for a report on Patrick's condition when he was found: "'It's amazing how good a condition he's in after being lost so long,' said State Police Sergeant L. Schmerheim. 'He was tired and thirsty but otherwise in excellent condition and was released from an Albuquerque hospital after a brief observation.'" I'm not sure how Patrick survived the distance he traveled and the mountains, but I'd like to know.

Patrick said that he remembered falling asleep under a tree with Kenny and he remembered walking away, but little else was to be revealed.

Michael Henley Jr.
Missing: 04/21/88-p.m. • 9 • Zuni Mountains, NM
Age at disappearance: 9 years

This incident happened at the far northwest corner of the state, just southwest of Grants, New Mexico. This father and son went to a location near the Oso Ridge area where elevations got to 8,400 feet.

On April 21, 1988, Michael Henley Sr. had taken his son, Michael Jr., on a turkey-hunting trip to the Zuni Mountains, specifically the Oso Ridge region. The two hunters somehow got separated, and dad could not find son. Michael Sr. returned to camp and notified the Cibola County sheriff's department. The sheriff's department responded swiftly and in force, getting three hundred people onto the mountain searching by the end of the first day. They believed they found one partial print in the snow, but immediately after Michael Sr. lost Michael Jr., snow started to fall, and this compromised search efforts.

Cibola sheriff's department got four Civil Air Patrol planes, an air force helicopter, a state police helicopter, and men on horseback and motorcycles, all looking for Michael Jr. Searchers commented that this was one of the biggest searches they had ever participated in. Specially trained dog teams were brought to the area, but they were unable to track any scent.

On June 23, 1990, a rancher was walking a fence line five to six miles from the location that Michael Jr. was last seen and observed a small amount of bones and clothing. He called the sheriff. There was a June 26, 1990, article in the *Roswell Daily Record* that had some notes about the questions Michael Sr. had: "Henley said he asked deputies why the remains weren't found in the search and that they described the area as being very rough." You can tell by the deputy's response that they never really answered the father's concerns. It seems like an appropriate question, since searchers claimed they had covered everything within a ten-mile radius of the point the boy was last seen. Articles that I found never absolutely confirmed that the partial skeleton found did belong to Michael Jr., even though deputies were fairly certain it was the boy.

This case has many of the elements we routinely see when we classify a case for the study. It seems very odd that the body was found in an area with many bushes but few large trees. How and why helicopters and planes never saw the boy and how he disappeared from camp so quickly seem to be the real questions.

Megumi Yamamoto
Missing: 06/09/09-4:00 p.m., Mount Baldy, NM
Age at disappearance: 26 years

This is another incident in the Sangre de Cristo Mountains of New Mexico. The precise location was Mount Baldy (Pecos Wilderness), approximately fifty miles north of Ledoux, the location of the disappearance of Celestino Trujillo Jr. The region around Mount Baldy can be very thick with big trees and steep mountains. In *Missing 411-Western United States,* I wrote about the strange disappearance of Mel Nadel, also in the Pecos Wilderness. This case had more strange events happen at different points in the story than just about anything I've ever written.

On June 9, 2009, New Mexico graduate student Megumi Yamamoto was camping in the mountains with her boyfriend, Paul Harrington. Megumi was a brilliant student who had graduated from California State University at Long Beach and was now a physics graduate student at the University of New Mexico specializing in nanotechnology and optics. Megumi was originally from Tokyo but had lived in the United States since 2003. She enjoyed the outdoors, and Paul offered to show her the beauty of New Mexico.

On June 9, Paul and Megumi were hiking the Sky Line Trail. Megumi was behind him, and somehow the pair got separated. Paul found three other hikers on the trail and asked for their assistance in looking for Megumi; they agreed to help. After thoroughly searching the trail area and yelling her name, Paul decided to head back to their Lake Katherine campsite to see if she had returned. She hadn't. Paul called law enforcement for assistance.

At some point while Megumi was lost, she was able to utilize her cell phone. She called 911 and stated she was lost, cold, and needed assistance. In one of the most bizarre stories I've ever read, Megumi did everything correctly, and something completely out of the norm happened. Seven times Megumi called 911 and did not get the emergency operations dispatcher; she got the nonemergency dispatcher, someone who did not have the ability to triangulate her cell signal. Only 911 emergency dispatchers have the triangulation ability. Dispatchers kept asking her to call back, and she kept getting diverted to nonemergency lines without any contact with emergency operators. A June 17, 2009, article on KOAT.com had the following headline: "Sheriff launches investigation into 911 problems." There is a partial transcript in this article of the conversation: "Solano said the investigation into why calls were routed to the wrong line is still continuing and could take several days to complete. A very frustrated Yamamoto is heard on the other end of those calls, "'Hello, I'm in the Pecos Wilderness and I'm lost. I don't know where I am now,' Yamamoto said. 'You are lost?' 911 dispatcher said. 'I am lost in the Pecos National Wilderness,' Yamamoto said."

Imagine that you lose your boyfriend on a major trail the first time you are in the wilderness. Somehow you become disoriented and have no idea where you are. She does the right thing and calls 911—and gets transferred seven times to the wrong number. Megumi must be thinking at this point that her luck is running out and she may never get off this mountain alive. Finally the call is routed correctly, and dispatcher triangulates her position and sends search and rescue teams to her.

As SAR teams are heading toward Megumi, the weather starts to change—clouds move in, temperatures drop, and it appears it might start to snow. It's getting late in the afternoon, and time is running short.

An April 1, 2010, article on the Abqjournal.com website had a short summary of the negative events that surrounded the rescue of Megumi: "During the search for Megumi Yamamoto on June 9, the report says some rescue team members refused assignments; an incident commander didn't have direct, real-time contact with the rescue chopper; and the choppers landing in the Santa Fe National Forest had no approval from forest managers." This came from an extensive report prepared after the event. Aircraft need special permission to land in wilderness areas; apparently they did not have that permission in Megumi's case.

Ground SAR teams got to Megumi and directed in a New Mexico State helicopter for evacuation. She was weak and cold, as snow had started to fall. Sergeant Andy Tingwall was the helicopter pilot and Officer Wesley Cox was the spotter as they maneuvered the helicopter into position to get Megumi inside. This was a high-altitude rescue in bad weather. The helicopter started to lift off, and something happened. Several news articles stated that it was theorized that the helicopter didn't gain altitude quickly enough and the tail rotor hit a tree, causing the craft to crash northeast of Baldy

Peak near the elevation of twelve thousand feet. Cox survived the crash and yelled at Tingwall through the night. In the morning, Cox walked out to get help even though his leg was crushed and he had serious back injuries. He eventually found help.

Rescuers found carnage at the crash site. A debris field extended eight hundred feet down the mountain. Andy Tingwall had died, and Megumi had perished.

If there was ever a definition of heroic efforts, it belongs to Andy and Wesley. They flew into horrific weather in an area they'd never been to save the life of someone they never knew. They are heroes!

Summary

I read this story several times and always came away with the same odd feeling: Megumi was never supposed to make it off the mountain alive. It seems that everything that could go wrong with finding and saving Megumi went wrong. The emergency 911 system failed her. If it wasn't for her smart, persistent, and patient demeanor, she never would've gotten through to the right system. The New Mexico state police later stated that this had never happened before or since. The girl was lost on a trail, not an easy thing to do in that area. All of the trails are readily marked and large. Luckily, Megumi had a cell phone and unbelievably had reception. Finally, the helicopter rescue: Who could've scripted a more depressing, fail-filled set of circumstances to end Megumi's life?

If you haven't noticed, I have been documenting a series of people who have gotten lost in the woods who were at the far end of brilliant. None of these people ever made it out of the wilderness alive. Several of these individuals have backgrounds in physics, quite a coincidence.

New York

Sex/Name	Date Missing • Age • State
M-Dayton Weaver	09/16/1890-10:00 a.m. • 3 • Greenport, NY
M-Eddie Nichols	05/25/1891-10:00 a.m. • 2 • Commac, NY
M-Stephen Parker	01/30/52-4:30 p.m. • 3 • Rome, NY
M-George Bombardier	11/29/71-5:00 p.m. • 55 • Brighton, NY

F-Kathryn Dekkers   07/24/81-3:00 p.m. • 10 • Ampersand Mountain, NY
M-Ronald Adams   09/07/85-p.m. • 21 • High Peaks, NY
F-Harriet Olsen   06/24/00-6:00 p.m. • 75 • Vermontville, NY

M-Dayton Weaver
Missing: 09/16/1890-10:00 a.m., Greenport, NY
Age at disappearance: 3 years

On the date of this disappearance, the city was called "Greenport Township." The location of this small hamlet is just northeast of Hudson. The area east of the city has many small bodies of water and can get remote and wild quickly.

On September 16, 1890, Mrs. George Weaver needed to take her six-week-old child with her when she went to a neighbor's house. She left her home at 7:00 a.m. and left Dayton with his mongrel puppy, Frank. Mrs. Weaver returned at 10:00 a.m. and couldn't locate Dayton or Frank. She searched for the boy nonstop through the day until George got home from his work at the mill. It was now 8:00 p.m. It was during the early evening that additional resources were requested.

On September 17 George told his boss that his child was lost. The boss closed the mill and committed everyone to finding the toddler. Heavy rain fell through the day, yet people stayed in the forest looking for the boy. A September 21 article in the *Philadelphia Record* related the feelings of searchers: "On Thursday it had cleared; but creeks and rivulets had become rivers and and when all of the searchers returned at night without a trace of the boy they did so in the belief that he was drowned and had been swept away by the floods." It had rained so hard that the press was using the word "floods."

On Friday two hunters heard of the fifty-dollar reward for finding Dayton, dead or alive. The men decided to hunt and search for the boy simultaneously. The guys were three miles from the Weaver residence in the late afternoon when they saw the child. He was sitting under a cedar tree with a rock in a tin can, making noise. Searchers didn't find the boy; hunters did.

Nobody could believe that Dayton had traveled as far as he did and was found in such good condition. He stated he was hungry but never mentioned being thirsty. There was never any mention of what happened to Frank.

M-Eddie Nichols
Missing: 05/25/1891-10:00 a.m., Commac, NY
Age at disappearance: 2 years

Commac is located on Long Island, approximately midway out the peninsula. On May 25, 1891, at approximately 10:00 a.m., Eddie was in a garden outside his residence with his six-year-old sister. The sister went into the house for ten minutes. When the girl returned, Eddie was gone. Eddie's mom and sister searched for the boy and then asked the village to assist.

A June 5, 1891, article in the *Daily Signal* explained the efforts to find the boy: "The neighborhood was aroused and a searching party of 800 men accompanied by a large pack of hounds engaged in the search for the lost child." The article stated that the area in a ten-mile radius surrounding Commac was walked by searchers. The story stated the men walked a "rod" apart throughout the area and could not locate the boy. The missing person was a boy, but the article stated that he left the area wearing a bright-red dress.

The afternoon and early evening that Eddie vanished, Commac was inundated with two large thunderstorms that dropped heavy rain in the area. By the end of the third day of search, there was talk that the boy may have been kidnapped and taken from the area. There was a complete lack of evidence that he was still in the area. There was one neighbor who had heard a child-like cry in the woods. Men went to the area and stayed in the region overnight but never heard anything else and found nothing. The exact location of this cry was never explained.

Eighty hours after Eddie went missing, there was a fascinating discovery as is explained in the June 1, 1894, *New York Times*: "Under great twin oaks on a hillside two miles from home of Stockton Van Brunt found him this afternoon nestling in a pile of leaves, face downward and almost unconscious." The find was two hundred feet from a major road. Van Brunt knew of the disappearance and had decided to go to an area where people thought the boy had been. The area had been searched many times and was in fairly close proximity to his home (two miles).

Eddie was taken to a local physician and was found to be in good condition with a slight fever. The doctor never stated he was dehydrated, and there was never a mention of what he was wearing when found.

Summary

I don't believe that any child who is two years old and is missing in the woods and goes without food and water for eighty hours would be considered to be in good condition when found. At the minimum, Eddie would have had to have found water and shelter to avoid suffering from exposure and dehydration.

The story mentioned he was found on a hillside and under a tree. This area was searched extensively. Thunderstorms hit the Commac area the day the boy disappeared, and searchers had stated that they felt the boy might have been kidnapped.

We study history for a reason. This same pattern that existed 120 years ago is found today in many missing person cases.

Stephen Parker
Missing: 01/30/52-4:30 p.m., Rome, NY
Age at disappearance: 3 years

This incident occurred ninety miles southwest of the High Peaks and twenty miles east of Syracuse. This area is very thick with ground cover and is a rural area, even by today's standards.

Little Stephen Parker was playing outside his home, four miles outside of Rome, NY. It was four thirty in the afternoon, and temperatures were plummeting when Mrs. Calvin Parker went into the backyard to check on Stephen. She found that the boy and the family dog had disappeared. She yelled for her son and did not receive any response. Mr. Parker called the local fire department and sheriff.

By 5:00 p.m., the woods surrounding the Parker household were crawling with over three hundred searchers. Soldiers were arriving from Griffith Air Force Base, and the New London fire department was sending crews to assist.

Two firemen and a sheriff thought they observed faint tracks in the snow some distance behind the Parker residence and started to follow them. The men tracked through the snow for over two hours and came to an area near Tannery Creek. A January 31 article in the *Post Standard* had a description of what the trio found: "Deputy Sheriff Richard Owens found the youngster on the ice half frozen and semi-conscious about 8pm." Stephen had traveled over five miles in four and a half hours.

I want readers to think about their child when they were three years old. Would that child have left your yard and walked five miles in subfreezing temperatures?

The Parker family dog returned to the yard shortly after Stephen disappeared.

In the book *Lost Person Behavior*, Robert Koester states that a lost three-year-old child will be found 95 percent of the time at a distance of two miles or less on flat ground from the point they were last seen. Stephen was found over double that distance and supposedly accomplished this feat in snow in just four and a half hours.

George Bombardier
Missing: 11/29/71-5:00 p.m., Brighton, NY
Age at disappearance: 55 years

The headlines in this story indicated the nearest city was "Paul Smiths in New York." Upon further research we found that the disappearance actually occurred in Brighton, New York, just one mile east of Paul Smiths. What is highly interesting is that this happened just eight miles west of the disappearance of Harriet Olsen in Vermontville, NY. Both of these areas have hundreds of small bodies of water, and both are very lush with thick forests.

George Bombardier was a lifetime hunter who always went to the same location to enjoy the outdoors and deer hunt. He was a retiree from the Rouse Point and Delaware Railroad, and he owned a hunting company in the area of Paul Smiths. George wasn't in perfect health. He needed daily medication for a blood condition. George was considered by friends and family an expert woodsman.

On November 29, 1971, George was hunting at his longtime favorite location, just outside the town of Brighton. It should be noted that three articles stated George went missing on November 29, and other articles stated November 27, 28, and 30. It's impossible to determine what the actual date of the disappearance was, so we will use November 29 because that was the date the majority utilized.

George went hunting alone and told his family that he'd be back late in the afternoon. George never made it home. The family contacted local natural resource officers and sheriffs. Many friends and family assisted in the effort to locate George in an effort that continued for over two weeks. Searchers did find George's truck but could not locate him. Hundreds participated in the effort, which was eventually terminated because of bad weather.

There was another push to find George in May 1972. Again, the search effort found nothing. A May 31, 1972, article in the *Press-Republican* had this statement about the feelings of family and friends: "No one who knew him believes he became lost."

It does seem coincidental that two people disappear just miles apart. One mature man, one mature woman, both with medical conditions, and both are never found.

F-Kathryn Dekkers
Missing: 07/24/81-3:00 p.m., Ampersand Mountain, NY
Age at disappearance: 10 years

I have described the High Peaks area of Northern New York in past books as a major cluster of missing people. Kathryn Dekkers's disappearance will be added to that group. Ampersand Mountain is seven miles southwest of Lake Placid and is in a rugged and wild section of the state.

Kathryn was hiking with a group as they were descending 3,365-foot Ampersand Mountain on a major trail. She was at the back of the line during the hike. When they arrived at the vehicles, the girl wasn't found.

A major search ensued. Helicopters with FLIR, conservation officers, law enforcement, wildlife wardens, Bloodhounds, rangers, and various volunteers scoured the mountain yelling and looking for the young girl. They found nothing for two days. On the third day, a volunteer, outdoorsman Jimmy Lamy, was three miles from the mountain on the far side of Ampersand Pond and found the girl. She had some scratches, but she was alive. Lamy took her to law enforcement, who then transported her to the hospital. She was released the following day in good condition.

Reporters and conservation officers attempted to interview Kathryn about her three-day ordeal, but her parents refused to allow it.

Professional searchers, Bloodhounds, and helicopters with FLIR could not find the girl. A volunteer who was hiking alone located her.

This is another in a long line of people who disappeared while they were last in line while hiking.

Ronald Adams
Missing: 09/07/85-p.m., High Peaks, NY
Age at disappearance: 21 years

The High Peaks region of northern New York has some of the highest mountains and the most rugged topography in the state. Lake Placid is the closest major city. I have documented several people who have vanished in this region, and it is one of the major clusters on the East Coast. The most famous disappearance in the High Peaks is probably Douglas Legg, missing since July 10, 1971. The eight-year-old boy was never found even though Bloodhounds allegedly tracked him around the High Peaks and over the top of the city of Lake Placid.

Bittersweet Farms is a facility in Toledo, Ohio, for young adults with autism. Seven residents and four counselors took a trip to the High Peaks area of New York to view the rugged and beautiful area. On September 7, 1985, they were visiting an area near Nye and Indian Pass. Sometime during the late afternoon hours, one of their residents, Ronald Adams, disappeared near Rocky Falls along the

Indian Pass Brook, an area of swamps and large boulders. Ronald was disabled, and his communication skills were severely challenged. Counselors with the group searched for the man and were unable to locate him. The group returned to the trailhead parking lot and made contact with department of natural resource officers.

The search for Ronald was a challenge from the beginning. They knew he had difficulty communicating and they hoped that playing music into the woods at night would draw him out; it didn't. The second and third days of the search, it rained hard and temperatures dropped below freezing. The five-day search included planes, two helicopters, ten Bloodhound teams, and hundreds of searchers.

During the effort to locate the young man, one of Ronald's boots was found. Later in that same day, Ronald's other shoe and a shirt were found. This was an unusual find, considering it was raining and cold.

A September 13 article in the *Toledo Blade* had the following information on finding Ronald: "An autistic Whitehouse man lost in New York's Adirondack Mountains was found yesterday lying in a swampy area about two miles from where he wandered from companions Saturday. Ronald Adams, 21, was found by a search party at 11am. He was suffering from trench foot and mild hypothermia, or subnormal body temperature, and was dressed only in his underwear, authorities said." Ten teams of Bloodhounds couldn't find Ronald. He had mild hypothermia, not enough to cause him to shed clothing and shoes.

Ronald was questioned at the hospital and could not remember specific details of his five days. The last paragraph in the same *Toledo Blade* article quoted above was this: "Mr. Dalton, also a ranger, said they had searched the area before, but Mr. Adams was not found." This is another case where the victim was found in a location that had been previously searched. The factors present in the Ronald Adams case are found in many of the searches documented in the four Missing 411 books.

Harriet Olsen
Missing: 06/24/00-6:00 p.m., Vermontville, NY
Age at disappearance: 75 years

I've researched thousands of cases of missing people from a variety of locations under a multitude of conditions. The disappearance of Harriet Olsen ranks as one of the strangest and quickest disappearances I've ever investigated.

The Olsen residence was on Fletcher Farm Road with an address in Vermontville, New York. The road parallels Franklin Falls Pond and is a very rural and lush area of northern New York. The home was located twelve miles north of Lake Placid and twenty-five miles south of Plattsburgh. There are hundreds of small bodies of water in the general area of the residence.

On June 24, 2000, at approximately 5:00–6:00 p.m., Harriet was in her residence preparing dinner while her husband, Henry, worked in the garage. When Henry came back to the residence, Harriet was gone. She hadn't said anything about leaving, and Henry had not heard anything unusual. He searched the area for over an hour and then called the sheriff. Searchers started their effort to find Harriett that night and continued for over three weeks.

The New York state police dispatched a helicopter with FLIR, and multiple canine teams were utilized along with hundreds of professional and volunteer searchers who worked areas miles from the Olsen residence.

The Olsens had lived in the area for over sixteen years. Harriet knew the area very well, and the idea that she was lost seemed ludicrous. Searchers could not find tracks or any other indicators that she had left the property. A June 27 article in the *Press Republican* had the following information about Harriet: "'We believe that she's in the early stages of Alzheimer's disease,' said LaRow. 'It hasn't been confirmed medically, but the indicators are there. She wasn't a hiker or walker. There was no communication between the subject and her husband.'"

The best information that investigators have determined was that Harriet disappeared between 5:00 and 6:00 p.m. She was last seen inside her residence while her husband was in the garage. Searchers could not find tracks leaving the area, and Bloodhounds could not pick up her scent in the outlying forest.

It's a major mystery what happened to Harriet Olsen.

North Carolina

Sex/Name   Date Missing • Age • State
M-Danny Hicks   12/03/80-2:00 p.m. • 2 • Raleigh, NC

Danny Hicks
Missing: 12/03/80-2:00 p.m., Raleigh, NC
Age at disappearance: 2 years

I've written about several cases in North Carolina that fit the criteria to be included in the Missing 411 books. The disappearance of Danny Hicks on December 3, 1980, fits the criteria and, from what you will read, raised the suspicion of the local sheriff. At approximately 2:30 p.m., Danny was playing outside his family's home with his two dogs. For some unknown reason, Danny and the dogs wandered off, and they wouldn't respond to calls. The Wake County sheriff was called.

Wake County covers all of Raleigh and extends into very rural areas with thick woods. This incident happened in the northern section of the county near an area of Falls Lake and Wake Forest.

The search for Danny was comprehensive and immediate. Hundreds of people participated, including Bloodhounds, teams of professional searchers, and hundreds of volunteers. At one point in the effort, the sheriff estimated more than one thousand people were participating in the effort to find the boy. On Friday, December 5, searchers were about to terminate their efforts when one of the dogs that disappeared with Danny, Honky, returned to the residence. The parents and the searchers prompted Honky to go back into the woods, where the dog led them to a small stream where they found tiny footprints. It was unknown if they were Danny's. The search was resumed again.

Unknown to the many searchers in the field were the visions of William Hal Caviness, a Creedmoor resident who had been having strong feelings about the boy for several days. The retired painter woke the morning of December 6 and decided to drive to a wooded area in Northern Wake County. At about noon William found the boy, as is described in this December 8, 1980, article in the *Herald*

Journal: "Caviness found the boy—dead and lying on his back in low undergrowth with his puppy, Fluffy, lying patiently by his side." Later in the same article was this description: "'He looked like he was asleep,' Caviness told the boy's parents as they sat in their mobile home Saturday. The area around the body had many large flat rocks covering the ground. He speculated the boy fell asleep Wednesday night, when temperatures dropped into the 20's, and never woke up." An autopsy showed that Danny died of exposure.

Wake County Sheriff John H. Baker was all over this case from the beginning. I think it would be fair to say that Baker was shocked that Danny was found just one mile behind the parent's residence. Danny and the dog never made any sounds. In the same *Herald Journal* article was this statement about the location of the body: "Investigators said the area where the body was found had been searched at least a half dozen times. Sheriff Baker said he was confident the search was thorough and complete as possible." In the December 11 *Herald Journal* was this statement by the sheriff: "Baker says that he still has some serious questions about the case, and it is still under investigation. 'There are some questions we are concerned about, and we're going back to the parents, relatives and neighbors.'"

There is no doubt that the sheriff was astounded that Mr. Caviness found Danny's body in an area so close to his residence and in an area that had been searched multiple, multiple times. I believe the sheriff had a hard time believing that someone hadn't placed the body there sometime after the last search teams cleared the area.

Summary

As readers of my past books know, this case is an absolute cookie cutter of dozens of others I have chronicled. Sheriff Baker wasn't aware of how many times children are found in areas that have been previously searched. It almost appears as if they are placed in an area where searchers will absolutely find them, almost in an area that can't be missed. The idea that searchers passed within feet of the body and never saw Danny, and the puppy never made a sound, is not believable.

Oklahoma

Sex/Name	Date Missing • Age • State
M-Jackie Landreth	12/03/39-p.m. • 3 • Cloudy, OK

Jackie Landreth
Missing: 12/03/39-p.m., Kiamichi Mountains, OK
Age at disappearance: 3 years

The small community of Cloudy, Oklahoma, did not have roads or general public access in 1939. It was a rural spot where people rode on horseback to get to. The community sits approximately twenty miles west of the Arkansas border in the Kiamichi Mountains. The Landreth family had lived in the community for ten months when during the afternoon of December 3, 1939, Jackie was playing in the yard with his pet kitten and his little brother. Apparently the cat ran out the gate, and Jackie ran out to get it. He didn't come back.

Jackie's parents called the community for assistance in finding their son, as he wasn't answering their calls. Over five hundred people from the surrounding communities responded to Cloudy to look for the boy. The Oklahoma Highway Patrol, Boy Scouts, WPA workers, and CCC youths all were in the mountains calling the boy's name.

Jackie's parents were interviewed about his disappearance. A December 7 article in the *Ada Weekly* had this statement from his mom and dad about what Jackie thought about living in the mountains: "The mountains were strange and fearful to the child. He never became accustomed to them, or to the towering trees which surrounded his home." This really does not sound like a boy who would run into the woods and go very far from his home.

On December 5, a searcher on horseback was five miles from the Landreth residence when he made a find that was documented in the same *Ada Weekly* article: "Sam Thompson, member of the posse which had searched the forests and canyons of this wild, remote section of southeast Oklahoma for 48 hours, almost rode his horse over the boy's body. It was hanging by the heels in the wire fence and physicians said the boy apparently had been dead since Monday afternoon."

Five miles is a very long way for a young boy to travel. The article states that a coroner determined that Jackie died the afternoon that he disappeared, and he traveled five miles during that small amount of time. This is not believable, especially since he had crossed very rugged terrain to get to the fence.

The Kiamichi Mountains are known as a location where there have been many strange events.

Oregon

Sex/Name	Date Missing • Age • State
M-Earl Gilliam	06/03/1893-p.m. • 3 • Heppner, OR
M-Samuel Ipock	10/10/77-5:00 p.m. • 22 • Tumalo Falls, OR

Earl Gilliam
Missing: 06/03/1893-p.m., Heppner, OR
Age at disappearance: 3 years

Heppner is a small rural community forty miles southwest of Pendleton and ten miles south of the Washington border. Pendleton was the location described in *Missing 411-Western United States* where little Keith Parkins vanished (4/10/52). At two and a half years old, he was found nineteen hours later twelve miles from his grandfather's ranch, over two mountain ranges and several fences. Yes, those numbers are correct.

The disappearance of Earl Gilliam happened on the afternoon of June 3, 1893, in a small town in the middle of a desert. The area around the city is void of any large trees.

The three-year-old boy somehow disappeared from the family residence on the perimeter of the city. City residents by the hundreds came out at night with lanterns and torches, searching for the small guy. In the early morning hours of June 4, searchers found small tracks near the Woodward ranch, four miles from the city. The Woodwards had found the boy on a lonely road late at night and put him to bed. He was still asleep and in good condition when searchers made it to the residence. A June 10, 1893, article in the *Oregonian* had this statement about the four-mile trip the boy made: "It seemed hardly credible that so young a child could have wandered so far." Considering Heppner sits at the bottom of a valley and all ranches are uphill from the young boy's house, yes, it is an amazing journey Earl accomplished.

There were no notes in the articles about what Earl was wearing when found.

Samuel Ipock
Missing: 10/10/77-5:00 p.m., northeast of Tumalo Falls, OR
Age at disappearance: 22 years

You are going to read about a man who should have never disappeared and should have never fallen off a cliff, and a search team that was completely baffled about where he was found. This story will make little sense.

Samuel Ipock was born June 13, 1955, in Bend, Oregon. He was born to be an outdoorsman, and he followed that path. He spent time hunting and being in the great outdoors with his father, uncle, and friends. He took an occupation as a timber faller, which placed him in the middle of desolate country, with him against the trees.

On October 10, 1977, Samuel and his father, Harry, went to an area northeast of Tumalo Falls to hunt. Samuel had been to this special location many times and knew it quite well. In the afternoon hours, Harry and Samuel split up to hunt with the agreement to meet back at camp before dark. Samuel never came back. Four hours after the agreed-upon meeting time, Harry called the Deschutes County sheriff, who in turn called the county search and rescue team.

The search for Samuel was not able to start until the morning of October 11 because of the rugged and dangerous topography of the area. On Wednesday morning, reporters interviewed a search coordinator, and this was the statement in the October 12 edition of *The Bulletin*: "'It's a real puzzling situation,' search coordinator Frank

Earl said Wednesday morning. 'Ipock is in excellent physical condition, he knows the area well and is an avid hunter.'" The weather in the area at the time of the disappearance and immediately after was cloudy and cold.

The search effort included planes, Bloodhounds, dozens of ground searchers, and cars patrolling the outer perimeter.

Just after noon on Thursday, October 13, witnesses saw birds circling in an area beneath cliffs that had been searched dozens of times. This was an area where Samuel may have been hunting, thus the big effort in the area. Samuel's uncle, Carl Ipock, went to the area and, to his shock, found his nephew's body. A coroner's report indicated that Samuel had major head and neck trauma. It was theorized that Samuel fell off a one-hundred-foot cliff and then slipped another 195 feet down a steep, boulder-strewn decline. According to an October 14 article in *The Bulletin*, "Ipock's body was found in an area searched extensively by ground crews, dogs and aircraft. Searchers Wednesday scoured the area around the cliffs without finding a trace of the body." This is a pretty clear statement that searchers were stunned by where they found Samuel. Later in the article, it states: "Much progress had been made and the crews had all but ruled out the cliff area." The teams of searchers were focusing their efforts at the base of the cliffs, not on top of the cliffs, because his dad knew he would not hunt in that area. This is another excerpt from the same *Bulletin* article: "Ipock was last seen Monday evening when he and his father separated to hunt the area surrounding the cliffs. Ipock's disappearance puzzled authorities because he was reputed to be an experienced hunter who knew the area well. Searchers say they are still puzzled as to why he was on the cliffs in the first place."

You will read many articles in my books where people are allegedly falling off cliffs even though close family members don't believe they would've been in that area, just as in this case.

This region of the Cascades has a horrid history of disappearances and deaths of hikers and hunters, deaths and disappearances that cannot be logically explained.

Pennsylvania

Sex/Name	Date Missing • Age • State
M-George Cox	04/24/1856-a.m. • 7 • Bedford County, PA
M-Joseph Cox	04/24/1856-a.m. • 5 • Bedford County, PA
F-Emma Grace Carbaugh	07/01/1887-10:00 a.m. • 22 mos. • Sabiliasville, MD
F-Minnie Parsons	04/04/1906-5:00 p.m. • 7 • Jamestown, NY
F-Alice Arnold	05/22/1911-a.m. • 4 • Ickesburg, PA
M-Kenneth Slagle Jr.	11/26/42-p.m. • 3 • Conemaugh, PA
M-Donald Curry	04/09/44-4:35 p.m. • 4 • Belleville, PA
M-Raymond Howe Jr.	07/15/46-5:00 p.m. • 9 • Pittsburgh, PA
M-Robert Haughney	07/16/58-a.m. • 6 • Strabane, PA

George Cox   Age at disappearance: 7 years
M-Joseph Cox   Age at disappearance: 5 years
Missing: 04/24/1856-a.m., Spruce Hollow, Bedford County, PA

Spruce Hollow is a rural community southeast of Pittsburgh in Bedford County. Samuel and Susannah Cox lived in their small cabin with their two boys, George and Joseph, and their family dog, Sport.

In the morning hours of April 24, 1856, the family was at the breakfast table when Sport was barking outside. The dog barked for an extremely long time, and Samuel thought it had treed a squirrel. He took his rifle and went outside to shoot whatever Sport had spotted.

At this point there are few details as to how and what transpired. It appears that Samuel was gone for approximately an hour or more and returned to find his wife upset. She couldn't find the boys. Some renditions of this story state that the boys went out and tried to follow their father; others state the boys just disappeared. The boys were gone, and Samuel did a brief search and then contacted neighbors for assistance.

The Cox family was immediately concerned about the welfare of their boys, as the weather had started to turn as soon as they vanished. The first night they were gone, snow started to fall around the Cox cabin.

The first eight hours brought 150 locals into the search. They covered every inch of area near the cabin and found nothing. The second day brought over one thousand people who volunteered to look for the boys, and this effort continued for days. One rendition of this story can be found on the Pennsylvania schools websites. The feelings of the locals are explained on the *www.bedford.k12.pa.us/c12* website: "By now the entire area was completely involved with the thoughts of what extreme misfortune the Cox family was experiencing. Rumors flew wildly as neighbors told stories to one another. They had drowned...they were killed by a man-eating beast seen prowling the forest...the parents had murdered them. Several neighbors went as far as to tear up the floor of the Cox cabin to relieve those acquisitions."

As the search went into the fifth and sixth days, community members were getting angry because they believed they had covered every possible area the boys could travel. They weren't finding any footprints or other evidence the boys were anywhere in the area.

The region the searchers were covering is now known as being on the border of the Gallitzin State Forest and Blue Knob State Park. I have chronicled several children who have gone missing in the area just southwest of this location.

Besides the website quoted earlier, many details about this incident came from a small book written by Charles R. McCarthy, *The Lost Children of the Alleghenies.* In one portion of the book, there is a description of the two boys: George had dark hair and blue eyes, and Joseph had gray eyes. There was another comment about George's intellect: "George was remarkably intelligent for one his age." The book states that there was inclement weather for much of the search, and the volunteers "failed to discover even a foot-print of their lost and starving children."

Searchers continued nonstop for ten days looking for the boys and finding nothing. On the tenth night, a man named Jacob Dilbert, who lived twelve to thirteen miles from the Cox cabin, had a dream, a dream that he had for three consecutive nights. In the dream was a series of mountain landmarks, streams, boulders, and logs that led him to the boys' bodies. After the third night of dreaming this scenario, he went to his wife's brother and asked for him to accompany him to the location in the dream. The brother stated that the location he described was five to six miles from the Cox residence and too far for the boys to have traveled, and they could never have made it over Bob's Creek to get to the location he had described. Jacob was adamant; he was going.

The following day Jacob and his wife's brother made the journey he had seen in his dream. This was a grueling trip from Jacob's residence but a trip he knew he had to make. They eventually came to a fallen birch tree; the stump could be observed from a distance. Jacob stated that if his dream was true, the boys would be at the bottom of the root. The men walked to the area and found both boys dead.

The bodies were described as thin with their limbs scratched and torn. Physicians felt the boys had been dead for three to four days. It was believed that the boys died of starvation and exhaustion. George and Joseph were placed on a sled and made the six- to seven-mile trip to the Cox residence.

Summary

The boys were found outside the search area because people did not believe they would wander that far and could cross Bob's Creek. Who am I to second-guess people who lived in the region? If those people didn't think the boys could cross the creek, then how did they cross?

Why would they cross, when they knew their cabin wasn't on the other side?

Doctors believed that the boys had been dead for three to four days, meaning they were alive and in the vicinity for five to six days with searchers in the area yelling their names. Why wouldn't the boys have observed or responded to the searchers?

Readers need to remember that there is not another state in the United States that has as many children who have disappeared under highly unusual conditions as Pennsylvania. We can now add two more small boys to the list. How many more victims are out there I haven't found?

F-Emma Grace Carbaugh
Missing: 07/01/1887-10:00 a.m., Sabiliasville, MD
Age at disappearance: 22 months

This case was placed in the Pennsylvania chapter because Sabiliasville is at the far northern area of Maryland directly on the border, approximately seventeen miles east of Hagerstown.

On July 10, 1887, The *Baltimore American* ran an article about this event with the following headline: "A Search for a Child, A Mysterious Case on a Mountain." On July 1, 1887, at 10:00 a.m., William Carbaugh (Last name also spelled Clabaugh in some articles) lived with his wife and two daughters in a small home on one of the main mountain roads in a very rural section between Emmitsburg and Sabiliasville (closer to Sabiliasville). This area of the mountains is now the home of the Emmitsburg Watershed. William needed to hike to neighbor David Bentzeil's home to buy butter. He walked out his front door and saw Bertha (four years) and Emma (twenty-two months) playing in the front yard. He walked toward the neighbor's fence two hundred years away, hopped it, and proceeded to the farmhouse.

William didn't know that Bertha and Emma had followed him. When they got to the fence, Bertha was able to get over the structure; Emma could not. Bertha continued down the path toward her father and left Emma behind in the family's fenced yard. Twenty-five minutes after going over the fence, Bertha and her dad returned to their front porch and met with the girls' mother. She asked where Emma was. Bertha explained the series of events, and a search was started. It wasn't long until William and his wife realized that Emma was not in the yard and started to contact neighbors for assistance.

This incident occurred on a Friday. Saturday and Sunday brought two hundred searchers who covered the hillsides walking arm in arm, ensuring they didn't miss finding the girl. In the same *Baltimore American* article cited earlier was this statement: "Some think the child was stolen, but are unable to determine a motive, as Clabaugh is a poor man who could offer no reward, and if the child had been stolen, the kidnapper would have been apprehended by some of the two hundred searching the mountains high to low. Some say the child might have been lost in the woods. That is almost impossible. The child was too young to stray off any considerable distance, and had it done so, would have been subsequently found."

On July 10, 1887, ten days after Emma disappeared, a gruesome discovery was made in the mountains near the Pennsylvania border. A July 17 article in the *Baltimore American* had the following description of the find: "The body [Emma's] with the head completely severed from it, was found in a grove about a mile and a half from the house. The head was found near by, and seems to have been severed from the body by a sharp instrument. Portions of the body have been devoured." Later in the same article were the findings of the coroner's jury: "Immediately upon the discovery of the body, a coroner's jury was summoned, and after a thorough investigation of the case, rendered a verdict to the effect that the child came to its death from cause-unknown to the jury."

Summary

This case is obviously disturbing from many fronts. How did the two hundred men miss the body when they were searching for Emma? Mountain men know what traverses the hills; they know the predators, and they know the type of injuries these animals could inflict. The coroner's jury could not determine what caused the injuries to Emma.

Readers of *Missing 411-Eastern United States* know that the number of children who have disappeared in the greater Pennsylvania area under highly unusual conditions is stifling. These disappearances started in 1880 and continued en masse until the late 1950s. This is one of the extremely rare cases where physicians, coroners, and civilian juries could not determine the cause of death.

Minnie Parsons
Missing: 04/04/1906-5:00 p.m., Jamestown, NY
Age at disappearance: 7 years

The location of this incident is just outside Jamestown, New York, just three miles north of the Pennsylvania border. The residence is ten miles southwest of the Allegheny National Forest and a cluster of missing people in Pennsylvania, thus it's included in the Pennsylvania section. For additional details about the missing people in this cluster, refer to *Missing 411-Eastern United States* and *Missing 411-North America and Beyond*.

On April 4, 1906, Minnie Parsons, her sister, and her little brother went with their cousin for a three-hundred-foot walk to Conewango Creek to go fishing. The kids did well and gave the fish to Minnie to take back to her family. They watched as she headed in the direction of her home. After a short period of time, the other children decided to return to the house for dinner. Once home, the kids learned that Minnie never arrived.

Minnie's father, William, and his wife started to search for the young girl and made a call for others to assist. Mr. Avery Hoyt did find tracks of a young person in the area where the children were fishing, but these soon disappeared. Slowly the search area got farther and farther away without finding Minnie.

An April 6, 1906, article in the *Grape Belt* had a good description of what searchers found the night Minnie vanished: "By this time the entire village was aroused and it seemed that if the child was on Earth, it could not be long before she would be found. This surmise was true, for about 9:30 p.m., one of the searchers stumbled upon the tiny body of the child lying on the bank fully four miles from the point where she was last seen. The child was sleeping peacefully, totally unconscious of all the fuss being made over her and of the heart-aches she had caused."

There are several key points to Minnie's disappearance that are important to the total missing person scenario. This entire incident occurred near water, Conewango Creek. She walked away from the creek with fish for her parents and was found asleep on the creek bank. As in many of the missing cases we document, victims are found unconscious, near a creek or river, and they can recall little about their time away. The only thing Minnie stated was, "I'm all right."

Minnie vanished at approximately 5:00 p.m. and was located at 9:30 p.m., four and one half hours without human contact. Where was Minnie, and why didn't she respond to the calls of searchers? What happened to the fish?

F-Alice Arnold
Missing: 05/22//1911-a.m., Ickesburg, PA
Age at disappearance: 4 years

This incident encompasses many of the elements I have discussed in past books: berries, inability to track, bad weather, allegations of kidnapping, and being found in an area previously searched. There were some discrepancies about the girl's age; some articles stated she was seven, but the majority stated she was four years old.

Ickesburg is near the geographical center of Pennsylvania and is just five miles west of the Appalachian Trail (AT). We have chronicled many unusual disappearances around the AT. The location of this incident was the Arnold ranch, two and a half miles east of Ickesburg in an area known as Marsh Run.

On the morning of May 22, 1911, the Arnold boys were herding cattle and moving them to pasture when Alice wandered over. The boys told her to go back to the house, but she initially refused. One of the brothers pushed her and yelled at her to go home. The house was in view, and Alice was seen heading in that direction. The brothers returned home in about an hour and found that their sister hadn't returned. The boys and their dad, William, searched the yard and found nothing. The local sheriff and state police were called.

The first two days of the search found nothing. Rain had inundated the area and had returned for several days. Law enforcement looked for assistance and found the best tracker in the state as is described in this July 20, 1911, article in the *Lock Haven Express*: "An Indian tracker from the Carlisle Indian School spent several days trying to pick up a clue. The nonsuccess of the searchers led to many wild stories about kidnapping and possible foul play." The tracker, Sylvester Young, spent three days and nights in the mountains north of the residence and stated that he found nothing to indicate the girl had been through the area.

While the tracker was working the mountains, over two hundred searchers were walking arm to arm through pastures and then into the mountains looking for the girl. They found nothing. A May 30 article in the *Easton Free Press* reported the feelings of law enforcement at the time: "The child disappeared so completely that the only idea now held by many of the searchers was that she was picked up by a party traveling through the country and taken away almost under the eyes of her parents." In that same article was this statement about the extent of the search: "The mystery surrounding the disappearance of seven-year old Alice Arnold from her home at Ickesburg last Monday grows deeper, and after a long search over five miles of mountain the parties admit that they are more puzzled than ever."

After ten days of intensive searching, the formal effort was terminated. There were no leads on this case for over a month.

On July 19 there was a major discovery as is described in the same *Lock Haven Express* article quoted earlier: "Huckleberry pickers working on the top of Tuscarora Mountain yesterday afternoon came upon a tiny skeleton, a whisp of light hair and little dress. And by this mute evidence of a tragedy was cleared away that much of the mystery surrounding the disappearance of Little Alice Arnold." The girl was found on top of a mountain, one thousand feet higher than her home and three miles from the residence. Later in the same article was this description: "It is plain from the position in which the skeleton was lying that the baby's face was pressed to earth when the end came." I have described this same type of event many times where the victim is found facedown on the ground. You may be thinking that it's strange that the searchers covered an area five miles from the residence, and the girl was found three miles away. The same *Lock Haven Express* article had these sentiments: "Now the people of this little community, which was the center of the excitement, are asking themselves how it happened that the organized search failed even to discover the dead body." The location where the body was found did disturb the searchers. They knew they had covered this area thoroughly.

Summary

I'm not sure how many articles need to be quoted to make the point that people disappear, searchers cover an area thoroughly, and the body is then discovered in an area that had been searched. I do not believe that ground searchers, airplanes, and Bloodhounds are missing the people. This scenario is replicated time after time, too many times to ignore.

In earlier books I have discussed the connection between the missing and berry bushes. I have stated that there is a distinct parallel between huckleberry bushes and missing people that usually ends with a death or not being found.

Alice was found at the top of one of the highest mountains in the area. She knew exactly where her home was at; why go to the highest mountain? Pay close attention to the many children I have documented—many are found higher in elevation than where they vanished, sometimes at the tops of mountains and peaks.

Law enforcement and professional searchers are experts at looking at the factual elements in the cases they research. These people are the best to make judgments about what is occurring. This is another incident where these experts state that a kidnapping may have happened.

The Ickesburg community was rocked by this tragedy. It's hard to reconcile the facts with the local knowledge of similar events. Until you look at the area on a grand scale, you'd never know that these events have happened dozens of times in Pennsylvania. The one state in the United States with the most missing children from rural areas: Why?

M-Kenneth Eugene Slagle Jr.
Missing: 11/26/42-p.m., Conemaugh, PA
Age at disappearance: 3 years

Conemaugh is twenty miles southeast from Bedford County and the location of the disappearance of George and Joseph Cox. The town is also twenty miles east from Somerset, the center point for a major cluster of disappearances in this region of the Keystone State.

On the afternoon of Thanksgiving 1942, Kenneth was playing in his yard with his pet collie, Fido. Somehow and for an unknown reason, Kenneth and Fido left the yard and disappeared. The family immediately started to get assistance from neighbors and friends, and a posse was formed.

Six hours after the posse was formed and as they were covering adjacent farm fields, one member was three miles from the Slagle farm and walking in a clover field when he found something he couldn't believe. There was a fresh depression dug into the ground, and there was Fido lying over something. When the dog got up, there was Kenneth, asleep in the hole. When he finally was woken up, he was fine. He explained that he followed Fido off the farm and he then fell asleep.

The Western Pennsylvania Humane Society gave Fido an award for saving Kenneth from the bitterly cold temperatures that existed the day of the disappearance. Mr. Slagle didn't think much of the award; he told the *Indiana Gazette* on April 20, 1943, his sentiments: "It was him that led my boy away in the first place. He can never come back to my home again." Fido was given to an appreciative neighbor.

Summary

This story is like so many others where a child on a farm or a ranch wanders off with his or her dog. This case is a bit different, because they gave the dog credit for digging the hole to protect Kenneth from the frigid temperatures that day. Why would the boy and the dog pick the middle of a large field to lie down and dig a hole? Why not pick a protected area in a barn or a nearby residence?

Donald Curry
Missing: 04/09/44-4:35 p.m., Belleville, PA
Age at disappearance: 4 years

Belleville is located in south central Pennsylvania, in a region that has had many unexplained disappearances. This case may seem mundane at the beginning—stay with it.

The Currys traveled with three other families for an April barbecue at a cabin in Greenwood Furnace State Park. The group arrived at 4:15 p.m., and immediately Donald and his seven-year-old brother, Eugene, wandered off toward a small creek. After twenty minutes, Mr. and Mrs. Curry became concerned about the boys and started to look for them. An April 11, 1944, article in the *Daily News* has an explanation of what was found: "A short time later, the elder of the two boys was found 300 feet from a path near the cabin. He was almost speechless and frantically told his parents that he was unable to find Donald." This is the first time I've read about a small boy being speechless at his inability to locate his sibling. Mr. and Mrs. Curry yelled and looked around the small creek for their son and then called authorities.

The first responding local emergency crews were the Belleville Volunteer Fire Department, followed by other fire districts. Boy Scouts from the region and volunteers all poured into the park to assist. The group rapidly rose to five hundred people looking for the four-year-old.

The interesting aspect to this case is the area where Donald vanished. Greenwood Furnace State Park is surrounded on three sides by mountains that rise as high as 2,100 feet. The only opening is the roadway to the southwest. Searchers believed that this is the direction that Donald must've traveled, because nobody believed he'd walk up and over the mountains.

Searchers were covering the area around the camp and park. Many groups were walking hand in hand to ensure they weren't missing anything.

Twenty-three hours after Donald went missing, two searchers were on their motorcycles heading home after a day in the woods. They were on a little-used road on Sand Mountain, northeast of Greenwood Furnace State Park. Ellis Zook and Glen Scott found Donald standing on the road. There was a brief conversation, and the one of the searchers told Donald to get on his bike for the ride back to his parents. Donald said he couldn't because his parents wouldn't let him ride on motorcycles. After a little prodding, Donald got on board. He was wet from last night's rain, had scratches over his body, and was nervous.

Donald was reunited with his parents and examined by a physician. A reporter got an opportunity to interview the boy as was documented in the April 12, 1944, article in the *Daily News*: "When questioned on his experience, the youthful pathfinder told tall stories about his adventures in wide eyed wonder. He complained that his legs burned him a little. His legs were slightly swollen and chapped. 'I saw a couple of bears and a bunny too,' he related, 'and some bad people back of bushes.'" I think it's fascinating that the reporter threw in his personal comment, "tall stories." As I have stated many times, it is remarkable how many times children who survive an ordeal similar to Donald's report seeing bears. New readers may completely discount the boy's recollection of "bad people in the bushes"; don't. In *Missing 411-North America and Beyond*, I wrote about the disappearance of Linda Arteaga from Saint Joe, Arkansas. The fifty-three-year-old hiker went missing for five days. When she was found, she told a physician that she saw people in bushes staring at her. She claims that she tried talking to them but was ignored.

The strangeness of Donald's journey hasn't yet been adequately explained. Earlier I described the valley that the Currys were visiting had an opening to the southwest. It appears that Donald went through the highest portion of the park to the northeast. He was found on Sand Mountain. News articles say the boy was located seven miles from where he vanished. I measured the distance on a map. It looked closer to a distance of twelve miles over several tall mountains and very thick forests. A four-year-old child in a mountain setting is found 95 percent of the time within 2.3 miles or less. Remember, Donald not only went over mountains and through thick woods, he accomplished this in a heavy rainstorm in just twenty-three hours.

I always go back in my mind to the location where Donald was originally lost. The human voice when yelling travels a long distance in the woods. You can bet that Mr. and Mrs. Curry were yelling very loudly for their son. Why didn't he respond?

Raymond Howe Jr.
Missing: 07/15/46-5:00 p.m., Highland Park, Pittsburgh, PA
Age at disappearance: 9 years

When I first read this case several years ago, I discounted it because there was the possibility it was a human-involved abduction.

After accumulating more information on the case, and after finding several missing person cases on the perimeter of Pittsburgh, I gave this incident a second look. I think there is ample ambiguity about the facts of this incident for it to be included.

On a warm summer day, July 15, 1946, Raymond Howe went with his three sisters and brother to Highland Park in Pittsburgh for an afternoon of swimming and fishing.

The group of kids went to the community pool and spent several hours swimming and having fun. Late in the afternoon, the group decided to go home, except for Raymond. Raymond told the group he was going to a nearby lake to spend some time there fishing, his favorite hobby. When Raymond never came home, his family called the police.

The police allocated significant resources to finding Raymond. Hundreds of people started searching the area of the disappearance. The police found one witness who claimed to have seen Raymond with a few fish walking along a road toward his residence. The witness felt that he might have been hitchhiking. One hundred and fifty Pittsburgh police officers walked the park shoulder to shoulder and said they found nothing of value. On August 9 there was a second effort to scour the park inch by inch, trying to find anything that could connect to Raymond. A group of Boy Scouts were going through the park, and Scoutmaster Blair Davis found a small plastic football in a far isolated corner. The football was given to police, who presented it to Raymond's mother. She confirmed that Raymond did have an identical toy. This really didn't prove much other than Raymond may still be in that area. A more comprehensive search of the area found nothing.

The disappearance of Raymond was probably one of the biggest news stories in Pittsburgh in the mid-1940s. Many headlines called this a "Mysterious Disappearance," and it seemed unreal to this part of Pennsylvania.

Approximately twenty miles southeast from Highland Park and forty-one days after Raymond vanished, Scott Terry was exercising his hunting dogs in an isolated park in Penn Township. A dog came upon the body of Raymond underneath a bridge at the end of a trail under a small group of bushes. There were no details about how the body was clothed. An August 26 article in the *Morning Herald* had the following details about the find: "Pathologist J.D. McMeans announced after the autopsy that the cause of death could not be determined because of the condition of the body. He said there were no fractures or bullet wounds, no broken bones nor any mutilation. The boy had been dead more than a month. Police said the position of the body—he was lying on his back with the right leg over the left—indicated the boy may have been fatigued and fallen asleep."

Summary
Raymond disappeared under highly mysterious conditions. It appears as though he was holding fish and walking near a rural road. He was missing forty-one days when his body was found. The coroner stated he had been dead approximately one month. Where was Raymond the other five to ten days? How did he get from one location to another? The police did make allegations that it appeared that Raymond may have been abducted, but no suspects were ever named.

The coroner being unable to determine the cause of death is a common factor in many of the missing person cases we have investigated. What happened to the fish and fishing pole?

Robert Haughney
Missing: 07/16/58-a.m., Strabane, PA
Age at disappearance: 6 years

I continue to be astonished at the distances it is claimed that some small children cover when they are lost. It challenges your belief system, and the facts supported by search and rescue guidelines. This is another one of those cases.

Strabane is located approximately fifteen miles south of Pittsburgh in a hilly and rural area. On July 16, 1958, in the morning hours, six-year-old Robert Haughney wandered away from his family's rural home. His parents quickly realized the boy had vanished and notified neighbors and law enforcement. A July 17, 1958, article in the *Perryopolis Junction* provided these details about the search: "Robert Houghney, 6, was found Wednesday night about 20 miles from his Strabane home after a search party which grew to 400 men had looked for him since mid-morning. Robert was found walking along a highway at Lone Pine, Washington County, by Charles R. Helmick, who didn't know the boy was lost but thought it was strange he was walking along the road."

The article states that the police debriefed the boy, but the content of the interview wasn't divulged, and there were no follow-up stories about the event, meaning law enforcement did not believe a crime had been committed.

If Robert went missing midmorning and was found at night, it means the boy couldn't have been gone more than twelve hours, meaning he was covering almost 1.5 miles per hour while he was missing. The area between the boy's home and where he was located is very hilly and rough country. It would be hard to imagine that the boy hadn't seen other cars or homes before seeing Helmick, if he was looking for assistance. I can't believe the boy traversed twenty miles of mountains and hills in the time he had to travel.

According to Robert Koester's book, *Lost Person Behavior*, a lost child between the ages of four and six will be found 95 percent of the time in mountain terrain within 2.3 miles or less.

This story is an ongoing legacy of very strange disappearances in Pennsylvania.

South Carolina

Sex/Name	Date Missing • Age • State
F-Tina Lucas	03/01/79-11:30 a.m. • 4 • Sumter, SC
M-Stephen Oleszczuk	10/03/81-3:55 p.m. • 4 • North Charleston, SC

Tina Lucas
Missing: 03/01/79-11:30 a.m., Sumter, SC
Age at disappearance: 4 years

Readers regularly e-mail us asking if there are missing person cases that occur on or near military bases. I have written about a few over the years; this is another.

Mrs. Olga Lucas was standing at her kitchen window watching her four-year-old daughter, Tina, playing in the front yard with the family's three dogs. A March 2, 1979, article in the *Sumter Daily* had a statement from Mrs. Lucas about how quickly the girl vanished: "'It wasn't even two seconds and she was gone. She's the kind of child who wouldn't answer when you call her,' Tina's mother said." Imagine, you look down from the kitchen window and look up two seconds later, and the dogs and your daughter are gone.

The family lived at 5424 Glen Street in Sumter. The residence is across from a creek and swamp and within one quarter mile of Shaw Air Force Base.

Tina's mom and brother immediately got into their car and started to drive the neighborhood looking for the girl and the dogs. They cruised for an hour and then called the local sheriff. The sheriff called for motorcycles, equestrians, and volunteers to search the area around the home. Four hours of intensive search efforts proved futile. The sheriff now placed a call into the air force base for a helicopter to assist.

The 703rd Tactical Air Support Squadron took to the sky in a CH-3 helicopter. Twenty minutes into their search, the team found the girl lying on the ground with her dogs nearby. The team landed and loaded Tina into the chopper for the short trip back to the base. Tina was found to be very wet and missing both her shoes.

Later in the same *Sumpter Daily* article was this quote from law enforcement: "Sheriff I. Byrd Parnell said Tina had braved some rugged woods before the Shaw helicopter spotted her. 'That gal's something. Part of the terrain she had been over men found it hard to get through. The later it got, the more concerned we got,' Parnell said."

Mrs. Lucas was interviewed about the family ordeal. She stated that she had never been so scared and worried that Tina had drowned or had been kidnapped.

Summary

Keep this case in your mind for how quickly Tina vanished. She was found to be wet and missing both shoes. The sheriff specifically made a comment about how rugged and difficult the terrain was for his men to cover. These are all important points in the overall spectrum of this book.

Stephen Oleszczuk
Missing: 10/03/81-3:55 p.m., North Charleston, SC
Age at disappearance: 4 years

Gerard and Becky Oleszczuk were living in the Pepperidge Apartments on the outskirts of North Charleston with their four-year-old son, Stephen. On October 3, 1981, Becky and Stephen were washing the family car. At approximately 3:55 p.m., Stephen told his mom that he was hungry. Becky went in the house, telling Stephen she would fix him something and she'd be right back out. Minutes after going into the residence, Becky was back out at the car, and Stephen was gone. She searched the area, yelling his name and looking in the woods and seeing nothing. Becky called the Dorchester County sheriff.

The sheriff got the community involved with local firefighters and emergency workers participating in the search. The sheriff drew a grid pattern starting near the residence and moving outward. Becky stated that nobody had been in the area when the boy was washing the car.

Just after 3:00 p.m. on October 4, a teenage neighbor, Seth Aldrich, was walking in the woods behind the victim's residence one quarter mile away when he found the boy lying on his side covered by a few branches. He was dead. The *Chronicle Telegram* interviewed law enforcement officials on October 5 about the location of the body: "About 100 rescuers including deputies, firemen, volunteers and friends searched the area three times Saturday night and Sunday morning without finding a trace of the boy." In the same article, Becky was interviewed: "'He is not a wanderer and has never done anything like this before, and I get along with him extremely well,' the child's mother said. 'He also was starving because we didn't have lunch and were going to have an early dinner. I really think he was picked up.'"

Sheriff's officials stated that Stephen's clothes were intact and did not appear to have been altered. Becky stated he was wearing the same clothes as when he was last seen. The sheriff stated that Stephen may have been lying on the ground and instinctively pulled braches onto him when he turned onto his side. There were no obvious signs of injury other than scratches on his face. The body was viewed by coroner's officials, who stated that they could not immediately determine a cause of death; more tests and a complete autopsy were scheduled to be performed. I did an extensive archive search and could not find the final autopsy results. It did get into the mid-forties the night Stephen was missing.

The sheriff stated in several articles that this was a "borderline" case. I believe the sheriff thought that Stephen somehow arrived at the location where he was found after the area was searched, and that was the confusion. There are many cases where small kids disappear only later to be found in an area that had been searched many times.

Tennessee

Sex/Name	Date Missing • Age • State
M-Henry Yarbrough	05/21/58-Noon • 2 • Jasper, TN

Henry Yarbrough
Missing: 05/21/58-Noon, Jasper, TN
Age at disappearance: 2 years

Jasper is located almost at the exact border junction of Alabama, Georgia, and Tennessee. It is a rural location with thick woods and marshes surrounding the region. There was some confusion about the boy's age; some articles stated he was two, and others stated three.

On May 21, 1958, at noon, Henry Yarbrough disappeared from his family's yard. His dad was away at the coal mines, and his mom was in the residence. When she came outside yelling for the boy, he did not answer.

The Marion County sheriff was placed in charge of the effort to find Henry. The sheriff gathered three hundred volunteers and National Guard personnel, who covered the forest yelling and calling the boy's name. Local pilots took to the sky and were also looking for the boy.

After three days of wandering the woods, Henry walked into a neighbor's yard. The sheriff gave an interview about the incident to the *Miami News* on May 26, 1958: "'The boy is old enough to talk but he couldn't tell the sheriff much about what happened to him,' Squire H.B. Killian said yesterday. 'He was lost in one of the worst looking jungles I have ever seen.'" Killian later stated that many of the searchers had given up, believing the boy couldn't live through the conditions and temperatures that existed.

I find this story interesting because Henry never said anything about what happened to him, a common trait of kids who have vanished.

Why didn't Henry answer any one of the hundreds of searchers who were calling for him?

Texas

Sex/Name	Date Missing • Age • State
M-Kevin Brown	09/21/06-Unk • 2½ • Alvarado, TX

Kevin Brown
Missing: 09/21/06-Unk • 2 • Alvarado, TX
Age at disappearance: 2½ years

Alvarado is located twenty miles south of Fort Worth in an area of hundreds of small bodies of water and swamps. Much of the area near the water sources is thick with lush vegetation and significant wildlife.

On September 21, 2006, Kevin Brown was playing in the front yard of his residence with his brother. His brother was bitten by a fire ant and entered the house to get aid. The brother and mother were in the residence approximately fifteen minutes. When they returned to the yard, they could not locate Kevin. They searched the area and called for Kevin but did not get an answer. It was at this point that the Johnson County sheriff's office was called, and they responded in force.

The search for Kevin was in its second day when Kevin's mom gave an interview to the *Fort Worth Star Telegram* on September 23, 2006: "Kevin Brown's parents asked the public for help, saying they are sure the boy was abducted. '"There's no words to explain the pain that I've been going through,' said his mother Karla Brown. 'Please all mothers out there, help me find my son.'" You can feel the pain that Karla was experiencing.

The search for Kevin was about to enter the seventieth hour when something miraculous happened, as is explained in the September 30, 2006, *Eugene Register*: "When a helicopter pilot spotted Kevin on Sunday night, the boy was nearly a mile from his home. Kevin was lying on his stomach at the edge of a pond as if he had been drinking, and the co-pilot jumped out, scooped him up and flew him to the hospital. 'This little fellow was gone 69 hours and 15 minutes. There's no way he should have been alive,' Johnson County Sheriff Bob Alford said." An interesting fact associated with the helicopter flight: this was the last effort the helicopter crew was making to find Kevin.

The sheriff was later interviewed about the facts surrounding the case and stated that he really didn't think the boy was abducted; he just walked off and was able to elude searchers. Kevin was treated for dehydration, minor cuts, and insect bites. Searchers did state that thunderstorms hit the area during the search and had no doubt scared the child. They also said that Kevin was lucky that he never encountered any of the coyotes, rattlesnakes, and bobcats that roamed the area of Alavarado.

It's hard to imagine that Kevin was in the area where he was found for sixty-nine hours. I don't believe that the searchers missed the boy if he was inside a one-mile radius of his residence. I do believe that parents have a sixth sense regarding their children. When Karla Brown stated that she believed her son was abducted, maybe we should've listened.

Utah

Sex/Name	Date Missing • Age • State
M-Reed Jeppson	10/11/64-1:00 p.m. • 15 • Salt Lake City, UT
M-Jerry Duran	07/24/13-4:00 p.m. • 21 • Hardware Ranch, UT

Reed Taylor Jeppson
Missing: 10/11/64-1:00 p.m., Salt Lake City, UT
Age at disappearance: 15 years

The location of the Jeppson disappearance was at the far eastern end of Salt Lake City up a road now called Emigration Canyon. This is a very steep and rugged mountain area, called the foothills.

On Sunday, October 11, Reed went with his mom and dad and eleven brothers and sisters to church and Sunday school. At approximately 12:45 Reed got home and went to his room, where he changed clothes, and then he went two hundred yards away from the main house to feed his two German shorthair pointers, one full grown and one a puppy. Reed loved the outdoors and training his dogs. This specific weekend had been good to Reed. Just a couple days earlier, Reed had scored the first touchdown for his Eastern High School sophomore football team.

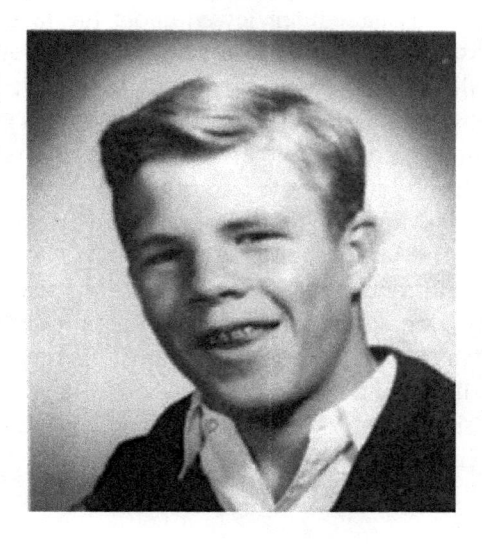

Reed left his wallet and valuables in his room when he went to the dogs. There were a variety of people who saw Reed after he fed the dogs. One person saw him walking the canines on the street toward the foothills, and another saw him in the hills above St. Mary of the Wasatch. According to the Utah Historical Society website *http://content.lib.utah.edu/cdm/ref/collection/,* here is a description of the location: "St. Mary of the Wasatch was an all-girls college funded by the Catholic Church and located on the east foothills of the Wasatch Mountains in Salt Lake City at approximately 1300 South. The school opened in 1926 and was demolished in 1972." There is an excellent photo on the website of the school and mountains. Reed was last seen in the mountains behind the school with his two dogs.

There was a massive search for Reed in which they found nothing of Reed or his dogs. In 2010 Reed's case got some life when his brothers and sisters worked with Salt Lake City police to publicize the disappearance. A May 25, 2010, article in the *Deseret News* had the following statement from one of Reed's sisters about what the family believes happened: "'He was taken against his will,' said his sister, Suzanne Tate."

Searchers tried again to find Reed in April 1965. Hard rain hit the area, and the search was suspended twice. In October 1965 the Salt Lake City police asked hunters in the area of Reed's disappearance to keep their eyes opened for any possible evidence. Nothing related to Reed Jeppson was ever found.

I know that some readers have keyed on the religious background of the victims and their families. I found one element about this quite coincidental to another case in this book, the Colorado disappearance of Bobby Bizup. Bobby was attending a Catholic summer camp when he vanished in the mountains behind the main buildings. You can read about the Bizup disappearance in the Colorado section. Reed disappeared in the mountains behind St. Mary of the Wasatch.

The Reed Taylor Jeppson case is the oldest active missing person case on the Salt Lake City police department's books.

Jerry Duran
Missing: 07/24/13-4:00 p.m., Hardware Ranch, UT
Age at disappearance: 21 years

Hardware Ranch is in Cache County near the Uinta-Wasatch-Cache National Forest in the far northeastern portion of the state. The closest major city is Logan, approximately ten miles west. The mountains in this area are steep and rugged and rise up to eight thousand feet in elevation.

On July 23, 2013, Jerry Duran had been camping with a large family group in the "Six Bit" area of the forest thirteen miles southeast of Hardware Ranch. At approximately 4:00 p.m., his family members realized Jerry had vanished, and a search was made that lasted several hours. After they failed to find the man, the Cache County sheriff was called. The deputies were dispatched at 3:00 a.m. and the formal search was started at 6:00 a.m.

The deputies had no idea where Jerry would go or what had prompted him to leave. An article published on July 25, 2013, on the website *http://news.hjnews.com* had the following information about Jerry: "The man, 21-year old Jerry Duran, has diminished mental capacity due to a previous traumatic brain injury, according to Cache County Sheriff's deputy Brad Slater. Duran functions on the level of a 7-year old child. Slater said the brain injury most likely altered Duran's ability to navigate through mountain terrain."

Later in the same article was information about how Jerry was eventually found: "Duran was found 10 to 15 miles away from the original camping spot along Ant Flat Road. Detectives en route to work on the case found him near the end of the road." Later in the same article was this: "Sheriff's officials say Duran has some difficulty communicating and couldn't explain about his time alone, He was missing some clothing when found."

For Jerry to travel fifteen miles in extremely rough mountain terrain in twenty-four hours is hard to understand. Since he can't explain what happened to him, we will never know the true facts about his journey and how he spent those hours.

Virginia

Sex/Name	Date/Time Missing • Age • State
F-Doris Dean	5/17/43-p.m. • 4 • Shenandoah National Park, VA
M-Brandon Beard	10/06/55-9:00 a.m. • 2 • Craigsville, VA
F-Letisha Faust	12/09/09-Unk • 50 • Franklin CO, VA

Doris Dean
Missing: 5/17/43-p.m. • 4 • Shenandoah National Park, VA
Age at disappearance: 4 years

When we imagine a national park, we tend to first think of isolation and serenity. Imagine finding those two factors just seventy-five miles west of Washington, DC, and that's where you'll find Shenandoah National Park. It's famous for its serene paths along Skyline Drive through the woods. It has two hundred thousand protected acres home to abundant wildlife and waterfalls.

The Dean family lived on the western edge of the park in a rural ranch where they had cows and other animals. On the afternoon of May 17, 1943, Doris followed her two brothers (nine and eleven years old) out to the pasture to get one of their cows. The boys walked into the pasture and grabbed the cow, expecting Doris to follow them home. She didn't. They arrived at their residence and realized she hadn't been following them.

The search for the young girl started quickly, and hundreds of locals participated. Sheriff Sam Callender led the search effort and made this statement in a May 19, 1943, article in the *Free Lance-Star*: "He said the widespread search for the missing child had exhausted her original volunteers that have numbered in the beginning 150 men, including 36 men from the government conscientious objectors camp at Grottoes." The countryside was so rugged, the volunteers became exhausted looking for the girl, and they got reinforcements. This was just after two days.

Forest rangers participated in the effort to locate Doris. All indications were that the girl had headed straight into Shenandoah National Park. Five days after she disappeared, twelve hundred persons were now involved in the search along with a Virginia Protective Force Company (not sure what that is). On May 22, 1943, Doris was found in a very hard-to-get-to location as is described in a May 23, 1943, article in the *Sunday Times Signal*: "Forest Rangers who directed a systematic search from maps of the area said she appeared to have moved doggedly toward the top of the Blue Ridge covering about five miles up the steep, rocky mountainside." She was located alive and taken by a stretcher for several miles to an ambulance.

Summary

Physicians examined Doris and stated that she had pneumonia and suffered from exposure, dehydration, and starvation. She survived.

The elevation of the Dean residence was 1,200 feet. The elevation where she was located was 2,400 feet. She had traveled up extremely steep and rugged boulder fields to reach a location very near Skyline Drive and the summit of that range.

If you believe in coincidences, the disappearance of Brandon Beard in this chapter occurred just fifty miles southwest and twelve years later than the Dean case.

Brandon Beard
Missing: 10/06/55-9:00 a.m., Craigsville, VA
Age at disappearance: 2 years

This story is about one of the few black children that fit the profile of the study. This is also another incident where a child disappears while visiting a friend or relative. Brandon lived in Baltimore with his mom and dad. His mother was a teacher and had left him with her mother in Craigsville, Virginia.

The tiny town of Craigsville sits fifteen miles east of the West Virginia border and adjacent to the Blue Mountains and between the George Washington National Forest and the Lesene State Forest. This region has very lush and thick forests and many water sources.

On October 6, 1955, at 9:00 a.m., Mrs. Fannie Beard (Brandon's grandmother) put him in his crib with his bottle for a nap. After carefully putting the child down, she went outside to work in the garden. After a short period of time (actual time not known), Fannie came back into the house to check on the boy and found he and the bottle were gone. She checked the home and the yard, and, upon failing to locate the baby, she called for assistance.

Searchers combed the yard and the surrounding woods for several hours without finding a clue. The boy's parents were notified and were en route to Virginia to assist in the search.

At approximately 4:00 p.m., searchers found Brandon in a dry creek bed four miles from his crib. He was still clutching his empty bottle. He somehow had lost his pajama bottoms and was found in bare feet. He was taken back to his grandmother's house and determined to be in excellent health except for a small sliver in one foot.

Summary

Two-year-old Brandon Beard walked four miles while carrying a bottle in less than seven hours. This was through mountain country while barefoot. He somehow managed to crawl out of his crib carrying his bottle, open the door to his grandmother's home, and escape through the yard without being seen. Does this seem believable? Would a two-year-old child continue to carry a bottle hours after it was empty?

Missing children fitting the criteria of this study are often found in dry creek beds. Brandon was too young to explain what happened during his journey.

Letisha Marie Faust
Missing: 12/09/09, Franklin CO, VA
Age at disappearance: 50 years

The facts surrounding this story are very similar to the disappearance of Emma Campbell in the outskirts of Christchurch, New Zealand, in May 2010. Refer to the New Zealand chapter for details.

Letisha Faust was a fifty-year-old woman living in Patrick County, Virginia. She was a graduate of the University of North Carolina and a longtime pharmaceutical sales representative. She was considered to be very well read and had a close relationship with her mother.

On December 9, 2009, Letisha drove her 1994 Honda Accord into Floyd County to shop at their pharmacy. After the shopping was completed, she called her mother and said that she was coming home. When Letisha hadn't returned to her mother's residence by late that night, her mom called the sheriff and reported her as a missing person.

There was no activity on the search until the Honda was located off the Blue Ridge Parkway on a remote section of Walnut Ridge Drive in Endicott in Franklin County. The car was found with its window rolled down and snow inside the car. It was parked adjacent to an abandoned home. The Franklin County sheriff's department realized the vehicle belonged to a reported missing person and started to search. Teams found Faust's purse, money, and purchased food inside the vehicle.

Search teams with canines found one of Letisha's sandals between her vehicle and a half-acre pond on the property. Rescue teams focused on the pond and did three different dives and a fourth using robotic cameras. Walnut Ridge Drive extends out to a point with steep drops-off each side. This is the highest point in the immediate area with an elevation of 2,400 to 2,800 feet. There were four different searches conducted, and only the sandal was found. Letisha's mom identified the footwear as belonging to her daughter.

Freezing rain and snow hampered search efforts from the beginning. After four comprehensive searches with multiple canine teams, divers, and planes, the sheriff called off the effort until the weather improved.

Authorities made several statements that they were not sure what happened to Faust and did not know if foul play was involved.

On March 21, 2010, there was an additional search of the area where Letisha's vehicle was found. There were conflicting stories as to how her body was located. One article indicated canines found it in a deep ravine 350 yards from the car; others stated a two-man team found the body. The sheriff's team processed the body for four hours and stated that it was identified through dental charts. A July 12, 2010, article in the *Franklin News Post* had the following details of the autopsy: "A Roanoke medical examiner has been unable to determine the cause of death for Letisha Marie Faust, whose body was found in May at Walnut Ridge." The inability to determine a cause of death is a common element in many of the missing person cases we research.

Letisha's mother was interviewed by various news organizations in regard to her daughter's disappearance. She stated that Letisha had no reason to be in the area where she disappeared, as she knew nobody who lived in the remote region.

Summary

I want readers to familiarize themselves with the disappearance of Emma Campbell, New Zealand. Emma also went missing at a high point on a street in a remote area. Her car was off the side of the road, and her shoes were found near the car. In both Letisha and Emma's cases, searchers had gone through the areas multiple times and could not locate a body. Twenty-two months after Emma vanished, her body was found 328 feet from her car. Letisha's body was found 350 yards from hers.

There is one clue in Letisha's disappearance that can't be ignored: the open window. The weather in December in this area of Virginia is very cold. We must ask ourselves why a woman would roll her window down just before exiting her vehicle. I know Honda Accords quite well. I used to own one. The visibility outside the car is very good, and the inside of the car is quiet. If Letisha had seen something outside the vehicle and driven to the point to observe it, maybe she rolled down the window to see if she could hear it.

The question that needs to be answered in both Emma's and Letisha's cases: Why did the women exit their cars, and why didn't law enforcement locate them in a timelier manner? The inability of the medical examiner to determine a cause of death is a recurring theme in the cases we investigate. Why are these people dying?

Washington

Sex/Name	Date Missing • Age • State
M-Julius Bakken	11/09/31-Noon • 21 • Wenatchee, WA
M-Jackie Helman	01/02/41-3:00 p.m. • 6 • Badger Pocket, WA
M-Joe Carter	05/21/50-3:00 p.m. • 32 • Mount St. Helens, WA
F-Joyce Abel	10/16/54-1:00 p.m. • 5 • Okanogan, WA
M-David Adams	05/03/68-5:00 p.m. • 8 • Tiger Mtn, Issaquah, WA
M-Donald G. Siskar	07/10/73-3:30 p.m. • 18 • Grass Mountain, WA
M-Stefan Bissert	01/20/92-p.m. • 23 • Olympic National Park
F-Paige Adriance	07/03/92-3:00 p.m. • 8 • Boardman Lake, WA
M-Bill McKinnon	02/14/93-p.m. • 28 • Church Mountain, WA
M-John Devine	09/06/97-2:00 p.m. • 73 • Olympic National Park
M-Zachary Weston	08/10/05-Unk • 22 • Mount Rainier National Park
M-Gilbert Mark Gilman	06/24/06-Unk • 47 • Olympic National Park
F-Hildegard Hendrickson	06/08/13-5:00 p.m. • 79 • Wenatchee Lake, WA
M-Bryan Lee Johnston	08/28/13-Unk • 71 • Olympic National Park, WA

Julius Bakken
Missing: 11/09/31-Noon, Wenatchee, WA
Age at disappearance: 21 years

This is another case of people vanishing around the Wenatchee Lake area. Julius went to the area with four other friends to hunt near Fish Lake, just one mile north of Wenatchee Lake. On November 9, the group decided to split up and meet back at noon. Julius never made the meeting, and law enforcement was called.

Snow was falling on November 9 and continued to cover tracks in the area over the next several days. Searchers spent two days searching the Fish Lake area and then moved their efforts just north to an area called Meadow Creek. Bloodhounds were used in both locations, and no scent of Julius was ever found. The last place his companions saw Julius was on Pole Ridge, just one mile from Fish Lake.

Search efforts continued for ten days, and they never found anything confirming Julius was in the region. The last article I found was published on November 19, and it confirmed that the search was being terminated. I could not find any other articles ever stating that his body was found.

The area around Wenatchee Lake is one of the strangest locations in North America for missing people. Three of my four books on missing people have notes about this region. I would consider Wenatchee Lake to be one of the major hot spots in North America for missing people over the last century.

Jackie Helman
Missing: 01/02/41-3:00 p.m., Badger Pocket, WA
Age at disappearance: 6 years

The Helman family lived in a rural home on the outskirts of Badger Pocket. This is a small city five miles southeast of Ellensburg and fifteen miles north of Yakima. The town is near the end of a small valley surrounded by large mountains.

At 3:00 p.m. on January 2, 1941, Jackie was in his backyard playing with a BB gun he had received as a Christmas present. He told his family that he had seen a pheasant and was going after it. This was the last they saw of the boy that day. The parents looked for him shortly after he made his statement, but he had vanished. His stepfather took a lantern and started to search the area around the home and the hills until his light went out. A call was made for local volunteer searchers, and the local sheriff was contacted.

Almost fifty searchers followed Squaw Creek through the mountains thinking they were following a smeared track. A January 3, 1941, article in the *Ellensburg Daily Record* described what searchers were following: "His feet dragged through the snow and the tracks wobbled from side to side." When I read this description, it reminded me of someone being dragged. Searchers never mentioned any tracks belonging to Jackie's two dogs and puppy that left with him. They also stated that they had problems following his trail, as they would lose it when the tracks left the snow.

Early on January 3, searchers made an amazing discovery as is stated in the same newspaper cited above: "Curled up in the snow under a greasewood tree on Squaw Creek, nearly eight miles away from his Badger Pocket home, little six year old Jackie Helman was found shortly after midnight last night by searchers who had followed his tracks for hours over the southeast rim of the valley." The article stated that Jackie was asleep and curled up with his puppy. He had taken off his coat and put it around his dog. The searchers stated his body was so warm that it had melted the snow around his body. Jackie was not able to walk and was carried on horseback back to his home.

The article never stated what happened to the BB gun.

Summary

This is a classic story of a disappearance with the same elements that have been described dozens of times in past books. In Robert Koester's book, *Lost Person Behavior*, he states that a four- to six-year-old child will be found in mountain terrain within 2.3 miles or less. Jackie was found eight miles away, and from the statements in the paper, he had walked up and over the rim in the valley. Many of my stories describe children who disappear with their dog. Jackie took three. Even though it was a frigid January night, Jackie was so warm that he removed his coat and then his body heat melted the snow around the body. Many of my cases indicate the child is found with a fever, thus high body heat. There was no mention of a fever in this case, but obviously his body was hot.

Jackie allegedly covered eight mountain miles uphill in less than nine hours, a phenomenal pace for an in-shape adult.

Joe Carter
Missing: 05/21/50-3:00 p.m., Mount St. Helens, WA
Age at disappearance: 32 years

Mount St. Helens has a long history of unusual occurrences going back over a century. The last time the mountain made international headlines was on May 18, 1980, when it erupted. Fifty-seven people were killed during the eruption, including the innkeeper of the famous Spirit Lake Lodge. Mount St. Helens is classified as a United States National Monument and is under the direction of the National Park Service.

This is another case of a disappearance involving a man who should never have vanished. Joe Carter had gone with a group of friends to climb Mount St. Helens on May 21, 1950. The group had brought their skis with the intention of climbing a portion of the mountain and skiing down. Joe had gone with a group of twenty climbers and brought his camera. As the group reached the point of skiing, Joe told them he would go down the hill and around a small corner and take photos as the group passed him.

Joe was a smart man and not your average skier. He was an employee of Boeing during the week and a member of the National Ski Patrol working at Milwaukee Bowl during the weekends. For readers who do not know, the National Ski Patrol has a high standard for acceptance. The testing is rigorous; you must be an outstanding skier with the ability to ski in control while pulling a three-hundred-pound toboggan and an injured party. Each National Ski Patrol member is dedicated to saving lives and treating injuries, and all have advanced first-aid training. Joe was well trained, a great skier, and knew the mountain's risks.

Joe had skied away from the main party and made a slight left-hand turn out of view. He set up to take the photos and somehow disappeared. People who later went to the spot found a discarded film box at the point where he had stopped. The location where the box was found is called "Dog's Head."

Skiers went around the corner and found that Joe was not there, and they continued down the mountain. The group believed that the National Ski Patrol member had gone on to the bottom and they would see him there. When the group reached the bottom, Joe never arrived, and they called for search and rescue (SAR).

One of the first SAR teams on Mount St. Helens looking for Joe was the Seattle Mountain Search and Rescue team with Dr. Otto Trott and Lee Stark. An August 1963 article in the *Longview Washington Times* had the following description of what searchers found on the mountain at the point where the film box was found: "From here, Carter evidently took off down the mountain in a wild death-defying dash, 'taking chances that no skier of his caliber would take, unless something was terribly wrong or he was being pursued,' says Lee, who was the first searcher to reach Carter's ski tracks. He jumped over two-three large crevasses and evidently was going like the devil. When Carter's tracks reached the precipitous sides of Ape Canyon, the searchers were amazed to see that Carter had been in such a hurry that he went right down the steep canyon walls. But they did not find him at the bottom of the canyon as they expected. 'We combed the canyon, one end to the other for five days.'"

There is no doubt that Joe Carter was acting in a very, very strange manner and skiing completely outside the bounds of any sane mountaineer; it appears as though he was skiing for his life. There were never any other tracks that were noted in the snow other than Joe's ski tracks. If the perceived threat to Joe wasn't coming from the ground (no tracks), that only leaves the threat being in the air.

In the same *Longview Times* article were the feelings expressed by searcher Lee while he was looking for Joe: "He said that every time he got cut off from the rest of the searchers during the long hunt, he got the feeling that 'somebody was watching me.'"

There was a ten-day search for Joe Carter; he was never found. There were some discrepancies in stories written about the incident. Some accounts stated that Joe skied straight off the end of the cliff, and others stated that the ski tracks stopped at the cliff and footprints were found going over the end. Neither scenario makes any sense.

Joe did have medical issues: he was diabetic and did not have insulin with him the day he vanished. He got separated from his group above the timberline and then got out of their view. He was a highly trained, advanced skier who should never have suffered the fate he did.

Summary

Mount St. Helens has history as a location of many strange stories and incidents. I won't mention them all here. Some of the people involved in the search for Joe Carter mentioned that they felt strange while they were looking for the man, an unusual statement for searchers to make. It is a bit of a coincidence that Joe was the designated photographer. Many photographers have vanished in the woods of North America. If Joe was injured and fell into the canyon, searchers should've found his camera, skis, poles, etc. Nothing was found. The statement that Joe was making a "death defying" run down the slopes is an interesting theory that should be taken seriously. Joe was not erratic; in fact, he was very stable. We must ask ourselves: What would cause you or me to ski straight down the side of a snow-covered volcano, knowing that whatever is at the bottom can't be as scary as what's behind us?

Joyce Abel
Missing 10/16/54-1:00 p.m., Okanogan, WA
Age at disappearance: 5 years

This incident occurred on the perimeter of the Colville Indian Reservation, a location of high strangeness over the years. The exact location is stated as twelve miles south of Okanogan in a very rural location. One newspaper article states that Joyce Abel disappeared from her grandmother's ranch, and another states the ranch belonged to her mom and dad. There is no conflict, however, in that this was a very rural ranch.

In the early afternoon of October 16, 1954, Joyce Abel somehow and for an unknown reason walked away from a rural location. The ranch can be better described as sixty miles northeast of Wenatchee

Lake, a place that readers would know well from other narratives about missing people.

An October 18, 1954, article in the *Reading Eagle* had this description of Joyce's trip: "A hardy 5-year old girl who sheriff's officers said walked 20 miles in 20 hours through the wilds of north central Washington wandered safely into a ranch yard 50 miles north of here yesterday as an army of men sought a trace of her." The article clearly states that searchers could not find any trace of the girl, and yet she was able to wander aimlessly and find a ranch in the middle of nowhere. Hiking twenty miles in twenty hours across a wild landscape would be a huge feat for a healthy adult. The idea that a five-year-old girl could manage this mileage is mind-boggling.

There was some discrepancy in the distance that Joyce covered. A farmhand from the ranch where Joyce disappeared had been attempting to track the girl when she wandered into another farm. He stated it was his belief that she had traveled eight miles from point to point, meaning she traveled eight air miles. People who hike in the woods know that there are no straight trails. Animal paths and trails meander. People in search and rescue know that lost children don't walk in straight lines; they wander based on the landscape. Water hazards and grades and inclines all come into play on how the child moves forward.

There can be no argument that Joyce made a very long trip in a very short period of time. According to the book *Lost Person Behavior* by Robert Koester, a child between the ages of four and six should be found 95 percent of the time in a mountain setting within 3.7 miles or less from the point they were last seen. Joyce Abel's trip is beyond the realm of any search and rescue guidelines.

David Adams
Missing 05/03/68-5:00 p.m., Tiger Mountain, Issaquah, WA
Age at disappearance: 8 years

Issaquah is a small community approximately ten miles southeast from Seattle and fifty miles southwest of Wenatchee Lake. Just twenty miles east of the city is a thickly wooded forest area with hundreds of small lakes and streams. The city of Issaquah has approximately thirty thousand residents with many more just outside its perimeter. One of those areas just to the southeast is a gorgeous 2,600-foot-high hill called Tiger Mountain. There are only a handful of roads that crisscross this area, and some of the mountain is still quite desolate. The area to the east of the mountain is very thick with lush woods and very few residents.

The Adams family had scouted much of Washington before deciding on Tiger Mountain as the location where they would build their dream house. In mid-April 1968, the Adamses and their family of seven moved into their home. Mrs. Adams was a stay-at-home mom, and Donald Adams was a captain in the United States Air Force reserve unit assigned to McChord Air Force Base near Tacoma. Donald had just been called to active duty because of the seizure of the USS *Pueblo*.

David's family was part of the religious community of Latter Day Saints. David made quick friends at church and at school. You could quickly recognize the eight-year-old by his vibrant blue eyes against his dark hair. In the late afternoon of May 3, 1968, David was visiting the home of his friend, Kevin Bryce. The Bryce residence was also on Tiger Mountain, and the boys had become quick friends. It was about 5:00 p.m. when Mrs. Adams called the Bryce household and asked them to send David home for supper. Kevin walked David down one of the small roads on the mountain and crossed a bridge at 15-Mile Creek. David stated that he was going to take a shortcut on a trail through the mountains and come up behind his home. Kevin said good-bye and walked back home. He was the last person to ever see David Adams.

Fifteen minutes after Mrs. Adams had called the Bryce residence, she called back again and asked if David had left. Mrs. Bryce looked at Kevin and asked if David was walking home; he stated he was stunned that David hadn't yet arrived. Mrs. Adams called a church member and asked for help looking for David. He in turn rallied one hundred other church members, and the mountain was crawling with people looking for the boy that first night.

The next morning King County investigators were at the Adams residence organizing additional searches and asking for more technical assistance.

A strange coincidence that we have found in many missing person cases is that the father is not at the residence when the child disappears. Mr. Adams was at Tinker Air Force Base in Oklahoma when David went missing. Once he heard about the incident, he was granted emergency leave and went back to Issaquah.

The search for David included over four thousand professional and volunteer searchers, an air force helicopter equipped with FLIR, Bloodhounds, and dozens of law enforcement veterans. It was a nonstop five-day effort that was halted when the involved believed that David was not on the mountain.

The thinking of most law enforcement in 1968 was that David was merely a missing person. This wasn't a location or a time when cops would immediately think about abduction by a pedophile. The mountains continued to be searched formally and informally; many of the searches were foot by foot.

There were many theories floated about what happened to David. There was a so-called "strange fellow" who was living on the mountain. The police did focus on him. There was some talk that he was given a polygraph near the time of the disappearance, and he might have failed it. The strange caveat to that: nobody can remember if he really took the test, as the results and the test are nowhere in the binders of documents associated with the case file.

Warren Kagarise was working for the *Issaquah Press* in 2009 and wrote a three-part series about this incident. On December 29,

2009, Walter released part three and addressed the canine search for David: "But the dogs like the searchers found nothing. Don Adams, now 77, recalled the follow-up visit from searchers after organizers called off the hunt for David. 'A few weeks later, they came back, and they said the dogs had never failed to find who they were looking for if who they were looking for was there,' he said. 'Based on that, I just assumed that somebody had taken him from the mountain.'" Later in the same article were a few statements from Mrs. Adams and her daughter, each of which I found fascinating: "'We've had a happy, good life,' Ann Adams said. 'Whoever was involved with this, I think I feel sorrier for them than I do for us. My life is just overflowing with good memories and happy days, but they must be carrying a terrible burden.'" The children biked, swam, hiked, and picked berries in the thick forest nearby. Still, questions about David remained. Jill Stephenson, the Adamses' oldest daughter, recalled how she walked through the woods as a child and wondered, "What if I came across him or his bones?"

The Adamses never moved from their residence and raised their family on the mountain. Yes, children roaming the mountain and picking berries with the concern they may find David's bones.

Summary

I truly admire the attitude and life outlook that Mrs. Adams was able to muster in a time of deep crisis. To move forward with your life and live with the daily reminder that your son disappeared on the mountain where you live shows strength of character.

I first looked at this case when I was initially starting to investigate missing people. I placed this file on the shelf and for some reason came back to it just recently. It wasn't until I started to understand the dynamics and elements associated with the missing did I understand how this case is relevant to the study.

Law enforcement and searchers eliminated any thoughts of an animal attack. David disappeared on a trail, not a roadway or even near a roadway. He was last seen crossing a bridge at a creek. Nearly four thousand searchers covered the mountain foot by foot, never finding any evidence of David being there. Bloodhounds could never find a scent. Helicopters with FLIR never found any heat signature. Air force and navy personnel along with specially trained search and rescue experts contributed countless hours to the effort to find David.

This is another one of the few cases I've found where the family had deeply religious roots and the father had strong ties to the military. I don't know if this is a significant element to these disappearances, but it is one that many of you have keyed on in the past.

This is another one of dozens of cases where a child disappears while visiting another person's home. It is also ironic that many kids disappear from the area of their new home after living in the area for only weeks. Many of these elements exist in the David Adams case.

I find many parallels between David Adams and Dennis Martin's disappearance in Great Smoky Mountain National Park (*Missing 411-Eastern United States* and the disappearance of Dennis Johnson at Yellowstone National Park (*Missing 411-Western United States*).

Name:	Dennis Johnson	David Adams	Dennis Lloyd Martin
Date Missing:	7/12/66	5/3/68	6/14/69
Time:	1:30 p.m.	5:00 p.m.	4:30 p.m.
Age:	8 years	8 years	6 years
Location:	Wooded area	Wooded area	Wooded area
Evidence:	None	None	None
Parents:	Living in same home	Living in same home	Living in same home
Disposition:	Case Open	Case Open	Case Open

The Martin and Johnson cases happened in national parks.

In all three cases, siblings were in the area of the disappearances. David's sisters were in his yard playing when he vanished, Dennis Martin's brother was playing with him when he disappeared, and Dennis Johnson's sister was in the woods with him when he was lost.

All the incidents occurred in the "magic hours" of disappearances, afternoon hours. In a very, very odd similarity, there was never any evidence found in any of the three cases.

It should be noted that the National Center for Missing and Exploited Children has case files on the Martin and Adams case.

The National Park Service has failed to send the information on Dennis Johnson to the agency, and the file doesn't exist.

I cannot begin to fathom the level of pain these families have endured. My prayers are with them daily.

M-Donald G. Siskar
Missing: 7/10/73-3:30 p.m., Grass Mountain, WA
Age at disappearance: 18 years

Grass Mountain is located just ten miles east of Enumclaw and four miles south of the Howard Hanson Reservoir. This area has very thick and lush forests and is part of the headwaters for the Green River.

The United States Forest Service (USFS) is the arm of the government that manages this area of the Snoqualmie National Forest. The USFS does not have the number of employees necessary to keep trails pristine and maintained, thus they contract with groups that go into the regions and do the work. On July 10, 1973, one of those contract groups, the Neighborhood Youth Corp (NYC), was clearing debris high up the north side of Grass Mountain. At approximately 2:00 p.m., the work group was ending its day and started to walk down the trail toward the bus.

Donald Siskar was part of the nine-member NYC team that started down the mountain. Donald was in the middle of the group on the trail when they came to a switchback and the guys at the back of the line cut through the woods to the front of the line; this put Donald at the back. The group was about one and three-quarters miles from the bus when Donald went to the rear.

Once the group got to the bus, the men boarded, and the bus started to head toward home. The bus driver didn't immediately realize that Donald was missing, but eventually he did. The bus driver returned to the trailhead, and two group workers went back up the trail to the point of the switchback but never found Donald. Another member stopped a USFS truck and had him take him to the top of the mountain with the possibility Donald went uphill, back to the site. He wasn't found. The USFS sent three rangers up the hill and then called for more assistance. It was now 6:30 p.m. The three rangers eventually returned and stated they found nothing.

The King County sheriff was called at 6:30 p.m. and took over as the primary law enforcement authority. The deputy determined that all of the men in the group were wearing work boots, but Donald was wearing cowboy boots. Searchers went up the trail to the switchback and attempted to find cowboy boot tracks, but they didn't.

The search for Donald was well organized and did have significant resources. Fifty-five ground searchers plus the USFS, the Boeing Company Amateur Radio Club, Explorer Scouts, the local ski patrol, 4x4 clubs, National Guard, German Shepherd Search Dogs of Washington, two helicopters, and multiple Bloodhound teams were on the mountain for seven days looking for Donald.

I have read thousands of search and rescue reports from hundreds of agencies. The missing person report I was presented by King County was one of the most comprehensive efforts I've ever read.

In March 2012 Detective Tom Jensen met with Donald's father at his residence. Jensen was attempting to get a DNA swab from the father to place into the national database should Donald be found. The swab was obtained, and Albert Siskar answered questions about his son's disappearance. In the case file report was the father's statement about the area where his son was working: "Albert said that he was at the search area and the terrain was extremely rugged." It was also stated: "He doesn't believe Donald left the area. He believes that Donald got lost and died and his body was never found because of the terrain."

Summary

It is difficult to understand how Donald could've gotten lost on the trail he was hiking. This path is very wide and clear of vegetation. I do not believe there is any chance that while he was following his group that he could've voluntarily wandered and been lost.

The man was wearing a silver hardhat, jeans, and cowboy boots. None of the clothing was ever found. Bloodhounds never picked up a scent. This was a very tough case because there were no leads.

In the dozens of missing person reports I've received from the National Park Service, I have never read about a NPS special agent conducting follow-up and obtaining a DNA swab from the victim's family members, ever.

You will find very little on the Internet about this case. Many of the supposed facts about this case that are on the Internet are incorrect. The information on this case was taken directly from the King County sheriff's reports.

Stefan Bissert
Missing 01/20/92-p.m., Olympic National Park, WA
Age at disappearance: 23 years

In the scope of this book you will read about a series of very intelligent young people who vanished, some never to be found. This is a story about a brilliant young man from Germany who was part of a foreign student exchange program between the University of Stuttgart and Oregon State University.

Olympic National Park is probably one of the biggest parks in the United States. The vast majority of it is never visited. The park has very rugged areas, an extremely diverse interior, and wildlife that would amaze the average visitor. There are trails in the park, but the majority of visitors are unwilling to pay the price to get to lonely locations of the interior. If you wanted to go to a national park and escape from crowds, I would head for Olympic.

Stefan Bissert was a physics major studying in Corvallis and visiting Olympic National Park with fellow German foreign exchange student Gerd Forstmann. The men had arrived at the park to hike the trails and enjoy the beauty. The pair had hiked from Soleduck to Deer Lake. They decided to separate as Bissert headed across the mountains to the Hoh River Valley and downhill to the Hoh Ranger Station. Stefan never arrived, and Gerd contacted local rangers.

The search for Stefan started quickly and was comprehensive. The second day into the effort to locate the hiker, snow started to fall and continued for several days. Helicopters took to the sky and found that the route Stefan had taken had had several avalanches. After six days and continual snowfall, the park services terminated their efforts to find the German national. On May 16, 1992, there was a secondary search for the man, which was completed after local snowmelt. Searchers still did not find any evidence of Stefan being on the mountain.

Stefan wasn't your average brilliant college student; he was a Fulbright Scholar. He wasn't studying just any normal college topic; he was a physics major. You are going to see that many brilliant people have vanished, and specifically, several of these people were involved in physics and two of the people specializing in physics were German. I find this a very, very strange coincidence.

Stefan's parents traveled to the United States and were on the scene during some of the search efforts. His body was never found.

Paige Adriance
Missing 07/03/92-3:00 p.m., Boardman Lake, WA
Age at disappearance: 8 years

Reid Adriance took his eight-year-old daughter Paige on a camping trip to an area approximately eighteen miles east of Granite Falls. At 3:00 p.m. Reid was hiking with his daughter on the Boardman Lake Trail when she decided she wanted to move faster and got ahead of him. After several hundred yards, Reid realized he could not find his daughter and started calling for her. He did not get a response. Reid went back to their campsite and called law enforcement for assistance.

The Seattle Mountain Search and Rescue group responded and started to look for the young girl. A July 6 article in the *Moscow-Pullman Daily News* reported the following: "Searchers worked until about midnight Friday, finding only the girl's pack, Woodall said. The search was halted at about 5pm because of heavy rain. Rain hampered the search Sunday, but crews of about 50 persevered until she was found." They located Paige at noon on Sunday, forty-five hours after she vanished. They located her in a steep valley near a creek, just one mile from their campsite.

Paige stated that she ate berries while she was lost. Searchers were interviewed about finding Paige and made the following statement (from the same article that was quoted earlier): "The girl was found in an area that had been previously searched, Woodall said."

Paige disappeared on a very well-established trail. There could be no mistake about where the trail went. Many children disappear when they are in front of or behind their parents, but out of sight. How could Paige have gotten so far from her dad that she couldn't hear his calls? How could searchers have missed her when they passed through the location where she was eventually found?

During the press conference, Paige dozed off several times. The Adriance family is very lucky to have their daughter back alive.

M-Bill McKinnon
Missing: 02/14/93-p.m., Church Mountain, WA
Age at disappearance: 28 years

The location of this disappearance is two miles south of the Canadian border, ten miles north of Mount Baker, one mile north of the Nooksack River, and just on the fringe of the North Cascades National Park. This is a very thick and lush area. Church Mountain has an approximate elevation of 6,200 feet.

Bill was a student at Western Washington University in Bellingham majoring in French. He and his roommate, Eric Hals, had planned a trip to the mountain pending good weather. On

February 14, 1993, Eric woke Bill and stated that they had the weather needed for a climb up the mountain. This was not a new effort for the pair; they had done it in past seasons. The roommates met a group at the trailhead, nearing two thousand feet in elevation, and started the climb to 4,200 feet. It was at this point the group encountered snow, and it appeared to get a lot deeper quickly. Bill realized that he wasn't dressed for that much snow and encouraged the group to go on, saying he'd wait.

The climbing group eventually made it back down to where they last saw Bill; he wasn't there. The group thought they'd find him at the parking lot; he wasn't there. It was at this point that people started to get worried, and phone calls were made. Late on that first night, Eric called law enforcement and reported Bill missing.

There was an extensive five-day search for Bill McKinnon that included SAR teams from Canada and the United States, army helicopters with FLIR, and canines. Searchers did find Bill's tracks heading up the trail to where he had separated from the group, but no tracks heading back downhill.

Bill was a smart and capable climber who had a high level of common sense, exampled by him deciding not to go further because he wasn't dressed appropriately.

During the five-day search, Bill's family conferred with a psychic, who stated that Bill was injured and in a location where you would not normally look. After hearing the psychic's report, SAR members looked everywhere within a two-mile radius where a person could hide; they found nothing.

During the search effort, it started to snow and continued to snow for the next three weeks, essentially terminating all search efforts.

Bill's family and law enforcement did consider the possibility of abduction. None of the possibilities of what happened to Bill made any sense. He wasn't going downhill—no tracks. He didn't go uphill any farther—no tracks. On May 8, 1993, the Whatcom County sheriff's office attempted one last search. They found nothing.

I did make a request to the Whatcom County sheriff's department for a copy of all reports associated with the disappearance of Bill McKinnon. Here was their response:

Dear Mr. Paulides,

I am writing this letter in reference to your public disclosure request of August 21 involving Mr. William McKinnon. Unfortunately, our records for that particular event have been purged and are no longer available.

Tara Tienhaara
Whatcom County Sheriff's Department

I followed this up with an e-mail inquiring why they would purge an active case file. Here is their response:

Hi Dave,

Per Washington State Retention Schedules, we did not retain this report. We keep reports for 5 years only. I am not aware of anywhere else you could obtain a copy of this report.

Tara Tienhaara
Whatcom County Sheriff's Office

Summary

If in fact the state of Washington only requires the retention of reports on active case files for five years, this is an abomination. How can a law enforcement agency throw away the facts behind someone's disappearance? Where is law enforcement's accountability? We might need federal legislation that requires all agencies to keep missing person reports until the individual is found.

John Devine
Missing 09/06/97-2:00 p.m., Olympic National Park, WA
Age at disappearance: 73 years

John Devine was a very experienced outdoorsman who regularly hiked the mountains. He would be classified as legally disabled, as he was blind in one eye.

On September 5, 1997, John was with his friend, Greg Blazer (46 years old). They established their camp in the Mount Baldy area of Olympic National Forest. On the afternoon of September 6, John left alone for a hike on the north end of the park along Gray Wolf Ridge with the intent to be back at his camp by early in the evening; he never returned.

Greg notified the National Park Service of his friend's failure to return, and a search was initiated. During the one-week search for John, there were five helicopters in the air, Civil Air Patrol planes, and four Bloodhound teams concentrating on an area between five thousand and seven thousand feet in elevation. John had snack bars and water when he vanished, but not overnight supplies. The weather was marginal at best during the search. Rain hit the search area for several days that the search was underway.

On Friday, September 12, a tragedy happened during the search. A Bell Helicopter 205-A1 with seven passengers aboard crashed at 4:00 p.m. near Olympic National Park, fifty miles west of Seattle, killing three and injuring several more. The chopper was from Heli-Jet in Eugene, Oregon, and on contract to the park service for search and rescue missions. It went down close to one of the landing zones near Mount Baldy in the Buckhorn Wilderness, just east of the park boundary. The helicopter went down in the area where John went missing.

A seven-day search did not find one piece of evidence that John Devine was in the park.

The helicopter crash and the death of three occupants was not an isolated incident in the realm of searching for people missing under unusual circumstances. There are several cases where aircraft has crashed, killing occupants in areas where there is high strangeness.

Zachary Weston
Missing: 08/10/05-Unk, Mount Rainier National Park, WA
Age at disappearance: 22 years

If we were to ever classify someone as an intellectual, Zachary Weston would fit the profile. He was a high school valedictorian; a senior at the Massachusetts Institute of Technology, majoring in aeronautics and aerospace engineering; and a scholar, poet, novelist, musician, and mountaineer. Zachary loved life and knew his way around both the mountains and textbooks.

On June 22, 2005, Zachary left alone for a long-planned hiking trip into Mount Rainier National Park. He had a significant history of hiking and enjoying the outdoors, and this trip was not outside his bounds. An August 14 article in the *Spokesman Review* had an explanation on how searchers started their trek to find Zachary: "Rangers began searching for Weston Friday [August 12], after his friend reported that he had not shown up to pick her up in Ashford. The car Weston was in was found parked at the Comet Falls Trailhead Thursday night."

The National Park Service knew the general area that Zachary had traveled and focused their efforts in the Van Trump Park and Kautz Glacier areas. The park service reported that they found tracks in these areas that matched the tread of Zachary's boots. An August 17, 2005, article in the *Seattle Times* had the following about where Zachary's tracks were lost: "They followed the boot prints along Wapowety Cleaver to an elevation of 10,000 feet 'at which point they petered out in the rocky terrain,' said Lee Taylor, a park spokeswoman."

The search for Zachary was terminated on August 20. An August 21 article in the *Record Journal* had the following statement from a park spokesperson: "The search for Zachary Weston at Mount Rainier National Park in Washington was called off Thursday night and the 22-year old city native is 'presumed dead,' said Lee Taylor, information officer for the park, said Friday afternoon. 'In a sense it means that we think the person is no longer alive, most likely,' Taylor said. 'We feel at this point, there is not much to be gained by further searching.'" I like the wording by the spokesperson: "most likely," meaning the weather hadn't been extreme, and he still could be. If he still could be alive, shouldn't they still be searching?

Readers need to understand, footprints and tracks don't last long at high altitudes on Mount Rainier because of the amount of precipitation the mountain annually receives. If they found tracks, they must've been fairly fresh. I'm surprised that they didn't make a longer effort to find Zachary. It seems very surprising they never found any of his camping equipment or a campsite. Where is all of his equipment, and where is Zachary?

Gilbert Mark Gilman
Missing: 06/24/06-Unk, Olympic National Park, WA
Age at disappearance: 47 years

When I speak about intellectuals who have disappeared under unusual circumstances, Gilbert Gilman may be near the top of the list in pure smarts. The last job that we know he held was deputy director of the State of Washington Retirement Fund. It is really Gilbert's past employment and history that resounds with intellect and intrigue.

Mr. Gilman was an army paratrooper, a psychological operations interrogator who was awarded two bronze stars. He had worked in Somalia for the United Nations and was a civilian contractor in Iraq. One of his former jobs also had him listed as working counterintelligence. He spoke five languages. He was not married but did have a girlfriend in Washington. One of his last jobs listed him as working for the Defense Intelligence Agency on counterintelligence related to weapons of mass destruction.

On June 24, 2006, Gilbert drove his 2005 silver Ford Thunderbird convertible to the Staircase Ranger Station in Olympic National Park near Hoodsport, Washington. As his car was parked in the lot and he was getting ready for a hike, he was playing his music loud—so loud that Ranger Sanny Lustig walked to the car and asked him to turn it down. He did. Gilbert exited the car wearing a bright green Hawaiian shirt, shorts, sandals, and no backpack. He carried a camera and was wearing prescription glasses. He was last seen walking down the trail.

Gilbert was supposed to meet a work colleague on June 25, a meeting that he never attended. His work colleague contacted authorities, and a search ensued. Law enforcement rangers found his car parked at the ranger station and found his dirty clothes in the backseat, as though he was going to the Laundromat.

There was a ten-day formal search for Gilbert that encompassed five thousand hours, Bloodhounds, helicopters, and underwater cameras that searched the deep holes in the creeks and rivers near the area he was visiting. Nothing was ever found indicating that Gilbert had been on the trails in the park. No hikers remembered seeing Gilman.

If this case strikes you as abnormal, you are correct—it struck the local sheriff's department the same way. A May 16, 2008, article on KIRO.com had the following statement regarding Thurston County Sheriff Dan Kimball: "He was the lead detective looking for Gilman two years ago and continues to offer assistance to park rangers regarding Gilman's disappearance. Kimball admits he's not sure Gilman is dead. 'His background is very different than most people who go missing. That's one of the things that raises some concerns for us.'" Gilman's bank accounts have never been touched since he disappeared.

Summary

Gilman's mother stated that her son was offered a position as a true-life spy, and her son told her that he turned it down. If Gilman refused to be a spy, there were probably many in the international community who would want him dead. What better place to kill him than an isolated national park trail? But I don't think this is what happened.

Gilman walked away from his car wearing sandals and a bright-green Hawaiian shirt, not normal wear for a hiker in the Olympics. He was playing his music loudly in the parking lot, almost as though he wanted to ensure that the ranger saw him and made contact. Gilman was single, had an ultra-top-secret clearance, and was near the top in trust at almost every agency he had worked at. If there was ever a man with the ability to disappear, possibly forever—high intellect, high trust, multilingual, no family ties to hold him down—it was Gilbert.

The real question in this disappearance is why and how was Gilbert transferred out of a national park without anyone observing the incident?

Hildegard Hendrickson
Missing 06/08/13-5:00 p.m., Wenatchee Lake, WA
Age at disappearance: 79 years

This is yet again another disappearance in the Wenatchee and Wenatchee Lake region. Readers need to refer to *Missing 411-Western United States* and *Missing 411-North America and Beyond* to read about the numbers of people who have disappeared in this area under highly unusual circumstances. They are staggering.

Hildegard Hendrickson is of German descent and came to the United States to attend college. She was able to get her bachelor's, master's, and doctorate at the University of Washington. She later joined Seattle University's MBA program and, during her thirty years as a professor, helped establish the Albers School of Business and Economics. She retired from the university in 1996.

Monte and Hildegard Hendrickson were married, and each enjoyed picking mushrooms in the forests of Washington. Both became experts and were members of the Puget Sound Mycological Society. In 1997 the society gave the pair one of its highest awards, the "Golden Mushroom," for helping and strengthening the organization. Hildegard wore a golden mushroom necklace around her neck. Many articles about Hildegard stated that she was a "legend" in the mushroom arena. Monte passed away, and this left Hildegard going into the woods alone to enjoy her hobby, a practice that fellow members of the club told her not to do. Everyone knew she was careful, never traveling more than one half mile from her car and never going off-trail for long distances. She had actually told friends that she wouldn't lose sight of her car while she was in the woods. Friends also knew that Hildegard had a bad knee that inhibited her hiking long distances and crossing logs and rocks.

On June 8, 2013, Hildegard drove her vehicle to an area fifteen miles north of Lake Wenatchee on Chiwawa River Road. She parked her car and left her purse inside, leaving the vehicle unlocked. She went north along Minnow Creek near the Basalt Peak Trailhead looking for morel mushrooms. This valley has very steep slopes and is thick with old-growth trees.

If you believe past articles about Hildegard, she was picking mushrooms while carrying a walking stick and a mushroom basket (these items were confirmed to be with Hildegard by witnesses who saw her just prior to her disappearance). She went to the trailhead area on June 8. Since she lived alone, nobody realized that she hadn't returned home until Tuesday, June 11. A friend of Hildegard's had recognized her vehicle parked for two days near the Minnow Creek Trailhead. This friend knew that she always went home to her residence in Seattle at the end of a day of picking. He became suspicious and called the sheriff. On the afternoon of June 11, Chelan County deputies found her vehicle parked at that location. Deputies contacted Hildegard's son by phone, and he confirmed that he hadn't spoken to his mother in a few days, and this might mean that she was possibly missing. An on-scene sergeant contacted Hildegard's cell phone provider to see if they could ping her phone. They determined that the phone was turned off. Deputies subsequently searched her light green 2012 Ford Focus and found the windows rolled down two inches, the doors unlocked, and her purse with wallet, credit cards, and cell phone inside. They also located a cooler in her trunk that contained food and water, which appeared to be untouched. In hindsight, finding the car in this condition would indicate that Hildegard didn't lose sight of her vehicle while she was out looking for mushrooms.

Deputies contacted Bloodhound teams and searchers and requested they respond to their location. The sheriff made a determination to close USFS Road 6210 at the Chiwawa Road junction. Fourteen ground searchers were divided into four teams to accompany the Bloodhound into the field to search. The group searched from 4:00 p.m. till 8:30 p.m. without finding anything of value.

On June 12 the search started at 7:45 a.m. Fourteen trained searchers and thirty-four total personnel were on scene working the area in a grid pattern. A search helicopter arrived at 11:30 a.m. and searched until approximately 1:30 p.m. The flight crew reported that they had minimal visibility through the forest canopy. They returned to base. Hildegard's son accompanied other searchers and was west of USFS 6210 when at 10:00 a.m. he heard what he described as a "whistling sound." I can confirm from contact with searchers in the area that a whistling-type sound was heard but was never identified. The command post sent several search teams into the area. Searchers found nothing of value.

At 1:00 p.m., deputies found a witness who had spoken with Hildegard on June 8 at 1:00 p.m. as she headed up the trail. They reported that she was wearing a tan vest and carrying a basket. They also found a USFS employee who reported they saw her at 1:30 p.m. on the trail before the first switchback.

This incident had significant press. A physician saw the media coverage and remembered speaking with Hildegard at the trailhead as he was hiking out and she was walking in. He reported that she was wearing a straw hat, a tan vest, and a colorful shirt under the vest. She was carrying a metallic bucket in one hand and a metal walking stick in the other. The physician told the deputy that he was concerned for her because she was alone and didn't appear in the best medical condition for her physical height. Hildegard was 5'4" and 180 pounds with short gray hair.

On June 13 and 14, there was a major push to find Hildegard with over seventy searchers and multiple canines, all producing nothing.

After the sixth day of searching, it was determined to terminate the effort. Chelan County deputies and SAR volunteers, Kings County SAR and canine handlers, and family volunteers and ten Bloodhound search teams all contributed to the effort to find the mushroom picker.

On June 16 at 4:50 p.m., the official search to locate Hildegard was terminated.

Deputies did return multiple times to the location to search. At one point, two deputies hiked over two hours into a location. They found nothing.

On July 9 Chelan County was conducting training for Explorer Scouts. They decided to use the location where Hildegard had disappeared. The area was again searched; again nothing was found.

On September 5 the county was conducting search and rescue training and again utilized Hildegard's last location as a training site. Two motorcycle teams were asked to check the shoulder of the roadway near the trailhead. One quarter mile north of the trailhead, on the east side of the road, deputies reported that they encountered a rotten or putrid smell. The wind was very light, and they couldn't locate the source. There was a steep embankment off the roadway, so search teams were deployed to the location. Searchers reported that the odor was prevalent at times but would often fade away. They never identified the source.

A six-day search ensued with ground teams, helicopters, and eight different dog teams with various breeds attacking the hillsides looking for a scent. They found nothing. They did not find Hildegard's walking stick, basket, nothing. Her car was found unlocked and the purse inside. It did not appear to be touched. Upward of eighty people attempted to locate Hildegard, including a search team member who contacted me. This individual stated that the searchers were befuddled at the lack of evidence and the amount of mushrooms in that specific area. The searcher did confirm that he and others heard strange whistles in the woods.

A June 18, 2013, article in the *Seattle Times* had the following statement from a law enforcement source: "Sheriff's sergeant Kent Sisso, who coordinated the search said, 'We need to step back and look at some other aspects of the case.' Regarding the possibility of foul play, Sisson said, 'You always investigate that side of any search.' But Hendrickson's purse and money were found in her unlocked car at the trailhead, making it hard to see what motive might have been for harming her, he said."

The day prior to Hildegard disappearing, she had traveled with friends into this same trailhead and discussed mushroom opportunities. Hildegard had agreed at that time that she wouldn't go out to this area alone.

Summary

Hildegard Hendrickson was not a very mobile person. She was older and used a walking stick. Searchers had excluded an animal attack as the reason behind the disappearance of the lady. The mountains in this area are so steep that the idea she climbed any hills near the trailhead is out of the question. This woman is one of many people who have vanished in the region around Wenatchee Lake.

In a past story about a disappearance, a member of the Chelan County search team had contacted me about the cases I've chronicled. He stated that these SAR teams know that very strange things are happening in the mountains. This particular searcher stated that he had been on search efforts in the past and had gotten strange feelings while looking for the missing.

Again, don't ever hike or go into the woods alone.

M-Bryan Lee Johnston
Missing: 08/28/13-Unk, Olympic National Park, WA
Age at disappearance: 71 years

There is significant ambiguity about this disappearance, and the National Park Service has refused to release details about what they know. I filed a Freedom of Information Act request for documents about this incident well over one month after it was reported. Their response indicated the reports were not finalized. I don't believe this. In my police days, your reports had to be completed before you went home. There is too much of a chance that details would be forgotten and then not documented if reports were not completed that night. I still don't have the reports.

I have learned that Bryan Johnston was a very handy man and had the ability to build almost anything. He had renovated his house in Ballard and had built another residence in Moses Lake. He received his bachelor's degree from the University of Washington and spent his military time in the air force. He retired from Seattle City Light.

I was able to put together basic details on this case from various articles.

Bryan Lee Johnston had planned a trip into Olympic National Park via the Ozette Loop Trail. This is a nine-mile roundtrip that could easily be accomplished in three days. Surveillance footage shows he went to a Safeway store and purchased a sandwich and two waters on August 22. His family reported him missing on August 28. Rangers found his truck at the Ozette Loop Trailhead parking lot after his family had filed a report.

Bryan's family was interviewed. They stated he took a sleeping bag and a daypack and told them he would be gone for two to three days. The National Park Service did comment that it was nearly impossible to get lost on this trail, as it was raised plywood over marshes and creeks and easy to follow. There is one segment that goes along the Pacific Ocean that is not raised plywood. Barb Maynes was the spokesperson for the park service and was interviewed for an October 27 article in the *Peninsula Daily News*: "About a week after the primary search ended, the park had several teams of dogs go over the same ground, Maynes said. There were no clues, no alerts, she said."

The National Park Service stated that they committed two and one half days to looking for Bryan on the ground and they had a helicopter in the air and found nothing. Bad weather and rain did hinder search efforts.

Jinny Longfellow was also interviewed in the same article that I quoted above and reflected on the assistance the family secured from other sources: "Longfellow said a paranormal researcher talked to her about the possibility of UFOs having something to do with her brother's disappearance. 'I told him I hadn't even thought about that, but if a spaceship came anywhere near my brother, he'd be the first one aboard,' Longfellow said."

As of the publication of this book, Bryan has not been found and the National Park Service never supplied their report.

Washington/Idaho Border

Sex/Name	Date Missing • Age • State
M-Arthur Leo Ivey	09/24/64-7:30 p.m. • 2 • Spokane, WA
M-Ryan Hoeffliger	01/11/84-7:30 a.m. • 2 • Hayden Lake, ID

Arthur Leo Ivey
Missing: 9/24/64-7:30 p.m., Spokane, WA
Age at disappearance: 2 years

The Washington/Idaho border near Spokane has a long history of unusual disappearances. The multitude of cases in this area could cause multijurisdictional issues and agencies not knowing that a city just across the border is working a very similar series of cases. If cases are within one state, communications and computer systems usually align and information is exchanged easily; issues in different states are sometimes jumbled and confused.

Many small children seem to disappear while they are visiting a relative or family friend's home, as in the case of Arthur Ivey, who went missing while visiting the home of James Stephens. At approximately 7:30 p.m. on September 24, 1964, little Arthur somehow slipped away from the adults and disappeared into the rural backyard twelve miles north of Spokane. This is a heavily wooded area with steep ravines. Once it was discovered that they could not locate Arthur, the local sheriff was called.

The sheriff's department contacted Fairchild Air Force Base and asked for assistance on the ground search. They also contacted local civil defense organizations and made a call for local volunteers. Hundreds of searchers were covering the area behind the home, yelling and looking for the small boy. The search went through the night without any success.

Early on the morning of September 25, three boys from a local high school decided to enter the woods and work together. After spending just fifteen minutes in the area of the backyard, they found Arthur curled up in the mud asleep, just three hundred feet from the home. He was alive and brought back to the residence. A September 25, 1964, article in the *Spokane Daily Chronicle* had the following statement about Arthur: "The lad seemed largely unaware of his ordeal or the stir he caused."

Search commanders asked the boys to explain exactly where Arthur was found. It was discovered that he was found in an area that 250 searchers had covered multiple times the prior night.

As is normal in the cases we highlight, Arthur was found unconscious or asleep. What I found very unusual is that he was lying in mud. Mud is wet and drains the body of heat, a location where it is difficult to sleep and be comfortable. I question how long Arthur had been there before he was found. I do not believe that searchers missed Arthur just three hundred feet behind the home.

Ryan Hoeffliger
Missing-01/11/84-7:30 a.m., Hayden Lake, ID
Age at disappearance: 2 years

Many of the loyal readers of my books will quickly realize that this story is different than every other missing person case I've documented. Once you get into the minutia of the details, you will understand why it is here.

This incident occurred in a cluster zone near the Idaho and Washington border just four miles northeast of Coeur d'Alene in a small town named Hayden. The specific area of the search happened at Hayden Lake on the east side of the city. The lake has a country club and residential neighborhood to the west, and mountains and a heavily wooded area covers the water's edge to the east. The lake has forty miles of shoreline and sits at an elevation of 2,239 feet.

The Hoeffliger family lived in a residence on East Dakota Road approximately one and a half to two miles from the west side of Hayden Lake. On the night of January 10–11, 1984, there were four people sleeping in the residence with one Doberman pinscher living in the backyard. Two-year-old Ryan had broken his crib and was sleeping in his sister Shawna's bed, in her room.

At approximately 5:00 a.m. on January 11, Shawna got out of the bed to use the restroom. She came back into the room and saw Ryan lying in the bed between her and the wall. She thinks she remembers hearing her family's dog barking, and she went back to sleep. At 7:30 a.m. Shawna awoke and found Ryan gone. She walked into her parents' room and woke them, and they looked around the house for the boy. They found all of the doors closed. The front door was unlocked, as the family knew they needed a new lock. Once the family knew that Ryan wasn't in the immediate area, the Kootenai County sheriff's office was called.

Once the deputy arrived, the parents explained that they had found all of the doors closed. They stated that Ryan knew how to open some of the doors but never closed them; these were all closed.

The deputy interviewed Shawna, and she said that she never heard or felt Ryan leave the bed and never heard her dog bark, which he usually did when doors were opened. The parents stated that they also never heard a door open or close and never heard the dog bark. The parents even commented that they believed that the Doberman appeared extremely lethargic and was acting outside its normal behavior.

The deputy called for additional assistance. Depending on the articles you read, it is one and a half to two miles from the Hoeffliger residence to Hayden Lake. A map shows that if you walked a direct route, you'd have to cross several roadways, a golf course and several fairways, and probably pass at least forty homes.

Deputies searched the home and investigated every possible point of entry. They found nothing forced open.

Approximately seven hours after Ryan was reported missing, a volunteer searcher found the boy's body underneath a dock on the west side of Hayden Lake. The dock belonged to a seasonal home that was vacant at the time. Deputies found the deceased boy wearing just a diaper.

The command staff at the sheriff's office immediately felt that something was odd. They did not believe that Ryan could've walked that distance in freezing-cold temperatures. They also found it unreal that he was able to leave the residence without waking his parents or causing the dog to bark. They looked at the child's feet and didn't see bruising or scratches that would be indicative of a long walk. They canvassed the neighborhood and the golf course and found nobody that had witnessed the boy walking that distance.

Ryan went to bed wearing pajama bottoms; these were never found even though multiple dive teams entered Hayden Lake looking for evidence. They found nothing. Searchers also scoured the area along a path that Ryan might have walked and found nothing. Ryan's body was sent to the coroner for an autopsy. A December 24, 1985, article in the *Spokesman Review* had the following; "Authorities initially cited murder as the probable cause of death; autopsy results indicated the boy drowned, though results weren't conclusive." If you've read my earlier books, you know that in many cases that happen under unusual circumstances, where a small child dies, the coroner cannot confirm the cause of death. The local coroner stated that drowning was a probable cause. The sheriff requested that the body be sent for further federal testing. The cause of death was not confirmed.

Because of the concern of Ryan's parents about the lethargic state of the family dog, the sheriff had the dog tested. It was found that the Doberman was not drugged or poisoned.

I have written about many cases where two-year-olds travel unreal distances, and the incident is not questioned. I applaud the Kootenai County sheriff for realizing the distance, time, weather, and circumstances make no sense. It seems like an impossibility that the event unfolded as it did. Ryan is sleeping between his sister and the wall; he leaves the bed, and the sister is not wakened. He allegedly leaves the residence with or without aid; doors are never heard opening or closing, and the family dog never barks. This almost appears as though everyone in this residence was in the deepest sleep of his or her life.

The deputies working this case have publicly stated many times that they do not believe that Ryan walked to the lake by himself and without aid. The diaper that Ryan was wearing at the time he was found was shown to his parents; this was not the type of diaper they used. Something very, very unusual happened inside the Hoeffliger residence between 5:00 a.m. and 7:30 a.m.

If Ryan was abducted, the suspect had the boy in his or her presence for only a very short period of time. Deputies started searching almost immediately upon arrival at the home, and volunteers and deputies were scouring the neighborhood continually. There is no suspect who would risk identification by dumping a body in a nearby lake with homes in the immediate vicinity when wilderness is just miles away.

This case reminds me of the disappearance of Ann Marie Burr from her residential home in Tacoma, Washington, on August 31, 1961. Ann's mom woke at 5:30 a.m. and realized her eight-year-old daughter was missing from inside the home. This story was covered in *Missing 411-North America and Beyond*. In the Burr incident, the family dog was inside their residence the entire night, and it never made a sound. Ann Marie was never found.

The Ryan Hoeffliger case is still an open file at the Kootenai County sheriff's office. As late as 2006, a cold case team worked the incident in an attempt to develop leads. No suspect has ever been named.

West Virginia

Sex/Name	Date Missing • Age • State
M-Robert Carr	01/11/49-2:00 p.m. • 7 • Davis, WV
M-Eston Carr	01/11/49-2:00 p.m. • 9 • Davis, WV
M-John Helmick	01/11/49-2:00 p.m. • 15 • Davis, WV

M-Robert Carr, age 7
M-Eston Carr, age 9
M-John Helmick, age 15 or 16 (Articles have conflicting information)
Missing 01/11/49-2:00 p.m.
Davis, WV

This incident occurred just outside of Davis, West Virginia, approximately twenty miles south of the Pennsylvania border. This is a bizarre story of how three boys disappeared in the woods where they grew up. Knowing that the boys went missing in an area that they trampled on a daily basis, you will have a difficult time understanding how this can happen. I should state at this early point, the sheriff involved in the case did not believe these kids were lost. He initially stated that he believed they ran away; they didn't.

The best way to explain how this event started is by quoting a January 14 article in the *Raleigh Register*: "The officer told this story: The Carr brothers whose home is off a strip mine road about five miles from here [Davis], had been boarding at the Helmick home while attending school. The Helmick youngster had been employed part-time at a sawmill operated by the Carr youth's father. The trio left the Helmick home en route to the Carr property about 2pm Tuesday [January 11] while a cold rain was falling, and never arrived there. A heavy fog followed the rain and snow and freezing temperatures came a short time later." The boys were on a well-worn path through the woods that led to the Carr household, a path they'd taken many times in the past.

Trackers were working through the woods looking for the three boys, a large group to be searching for. It was raining when the boys had left for the home, but fog did not set in until the following night. The boys had had plenty of time to make the Carr household before the weather turned treacherous.

A June 17 article in the *Cumberland Times* had the following statement about the search's progress: "John Helmich, 16, was found shortly after noon yesterday [January 16] on the bank of Beaver Creek about ten miles from Davis, alive but in critical condition." Helmick was taken to the hospital, a six-hour trip, and found to have double pneumonia, frozen feet and hands, and some gangrene. Both of his feet were amputated. Helmick was found next to a creek lying under a patch of wild laurel.

Later in the same *Cumberland Times* article quoted above was the following: "Six hours later [after finding Helmick] Robert Carr, 7, Eston's brother, was found dead two miles further away." Later in the same article was this: "The sheriff stated the terrain is the most rugged in West Virginia." Both Helmick and Carr were transported on litters over five miles before they could reach a road. Robert Carr was found on the bed of an old tram railroad that was called the Dobbin Trail and was used to haul lumber. The claim was made that Robert died of exposure and hunger.

Later in the same *Cumberland Times* article was the following about the location of the bodies: "Sheriff Costen said that the Helmick youth was found about 12 miles from Davis and that Carr's body was about 14 miles away. Helmick is believed to have left the other two younger boys alone with the idea of going for help but he was overcome. Helmick was found within 50 yards of a hunter's cabin which he apparently did not see." Many, many missing people are found in areas where they are easily located or will be seen by others.

Searchers made many interesting notes while they were looking for the boys. One searcher noted they found pine boughs woven into a bed that they felt the boys made—fascinating. There have been several cases where searchers have found the same thing while looking for others. Other searchers stated that they found a pile of stones and braches that appeared to be purposely made. Searchers were shocked at where they found the body of nine-year-old Eston Carr, as is described in this January 19 article in the *Thomasville Times*: "The frozen body of nine-year old Eston Carr was found in a huddled heap high on a mountain side yesterday, completing the search for him and two other boys missing a week."

Three hundred searchers who knew the countryside like their backyard could not find the majority of these boys for over five days. If the weather was as treacherous as described, how did the boys travel the distances they did in just a few days? The million-dollar question is how three boys, all with knowledge of the area, got lost and ended up so far outside of normal search and rescue guidelines. John Helmick was the only boy who survived.

Wisconsin

Sex/Name	Date Missing • Age • State
M-Michael Janiko	09/10/1917-2:00 p.m. • 4 • Ashland, WI
F-Helen Kockman	04/23/1930-6:00 p.m. • 3 • Quinney, WI
M-Joseph Stallman	01/19/87-5:00 p.m. • 2 • Washington, WI

Michael Janiko
Missing: 09/10/1917-2:00 p.m., Ashland, WI
Age at disappearance: 4 years

Ashland is located at the southwestern tip of Lake Superior thirty miles east of Duluth and twenty-five miles west of Porcupine Mountains State Park. There are hundreds of small bodies of water and swamps within ten miles of this location.

On September 10, 1917, at approximately 2:00 p.m., Michael Janiko was playing in the yard of his rural home when he vanished into the woods. His mom searched for him briefly and then contacted local neighbors for assistance. At the onset of the rescue effort, there were almost one thousand volunteers looking for Michael. A September 14, 1917, article in the *Milwaukee Journal* described search conditions: "Monday and Tuesday were freezing nights and for the last twenty four hours of his wandering rain fell continuously."

The search lasted three days and three nights with searchers not finding any evidence the boy was in the area. They weren't finding tracks, and they heard nothing. On September 14 their luck changed. An eight-year-old boy, John Jablonsky, was searching with his father and another farmer when the young boy found Michael near a tree. When rescuers found the boy, he was without his clothes and undergarments, and even his shoes were missing. A September 14, 1917, article in the *Eau Claire Leader* had the following about Michael's actions after he was found: "Effort was made to have Michael drink a glass of milk, but he was unable to do so. The boy either is too frightened to talk or has lost the power of speech." Many of the cases I have chronicled explain that children in these instances act in the same manner as Michael and won't or can't talk about what happened to them. Later in the same *Eau Claire* article was the belief by searchers about how far Michael had traveled: "He was found nearly four miles from where he disappeared and evidently walked around in almost a circle, traveling it is estimated at least 30 miles."

Michael was first taken to his home and then on to the hospital. The thought that the boy was found naked in the woods after four days in freezing weather in Wisconsin and survived is mind-boggling. After two days of hospitalization, Michael did make a few fragmented sentences, which are intriguing. The statements appear in the September 14, 1917, article in the *Milwaukee Journal*: "'One night I crawled into a log to get away from a big dog.' This and other fragments, uttered by little Michael Janiko, 4, are being used to piece out the wonderful story of the child's experiences during the three days and three nights during which he wandered. The tot is rapidly recovering from the effects of exposure and shock of fear, but it is impossible to get a connected narrative from him." I'm not sure why the writer described the experience as "wonderful"—maybe it's because he was alive.

Summary

How Michael survived three days and nights in freezing rain without clothing is the major question. Do you believe that a four-year-old boy could travel thirty miles in three days under the described conditions?

Helen Kockman
Missing: 04/23/1930-6:00 p.m. • 3 • Quinney, WI
Age at disappearance: 3 years

The area of this incident would be considered prime based on the geographical areas we've found in prior cases. Quinney is located forty miles south of Green Bay directly on Winnebago Lake. It is six miles west of Collins Marsh State Wildlife Area and four miles west of Killsnake State Wildlife Area.

The headline of an article we found in the *Milwaukee Journal* of April 30, 1930, grabbed me: "Girl, 3, Out in Rain All Night Found." Helen Kockman was playing in the yard of her rural home when she somehow wandered away. The parents realized the girl was missing and searched the immediate area without success and then ran to the Quinney Store and asked for assistance. Neighbors and friends conducted the search for Helen on Wednesday night. By Thursday morning Sheriff John Dietrich was on the scene and running the operation. Weather was not the searchers' friend, as it rained continuously through the night and early morning.

By early Thursday morning, searchers and Helen's parents had started to talk about kidnapping and murder because they hadn't found a trace of the girl and couldn't understand how she had managed to get away from the house. Searchers combed an area one mile around the family residence and continued to find nothing. On Thursday afternoon, one searcher was one half mile from the home and found the girl. No details were available on her condition other than she was alive and talking.

Searchers and law enforcement tried to question Helen about how she got away from her home and where she had gone. In the same *Milwaukee Journal* article quoted above was Helen's response: "She was unable to explain how she happened to wander away from the home."

Summary

As I've stated dozens of times in the past, don't focus on the story; focus on the details. In this incident, Helen went missing during a rainstorm. Weather is a continual theme in many of the cases in the Missing 411 books. Searchers had covered the area around the home and then the girl is found a short distance away the following afternoon. In many of these instances, people close to the family and law enforcement start to think that a crime has occurred because the facts surrounding the missing are baffling and make little sense, as in Helen's case. Finally, the victim cannot explain how she wandered away from the home. Memory loss is a constant and consistent element in many of these cases.

Joseph Stallman
Missing: 01/19/87-5:00 p.m., Washington, WI
Age at disappearance: 2 years

The town of Washington, Wisconsin, is located just south of Eau Claire. It is a small city with a farming culture. The town has several water sources to the north and many ponds and swamps surrounding the area. This case has one element that is not seen in the vast majority of the cases we quote: the Bloodhound at the scene *was* able to track a scent, or got very lucky.

Joseph Stallman (two and one half years old) was at home on January 19, 1987, with his mother and his seven-month-old sister on the family farm. The last member of the family with the group was Coco, their Labrador retriever, who was the kids' constant companion. At approximately 5:00 p.m., the temperature was a frigid seven degrees, and Joseph was riding his bike in the yard. Mrs. Stallman was in the barn feeding the calves and returned in five minutes to find Joseph and Coco missing. She looked for the pair, yelling and calling their names; no answer. After fifteen minutes of searching the yard, barn, and vehicles, she called law enforcement.

The La Crosse County sheriff made a community call for volunteers to look for the missing boy. One hundred and fifty locals responded and within one hour were in the cornfields and pastures looking for Joseph.

Searchers did not have any luck finding the boy, but a law enforcement canine responding to the scene did pick up his scent. A January 21 article in the *Milwaukee Sentinel* had the following description of the event: "A Sheriff's department tracking dog picked up the boy's scent before searchers found tracks from the lost pair, Tiedt said. The tracks led to the boy's discarded clothing and then to the dog and child. The two were found about a mile south of the main buildings on the farm and some people estimated they may have walked up to three miles to get there, the Stallmans said." Coco was found lying on top of the unconscious boy, keeping him warm. Earlier in the same article was this: "The boy was without mittens, boots or socks and his face was cut and bleeding, possibly from walking through the cornfields, police said. His feet were numb, but an examination at St. Francis Medical Center indicated he was not seriously hurt."

I read these stories several times attempting to understand how Joseph could get away from his mother so quickly that he could not hear her calls. For a little two-and-a-half-year-old boy to travel three miles in two hours is a major accomplishment, something that's hard to believe. I'm also surprised that Coco didn't return and respond to the call from Joseph's mom. The last point that is baffling—it was seven degrees. Joseph was gone two hours—why would he be stripping clothes and shoes, and why didn't his feet and hands suffer extreme frostbite? It does not seem possible that a child would not have suffered serious injury if he was outside in the frigid cold for two hours.

This is another in a very long list of cases where small children disappear with the family dog.

Wyoming

Sex/Name	Date Missing • Age • State
M-Kerry Smith	05/03/53-1:00 p.m. • 10 • Middle Fork Powder River, WY
M-Edward Eskridge	02/19/63-5:00 p.m. • 16 • Green River, WY
M-Nicholas Dailey	07/03/82-a.m. • 2½ • Muddy Mountain, WY

Kerry Smith
Missing: 05/03/53-1:00 p.m., Middle Fork Powder River, WY
Age at disappearance: 10 years

Mr. Gerald Smith and his son, Kerry, were fishing on the Middle Fork of the Powder River twenty-seven miles west of Kaycee. They were accompanied by one of their hometown police officers from Casper, John Manning. The group was fishing in an area near the Bar-C Ranch, in a location where they could park relatively close to the river.

At approximately noon on May 3, 1953, a severe storm with heavy winds and rain inundated the area and caused Kerry to get cold. A May 5, 1953, article in the *Billings Gazette* explained the details of what followed: "He complained of suffering from the cold and started back to their car, parked almost within sight of the Bar-C Ranch. His father and John Manning, a Casper police officer, forgot the car was locked." When the men returned to the vehicle at 1:30 p.m., Kerry was nowhere in sight.

It was at this point that the men did a quick search of the surrounding area and then went to the ranch for additional assistance.

Searchers responded en masse. Fifty cowboys on horseback and the sheriff's department came to assist. Kerry knew that his dad and friend were fishing downstream from the car, so the search effort focused in that area. That first afternoon of the search produced no results.

On May 4, a few searchers rode upstream into the Outlaw Canyon where the walls are one thousand feet high and look quite different than where the group was fishing. To the shock of everyone, Kerry was found seven miles up the canyon amid the cliffs. He was found in the exact opposite direction of where the group was originally fishing and in very rough terrain. Kerry was dead. It was declared by the coroner that he had died from exhaustion and exposure. There were no details on what he was or wasn't wearing.

Summary

I have stated in past books that you never hear about coroners citing exhaustion as a cause of death in the twenty-first century. The storm that hit the area was so severe it knocked out telephone lines in the ranches in the area. It did rain heavy. A ten-year-old boy is very aware of his surroundings, and I seriously doubt that he would get confused to the point of walking up Outlaw Canyon.

Edward Eskridge
Missing: 02/19/63-5:00 p.m., Green River, WY
Age at disappearance: 16 years

During the summer of 2013, I made a trip north through the valley where this incident occurred. The drive from Green River to Pinedale is desolate, dry, and lonely. There was little happening in this area other than a new oil rig. The Green River bisects the valley, which is mainly managed by the Bureau of Land Management. There's a lot of sage brush in the area and the ground cover would remind you of a desert.

Brothers Edward and Richard Eskridge were spending a long weekend with their grandparents, as their father was away. On February 15, 1963, Edward drove one of his grandfather's cars and with Richard, age thirteen, he traveled to an area in the desert twenty-nine miles north of Green River for rabbit hunting. The weather turned very cold, and the boys were en route back when Edward flipped the car and seriously injured Richard. Edward apparently dragged Richard from the car, placed him next to it, covered him with additional clothes, and built a small fire. Richard was injured to the point that he could barely move. Edward knew he had to get assistance and left Richard at the vehicle as he started walking across the desert.

Early in the evening of the accident, Richard's grandparents got concerned that the boys had not returned and called the sheriff. Patrol units did not have success finding the boys the first night, and the effort went to the air. On February 20 a search plane saw Richard lying next to a crashed car and directed ground teams to the scene. They found the boy unconscious and severely injured. He was immediately transported to a hospital in Rock Springs. Richard did gain consciousness at the hospital and was asked about the incident, but he couldn't remember anything. Richard was paralyzed from the chest down and had double pneumonia. He died hours after his brief conversation.

Ground and air teams were still in the desert looking for Edward. A February 22, 1963, article in the *Billings Gazette* had a summary of what was found: "The searchers led by Sheriff George

Nimma, followed Edward's tracks in the snow for several miles Sunday, but lost the trail on a rocky ridge and in fresh snow." One hundred searchers stayed at the effort for three additional days and found nothing. There were no additional tracks, and Bloodhounds brought from a state penitentiary could not locate a scent.

Summary

It is baffling that airplanes, Bloodhounds, and ground teams could not find Edward Eskridge. There are no large trees or significant cover in the area. Where did this boy go?

Nicholas Dailey
Missing: 07/03/82-a.m., Muddy Mountain, WY
Age at disappearance: 2½ years

You will read a few stories in this book that almost describe some type of divine intervention. This story may be one of those events.

Nicholas and his parents had gone to the mountains twelve miles south of Casper for a weekend. They had traveled to the Lodgepole Campground at the base of Muddy Mountain at an elevation of approximately seven thousand feet. This area has acreage without large trees and some areas with big trees.

On the morning of July 3, Nicholas was playing with other children near the perimeter of the campground and disappeared. Parents started calling for the boy, and many gathered to search the surrounding area. After two hours the family called for additional assistance. The local sheriff responded, and he gathered more searchers. The sheriff also brought Bloodhounds from Great Falls in an attempt to track a scent.

The search for Nicholas got bigger until over two hundred people were scouring the countryside and searching the area near the campground foot by foot. The Natrona County sheriff was leading the effort to find the boy and was getting frustrated because they weren't locating any evidence that he was in the area.

On July 6, fifty-six hours after Nicholas had vanished, an unusual event happened as is described in the July 6 *Youngstown*

Vindicator: "A 2½ year old child missing from a nearby campground for three days was found safe Monday evening by a man who says he 'sat down, said a prayer, walked three steps and found him.'" Bruce Luick was a motorcycle repairman who had traveled into the mountains hoping to assist in the search for Nicholas. Later in the same *Youngstown Vindicator* article was this: "Luick said he found the child 300 yards from the campsite where he was last seen Saturday." Again, later in the same article: "Natrona County Sheriff's deputies and other searchers had twice before scoured the area where the child was found, but they said high grass and heavy woods had apparently hidden the 3-foot tall youngster from view."

I can understand how searchers may have missed the boy, but what about the canines that never picked up the scent? If the boy was in the area for three days, why didn't he yell out to the people in the area? If he was that close to the campground, he must've smelled food and heard chatter. What was the child doing during the daylight hours?

This is an amazing story that almost seems as though the searcher was given some type of message about finding Nicholas.

This is one of those dozens of cases where a child is found in the midst of the searchers after the area had been covered multiple times. It's almost as though the child was placed in a location where he'd be easily found.

CHAPTER TWO: CANADA

Alberta

Sex/Name
F-Helen Bogen

Date/Time Missing • Age • State
08/07/50-10:00 a.m. • 2½ • Monitor, AB

Helen Bogen
Missing: 08/07/50-10:00 a.m. • 2½ • Monitor, AB
Age at disappearance: 2½ years

    Monitor is an extremely small city nearly two hundred miles southeast of Edmonton. It's approximately ten miles southeast of Gooseberry Lake Provincial Park and in an area of hundreds of small swamps and ponds. The Bogen farm was ten miles north of the small city.
    On August 7, 1950, at 10:00 a.m., a few of the Bogen children were mounting horses for a ride to their grandparents' home. Helen asked to go on the trip and was told by her parents that she could not. The kids rode off, leaving Helen alone in the garden. Sometime after the kids left, Helen disappeared. Mr. and Mrs. Bogen searched the yard and surrounding farm and found her nightgown near a gate on their property. It was at this point that they made a call to neighbors to help in the search. It wasn't long after that first call that 150 neighbors responded to the Bogen farm, yelling and calling for Helen.
    The neighbors searched nonstop for that first twenty-four hours. They lit fires and yelled for the girl while not getting a response. Bloodhounds from Westlock were brought to the farm, and they couldn't pick up a scent. Two private planes from Provost also responded and flew the skies above the farm without finding anything

of value. A total of 450 area residents responded to the Bogens' call for assistance.

Thirty hours after Helen had vanished, an abandoned farm was being searched when a severe thunderstorm hit the search area. All searches were stopped. Searchers found nothing on the farm. An hour after the rain stopped, Mrs. Douglas Tainsh was back at the same abandoned farm that was searched an hour earlier and found Helen. An August 9, 1950, article in the *Lethbridge Herald* explained what Mrs. Tainsh found: "Naked and splashing happily in an old tub of dirty water inside a shed on an abandoned farm, 30 month old Helen Bogen was found Tuesday night." She was hungry, weak, and happily, she was alive. She had scratches over her body.

An August 9, 1950, article in the *Edmonton Journal* reported the feelings of searchers about the discovery of Helen: "Observers termed it a miracle that she had survived the 30 hour period, unclothed, unfed, plagued by insects and exposed to a rain shower and overnight temperatures that dropped to about 40 degrees."

Helen was taken to the hospital for observation and an evaluation. Helen made only a few statements to her father the first morning after she was found. She stated that the night she was gone she spent on a hill and "rested and listened." She made no mention of the dozens of searchers that had to have been in the area or the fires that were built to attract her attention. She also said nothing about being cold, even though temperatures were in the low forties.

Summary

This case is important because of the details that emerged. Searchers had gone through the abandoned farm just before a major thunderstorm hit the region. They were calling Helen's name and looking in the area. Helen wasn't found, no tracks were located, and she didn't respond. The thunderstorm hits, the farm is searched again afterward, and Helen is found playing in a tub. We know that weather plays some role in disappearances. This case makes it even more obvious.

Helen was out in the elements naked, yet she never complained about being cold and did not suffer from hypothermia.

The region of the Bogen farm is literally covered with hundreds of small bodies of water.

British Columbia

Sex/Name	Date/Time Missing • Age • State
M-Leo Gaspard	7/31/51-Unk • 60 • Pitt Lake, BC
F-Rachael Bagnall	09/08/10-Unk • 25 • Pemberton, BC
M-Jonathan Jette	09/08/10-Unk • 34 • Pemberton, BC
M-Raymond Salmen	05/28/13-Unk • 65 • Harrison Lake, BC

Leo Gaspard
Missing: 7/31/51-Unk • 60 • Pitt Lake, BC
Age at disappearance: 60 years

This story centers on an old gold mine near the headwaters of the Pitt River, forty-five miles northeast of Vancouver, British Columbia.

The stories about this incident vary slightly, but they all begin in 1890. An Indian named Slumach or Slummack was prospecting in the headwaters when he supposedly found a very wealthy vein of gold. Slummack was a very private person, but it was noted that he had returned to civilization with bags of fine gold. Sometimes he would realize he needed more gold, and then he would disappear for forty-eight hours and return with another bag, some nuggets as big as walnuts.

Slummack wasn't a model citizen. One story stated that he murdered a person and was hanged on January 16, 1891. Another story, more complex than the first, indicated that he brought a Native American woman with him on each trip to cook for him. Each time he returned alone and said that the woman either died of a variety of reasons or disappeared. On one return trip, other miners found his female companion in a river with Slummack's knife in her back. He later confessed and was supposedly convicted of eight murders. He was offered life in prison if he told the court where his mine was located. He refused. Between 1891 and 1951, twenty miners reportedly entered the headwaters of the Pitt

River looking for the Lost Creek Mine and disappeared, never to be found.

There are strange stories associated with this area of the Pitt as were described in the February 21, 1943, *Milwaukee Sentinel*: "Strange lights recently have been flickering in the skies above the Pitt Lake Mountains in the icy wilderness of British Columbia. The aged Indians of the district say the weird illumination is caused by the spirits of the 11 murdered squaws of Slummack, a strange Indian killer who disposed of women to protect the secret of his fabulously rich Lost Creek mine."

In July 1951, Leo Gaspard entered the offices of Okanagan Air Services and asked to be helicoptered into the headwaters of the Pitt River. He stated that he wanted to contract for four hundred pounds of food to be dropped four months after he originally left. Carl Agar was the manager of the air service and the man who Gaspard spoke with. He stated that Gaspard was one of the few legitimate and well-prepared prospectors he had ever met. He said that ten to twelve people a year ask him to drop them at the Pitt, and he normally refuses. He said that Gaspard was one of only two he has agreed to allow his pilots to fly in. Agar stated that the area is too dangerous for anyone who isn't extremely experienced in mountain life and well prepared for all types of weather.

After Gaspard was originally dropped on the Pitt, two other prospectors remembered seeing him hiking north into the woods. After this initial observation, the prospector was never seen again.

In October 1951, two RCMP officers went into the headwaters to search for evidence of what had happened to Gaspard. The area had incurred snow, and it rained on the officers during their search. They spent two weeks in the rugged wilderness and did not find any information about where the man had set up camp or any evidence of his death. Every news article that I reviewed indicated that Gaspard was the twenty-first victim who had gone into this area in an attempt to work the Lost Creek Mine. He was never found.

Summary

I've always been interested in this area of British Columbia. The region is considered some of the roughest mountain landscape in all of North America. Many segments of these mountains have probably never been walked by humans. There have been several First Nations stories about this area being a place just for Indians and not for white people.

In another odd twist to the Gaspard story, he left a letter for relatives to read should he disappear. In the letter he stated, "By the time you are reading this note, I have passed on." Yes, he had a premonition about his own death on this last trip of his life.

Rachael Bagnall, age at disappearance: 25 years
Jonathan Jette, age at disappearance: 34 years
Missing: 09/08/10, Pemberton, BC

Significant research went into this case. It was one of the missing incidents that struck me as even more unusual than the majority I've documented, if that is possible. In *Missing 411-North America and Beyond*, I documented a series of double disappearances. This incident would qualify for that section of the book. When I first started to read about the background, education, climbing history, and love of the outdoors that this couple had, I knew this story was going to be unusual. Just prior to this book being published, I was contacted by Jonathan's mother and asked if we were looking into her son's disappearance. I reassured her that we were and that this case would be getting significant press by our organization.

Rachael Bagnall was raised in Prince George, British Columbia. She was a brilliant student in her third year of medical school residency at the University of British Columbia in Vancouver. She loved the outdoors and had hiked in the United States and throughout Canada and always read books about the areas before she traveled. She knew the dangers of the outdoors and took appropriate equipment.

Jonathan Jette was raised in Quebec and was also a lover of the outdoors. His parents owned a restaurant. They knew their son's love of Canada's mountains and endorsed his interests. Jonathan was a governmental attaché for the Canadian government in Quebec and living in Vancouver.

Rachael and Jonathan initially met at a climbing gym, and their relationship blossomed. They both were in outstanding physical condition and seemed to thrive off each other's interest and intellect. They had planned a two to three day trip into an area north of Pemberton. The couple knew that this was going to be their last weekend together before they had to separate for a year. Rachael was going to South America to help the underprivileged utilizing her medical background, and Jonathan was staying in Vancouver.

They had purchased the book *Scrambles in Southwest British Columbia* by Matt Gunn. They had brought climbing helmets, an ice ax, backpacks, and food, but no ropes. The couple left early in the morning of September 4, 2010. Credit card receipts show they stopped at Tim Horton's in Squamish at 7:42 a.m. and purchased coffee and hot chocolate. The couple continued driving north through Whistler, Pemberton, and toward their destination, the Spetch Creek Forest Service Road, 8.7 miles from Mount Currie. At this point they parked their car and started a five-hour hike, presumably toward Valentine Lake. The hike would take them into the shadows of Cassiope and Saxifrage Mountains. The trail was large and well maintained, and it would be obvious to all what direction you were supposed to travel.

The Labor Day weekend trip was supposed to be two to three days. On September 8, 2010, Rachel had not returned to her sister's residence, and her sister called the RCMP.

Two days after the initial missing person report, RCMP found the couple's vehicle. They saw cups inside from Tim Horton's. There were no other clues found with the vehicle. The police asked Rachael's sister to search her room in an attempt to determine what she had and had not taken. They then went on to search Jonathan's residence looking for clues as to how long the couple would be gone and what he had taken. All indications pointed to the couple taking a two to three day hike.

The RCMP put a major effort into locating Rachael and Jonathan. Bloodhounds were brought to the vehicle, and they did not pick up a scent leaving that area. News articles did state that rain and clouds hampered searchers; this may have been a contributing factor in the disappearance. Dozens of search teams from Pemberton, Whistler, Vancouver Island, Ridge Meadows, and more all converged into the area to assist. A commercial and an RCMP helicopter took to the sky when the weather permitted to look for traces of the two. The initial search was for ten days and nothing was found. There have been no less than four additional searches that were initiated by family and friends. The family actually hired professional guides from the area to search for the pair. Nothing was found. Over 2000 search hours went into the effort to locate the couple.

Jonathan's family did state that he had an injured knee and they believed there was a possibility that he injured it further and the couple may be stranded somewhere. This statement was found in one article and seemed to be a side note of the family looking for answers.

The lead investigator on this case is Steve LeClair, staff sergeant from the Whistler/Pemberton RCMP Detachment. I sent the sergeant a series of e-mails inquiring about specific facts surrounding the case. The sergeant confirmed that canines never found the couple's scent at any location. He also stated that they didn't find any of the pair's cookware or used campsites. I asked if anyone on the trail or at the lake reported seeing the pair. LeClair stated that there was nobody else in the Valentine Lake area when Jonathan and Rachael walked in. He said that this would not be unusual based on the area's remoteness and the bad weather at the time. Imagine walking into a massive forest and not having anyone in the area—it sounds heavenly but apparently turned deadly.

Summary

I've read too many search and rescue reports to not know that there is something very wrong with this case. The parents have stated that they believe there may be foul play involved in the disappearance. They have also questioned whether their children are actually still in the area.

Bloodhounds could not locate a scent. Rain and clouds restricted search operations. People intimately involved in the search effort talked about foul play. There are too many commonalities with other cases I've researched for this incident not to be included in this book.

There are posters in the area of Valentine Lake about the disappearance of Rachael and Jonathan. There hasn't been one clue found regarding their whereabouts.

Raymond Salmen
Missing: 05/28/13-Unk, Harrison Lake, BC
Age at disappearance: 65 years

This will be recognized by longtime readers as an unusual case. I have stated that I will not include stories in the books that deal with the possibility of drowning. I probably would've excluded this story early in the study, but not now. Canadian officials state they believe that Raymond drowned. I don't think so.

Raymond Salmen was an experienced outdoorsman, camper, and hunter. He left his home with his two dogs and told his wife he'd be camping at Harrison Lake and he'd be back in two weeks. He was going to be spending time in the outdoors, a place he loved. He drove his pickup with a camper to an area west of the lake where there are no established campgrounds. Nothing was heard or seen of Raymond after May 28. There was no cell phone reception in the area.

On June 9, Agassiz RCMP responded to the area of Raymond's camper on the report of shots fired. Officers found Raymond's camper with his two dogs inside, but no Raymond. They started an intensive search of the area. RCMP called for search reinforcements in an area known as the "48 kilometre mark." Several search groups from throughout British Columbia responded and started a grid search of the area around the camper.

Four days after the initial call of shots fired, an unusual discovery was made as is described in the June 18, 2013, edition of *The Province*: "On Thursday, just after 3pm, crews on board an RCMP chopper spotted balloons about 400 meters north of the abandoned campsite at a secluded beach. Police then uncovered what's believed to be Salmen's clothing, as well as a rifle and spent casings nearby." What they found exactly was the man's backpack in the bush, his shoes, socks, rifle, and shell casings on a small beach. His knife and belt were not found (although there is no absolute proof he had them).

The RCMP believed that Raymond had gotten down to the beach, gotten stuck, and started shooting to draw attention. If he did shoot his rifle, he hit parked cars, and this was reported. The RCMP stated that they think he ditched almost everything he owned and then tried to swim across the lake and drowned, at night. They did put divers into the lake and found nothing. Raymond's wife hired a recovery team with a robotic camera that had recovered over ninety bodies. The recovery team covered every inch of the lake bottom and found nothing.

Raymond's brothers don't believe in the RCMP's theory. They think it's possible that Ray ran into foul play. They stated that he had seen odd things out in this area on past trips.

If Raymond were well enough to get down to the beach, why wouldn't he be in good enough condition to get himself out? There is one huge wildcard in this mystery. Raymond wouldn't go anywhere without his dogs, and they were found locked in the camper. A June 12, 2013, article on CTV.com had this: "'It's all these mysteries. My mind keeps thinking what could have possibly happened that he would go without the dogs,' his wife Daniela Salmen told CTV News." My question: What if the dogs refused to leave the camper? Raymond obviously went looking for something dangerous and went prepared. He had his backpack and supplies and took his rifle with extra ammunition. He got to the beach, and something deadly confronted him—or why would he be shooting at cars trying to attract attention?

Summary

The RCMP believes that Raymond drowned. The officers' dive team searched the area, and this was followed up by a specialist in recovering bodies. Nothing was found.

The RCMP wants to close the case and ignore all other outside possibilities. There is a reason that Raymond didn't have the dogs with him. Remember, canines play a role in many of the disappearances I've chronicled. I don't believe that Raymond would strip his clothing, shoes, and rifle and leave them behind as he swam. If there were a choice, he would've waited for daylight and then shot rounds to draw attention. I don't think he believed he had that choice.

Manitoba

Sex/Name	Date Missing • Age • State
F-Madeline Grisdale	07/06/86-Unk • 49 • Manitoba

Madeline Grisdale
Missing: 07/06/86-Unk, Fort Alexander Indian Reservation, Manitoba
Age at disappearance: 49 years

This disappearance happened on the Fort Alexander Indian Reservation, which is located at the southeastern end of Lake Winnipeg in Manitoba. It sits approximately thirty miles west of the Ontario border.

On July 6, Madeline walked into the bush to pick blueberries with her small puppy. Friends knew the woman wouldn't go far because of a stroke she had suffered ten years earlier, which left her with a severe limp. Madeline was also considered disabled because she was a mute. When the woman didn't return to her resident care facility, the RCMP was called.

There was an initial response by thirteen officers followed by fifty-five members of the Canadian armed forces. The search was intense and nonstop. The area of the search was swampy, wet, and thick with bushes.

Six days after Madeline vanished, she was found 2.1 miles from where she was last seen. Searchers found her lying under a tree adjacent to a trail, dehydrated, weak, and alive. Her puppy was sitting by her side. Searchers described her as very scared. She was airlifted by helicopter to a medical center in Pine Falls and declared to be in stable condition.

A July 14, 1986, article in the *Leader Post* described how Madeline was found: "A group of 20 searchers, including McKenzie and two other of Grisdale's children went into a previously unsearched area around 10am and were lost for some time before they discovered the woman. 'We went one direction and then we came back along the trail and we found her,' said Willy Grisdale. He added he didn't know how his mother got to the spot, why she couldn't return home, or if she had eaten during the ordeal."

Summary

Madeline was found just off a trail that had been searched just prior to her being found. Even her family couldn't understand how she had gotten to where she was found or why she hadn't made it back home.

Because of Madeline's disability, she couldn't explain details of what happened while she was missing.

Nova Scotia

Sex/Name	Date Missing • Age • State
M-Howard Newell	01/22/55-Noon • 6 • Little River Harbour, NS

Howard Newell
Missing: 01/22/55-Noon, Little River Harbour, NS
Age at disappearance: 6 years

Little River Harbour is at the far southwestern end of Nova Scotia in a very rural section of Yarmouth County. Even today the region has few homes and a small harbor. The forests in this area are thick, lush, and pristine. If you drew a line directly east from Acadia National Park in Maine and traveled fifty miles, you would hit Little River Harbour. The small town is located twenty miles northwest of Shag Harbour, Nova Scotia. This incident occurred ten miles outside the small city in an extremely rural region.

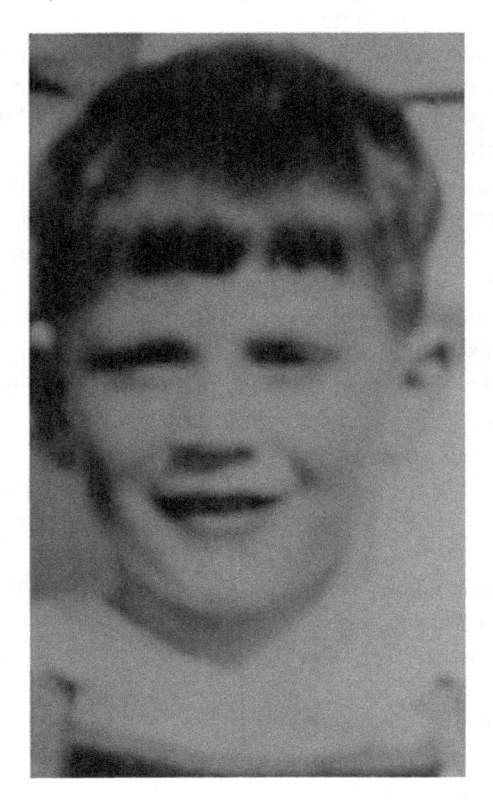

On January 22, 1955, at approximately noon, Howard was with a group of family members, led by his uncle, who were cutting firewood on a lot near his home. The group was getting ready to head back to their residence when Howard told the group that he was taking a shortcut through the woods. With nobody anywhere in the area but the group, Howard took off by himself, headed in the general direction of the residence. His cousins last saw him running through the snow, putting on his coat.

The group returned to the residence, and family members asked where Howard was. A June 9, 2008, article in the NovaNewsNow.com interviewed family members about the day Howard disappeared. The reporter interviewed Howard's sister Zita, twelve at the time, about the incident: "Her uncle said he was coming behind them but the sister didn't hesitate. She ran into the woods calling out her brother's name. There were no tracks. No Howard. What had she missed, she wondered? 'So I started retracing my steps and calling his name, stopping and listening in case he had fallen down.' But there was nothing. 'Then I kind of started panicking. My sister and one of my cousins appeared; we split up to search.' Still nothing."

This point in time started the search for Howard. Brian Newell was Howard's eight-year-old brother at the time and remembers going with others into the woods looking for Howard. He remembers those first moments of the search and explains what he did in the same article as quoted above: "Like the others, Brian went looking for his brother. 'It started to snow just as I got in the woods, big heavy snowflakes. So within an hour any tracks that you could have followed were all covered,' he recalls."

Nova Scotia threw every imaginable resource into the effort to find Howard Newell. Here is a partial list of the groups that were searching:

- Canadian army reserve from Yarmouth
- Naval training recruits from Cornwallis
- Helicopters from Shearwater
- Firefighters
- RCMP
- Bethany Bible College students and staff
- High school students who responded after the school was closed

Over one thousand people from throughout Nova Scotia walked shoulder to shoulder looking for the small boy. They didn't find anything.

Harold Newell was Howard's father. He remembers coming straight home from his construction job after hearing of the disappearance. He stated that he went straight to every water source he knew. He found no ice was broken and that it was too thick for his young son to crack. Harold worked for Kenney Construction. The owner shut down the company for days so employees could search for Howard.

There were rumors about what may have happened to the young boy. One of the biggest claims in the area was that a truck had hit the boy, and the driver had taken his body and burned it. In 1988 the RCMP took this incident as a cold case and looked into all possibilities. They found one of the occupants of the truck and had him take a polygraph test. He passed, proving there was no involvement and the truck story had no validity.

The RCMP reopening this case and handling it as a cold case is fascinating. Every document from them regarding this incident claimed it was a drowning. After the case was reopened and there were no new developments, they still claimed it was a drowning. Why did they have a cold case team investigate the disappearance if they were positive about their findings?

Howard Newell's relatives believed the child was very smart. In the same Novanewsnow.com article of June 9, 2008, his siblings were quoted: "Just in grade 1, attending a two-room schoolhouse in Melbourne, not only could he print his name, but he could write it too they say. 'He could do my homework, where I didn't have a clue,' says Brian [eight years old at the time]. Zita calls him 'One of those smart kids. And he was religious,' she says. Yes, he was still the type of kid to play in the dirt, but when it came time for the children to place their Christmas wishes—for that one special gift that they wanted—Howard's special request isn't what you would have expected a six-year old boy to ask for. 'He wanted a picture of Mary and Jesus, he wanted the Immaculate Heart,' Zita says." He hung the photo over his bed so it was close to him at night.

An eleven-day nonstop search failed to find any trace of Howard Newell. A follow-up search the following May also failed to find any evidence of a body floating to the surface or anything on land indicating where the boy may be.

Summary

I don't think I ever recall hearing such an explicit description of a young boy's intellect as I did in Howard's case. His religious beliefs and affiliation also strike a strong chord. It's obvious that Howard was a very smart and happy boy.

I am in Harold and Brian's camp on their beliefs about what happened to Howard. Harold didn't believe his boy went into the water. Brian is the lone sibling still living in the area, and he also does not believe his brother went in the water. The number of options for what happened to Howard is slim. There are no animal predators out moving in the bush in the month of January, when temperatures are near or far below zero. The idea that a human predator is walking in the woods in the middle of an extremely remote region of Nova Scotia seems unbelievable.

This story pulled at my heart.

Ontario

Sex/Name
M-Jack Ostrom

Date Missing • Age • State
05/29/57-Unk • 74 • Jawbone Lake, Ontario

Jack Ostrom
Missing: 05/29/57-Unk, Jawbone Lake, Ontario
Age at disappearance: 74 years

I've written about a series of unusual disappearances that happened in Ontario in a one-hundred-mile radius of Timmins. Jawbone Lake is located seventy-three miles south of the city and twenty miles north of the Trans Canadian Highway. It is surrounded by hundreds of small bodies of water and very rugged terrain. The majority of the articles researched for this event listed the man's name as Ostrom; one article spelled it Ostrum.

Jack Ostrom had taken his son, Harry, and fellow prospector, Ivan Anderson, by floatplane from South Porcupine to Jawbone Lake. Ostrom had a prospecting claim in the area and was going to work the zone for two weeks. On May 29, 1957, Ostrom set out with his ax and a compass to head one mile north and said he'd be back at the end of the day. He didn't return. Harry and Ivan searched nonstop for two weeks but were unable to find the man.

On June 12 the floatplane arrived to pick up the men, and the pilot was told of the disappearance. The plane returned to South Porcupine and gathered searchers for the return trip. The Royal Canadian Air Force was advised of the disappearance. They looked at topographic maps and said the area was too dangerous and refused to participate.

Friends and veteran bushmen did go into the area and allegedly found tracks. A June 18, 1957, article in the *Windsor Daily Star* had the following: "Two members of the ground party looking for the missing man reported Tuesday they have been following tracks for three days. Ostrom now is believed to be in a triangle formed by Mile and McKee Rivers, which meet six miles south of Jawbone Lake, and two parties of searchers have been dispatched down each river in canoes." It's fascinating that searchers were following tracks six miles south of the lake, and Ostrom was heading north. He had a compass and knew the area from past trips.

There was an article published on July 24, 2012, in the *Timmins Times,* which discussed a series of missing people around Timmins. Many of the missing they discussed have been written about in prior Missing 411 books. The article made a special point that many of the missing were berry pickers that were never found.

There is a cluster of missing people in and around Timmins. Most of the missing are older males.

Jack Ostrom was never found.

Quebec

Sex/Name	Date/Time Missing • Age • State
F-Grace Cooper	08/08/1913-1:00 p.m. • 5 • Lake Timiskaming

Grace Cooper
Missing: 08/08/1913-1:00 p.m., Burnt Island, Lake Timiskaming, Quebec
Age at disappearance: 5 years

When I explain water-related disappearances and their relationship to missing people, this incident would exemplify my point. Burnt Island is in the middle of Lake Timiskaming on the border of Ontario and Quebec. It is approximately seventy miles southeast of Timmins, a location where there are several missing people. The island is approximately two miles across at its widest. It can be very thick and lush and has cliffs on the east side.

The details of exactly how Grace Cooper managed to get away from her family are vague. On August 8, 1913, at 1:00 p.m. she was missing. Over eighty searchers joined her family in a comprehensive search of the south shore of the island, the location everyone believed she would travel. Several days were spent searching every inch of this area without finding a clue.

On the fifth day of the search effort, C. H. Burton and John McLennan decided to move away from other teams and head east. The east side is extremely rough as is described in the August 14, 1913, article in the *Toronto World*: "The bush in many places in almost impenetrable to a strong man, and a want for food and wet and cold weather might have caused the death of many a seasoned bushman lost for such a period." During this time a large storm hit the island and made travel and searching difficult. Rain and cold temperatures lingered in the area for two days.

Just as Burton and McLennan were at their farthest point from the Cooper family camp, they located Grace, on the fifth day. Where they found the girl is very peculiar as is described in the same *Toronto World* article: "Her head was resting on one log and her feet on another and caught in this position, she had been evidently unable to free herself." Readers of my past books have been told of other children who went missing who were found trapped and unable to move in dangerous locations. Grace was two feet from a one-thousand-foot cliff and water. It seems pretty timely that she was caught and pinned in that exact location.

The same *Toronto World* article had an interesting statement near its end: "How the child reached the other side of the island and was found alive is a mystery."

Summary

Grace Cooper disappears on an island that is essentially two miles by two miles—four square miles. The eastern end of the island is the most difficult to travel, and many have died in that area. Searchers go to this region and find her pinned and unable to move. She lived five days through a major storm. Searchers are mystified she got to the location where she was found and equally amazed as to how she was alive.

Saskatchewan

Sex/Name	Date/Time Missing • Age • State
F-Hazel Scraba	05/23/37-Unk • 11 • Pelly, Saskatchewan, Canada
F-Ludvina Machishyn	05/23/37-Unk • 10 • Pelly, Saskatchewan, Canada

Hazel Scraba   Age at disappearance: 11 years
Ludvina Machishyn   Age at disappearance: 10 years
Missing: 05/23/37, Pelly, Saskatchewan, Canada

Pelly is ten miles west of the Manitoba border in an area with hundreds of small bodies of water. The region is known for its farming and wildlife. The area of this incident can get very wild in the areas surrounding the farms and is a mecca for fisherman and hunters.

On May 23, 1937, best friends Hazel and Ludvina were at the Machishyn ranch and were asked to go into the fields and look for lost cattle. The children knew that many of the areas around the property were swampy and wet. The girls went into the fields and apparently got lost. Ludvina's father called upon the residents of Pelly for assistance. The Royal Canadian Mounted Police (RCMP) also responded in force.

Two days and seven miles from the ranch, searchers found small footprints that they believed may be the girls but weren't sure. The rescue teams were challenged in their efforts by severe rain, which had been in the area since the girls disappeared.

According to Robert Koester's book, *Lost Person Behavior*, children ten to twelve years of age, if traveling on flat ground, should be located 95 percent of the time within 6.2 miles or less. A

May 27 article in the *Calgary Daily Herald* had this statement about what searchers found: "Ludvina was found yesterday afternoon by a roving band of Indians 20 miles northwest of her home." This means that Ludvina traveled twenty miles in less than three days across fields and swamps while passing many farms, ranches, and roadways. This is an unbelievable distance for anyone to travel in that time frame.

After Ludvina was found, the girl was questioned extensively about what had happened to her friend. She stated that they separated on Monday after they argued about what they wanted to do. RCMP now went back to the location where Ludvina was found in hopes that Hazel was in that same area.

On May 27, 1937, Joe Malonowich was driving a wagonload of food from Pelly to the search teams up north. A May 29, 1937, article in the *Montreal Gazette* explained what Joe found: "Malonowich heard Hazel's shrill cries near the Swan River. Jumping off his wagon, he plunged into the bush and found her sitting under a fir tree on a high piece of ground that had been cut off from the mainland and transformed into an island by the rising river." Hazel was taken to a local farmhouse where she was given food and shelter. In the same article, the girl explained her travels: "At another time, 12 small brown bears passed near her but, 'they didn't even growl,' Hazel said." She said that she drank water and ate berries.

Summary

When you read all of the stories in the four Missing 411 books, children seem to see bears in an inordinate amount of occasions. Many claim to see the animals sleeping and under other unusual conditions, and they never have a negative encounter. The opportunity to see twelve bears at any one time seems highly unusual.

It seems odd that both girls weren't found by the hundreds of searchers, planes, and RCMP that were looking for them. When Malonowich located Hazel, she was found completely surrounded by water, a very unusual location. She obviously didn't see Joe, because he hadn't seen her from the roadway. Was that Hazel's loud scream that had alerted Joe?

Many lost people are found in, near, or adjacent to creeks and rivers, exactly as Hazel was found.

If I wrote a movie script where one girl disappears and is found on an island in a river, while the other is found twenty miles from where she was last seen, would that be believable?

CHAPTER THREE: AUSTRALIA

New South Wales

Sex/Name	Date/Time Missing • Age • State
M-Mrs. Farrell's Son	10/12/1875-8:00 a.m. • 4 • Tenterfield, NSW
F-Glenis M. Gilbert	04/09/28-4:00 p.m. • Unk • Leura, NSW
M-I. Shields (Son)	08/31/31-Unk • 4 • Mossgiel, NSW
F-Anna Gullett	09/10/32-5:00 p.m. • 48 • Leura, NSW
F-Joyce Fielding	02/03/36-Unk • 22 mos. • Goondiblule, NSW
F-Silvia Green	03/24/53-7:00 p.m. • 26 • Katoomba, NSW
F-Mary Lewis	06/16/53-Unk • 83 • Wentworth Falls, NSW
F-Isabel Davies	07/07/53-5:00 p.m. • 75 • Blackheath, NSW
M-Timothy Farmer	05/05/54-11:00 a.m. • 2½ • Linden, NSW
M-David Ashley Cusiter	03/04/62-3:00 p.m. • 17 • Katoomba, NSW
M-Stephen Crean	08/06/85-2:40 p.m. • 37 • Charlotte Pass, NSW
M-Prabhdeep Srawn	05/13/13-Unk • 25 • Charlotte Pass, NSW
M-Gary Tweddle	07/16/13-Unk • 23 • Leura, NSW

Introduction

I became aware of the Katoomba, Leura, Wentworth Falls, and Blackheath areas with the disappearance of Gary Tweddle. As I dug deeper into the story, I found that there was a lengthy history of odd disappearances in this area. I want readers to pay close attention to the details surrounding the incidents and their locations. I have never found an area of such tight geographical boundaries that has this number of strange cases.

There is a remarkable coincidence regarding the area around Katoomba, as it relates to my stories of missing people in North America. The city is almost surrounded by one of the most popular national parks in Australia, the Blue Mountains National Park. Australian National Parks states on its website that the park is a

World Heritage site "listed for its remarkable geographic, botanic and cultural values, including protecting sites of aboriginal significance. This huge park boasts more than 140 km of trails and walking tracks and there are great places to go camping, including Euroka or Blue Gum Forest where you can pitch your tent beneath the shade of a majestic eucalypt."

I'll start the chapter with a short story where I could find only one article. The information I located wasn't enough to establish a stand-alone case, as are listed below, but it does add to the mix of strangeness in the focus area.

The following details were found in *The Age* newspaper dated September 13, 1932: "The happening recalls the strange disappearance of Mr. David Joel and his wife in the Wentworth Falls district in May, 1918. A wealthy man, Joel and his wife, who was very delicate, went to Wentworth Falls for a holiday. They left the train and in misty rain commenced to walk back towards Lawson, but off the main road. This was the last seen of Joel. Mrs. Joel, who tore the clothes from her body in hysterical racings, was found starving a few miles from where she had been last seen. When rescued, she slipped into unconsciousness and died shortly afterwards in a Penrith hospital. No trace was ever found of Joel."

As a stand-alone story, the disappearance of the Joels may not have much meaning. When you take into account the bad weather and the other missing people surrounding this region, there is a consistency that can't be ignored.

As you read the stories, go to Google and map the locations of the disappearances. You may be surprised at their proximity to each other.

Mrs. Farrell's Son
Missing: 10/12/1875-8:00 a.m., Tenterfield, NSW
Age at disappearance: 4 years

This incident occurred four miles northeast of Tenterfield just off Timbarra Road in an area of many rivers and swamps. It is just seven miles east of the Queensland border and on the border of Basket Swamp National Park.

On October 12, 1875, at about 8:00 a.m., Mrs. Farrell sent her three sons into the bush with the family dog to gather the cattle and calves. About a mile from their residence, the boys startled a kangaroo, and each wanted to chase it. The two older boys realized their younger brother wasn't able to keep up and ordered him home. They put him on the path back to their residence and walked away from him. An hour after they sent their youngest brother home, the boys returned home for breakfast. Mrs. Farrell asked where the youngest brother was; they were shocked he wasn't at the home. The brothers were sent out into the bush to bring him home. Hours later they returned and stated they couldn't locate the young boy. It was at this point that the community was notified and searchers started to respond. Late in the afternoon, the area was hit by two severe thunderstorms, which restricted search operations.

Hundreds of neighbors responded and searched every nook and rock for a six-mile distance without finding even a trace of the boy.

Searchers continued to grow in number for four days without anyone finding anything related to the boy.

On the fifth day, a police officer was on horseback. He dismounted at Clear Creek in an effort to find any tracks. Sergeant Goldrick saw the boy near the creek in high weeds looking at him. He was alive. An October 30, 1875, article in the *Sydney Mall* explained the area and the find: "The place where he was found was fully nine miles from where he was lost, and he had gone over some of the wildest and roughest country in the district, and that is saying a good deal. Some of the places where he had gone down were too steep to bring a horse with any degree of safety." The boy had lost his shoes, and his feet were swollen with splinters. He was gone a total of eighty hours without food. He was found to be in good condition.

Summary

This four-year-old boy had traveled nine miles in eighty hours. He had traveled without his shoes through dangerous and steep terrain. This happened just on the edge of a state park near Sandy Hill.

A four- to six-year-old child in mountain terrain should be located within 2.3 miles or less, according to Robert Koester's book, *Lost Person Behavior*.

The thunderstorms, the extraordinary distance traveled, and the lost shoes all mimic cases I have written about in North America.

Glenis M. Gilbert
Missing: 04/09/28-4:00 p.m., Leura, NSW
Age at disappearance: Unknown

Luera is the city immediately to the east of Katoomba.

On April 9, 1928, at 4:00 p.m., Glenis was seen at the seventeenth tee of the Luera Golf Links. Nobody knew where she went after that, but she didn't return to her home in Luera. Her husband became concerned and notified local authorities that she was a missing person.

Searchers started to comb the area near the golf course. Near the course's pumping station, a searcher found a walking stick that was identified as belonging to Glenis. This was approximately one and a quarter miles from the Gilberts' residence. Searchers now started to check cliffs in the area and found a place where they believed Glenis had rested. Many thought she had been there for several days. Near this spot, searchers found Glenis's false teeth.

A May 7, 1928, article in the *Sydney Morning Herald* had a summary of what searchers did next: "With these definite clues, an intensive search was made. Mr. Nettup's party went down a difficult gully, where it seemed impossible for Mrs. Gilbert to have wandered, but the searchers were rewarded. Mr. Nettup discovered the body of the missing woman in a remarkable state of preservation. She was missing her shoes and stockings and leaning against a rocky ledge, dead."

Prior to the discovery of Mrs. Gilbert, local officials had stated that this was one of the most thorough searches ever in the area. They claimed that Mrs. Gilbert would not be found anywhere in the district. They were wrong.

Summary

This case is important for several reasons. Searchers were astounded that they found Glenis where they did. They had a difficult time getting to the area, and they were shocked that she made it. The more important fact is Glenis's state of preservation. Why is this fact important? Glenis disappeared on April 9 and was found May 7. If the search for the woman was as thorough as authorities claim, is it possible that she wasn't in the area when they were searching? Why would any woman remove her dentures and shoes if she was alive and knew she'd be moving around?

There was never an article stating Glenis's cause of death.

M-I. Shields (Son)
Missing: 08/31/31-Unk, Mossgiel, NSW
Age at disappearance: 4 years

The tiny town of Mossgiel is located approximately 420 air miles west of Sydney. It sits in an area with light ground cover. Just on the outskirts of the city is Willandra National Park. It's an entirely different landscape with water, campgrounds, and a gorgeous environment for hiking.

On August 31, 1931, the four-year-old son of Mr. I. Shields disappeared from his home. Articles state that searchers scoured the neighborhood and couldn't locate the boy. In the late 1800s and early 1900s, this area was known for sheep farming. The local shearers left their jobs and joined searchers looking across the countryside for the youngster.

After several days of looking, some of the people started to believe the boy was dead and walked away. A September 7, 1931, article in the *Sydney Morning Herald* had the following description of what happened next: "After wandering aimlessly for five days through the scrub, the four year old son of Mr. I. Shields, of Mossgiel, was found on Saturday afternoon near Hillston, 45 miles from his home."

The boy made a few vague comments about eating grass and being cold at night. The article also noted that his clothes were "torn into rags."

According to the book *Lost Person Behavior* by Robert Koester, a four- to six-year-old missing in relatively flat country should be found at a distance of 6.6 miles or less 95 percent of the time.

When looking at the area between the two cities, you'll find that the boy would've had to cross at least five rivers.

The boy was found in such good condition that it says he was just driven home. There are no notes indicating he ever saw a doctor.

Is this believable? Do you know a four-year-old who could make this trek?

Anna Gullett
Missing: 09/10/32-5:00 p.m., Leura, NSW
Age at disappearance: 48 years

Anna was a resident of Rose Bay but was staying at the Leighton Lodge in Leura. Leura is the city immediately to the east of Katoomba.

On September 10, 1932, at 5:00 p.m., Anna left the lodge to take a walk around the city. When she didn't return by the end of the night, the lodge became concerned and notified the police. On September 11, searches of the city started.

Police knew that the night of September 10 was unusual as there was a heavy mist and fog that had engulfed Leura. People were concerned for Anna because she wore thick glasses and her vision wasn't the best.

As searchers were pressing forward to find Anna, heavy rain continued to inundate Leura and cause the searchers to have problems with visibility.

On September 12, there were almost two hundred people working in and around the city looking for the woman. One group was at the bottom of Northcote Street in a swampy area approximately one mile from the lodge. A September 13, 1932, article in the *Sydney Morning Herald* had a description of what was found: "He pushed aside the tall reeds, and stepped forward. Looking down, he was horrified to see the missing woman's body lying at his feet. Miss Gullett was lying on her back. Her umbrella was lying close beside her. The body was taken to the morgue pending a post mortem exam."

There were rumors that Anna had been sick, but that was never clarified.

There was never any clarification on what the woman was or was not wearing. There was some conjecture that police felt she wandered into the swamp when she was lost and collapsed. If you've read my other missing books, there is something about swamps and missing people that is not understood. Anna was lost during bad weather, something that is a common theme in the profile of the missing we've developed.

I could not find an article clarifying what the medical examiner determined to be the cause of death.

Joyce Fielding
Missing: 02/03/36-Unk, Goondiblule Station, NSW
Age at disappearance: 22 months

Goondiblule Station is near Mingindl in New South Wales.

On February 3, 1936, Joyce Fielding was in the yard of her parents' rural home when she disappeared. Area residents responded and assisted in the search. Four hundred people from throughout the area responded, and all contributed their time to finding Joyce.

Three days after Joyce disappeared, an aboriginal tracker, George Qombo, found the girl sleeping beside a log under a bush. She was alive. She was taken home and later evaluated by a physician and found to have a slight fever.

The reason this story is in the chapter is what is described in the *Sydney Morning Herald* of February 6, 1936: "Although she was only five miles from the place she was missed, it is estimated that she wandered 15 miles." A twenty-two-month-old girl is claimed to have walked fifteen miles in less than three days.

It was found that Joyce had lost one of her sandals and made part of the trip in bare feet. She also had removed a portion of her clothing. Witnesses stated that she had many scratches on her legs and arms.

Many of the missing children who are found are located asleep or semiconscious. I have stated in past books that many children are also found with a slight fever, but no cause can be found.

Silvia Green
Missing: 03/24/53-7:00 p.m., Katoomba, NSW
Age at disappearance: 26 years

Ms. Green was described as an attractive, six-foot-tall blonde. She was a receptionist at a Katoomba guest house on Waratah Street. On March 24, 1953, the blonde left Katoomba by train to meet a date in Penrith. The two spent the day picnicking on the Nepean River. Detectives later interviewed the man and confirmed that he drove her back to her residence at the guest house at 7:00 p.m.

On March 25, 1953, Mrs. M. Pole, the proprietor's wife, went to check on Silvia. She found that she hadn't slept in her bed. It was at this point that local police were called.

Searches continued for six days without any new clues. On March 30, 1953, police made a gruesome find as is described in the March 30 article in the *Sydney Morning Herald*: "The party descended into the Jamieson Valley on a carriage of the scenic railway and made their way along the Federal Pass until they were directly below Echo Point. The police officers made a grueling climb of 400 feet up a steep and rugged slope to where they found the body, about 50 feet from the cliff face." The article states that every bone in the woman's body was broken.

As officers were recovering the body, something extremely unusual happened, which is described in the same article quoted above: "While recovering the body, Detective-Sergeant Fisher was struck on the ankle by a boulder. The ankle became discolored and swollen and he later had it X-rayed. Other members of the police party narrowly escaped being struck by a bottle and a stone thrown from the lookout above." The article also clarified that Silvia's body had fallen one thousand feet.

If life in Katoomba and the surrounding regions seems a little strange to you, you are not alone.

Mary Lewis
Missing: 06/16/53-Unk, Wentworth Falls, NSW
Age at disappearance: 83 years

This story appears in the chapter because it fits the pattern of high strangeness existing in the Katoomba, Leura, and Wentworth Falls area during the early 1950s. The falls are less than three miles east of Katoomba with Leura sitting in between the two.

Mrs. Mary Lewis lived in Collaroy but was vacationing with her daughter at a cottage on West Street in Wentworth Falls. On June 16, 1953, Mrs. Lewis went for a walk from the cottage and never returned. The police conducted an extensive seven-day search and then terminated their effort. They never found any evidence of where Mary may have gone.

The police did make a statement that they did not believe that the woman would have wandered into the bush, but they had no explanation on where she did go. I did an extensive archival search and found two short articles on the incident, but never anything about the woman being found.

Summary

I do find it highly unusual that three women vanished from this area in an eleven-month period between 1953 and 1954. I did a search for all years, and these are the only incidents that came up matching the profile of what we were looking for.

Isabel Davies
Missing: 07/07/53-5:00 p.m., Blackheath, NSW
Age at disappearance: 75 years

This incident occurred just four miles north from downtown Katoomba.

Isabel Davies lived on Prince Edward Street in Blackheath. She had a bachelor of arts degree from Sydney University. In 1903, she founded the Roseville Girls College and owned the property where it sat at the time she disappeared. She was well known in the small city.

On July 7, 1953, at 5:00 p.m., a resident remembered seeing Ms. Davies walking toward Blackheath Golf Course. This was the last time she had been observed, and this raised concern among the neighbors. Police started to search for the woman. Authorities expressed concern that maybe she had fallen and injured herself or had a heart attack. She was known to take daily walks around the city, and it was thought she was in good health. When news struck that she was missing, relatives from throughout the area came to Blackheath.

Searchers were focusing near the south end of the city around the golf course and then slowly started to change their focus. As the days started to tick off, police started to look toward the cliffs in an attempt to understand where the woman may be.

Nine days after Isabel was first reported missing, a discovery was made on the cliffs. A July 16 article in the *Sydney Morning Herald* stated: "Body of missing woman found on mountain ledge." The article stated that many of her bones had been broken, and she was deceased. She had fallen off a twenty-foot cliff and then rolled thirty feet to the ledge. The article stated: "The ledge is swampy and reeds grow thickly over it." The article goes on to explain that this area had been searched multiple times in the past. The exact location was Phillips Lookout near Govett's Leap. In one of the articles I reviewed, it was stated that it was believed that Isabel had wandered too close to the cliff at dark and fell. Others stated that Isabel went to this area regularly, and it was doubtful she'd make a mistake by getting too close. There were railings in place at the time of this incident, according to the articles.

Keep track: this is another case where the body was found in a location searched multiple times.

Timothy Farmer
Missing: 05/05/54-11:00 a.m., Linden, NSW
Age at disappearance: 2½ years

Linden is eight miles east of Wentworth Falls in Katoomba. It's in very rough country. An observatory is just down the road from the family home on Glossop Road.

On May 5, 1954, at 11:00 a.m., Mrs. Farmer was hanging clothes in her backyard. She had placed Timothy with his fourteen-month-old brother under the veranda in the front yard. When she returned after a few minutes, Timothy was gone. She called for the boy, searched the surrounding yard, and didn't get a response. She called neighbors for additional assistance.

The search hadn't gone on long when police asked for additional volunteers. A row of cars filled with volunteers left Sydney and drove to the small community. It wasn't long before hundreds were looking for the boy.

Mrs. Farmer told authorities that her son had never walked off before. She was concerned that he may have followed their road to the main highway and been picked up by another car. A May 6, 1954, article in the *Sydney Morning Herald* had a statement from an astronomer at the local observatory: "I think we will find him alive this morning somewhere in this area, which is rugged and practically impassable." You read that correctly—they were in some of the roughest country in the Blue Mountains.

On May 6, searchers found one of Timothy's shoes. More searchers went to that area and spread out in a triangle formation. One of the searchers brought his German shepherd, Dell, and the dog took off in another direction and started barking. They dropped down into a gorge and were standing in front of a waterfall. In a May 6, 1954, article in the *Sydney Morning Herald* was a description of what the dog handler found: "Mr. Whitburn said later: 'When Dell continued to bark and jump up and down, I made a closer inspection and could see a cave, partly hidden by ferns at the back of the waterfall. I parted the ferns and was amazed to see the boy curled up like a possum in a cave. At first I thought he was dead by the way he was staring, but when he said "puppy," and waved his hand, I knew he was alive and I rushed forward and picked him up.'" Later in the same article was a description of the conditions near the falls: "Police and searchers were amazed that Timothy had made the rugged journey without serious injury. Police and bushmen, as well as the dog Dell, had to receive assistance to climb down to the bottom of the gorge."

Summary

I must admit that I was dumbfounded when I first read this story. How did the boy find the cave? How did the boy make it safely around the water and into the cave? How did Timothy make it safely down into the gorge? Why did the boy leave his home?

Readers of my past books know that the majority of the children who are found are located in a semiconscious or unconscious condition. If you are ever able to find photos of these children after they are found, they do have very wide eyes and an unusual stare.

David Ashley Cusiter
Missing: 03/04/62-3:00 p.m., Katoomba, NSW
Age at disappearance: 17 years

This is another case from the Katoomba area. Start paying special attention to the details of these cases.

David was a student at Katoomba High School and lived on Commonwealth Street in the city. He was last seen in his room at his residence at 3:00 p.m. on Sunday afternoon. He was studying. Once his parents realized he was missing, they reported the disappearance to police at 8:30 p.m. A March 4 article in the *Sydney Morning Herald* had the following information on what police found during their search: "A police search today found a handkerchief believed to belong to the youth and footprints believed to have been made by him. The handkerchief was found near Leura Falls. The footprints were along a narrow track and ended at a narrow outcrop of rock 800 feet above Jamieson Valley." Police stated that they felt the boy may have fallen somewhere in this area, but they could not locate him. March 5-9 police were lowered down the cliffs were the footprints were last seen in an attempt to locate a body. A May 9 article in the *Sydney Morning Herald* updated the search effort: "The fatigued men, drenched to the skin by heavy rainfalls, returned to Katoomba late this afternoon without finding any trace of the boy."

Close to one hundred searchers had been combing the cliffs around Leura in an effort to locate David without success. Articles stated that this was the largest search in the history of the Blue Mountains to date.

A March 11, 1962, article in the *Sydney Morning Herald* had the headline "Body Found" and the following notes: "The body of a Katoomba school boy David Ashley Cusiter, 17, was found yesterday on a narrow ledge 400 feet below Elysian Rock, near Leura." The article states that four bushwalkers were one hundred feet below the Elysian Rock Lookout when they saw the body. The bushwalkers were members of the Sydney University Mountaineering Club. Police officers were lowered down the cliff and recovered the body. I could not locate any notes on the condition of the body or the cause of death.

Summary

The location of David's body appears to have been in very close proximity to the fall and death of Gary Tweddle. Between the date that David went missing and the date he was found, there were heavy rains in the area. How did the emergency crews miss the body for a week when they had been on ropes on the cliffs searching the area the previous four days?

Stephen Crean
Missing: 08/06/85-2:40 p.m., Charlotte Pass, NSW
Age at disappearance: 37 years

Stephen Crean was born into the life of a politician and the world of government. His father was a former deputy prime minister, and he was the head of administration for the federal department of road safety and transportation in Cranberra. He was a university graduate and was known as a quiet and respectful man with a wife and three children.

On August 6, 1985, at 11:00 a.m., Stephen purchased a lift ticket at the Charlotte Pass Ski Resort inside Kosciusko National Park. He had told friends that he intended to cross country ski from Charlotte to Thredko Ski Resort. This wasn't a difficult trek, and he should've made it easily. He told his friends that he'd be back just after lunch. At 2:40 p.m. his friends reported Stephen as missing.

When Stephen had left, the weather had been starting to cloud up. By the time he was reported missing, it was raining and snowing with heavy winds. Rescue personnel found a couple who had seen someone matching Stephen's description at 3:00 p.m.; this was never confirmed.

The search started slowly because of the bad weather and was terminated after only four days. Searchers believed a thorough search of the area the following summer would allow them to find Stephen's body.

The regional search and rescue teams put hundreds of volunteers and professional searchers back into the area Stephen was supposedly in. They also placed multiple helicopters in the sky with the ability to see beer cans in the creeks. Searchers found a fifty-year-old broken ski and mittens. They searched under every crevice and rock in the area. A May 12, 1986, article in the *Sydney Morning Herald* had this statement about the search: "The park's chief ranger and a search coordinator, Mr. Russell Knutsen, says: 'I believe that if he was still up there, we would have found something by this time.'" Stephen was carrying a small backpack; he was on cross country skis and wearing heavy clothing. Nothing was found. Later in the same article was this: "The searchers believe that Mr. Crean most probably fell into the upper reaches of the Snowy River, which he had to cross to reach Foreman's Hut. They say he may have fallen through the dense snow which blankets the river in winter."

Stephen's relatives told searchers that he had suffered from gout, kidney issues, and high blood pressure. They weren't sure if this contributed to his disappearance. Searchers were already baffled by the lack of any evidence of Stephen, and the case only got murkier.

Nothing much happened on this case for nearly eighteen months after the disappearance. Police in Khancoban then received Stephen's wallet, credit cards, birth certificate, and the remnants of two bank notes. There was a note in the wallet that made a statement that it had been allegedly found in Kosciusko National Park. The letter wasn't signed, but it was postmarked in Shepparton. Police thought it was very odd that it was mailed anonymously and not personally handed in to the police. Through diligent investigation, they interviewed postal workers and determined it had been sent by a fruit picker from New Zealand who was working in their area. They found a twenty-six-year-old man who took investigators to his hut and gave them a skull that was later identified as Stephen's. This man stated he would show investigators where he found the skull, and they went in a helicopter. The man took them to the wrong location and was later arrested. After a lengthy process, the man admitted he had found the skull and wanted to keep it and any human bones that he had found. The man, Stephen James Forsythe, was charged with interfering with human remains and giving a false report to police. Police determined that Forsythe had randomly found the skull while he was hiking in the park. Exactly where the skull was found was not released.

Police eventually found some remains. The specifics of what they found were not in any of the articles we found on this incident.

Summary

The Crean disappearance and how the search was handled made big press in that region. There were many questions about the initial response and why he wasn't found by the multitude of searchers in the area.

The true question in this case is why Stephen's remains were not found by the organized search. They were located by a random hiker. Where are the rest of Stephen's remains and equipment? These were never mentioned in the articles we found.

Stephen disappeared just as inclement weather hit the region. He had a history of medical conditions.

The similarities in cases between the United States and Australia are noteworthy. I've written about the strange disappearances of skiers and how they weren't found in a timely manner.

Prabhdeep Srawn
Missing: 05/13/13-Unk, Charlotte Pass, NSW
Age at disappearance: 25 years

This incident also happened in the Charlotte Pass area of Kosciuscko National Park, same as in the case of Stephen Crean. As I have stated in past books, if these cases had occurred in back-to-back years, they would raise the suspicion of local law enforcement and SAR leaders. But there are almost twenty-eight years between these two disappearances, and almost a full contingent of local government leaders have retired in that time frame. The people who would remember and maybe participated in the Crean incident have moved on in life. But the similarities in the two disappearances are obvious.

Prabhdeep was a resident of Brampton, Ontario, Canada. He was a student at Bond University in Brisbane, Australia. He was a former Canadian army reservist who was trained in wilderness survival.

On May 13, 2013 Prabhdeep rented a car, purchased a black-and-red ski jacket, and drove to Charlotte Pass Village in the national park. He had researched his trip on his laptop, and it showed that he was going to climb in the area of Mount Kosciuszko and Mount Townsend. It was believed that he walked along the main range trail from Charlotte Pass in a counterclockwise direction toward Mount Townsend and Mount Kosciuszko. Kosciuszko is the tallest mountain in Australia at 7,310 feet. The area around the mountain is boulders and dirt with no trees. As you go lower in elevation, there is sparse cover. Up until 1977 there was a dirt road to the summit. In an effort to preserve the environment, the government removed the road. You can take a ski chairlift ride to the top of Charlotte Pass and easily make the three-and-a-half-hour walk to the summit and get back in daylight. The hike has been described as a fairly easy walk.

One week after Prabhdeep left for his hike, it was realized he hadn't returned. A SAR mission with limited resources was started. When he had left for the hike, the weather was perfect. In the late afternoon, rain, snow, and wind hit the mountain and made conditions horrible.

There was a two-week SAR that included twenty members and volunteers. Prabhdeep's family from Canada came to assist and was critical of the effort made by local authorities. The search was eventually abandoned on June 1.

Prabhdeep's family never gave up. They hired eighteen Canadian search team members and flew them to Australia. This effort cost the family $50,000. They found nothing. The family posted a reward of $100,000, which has produced nothing. In one effort, the Australian Swiss Dog Association worked the area for several days and eventually had to leave because of inclement weather. The dogs found nothing.

The strangest incident to occur during the search happened on Wednesday, May 22, 2013. Ruby Singh Sahota, Prabhdeep's cousin, described the incident on *CTV News* on May 25, 2013. She stated that searchers were on the mountain and heard a man's call for help. They couldn't determine where the cries were coming from and spent two days trying to find the precise location. They never could find the origin of the calls. This is very similar to what was heard in the disappearance of Mitchell Dale Stehling from Mesa Verde National Park in Colorado on June 9, 2013. Searchers in that incident heard a man's cry for help and couldn't locate the source (see the Colorado chapter).

A drone was used to cover the countryside on June 10 in Kosciuszko National Park. The family offered to pay for the effort, but the company was using the drone to map the topography and volunteered to utilize the craft in the SAR. Nothing of any evidentiary value was located.

As of the publishing of this book, Prabhdeep has not been found.

Gary Tweddle
Missing: 07/16/13-Unk, Leura, NSW
Age at disappearance: 23 years

This story is truly mind-boggling. It doesn't make any sense and will challenge your analytical skills to develop a rational explanation for what transpired.

I must first tell readers that without the assistance of a resident of Leura, this story would not be nearly as complete as it is. I will call this person "PM." He is a retired professional who lives in the neighborhood where Gary disappeared. We crossed paths on the Internet, and he was responsible for giving his views on the path Gary took and the feelings of the local community. He and his family are equally disturbed with what happened and are at a loss to explain why and how Gary ended up where he did. Thanks, PM!

Gary was born in Cremorne, England, and later lived in Reading. His father is a British military officer. Gary and his dad traveled to Scotland and the Welsh mountains, where they went mountain climbing together. In 2005 he moved from Britain to the Gold Coast of Queensland and later moved to the lower north shore of Sydney. He was a regular participant in early-morning boot camp for young athletes. He was in great physical condition and known by his family and friends as a "junior Bear Grylls."

Gary landed a job in Australia as a business intelligence sales representative for Oracle Corporation. Oracle is based just twenty-five miles from where I lived in the San Francisco Bay Area. They are known as a great technology company that hires some of the brightest young people in the world. Gary was obviously doing well in his job, as he was invited to the company's business conference at the Fairmont Resort in the Blue Mountains adjacent to the Blue Mountains National Park.

MISSING
GARY TWEDDLE

Gary Tweddle

Missing From: Fairmont Resort, Leura NSW
Date Missing: Tuesday 16 July 2013
Age: 23 years
Sex: Male
Height: 170cm
Weight: 85kg
Build: Medium
Eyes: Brown
Hair: Short brown
Race: Caucasian
Clothing: Dark jeans, checked shirt

PLEASE CALL WITH ANY INFORMATION
Crime Stoppers 1800 333 000

We ask all local residents to please check any sheds, outhouses, underneath houses and any unoccupied houses in your area.

On the night of July 16, 2013, Gary went with other members of his business group to the Silk's Brassere restaurant in Leura. This is known as a high-end restaurant that serves excellent food. All indications are that the group had a good time and returned by taxi to the Fairmont. After they arrived, Gary is seen on video leaving from the front of the hotel and talking on his cell phone.

Shortly after leaving the resort, Gary called his friends back at the hotel and explained that he was lost. His business associates described him as being initially calm but apparently worried that he didn't know where he was. He said that he was turning toward "a light on the hill" and then after a seventeen-minute conversation, he terminated the call because he was afraid his phone would go dead.

There is some confusion and conflict among the many news sources about the content of the call. One of the accounts states that Gary could be heard running through the bush. Nobody was sure why he'd be doing this. It's also unclear what light on what hill Gary may have seen, the one he said he was walking toward. After that initial call, Gary wasn't heard from again. He disappeared.

Local SAR teams responded in force. Hundreds of hours of helicopter searches and over ten thousand search hours committed over twelve days found nothing. Law enforcement was baffled at the lack of evidence and their inability to find the missing man. Helicopters combed the hills and the area around the resort and found nothing to indicate that Gary was in the area. Family from England came and monitored the search. Gary's girlfriend was a frequent observer to the SAR effort.

Gary was reported missing on July 16. On September 2, a New South Wales Ambulance Special Casualty Accident Team (SCAT) was on a training mission flying a helicopter off the cliffs in Leura and Katoomba. The team had a flight plan but decided to deviate slightly and fly over an area called "Sweet Dreams," the same area Gary was last thought to be in. A September 7, 2013, article in *The Telegraph* described what pilots observed: "To maintain the hover as they ran through hypothetical rescue missions, the pilot had to pick a reference point on the cliff as a marker. The sun flickered on something slumped backwards over a fallen tree branch that caught the pilot's eye." Later in the same article was this: "It was slumped backwards over a fallen tree branch, clothed in dark blue jeans or pants, and a tattered shirt partially covering what appeared to be a bare torso. Two legs could be clearly made out and, the way the object was lying, just one arm was visible." They had found Gary Tweddle.

The helicopter crew made a determination that the person was deceased. This was only a kilometer from the Fairmont, and the pilots believed they had found the body of the missing businessman. Crews responded and recovered Gary.

The real mystery to this story is how Gary got to the location where he was found and why he became lost in the first place. In the same *Telegraph* article quoted above was this statement from a search volunteer: "Leura's Kevin McDonald who volunteered in the search for Mr. Tweddle, said it staggered him how someone could plunge from that cliff, given the edge was several hundred meters from the roadway: 'It's not like you come to the end of Sublime Point Road and bang, you drop off the cliff,' Mr. McDonald said. 'You've got to walk for a good way through seriously rugged bush, before you fall off.'" The mystery didn't end with this.

Gary was found September 7, 2013. It takes six weeks to get toxicology results, and an autopsy is usually done immediately after the body is recovered. It's now May 2014, and the police and coroner's office in Australia have not released any official statement about the cause of death. Why?

PM did offer some clarity on the path that Gary must have taken the night he disappeared. He walked out of the Fairmont and turned left onto Sublime Point Road. This is a very nice area of expensive homes and well-maintained roadways. He walked through an area of heavy bush on each side of the road and past a few small streets. The road eventually comes to a dead end, but there is not a definitive cliff in that area. There is a walkway with guardrails.

PM makes an important point about the location where Gary must've fallen. To get to that location, it would've taken a big effort through some very heavy bush. Many people cannot believe he got to that point because of the ruggedness and because the trail is almost impossible to find unless you knew it was there. From the front of the Fairmont to the end of Sublime Point Road is a fifteen-minute walk. With expensive homes and great roadways nearby, why would anyone leave the roadway and start running through the bush? This makes zero sense. Gary knew cliffs were in the area, if he knew where he was located. Nobody can definitively state what the "light on the hill" might have been that Gary claimed he was walking toward. Why would he be walking toward that light?

Many residents in the Leura community are puzzled how the initial searches from helicopter and land failed to locate Gary. As many readers know, this isn't uncommon in the cases we have highlighted in the Missing 411 books. This is not meant to be critical of the searchers or their efforts; it's a comment associated with the strangeness of these disappearances. There was not any mention in any article that searchers found Gary's phone or regarding the condition of the body (other than what I mentioned from the helicopter crew).

If the body had been in that location during the entire time he was missing, it should've been in deep decomposition.

Summary

As in all of this research, it's not about one case, and it's not about one unusual aspect; it's about the totality of the circumstances and the history of the region. This is another case to add to the total in the world's national parks.

Queensland

Sex/Name	Date/Time Missing • Age • State
M-Johnny Connors	5/26/1904-p.m. • 2½ • Packsaddle Bore, Australia
F-Vivienne Goldstiver	12/25/37-Unk • 7 • Toonpan, Australia
M-Eric Taylor	07/13/88-4:30 p.m. • 2 • Cooktown, Australia

Johnny Connors
Missing: 5/26/1904-p.m., Packsaddle Bore, Queensland, Australia
Age at disappearance: 2½ years

This incident happened at the northern end of Queensland in an area of desolation and dryness. Packsaddle Bore is located approximately 130 miles northeast of Broken Hill. There is a series of small lakes approximately fifteen miles northwest, and the Norman River is the same mileage to the northeast.

On May 26, 1904, in the afternoon hours, Johnny Connors was on the outskirts of his yard looking for mushrooms. As the afternoon turned to early evening, Mrs. Chris Connors couldn't locate her son and asked neighbors for assistance. As darkness hit the area, six people were looking for the boy. Meanwhile, Mrs. Connors wandered deep into the bush and claimed she also got lost and spent the night in the dirt. Early the following morning, Mrs. Connors found her way home and discovered her boy still hadn't been found.

The weather during the search was described as "bitterly cold," and this concerned family and searchers. Johnny disappeared on a Thursday afternoon. On Sunday afternoon one of the searchers made an interesting discovery as is described in a June 4, 1904, article in the *Sydney Morning Herald*: "On Sunday afternoon Mr. Becks, one of the searchers, found the child about nine miles from his home, trudging along quite happily." The boy was asked where he was going and he stated, "I don't know." The searchers stated that the boy was moving like he was coming back from school.

It's hard to understand how a baby can survive bitterly cold nights and three days without food or water and be walking so briskly when found. It appears the weather had no effect on the child.

Summary

Search manuals indicate that a child one to three years old traveling on flat ground will be found 95 percent of the time within two miles or less. Johnny was found more than four times that distance.

These stories of children covering vast distances may start to sound boring and repetitious. Understand, these stories are so far outside the bounds of any normal missing person incident it is newsworthy, and this is why they appeared in local papers.

I could've almost classified this as a double disappearance because of Mrs. Connors vanishing for one night. It would have been interesting to have had the opportunity to interview her.

Many of the missing people I have chronicled in North America were performing tasks such as mushroom and berry picking when they vanished. The similarities between the US and Australian cases are noteworthy.

Vivienne Joyce Goldstiver
Missing: 12/25/37-Unk, Toonpan, Australia
Age at disappearance: 7 years

Toonpan, Queensland, is located adjacent to Bowling Green National Park and the Ross River Dam. The park is in a mountainous area that can be rough and remote.

On Christmas Day in 1937, Vivienne was visiting her grandmother in Toonpan when she wandered from the home. The family immediately started a search with assistance from the community. A December 31, 1937, article in *The Age* described the rescue effort: "The search, in which hundreds of persons, with police and black trackers participated, was the biggest ever organized in North Queensland. Aeroplanes also cooperated with ground parties."

The search continued for six days until a discovery was made. This is described in the same article quoted above: "The body of Vivienne Joyce Goldstiver, 7 years, daughter of Mr. and Mrs. R. Goldstiver of Richmond, for whom the police and civilians have been searching since Christmas day, was found today by her uncle, Vincent Young, eleven miles from her grandmother's residence at Toonpan. A post mortem examination revealed that the death was due to heat, exhaustion and thirst. The child had lost her shoes in her wanderings through the rough range country. It is believed that death occurred on Sunday or Monday." The revelation from the medical examiner means that Vivienne traveled the eleven miles through very rough terrain in one, maybe two days.

Summary

The similarities in North American and Australian cases are mind-boggling. I have stated many times that children disappear too many times when they are visiting a relative or friend's home. This is another in an extremely long list of children who lost their lives and lost their shoes.

According to Robert Koester's book, *Lost Person Behavior*, children seven to nine years are found in mountain terrain 95 percent of the time within five miles or less from the point they vanished.

Eric Taylor
Missing: 7/13/88-4:30 p.m., Cooktown, Australia
Age at disappearance: 2 years

Cooktown is in Queensland, Australia, near the far upper northwest location of the country. The Taylor family owned a farm approximately twenty miles south of the city in an area of heavy foliage adjacent to Black Mountain National Park.

On July 13, 1988, at approximately 4:30 p.m., Eric was playing outside his residence when he inexplicably disappeared. The family immediately notified adjacent residences and local law enforcement, and the hunt was on. Over three hundred people responded and scoured the landscape, hollering and looking for the lad. State emergency workers brought canines and additional assistance to the rescue effort.

July is the coldest month of the year in this section of Australia with nighttime temperatures as low as sixty degrees.

The searchers went three days without finding a trace of the two-year-old. Searchers were about ready to give up hope of finding the boy alive. On July 17 at 3:00 p.m., they made an unusual find in an unlikely location. A July 18, 1988, article in the *Albany Herald* had this: "Eric grinned and held out his arms when he was discovered by rescue workers 400 yards up a mountain track and more than a mile from his home." A July 18, 1988, article in the *Glasgow Herald* had more information about what searchers determined: "Rescue workers believed the little boy had walked and crawled at least 12 miles." In the same article was this: "When a search party found him yesterday, sitting naked in a scrub patch, the boy grinned and stretched out his arms for a cuddle."

I believe that the rescue workers made the above statements to the newspapers. It's hard to believe the boy actually made the journey that is described. He was found twelve hundred feet up a mountain after being gone for almost four days without water. When people are dehydrated, they rarely exert significant effort. When small children are missing in the woods, the majority of the time they do not climb mountains, naked.

Doctors stated that Eric had a significant amount of scratches and was dehydrated. There were never any statements about the boy suffering from exposure. A July 18, 1988, article in the *Albany Herald* also had this: "Police sergeant Ken Salmon, the search coordinator, said that the area where Eric was eventually found had been scoured a number of times. 'Believe me, it's rugged, treacherous country,' he said. 'We are both stunned and jubilant at finding the boy.'"

Eric was found in Black Mountain National Park.

Summary

I think the facts of this story speak for themselves. Rescue workers were stunned that they found Eric alive on the side of a mountain. I can't imagine any twelve-year-old hiking through the woods for twelve miles in four days, much less a two-year-old.

South Australia

Sex/Name   Date/Time Missing • Age • State
F-Daughter of Mrs. Starkey 04/26/39-a.m. • 5 • South Australia

Daughter of Mrs. Starkey
Missing: 04/26/39-a.m., Andamooka Station, South Australia
Age at disappearance: 5 years

This is another case where the distances traveled by the child are mind-boggling and a reminder of the similarities between the North American and Australian cases.

This incident occurred on the outskirts of Andamooka Station, a small opal-mining community 375 miles north of Adelaide. While the city may be small in size, it is huge in the opal industry. The city sits just five miles west of giant Lake Torrens and is surrounded by hundreds of small lakes, swamps, and rivers.

In the morning hours of April 26, 1939, Mr. Starkey left the family residence to fix a fence at the outer reaches of their ranch.

Unknown to family members, Starkey's five-year-old daughter had attempted to follow him. After a short period of time, the family realized the girl wasn't in the home. The area around the home and the land between the residence and the fence were searched, and the girl wasn't found. A message was sent to town that a small child was missing, and searchers responded.

Native aboriginal trackers were brought to the homestead to follow the tracks. A May 2, 1939 article in *The Age* had the following about the success of the search: "Search parties, including black trackers and horseman went out, but she could not be found." Early efforts couldn't find any evidence of the girl being in the area.

On April 28 searchers continued to look for evidence and got lucky, as is described in the same *The Age* article: "After having been lost in the bush for almost 36 hours, during which she wandered barefooted for 34 miles, the five year old daughter of Mr. and Mrs. Starkey of Andamooka Station, 60 miles from Pimba was found on Friday afternoon about 15 miles from her homestead."

Just for perspective, according to Robert Koester's book, *Lost Person Behavior*, a child between the ages of four and six if traveling on flat ground will be found 95 percent of the time within a distance of 6.6 miles or less. This girl allegedly traveled more than five times the distance quoted in SAR books. The other bizarre part of this incident: the girl wasn't wearing shoes.

It would be difficult for anyone of any age to hike thirty-four miles in less than thirty-six hours. The last paragraph in the same *The Age* article was this: "Although she had been without food and the night was bitterly cold, the child was little affected, but her feet had been badly scratched by prickles. She had dug a hole under a tree and slept when she found that she was lost." This means that she had actually traveled the thirty-four miles in far less than thirty-six hours, making this even more unbelievable. There are a few instances where I've written about a missing person being found under a tree. This is the first time a claim has ever been made that a five-year-old dug a hole to sleep under a tree. It would seem that it would take several hours to dig a hole large enough for a five-year-old to get into and "sleep in."

There was never any mention of what the girl remembered or said about the time she was missing. She was seen by a doctor and found to be in very good condition except for the scratches on her feet.

Victoria

Sex/Name
M-Patrick Hildebrand

Date/Time Missing • Age • State
06/27/87-1:50 p.m. • 9 • Wilsons Promontory National Park, Victoria, Australia

Patrick Hildebrand
Missing: 06/27/87-1:50 p.m., Wilsons Promontory National Park, Victoria, Australia
Age at disappearance: 9 years

This is the description of Victoria's Wilson's Promontory National Park directly from its website: "The Prom is one of Victoria's most loved places. At the southern most tip of mainland Australia, it offers spectacular scenery of huge granite mountains, open forest, rainforest, sweeping beaches and coastlines." The park is located ninety-seven miles southeast of Melbourne on a gorgeous peninsula. It's known as a location where visitors travel and stay for one to three days, either to enjoy the ocean and beaches or the mountains and wildlife.

On June 27, 1987, the Hildebrand family made the trip from their residence in southeast Melbourne to "The Prom." Participating in the family trip was nine-year-old Patrick and his sister. He was a unique child. He had a highly unusual type of epilepsy called Lennox-Gastaut Syndrome. He also had a slight speech defect. The boy enjoyed the outdoors and wanted to walk the trails in the park.

At 1:00 p.m., the family was hiking the Lilly Pilly trail. They had hiked their way two and a half kilometers down when they noticed that Patrick had gone ahead out of sight. His sister ran ahead to look for her brother and couldn't locate him. A group of adults now started an extensive search of the area they believed he probably was. The family retraced their journey back to their car and drove five kilometers to the ranger station where they reported the boy as lost. A July 6 article in *The Age* had the following information about search efforts: "The rangers immediately embarked on a piecemeal search, but were thwarted when evening fog closed in." Weather issues are a very common theme in the cases we write about.

Rangers gathered almost fifteen searchers by Sunday morning. They did find a cap in a bed of ferns several hundred yards from where Patrick was last seen. One article I located stated that the cap belonged to Patrick. Once the fog cleared, helicopters took to the sky with FLIR. They found nothing of value.

Searchers made several optimistic statements early in the effort. After five days of searching, the attitude started to change. Authorities now brought in aboriginal searchers to assist.

The trackers were brought to the scene after hundreds of people had crumpled the bush and obliterated any possible footprints. There was controversy surrounding the reason why officials waited so long to bring in the native trackers.

The Lilly Pilly Gully ran down toward a large swamp, a location that concerned searchers. Some felt that Patrick would walk uphill and not down to the swamp; others believed if he went to the swamp, he would be in great danger.

Readers of other books know that swamps are some type of magnet for missing people. This issue is not understood, but the facts indicate that people go into the swamps for some unknown reason. Missing people have been found in swamps up to their necks.

The aboriginal trackers were unable to find any trace of the boy. A seven-day search failed to find any convincing evidence that the boy may be alive, and the search was terminated.

There were many articles that addressed the controversy among the search groups on this effort. Some claimed the strategy was flawed, and others defended the effort.

Summary

Patrick fits the profile of many missing children with disabilities. They get ahead or behind the group on the trail and vanish. Searchers have a difficult time finding evidence, and the child may not be found. The inclusion of fog into the equation is another weather element that inhibited and delayed the ability of searchers to locate the boy.

The continent of Australia has many missing cases that mimic missing person cases in North America. I think it's noteworthy that this case also occurred in a national park.

Western Australia

Sex/Name   Date/Time Missing • Age • State
F-Caroline Chamberlain   05/19/62-4:30 p.m. • 2 • Kojonup, WA

Caroline Chamberlain
Missing: 05/19/62-4:30 p.m., Kojonup, WA
Age at disappearance: 2 years

Kojonup is approximately 150 miles southeast of Perth at the far southwestern edge of Australia. This incident occurred thirty-five miles west of Kojonup in a region surrounded by water and swamps. Stirling Range National Park is just to the south, and Lake Magenta Nature Reserve is to the east. The small city is known for its pastureland and farms. The population of the actual city is just over six thousand but goes much higher when you start to include the surrounding countryside.

On May 19, 1962, Caroline Chamberlain was playing in her yard with her twelve-year-old sister, Shelly. At approximately 4:30 p.m., Shelly came into her home and told her mother that Caroline had wandered away. Mrs. Chamberlain went into the yard and surrounding area, calling the girl's name and trying to find her. After an hour, it was apparent that the girl was nowhere in the vicinity, and a call was made for searchers.

The first twelve hours of the search produced no evidence that the girl was anywhere close to her home. At 10:30 p.m. on May 20, there was an interesting discovery by someone who was probably very surprised, as is described in a May 22, 1962, article in *The Age*: "Farmer Frank Smith of Cranbrook, found Caroline huddled on her hands and knees with her head on the ground. She had lost one of her slippers and the bitter cold had stiffened her limbs." The farmer wrapped the girl in a blanket and brought her into his home.

Caroline was found two miles from her home. Later in the same article quoted above was this: "Men on horseback and on foot must have passed within a few yards of her during yesterday's extensive search." Searchers were surprised the girl hadn't heard them calling her name or seen the men on horseback. Later in the same article was a statement about what Caroline said: "She had no recollection of having been lost and told her mother that the family dog had caused the scratches on her limbs."

The girl was found in the city of Cranbrook. It is located on the edge of Stirling Range National Park. There are hundreds of small bodies of water just to the northeast of the city.

Summary

The elements associated with Caroline's disappearance and later discovery mimic the facts surrounding missing children in North America. They are found in and near national parks. Children are located near bodies of water and are many times located by people uninvolved with the search effort. Searchers are surprised they didn't find the girl sooner, as she was found in an area that was previously searched. One of the more fascinating elements—which matches many of the missing children cases we've chronicled—is the child doesn't remember anything about being lost.

CHAPTER FOUR: BORNEO

Sex/Name	Date Missing • Age • State
M-Ng Boon Heng	10/22/88-Unk • 26 • Mount Kinabalu, Borneo
M-Lau King Thong	10/22/88-Unk • 34 • Mount Kinabalu, Borneo
F-Ellie James	08/16/01-Unk • 17 • Mount Kinabalu, Borneo

The stories in this chapter center on the tallest mountain in Southeast Asia, Mount Kinabalu. It's situated in Kinabalu National Park and is reportedly climbed by thirty thousand people each year. The website climbmtkinabalu.com states that "it is one of the easiest peaks in the world to conquer." The mountain is usually summited in two days, and the lone night can be spent at one of many guest homes in the area. The elevation of the mountain is 13,454 feet (source-BBC 8/19/01), and it is located on the northern corner of the island.

Ng Boon Heng Age at disappearance: 26 years
M-Lau King Thong   Age at disappearance: 34 years
Missing: 10/22/88-Unk, Mount Kinabalu, Borneo

On October 22, 1988, five employees of a bottling company in Kuching decided that they would try to summit Mount Kinabalu. The group started up the well-marked trail with ropes guiding their path.

At 12,500 feet, Boon and Lau told the three others in the group to go ahead and they would rest. As the pair sat, a Singaporean and her guide also passed and continued up the mountain. These were the last two to ever see Ng and Lau. Bad weather moved in, and the pair disappeared.

The Sabah Parks department spent over $200,000 searching for the two. Thirty park rangers and twenty police officers spent almost two months of searching nonstop and found nothing to indicate they were on the mountain.

While the search was ongoing, on November 24 the parks department constructed a series of huts along the hiking route to allow people to rest with some defense against the weather.

It should be stated here that I've seen photos of the mountain. It is not a dangerous or difficult hike, but it does reach high elevations. There is no place on it to get cover, other than the huts. There is nothing on the mountain but many, many large boulders. I have no idea where these two men could've gone.

In *Missing 411-Western United States,* I wrote about the disappearance of Carl Landers on Mount Shasta in Northern California. The search coordinator in that incident had supervised hundreds of SARs and stated that he was completely baffled about where Carl could have gone. I feel the same about the disappearance of these two men. As you read the next story, you'll hear about a fourteen-year-old boy who was also was lost and never found on this mountain.

Ellie James
Missing: 08/16/01-Unk, Mount Kinabalu, Borneo
Age at disappearance: 17 years

The James family from Cornwall, England, had traveled to Borneo for a fourteen-day vacation. On August 16, 2001, the family decided to try to summit Kinabalu. As the James family was climbing with a group of British trekkers, the weather turned bad. Ellie was with her fifteen-year-old brother, Henry. Winds started to pick up, and rain inundated the mountain. The two were following a rope trail down the mountain when Henry sat down and stated he'd wait for the others behind him. Ellie told him she'd go get help and left the rope. Henry was found hours later on the rope and was brought down the mountain; Ellie was lost.

Borneo sent troops up the mountain in an effort to find the young girl. An August 23, 2001, article in *The Item* had the following statements from a local guide who was assisting in the rescue: "We heard Help me…Help Me…and ran back and forth to try to locate the area from where the cries were coming, but our efforts were in vain because of strong winds, the mountain echo and low visibility." There were others who heard a cry for help, but nobody could identify where the calls were coming from.

It rained nonstop for four days after Ellie went missing. Conditions for searching were some of the most treacherous the guides and local officials had seen in ten years.

There was an article printed on August 21 that explained that rangers found a makeshift bed of ferns and empty banana peels at the 1,500-meter elevation. They actually entertained the idea that this was Ellie. They could not prove it.

On the sixth day of the search for the seventeen-year-old, searchers were covering an area near 12,270 feet that had been covered multiple times in previous days, and they found Ellie. She was still wearing her bright-pink coat and was lying facedown at the base of a steep cliff. Her body was removed, and later an autopsy was conducted. It was determined she died of exposure.

Everyone on the mountain believed that Ellie had gone downhill to get assistance for her brother. It was now believed that she was found uphill from where she left Henry.

Summary

This book contains other stories where searchers hear a victim calling for help and they can't be found. In this instance, the area where Ellie was found had been searched before.

While doing the research for this story, I discovered a three-line note about the disappearance of fourteen-year-old Ng Chong. He disappeared on a school outing sometime in 1978. Ng was never found. The only item searchers found was one of his shoes. Because I can't confirm a date or any other specific details about the disappearance, I won't write a stand-alone article about the boy.

CHAPTER FIVE: ECUADOR

Sex/Name	Date Missing • Age • State
M-David Byrd Felker	07/22/02-Unk • 20 • Zamora, Ecuador
M-August Reiger	06/16/13-Unk • 18 • Banos, Ecuador

You are about to read about two unusual young men who disappeared in the wilds of Ecuador. Both of these students were highly intellectual, bordering on genius. These are the only two Americans I could find who disappeared under similar conditions in a South American country.

David Byrd Felker
Missing: 07/22/02-Unk, Zamora, Ecuador
Age at disappearance: 20 years

If you tried to find a couple who could come together to give life to a highly intellectual man, that may be Maggie Felker and Mike Byrd. Mike was a professor of philosophy at the University of Wisconsin at Madison. Maggie was a registered nurse at Saint Mary's hospital in Madison.

David Byrd Felker showed extreme intelligence at a young age and continued to push his intellectual limits through July of 2002. At twenty years old, David spoke four languages fluently and had traveled to many far reaches of the world.

David was a full-time student at Beloit College. He had told many family and friends that he wanted to join the Peace Corps when he finished college. During the summer of 2002, he traveled with fourteen other Beloit students to the capital of Ecuador, Quito, to study Spanish literature and German in a special program sponsored by his college. During his time out of class, the young man taught children to read. His Ecuadorian college was Pontificia Universidad Catolica del Ecuador in Quito.

In early July 2002, David had some time away from college and decided to travel fifteen hours south of Quito and visit Podocarpus National Park. It features 360,000 acres of lush woods and jungle with trails crisscrossing the countryside. He checked into a hotel and dropped his supplies. Hotel employees remembered seeing him and believe he took park maps when he left. He was never seen again.

Fast forward to August 12, 2002, and O'Hare International Airport in Chicago—there waited Maggie Felker for David to disembark from his flight. He wasn't on it. This started an agony-filled journey of parents trying to find their son. They had few leads and were working in a country with a limited law enforcement infrastructure.

Maggie Felker pulled some heroic efforts to get to the point where she found her son's belongings at his hotel. She was presented with David's journal. Inside the journal he explained that he had visited the park, and he checked into the hotel on July 22 at 10:00 a.m. All indications were that he was headed back to the park. It did not appear to hotel staff that his bed had been slept in.

Mom went to the US embassy and got someone interested in the case. This support rallied more with the FBI becoming involved. Maggie also was able to convince a search team from Tampa Bay to travel to Ecuador to assist. They spent ten days in the jungle searching at a cost of $60,000. Nine canine teams of search and cadaver dogs from the United States found nothing. They found nothing indicating that David had ever been in the area.

The FBI eventually got back to the Felker-Byrd family and indicated that their investigations revealed that there was no foul play they could find.

David has never been found.

Summary

The loss of a family member is one of life's most difficult challenges. Not knowing what happened to a loved one is horrific and follows you forever. A July 21, 2012, article in JSonlinenew.com had an article that addressed what Mike and Maggie did after it was determined that David may never be found: "Mike and Maggie rented out their home in Madison and became volunteers at the Working Boys' Center in Quito, a school for the city's multitude of impoverished children and their families. A medical emergency—Maggie suffered a transient ischemic stroke—brought them back to Madison. They decided to remain, at least until Rachel finished college. They returned to the center in 2007 and remained there for three years."

Pray that the family finds peace with their loss.

M-August Reiger
Missing 06/16/13-Unk • Banos, Ecuador
Age at disappearance: 18 years

During the spring of 2013, eighteen-year-old August Reiger was attending the Classen School of Advanced Studies in Oklahoma City. He was fluent in Spanish, had won a science fair, and played the guitar and piano. In June, August graduated as a National Merit Scholar and an International Baccalaureate Valedictorian. He was granted a full-ride academic scholarship to the University of Oklahoma. As a graduation gift, he had asked his parents for a vacation to a Spanish-speaking country.

On June 11, 2013, the Reiger family landed in Ecuador and drove to the resort town of Banos, one hundred miles south of Quito. This is known as a safe and lush resort region with gorgeous views and thick jungles. The family checked into their hotel and traveled for the first few days. On the morning of June 16, the family took a trail adjacent to the hotel that went to a peak that overlooked the city. As they were hiking, August stepped ahead of the family and stated that he'd meet them at the top. The trail is very easy to follow, and there was only one way to the top. There was a trail that forked and went downhill, but that was obvious. The family hiked to the top, experienced nothing unusual, and waited for their son. This was the last time the young man was seen.

The family contacted local law enforcement and emergency personnel. There was a massive search and a committed effort to finding the student. In the beginning it was believed that August might have fallen. After a thorough search, that belief evaporated. Canines were brought to the trail, and they couldn't locate a scent.

The family has gotten increasingly frustrated at the lack of evidence. A June 21, 2013, article on CNN.com shared the thoughts of August's father: "'Nothing makes sense to me…Everyone's baffled, because it's not a dangerous place,' his father, Chris Reiger, told CNN. 'There's no rebels or something like that who kidnap people. I can't come up with a scenario that could make sense.'"

The local director of the provincial police has stated that they don't have any clues or thoughts about what may have happened to August. He did state that over 150 searchers thoroughly covered the area where August was last seen.

Summary

August's father, Chris Reiger, has stated that he believes that his son was either kidnapped or fell off the trail. Since the trail has been thoroughly searched multiple times, that leaves kidnapping.

Our prayers go out to the Reiger family.

CHAPTER SIX:
UNITED KINGDOM

I am going to handle the following story a little differently than the majority I've chronicled. I don't know the names of the involved children or the exact date of the incident. This story comes from a book, *Mysteries, Solved and Unsolved* by Harold T. Wilkins. I was made aware of the book and subsequent story by a reader from Finland. Thank you!

Harold Wilkins wrote about this incident with great insight and passion, as he was one of the searchers for the children. It's an old story, but you will understand why it's here.

It was a June day in 1906 in Gloucester, United Kingdom. A ten-year-old boy and his two sisters, age three and five years, had gone into a large field that was adjacent to a locomotive shed for the Midland Railway. This property was known to locals as "Forty Acres" and was located just one mile out of town. People observed the kids walking into the field but nobody saw them come out.

The Gloucester community organized and put forth a major effort to find the children. Searchers were almost hand to hand as they walked through the field, ensuring that they did not miss anything. After three days of nonstop effort, the children could not be found. This incident made major headlines in local newspapers. There were rumors that the kids may have been abducted by some local crazy person, but taking three kids at once seemed absurd.

Just as the search was winding down, at 6:00 a.m. on the fourth morning, a ploughman was working in an adjacent field and looked over a large hedge in Forty Acres and saw three children lying in a ditch. The man went into the field and found the kids groggy and sleeping.

There was a large reward for finding the children, and the ploughman attempted to claim the money. The local police superintendent did everything except directly accuse the man of abduction.

The ploughman never recovered the award. All three kids were in good condition. An investigation into where the ploughman lived and the possibilities that he may have had the opportunity to abduct the children proved he could not have done it.

Author Harold Wilkins located the boy who was in the group that vanished. He was questioned in the 1960s about the incident. He stated that he has no recollection of the event from the time he and his sisters went missing until the time he was awakened in the ditch.

Summary

The facts of this case are slim, but the basic elements mimic much of what I've chronicled in past books. The kids disappear, a thorough search is completed, and days later they are found. I've said numerous times that the missing are often found semiconscious or unconscious; the same happened here. The fact that the male who was questioned had no recollection of the event is also a classic element I've documented numerous times.

Sex/Name	Date/Time Missing • Age • State
M-Owen Parfitt	06/1768-Unk • 70 • England

Owen Parfitt
Missing: 06/1768, Shepton Mallet, England
Age at disappearance: 70 years

We study history in school for a reason. I recount historical cases to show a pattern that has never been revealed. Without a historical record, the scope of the study changes, and this may alter our perception of what is occurring. This is an important case, and you will soon understand why.

Owen Parfitt led a very interesting life for someone living in the late 1700s. He was a soldier who had fought in Africa, and it was alleged that he was involved in some questionable conduct regarding slavery. He was tough and spoke in a military dialect on a regular basis. He had a volatile temper, and he let others around him know that he liked to use it.

Some articles stated that Owen suffered a stroke when he was in his younger years, and this left him a "cripple." He managed to earn a salary as a tailor and lived with his sister in Shepton Mallet, England. This was a relatively small community of four to five thousand residents. The village is still surrounded by agricultural fields and sits in the southern portion of the country between Exeter and Bristol.

It was a clear day in June 1768 when Owen's sister and a woman assisting in the house lifted him from the bed and placed him on the front porch in a chair. They covered him with a gray blanket and went back to change the sheets. The assistant left, and the sister completed the bed. After fifteen minutes, the sister yelled out to Owen to see if he needed anything. There was no response. She walked downstairs and found the blanket draped across the chair and Owen missing. The sister knew that Owen had been crippled for years and didn't have the strength to walk anywhere. She searched the area and then started asking people in the village for assistance. A February 1, 1877, article in the *Detroit Free Press* had the following details at this point in the story: "Susannah Snook further said that the weather had been fair during the day, but after the alarm was given it began to thunder and lighten, with a heavy fall of rain, which continued for some time. She herself was wet through in returning to her house."

The village rallied around the disappearance, and thousands searched the fields, creeks, rivers, and gullies but found nothing. The article I quoted did state that Owen was regularly placed in the front of the house so he could get fresh air and sun. It would've been a common practice for his sister to put him there. The day of the disappearance had people in the fields working up until the time the storm hit. It was believed that if Owen had walked away or been taken away, people would've heard or saw the man.

Owen was never found.

Summary

This disappearance has many similarities to the case of Rose Jewett, a ninety-five-year-old woman who disappeared from a campsite in Elk River, Idaho, on August 11, 1957. Rose was disabled because of a stroke and was completely incapacitated. Her children left her in a chair when they went to pick huckleberries. The group returned and couldn't locate Rose. An extensive search failed to find any evidence of how she managed to leave the area. (Refer to *Missing 411-Western United States*, pages 15–16, for details on this case.)

The article that I found on Owen Parfitt's disappearance had been printed many times in the years since. The final paragraph is interesting: "The day had been fine up to the disappearance of Owen Parfitt, which was followed by a terrific storm of thunder and lightning, and rain. He had been wicked—perhaps, a frightfully wicked man in his youth. Putting this and that together, there could be no doubt about the matter. The old soldier, slaver and tailor had been carried off by the devil."

Just for absolute clarity, I'm not alleging that Owen was taken by the devil. I am merely reporting what the article stated. His disappearance does have several elements that are in many of the cases I've documented. He was disabled, he disappeared during a storm, and people have alleged that he was abducted.

CHAPTER SEVEN: NEW ZEALAND

Sex/Name	Date Missing • Age • State
F-Masami Somaki	02/12/94-1:00 p.m. • 32 • Mount Cook, NZ
F-Emma Campbell	05/01/10-5:45 a.m. • 29 • Port Hills, NZ

We've never focused on New Zealand as a land where people disappear under odd circumstances. This country has some of the most beautiful landscapes in the world. If you are a fisherman, some of the best trout fishing you can imagine is here.

Here are some statistics about New Zealand, taken from its governmental website:
Resident Population (as of 6/30/13): 4,470,800
Size: 103,738 square miles
Compared to Oregon:
Resident Population (as of the 2012 census): 3,899,353
Size: 95,988 square miles

Several readers of past books have asked us to look into a series of disappearances and see if they match what we are studying. Information on disappearances in New Zealand is even harder to get than in the United States and Canada. We were able to find a few, though, that add major intrigue to our study.

Masami Somaki
Missing 2/12/94-1:00 p.m., Mount Cook, NZ
Age at disappearance: 32 years

Ms. Somaki was traveling with her mother and decided to climb Mount Cook, located in Aoraki/Mount Cook National Park. It has an elevation of 3,700 meters and is located in Canterbury, approximately two hundred miles west of from Christchurch. The mountain can be found near the western coast in a very rugged range.

On February 12, 1994, in the morning hours, Ms. Somaki and her mother started to hike a major path, hoping to summit Mount Cook. The first significant stop on the trail is a location called the Mueller Hut, which is at 1,800 meters in elevation. This hut is really a moderately sized house where climbers can rest during their journey. Ms. Somaki and her mom had not yet made it to the hut when her mom stated that she was going to wait behind as her daughter continued up the trail. Ms. Somaki did hike farther up and made the Mueller Hut. She was last seen at approximately 1:00 p.m. leaving the hut and moving upward. When she did not return to her mother, the local search and rescue was called.

The first searchers were on the trail at 9:30 p.m., quick by any standards. The New Zealand Air Force Iroquois took to the air over the following four days along with fifty searchers, all finding nothing. Searchers also put a helicopter equipped with FLIR in the sky, which also found nothing.

Search coordinators were stumped that they could not spot the woman, as she was wearing yellow trousers and a bright-pink sweater.

A March 10, 2009, article on the website stuff.co.nz titled "Search for Missing Tourist Reluctantly Called Off" had the following information about the frustration level with searchers: "Long-serving Lake Tekapo police officer the late Bill Apes described the search for Miss Somaki as one that continued to frustrate him years later. 'After the first hour of searching, we said "hello, there is a problem, we can't find her,"' he said. 'When it hit the hour we knew there was something really wrong. After a couple of days we got to the stage we were looking at each other and asking if anyone had seen a strange light in the sky.'"

After four days of intensive search efforts, Ms. Somaki was not located. She is still missing.

I am going to keep the following case within the context of the Somaki case because there is no definitive data when this incident occurred, and comments are similar.

This next case happened on Canterbury's Mount Grey. The mountain is just nine hundred meters in elevation and just twenty-five miles north of Christchurch.

Ray Cassidy was a healthy seventy-three-year-old climber who wanted to spend the day enjoying the beauty of Mount Grey. Searchers stated they can validate that Ray was seen one minute on the trail and was gone the next. On the website wildernessmag.co.nz, a July 1, 2012, article had the following from a search and rescue coordinator with fifty years of experience about the search for Ray: "I've been involved with SAR for over 50 years and every now and again one of these cases pops up where you're completely baffled because there is no logical explanation." Later in the same article was this description of what searchers thought happened to Ray: "'It was just as though someone had come down from above and zapped him up into a flying saucer,' Fiddler said. 'For the last three months after that I kept going up there on weekends or when I had a day off.'" Ray Cassidy was never found.

In the same article on the stuff.co.nx website were statistics on missing people in New Zealand. Here is an exact quote from the article: "While more than 40 of the 225 people who have died in the national park have never been found, they have generally gone missing at high altitude, not on tracks close to the village." I read this statement multiple times in an attempt to understand why it was written. The national parks in New Zealand appear to classify people in the same way we do in the United States, "missing and presumed dead." It is a clean way to wipe the "missing person" slate clean so there are no missing people, statistically. One question for the United States and New Zealand parks departments: How do you know these people are dead?

Emma Campbell
Missing: 05/01/10-5:45 a.m., Port Hills, NZ
Age at disappearance: 29 years

Emma was a caretaker for disabled and elderly people. She lived with a friend in a flat in Christchurch. She enjoyed taking day trips, and it wasn't unusual for her to tour the countryside alone.

On May 1, 2010, at 5:20 a.m., Emma entered her blue 1994 Toyota Corona and drove to a gas station in Port Hills. She paid thirty dollars for fuel, reentered her car, and drove two and a half miles on Dyer Pass Road to its highest point. It was at this location that something unexplained happened.

The Toyota went off the right side of the roadway and down a small embankment. There were no skid marks on the road and little damage to the vehicle. Police described the event in a May 12, 2010, article in the *New Zealand Herald* as "a very low impact crash." Emma could not be found, and a major search ensued. In the same article, police explained they were baffled they couldn't locate the woman. They called in the New Zealand Defense Forces (army) to assist in the search. Tracking dogs had responded to the scene days after the accident and found something unusual, as is described in a May 4, 2010, article on the TVNZ website: "Her shoes were found on a nearby path and that is something that has baffled police and her family who say the disappearance is totally out of character." Tracking dogs found the shoes and also located her watch a short distance from the footwear. The shoes were located just below the car.

In another effort to locate Emma, police utilized a helicopter with FLIR. They reported finding deer on the hillside, but no body. Family members, local volunteers, police, and the army covered a massive area around the crash site without finding the body.

Police continued to speak to the press about the peculiarities of the case, questioning why the woman didn't return to the roadway after the accident. They were obviously confused about finding the shoes and Emma's watch. Reporters continually used the word "mystery" to describe the event. Law enforcement also publicly stated that the accident may have been staged and there was a possibility that foul play was involved.

On March 9, 2012, a pig hunter was on the hillside where Emma had crashed. He was one hundred meters from the crash location in a small ravine when he found a body and called police. Law enforcement originally stated that they were sure it was Emma. Days after the body was found, the police then stated that they couldn't conclusively state it was Emma and further testing needed to be done. Days later, they came back and stated the body was Emma Campbell. I could not locate documentation stating what she was wearing when found or the cause of death. I found it very strange that the police and the coroner couldn't immediately identify the body.

It's a complete mystery how police, defense forces, helicopters with FLIR, and tracking dogs failed to find Emma 328 feet from her car.

After police confirmed the body was Emma, her brother, David, made a public statement on March 12, 2012, to 3News.co.NZ: "It is fair to say at this time we are at a complete loss to understand what has occurred."

Summary

A low-impact crash on a rural mountain road near its summit leads to a missing woman. The woman's shoes are found just below the vehicle, and her watch is found nearby. Readers know that missing people in the cases we chronicle remove their shoes in many instances. If you were walking into the woods, you wouldn't be removing your shoes. Safety for Emma was on the roadway, the place she had just left. Why walk downhill? *Did* she walk downhill?

I've stated dozens of times, I don't believe that searchers are missing people as many times as I've outlined in each of my books. Technology doesn't fail—FLIR is effective at finding bodies. Why can canines find watches and shoes, yet not find a body?

If you look at this scenario from a logical standpoint, Emma's body wasn't there when the searchers were on scene. You can't believe in proven efforts to locate people—technology, canines, police, law enforcement, etc.—and believe that each and every level of the effort failed.

CHAPTER EIGHT:
SWITZERLAND

<u>Sex/Name</u> <u>Date/Time Missing • Age • State</u>
M-Jonathan Robinson 12/22/09-2:50 a.m. • 23 • Switzerland

Jonathan "Myles" Robinson
Missing: 12/22/09-2:50 a.m., Wengen, Switzerland
Age at disappearance: 23 years

    If there was ever a story that had international intrigue, a beautiful setting, and a highly intellectual victim, this is it. The disappearance of Jonathan Robinson defies conventional explanations.
    Jonathan went by the name of Myles. He was a recent graduate of Newcastle University, majoring in math and economics. He had a gorgeous girlfriend and tight family bonds. Every year for fifteen years, the Robinson family flew into the Swiss Alps and took the cog train to the small community of Wengen for their Christmas getaway. If there was a picture-postcard community for the Alps, it is Wengen. Sitting at the base of Eiger, it is a majestic location. This small community can be accessed two ways, either by making a five-hour mountainous hike in the summer or by taking the cog train from Lauterbrunnen. The train runs from early morning to midnight.
    On December 21, 2009, Myles left the Eiger Hotel with his parents, sister, and family friends for dinner. After the meal, Myles, along with family friends and his sister, walked to the Blue Monkey Bar for a night of playing pool and drinking. The socializing continued until 2:00 a.m. when the group decided to walk back to their respective hotels. Myles walked a female family friend, Amy O'Brien, back to her hotel. The pair was caught on closed circuit television (CCTV) leaving the bar at 2:19 a.m. The two friends talked for a while, and Myles left the hotel at 2:50 a.m. en route to his family's

hotel. The walk between the two hotels was two hundred yards. Myles never made it back to his room, and his parents notified Swiss authorities.

From the beginning of the investigation, the Swiss police weren't moving fast enough for the Robinsons. They classified the case as a "typical" missing person investigation, and this had the family disturbed. A December 29, 2009, article in the *Belfast Telegraph* had the following statement from Cara Robinson: "Mr. Robinson's sister Cara, 25, yesterday called for Swiss Police who are treating the case as a missing person hunt, to upgrade their investigation. Referring to her brother she said: 'This is 100 per cent out of character. Without a doubt, something strange has gone on.' His mother, Sarah, 59, who is a senior figure in the British Skiing administration added: 'My son does not care for hiking or spontaneous craziness. He always at least sends a text message if he changes his short term plans. We are convinced there is a crime.'"

The police did respond immediately to the missing person claim. Tracking canines, helicopters with FLIR, and ground teams combed the small city. There was never a scent found, and his body wasn't located. The Robinsons had political clout and the resources to gather additional forces to locate their son. The family organized and actually went door to door in Wengen, asking people to search their residences. They were convinced that Myles was being held against his will somewhere.

If Myles had been physically taken, it would not have been an easy task. He was six feet, five inches tall and in perfect physical condition. He had always played team sports.

On December 28, 2009, a small team of professional searchers hired by the Robinsons made a grim discovery. They located Myles's body 330 feet down a cliff just outside of Lauterbrunnen. The body was found at 4:00 p.m. Remember, Myles disappeared at 2:50 a.m. The cog train to Lauterbrunnen was not operating, and it was a five-hour hike in deep snow, a hike nobody makes during the winter. Swiss police found his cell phone and determined that his BlackBerry made a call at 3:26 a.m. on December 22. The call was made to the first person listed in his phone directory, meaning it was probably automatically dialed. Police surmised that the phone made the call because of the severe impact from falling off the cliff. The phone stopped sending a signal just after 5:00 a.m. on December 22. A March 24, 2011, article in the *Telegraph UK* reported the following: "Westminster coroner Dr. Paul Knapman recorded an open verdict after hearing foul play could not be ruled out, but concluded that it was most likely a tragic accident. Six days after disappearing he was found at the bottom of a 330 foot cliff in Switzerland, missing his shoes and socks." Read those last five words again. Myles was missing his shoes and socks when he was found! This was the middle of winter, and he wasn't wearing his shoes—a classic feature of the missing people I have chronicled.

The coroner determined that Myles's blood alcohol level was twice the legal driving limit and he had amphetamines in his system. The amphetamines aren't that surprising, as they could've been taken with medication, and this would counteract any drowsiness caused by the alcohol. In fact, US fighter pilots are given amphetamines to stay awake and maintain their edge while flying. Any idea that this drug inhibits judgment is false. The CCTV footage of Myles did not show he was staggering or couldn't take care of himself, and friends and family never indicated he was in any danger. The information about Myles's blood alcohol level is irrelevant in determining how he got to where he was found. It seems to be all but impossible to travel at 2:50 a.m. from where he was last seen to where his body was located. (FYI, there are no cars allowed in Wengen or Lauterbrunnen.)

If the coroner didn't rule out foul play, what happened to the police investigation? How did the Swiss police rationalize Myles's body being in the location where it was found, especially if they believed he went off that cliff the night he disappeared? How did Myles transport himself from the middle of Wengen to a cliff in Lauterbrunnen?

Summary

The disappearance of Myles Robinson has many similarities with the case of Gary Tweddle from the Blue Mountains in Australia (July 17, 2013). Both men were raised in Great Britain, both were twenty-three years old, and both had been drinking prior to their disappearance. Gary and Myles were both extremely smart and disappeared under very unusual circumstances. Both men were found at the bottoms of cliffs that were nowhere near where they were last seen, and both should've never been in the area where they were located. (Please refer to the Australia section of this book for details on Gary's disappearance.)

I do believe that Myles's parents were correct. Something very unusual happened to their son.

CHAPTER NINE: AUSTRIA

Sex/Name Date Missing • Age • State
M-Helmut Simon 10/15/04-5:00 p.m. • 67 • Salzburg, Austria

Helmut Simon
Missing: 10/15/04-5:00 p.m., Salzburg, Austria
Age at disappearance: 67 years

In September 1991, amateur hikers Helmut and Erika Simon of Germany were vacationing in Austria and took a high-altitude hike in the Tyrolean Autz Valley near the Italian border. The couple found the 5,300-year-old mummified remains of Ötzi the Iceman partially protruding from ice. The Simons went back to the city and notified the authorities, who recovered Ötzi's remains. This was one of the most significant finds in decades. He is Europe's oldest known natural human mummy.

Helmut and Erika continued their recreational hiking and went back to Austria in October 2004. On October 15, Helmut embarked on a four-hour hike from Bad Hofgastein in the Alps with the goal to hike Gamskarkogel Peak. Helmut did not return, and Erika notified authorities.

Just as searchers were organizing, snow started to fall and got continually heavier. Austrian rescuers utilized airplanes, canines, and over one hundred ground searchers.

The effort to find Helmut continued for eight days when rescuers discussed suspending the search. A hunter who was not involved in the rescue effort was walking along a stream and found Helmut facedown, dead. They theorized that he had fallen three hundred feet into the creek. There was never any mention of if there was snow on the body or if he had all of his clothes and shoes. I could not find any article that mentions what Helmut's cause of death may have been.

Summary

What is truly fascinating about Helmut is his association with Ötzi and the parallels made between his death and the death of others associated in some way with the body and the maintenance of the body.

A BBC article on November 5, 2005, reporting the following:

Four other people associated with Ötzi have died, prompting rumors of a mummy curse:

- Rainer Henn, 64, a forensic pathologist who handled the body. He was killed in a car crash the following year.
- Kurt Fritz, the mountaineer who led Dr. Henn to the body. He was killed in an avalanche shortly after Henn died.
- Rainer Holz, 47, a filmmaker who made a documentary about removing the body from its block of ice. He died of a brain tumor soon afterwards.
- Konrad Spindler, 66, an archaeologist who was the leading expert on the body. He died of complications related to multiple sclerosis.

CONCLUSIONS

Cornerstone Cases

I want readers to read the cases on the list and then go back and read the corresponding sections again. I believe it's very difficult to come to a rational explanation for these cases. Many of the cases have statements from law enforcement that they found the circumstances highly unusual.

The other Missing 411 books have cases that mimic what I have outlined below. These are not isolated cases. In past books I have written about children who disappeared from inside their homes— one home had an alarm that wasn't activated. How can this be happening?

Sex/Name	Date Missing • Age • State
F-Margaret Turner	10/09/24-a.m. • 20 mos. • Durango, CO
F-Patricia Connolly	01/29/42-Unk • 2 • Menlo Park, CA
M-Al Snider	03/05/48-5:00 p.m. • 28 • Sandy Key, FL
M-C. H. Trotter	03/05/48-5:00 p.m. • 48 • Sandy Key, FL
M-Don Frasier	03/05/48-5:00 p.m. • Unk • Sandy Key, FL
F-Helen Bogen	08/07/50-10:00 a.m. • 2½ • Monitor, AB, Canada
M-Jimmy Howard	02/25/51-11:30 a.m. • 2 • FL
F-Myrtle Gray	07/30/53-Noon • 3 • Churchton, MD
F-Barbara Sue Jones	11/25/53-Unk • 22 mos. • Marianna, AR
F-Susan Jackson	07/07/54-5:00 p.m. • 3 • Rockville, MD
M-Dr. Maurice Dametz	04/29/81-3:45 p.m. • 84 • Pike National Forest, CO
M-Ryan Hoeffliger	01/11/84-7:30 a.m. • 2 • Hayden Lake, ID
M-Jonathan Robinson	12/22/09-2:50 a.m. • 23 • Switzerland
M-Emmett Trapp	08/02/10-8:00 p.m. • 2 • Dewey, AZ
F-Hildegard Hendrickson	06/08/13-5:00 p.m. • 79 • Wenatchee Lake, WA

F-Margaret Turner   10/09/24-a.m. • 20 mos. • Durango, CO
Margaret disappeared from her home on the outskirts of Durango. She was found days later on the top of a barren peak five miles away, which was surrounded by searchers.

F-Patricia Connolly   01/29/42-Unk • 2 • Menlo Park, CA
The young girl disappeared from her family's residence on a stormy night. Everyone believed she fell into a flooded creek and went to the bay. Her body was found in the mountains. She traveled over a 650-foot mountain and upstream from her residence.

M-Al Snider   03/05/48-5:00 p.m. • 28 • Sandy Key, FL
M-C. H. Trotter   03/05/48-5:00 p.m. • 48 • Sandy Key, FL
M-Don Frasier   03/05/48-5:00 p.m. • Unk • Sandy Key, FL
Three men were fishing within sight of a yacht. Bad weather quickly engulfed the men, and those on the yacht lost sight of them. They were fishing in water just feet deep. After an extensive search, no one was ever found.

F-Helen Bogen   08/07/50-10:00 a.m. • 2½ • Monitor, AB
Helen went missing from her family's farm. She was missing for thirty-one hours. A local abandoned farm was searched, and nothing was found. After a severe thunderstorm, the farm was searched again and the girl was found naked playing in an old dirty bathtub. Temperatures were in the low forties while she was missing, yet she never had hypothermia.

M-Jimmy Howard 02/25/51-11:30 a.m. • 2 • FL
The Howard family parked their trailer in a rural area. They left Jimmy asleep in the trailer while they collected firewood. The parents returned and found that Jimmy is gone. He did not respond to calls. Sheriff responded and couldn't find the boy. He made statements indicating that he didn't believe the boy could go very far. Jimmy was eventually found two and a half miles from the trailer in an area already searched. **This case mimics events surrounding the disappearance of a Jimmy Duffy, who went missing from his camper in Washington (see *Missing 411-Western United States*).

F-Myrtle Gray   07/30/53-Noon • 3 • Churchton, MD

Myrtle was playing in the woods with her brother. The brother had a disability and couldn't speak. He returned from the woods without his sister. A large three-day search found no proof she was in the area. At the end of the third day, she was found alive. She refused to say what happened, and law enforcement believed she had outside assistance while she was missing.

F-Barbara Sue Jones   11/25/53-Unk • 22 mos. • Marianna, AR

Sheriff stated that it was impossible for the small girl to get outside the one-mile radius around her farm because of bogs and swamps. She was found dead from exposure and starvation ten days after being reported missing.

F-Susan Jackson   07/07/54-5:00 p.m. • 3 • Rockville, MD

This is the second Maryland case to make this list. Susan disappeared from her home during a violent rainstorm. She was found eighteen hours later in an area that was very wet, yet Susan was completely dry. She refused to make any statement about her eighteen-hour journey.

M-Dr. Maurice Dametz   04/29/81-3:45 p.m. • 84 • Pike National Forest, CO

Reverend Dametz was with a friend searching for rocks in the forests of Colorado. He had severe disabilities that made it difficult for him to walk fast or far. He disappeared. His wife wrote a letter to the Colorado governor asking him for assistance because she felt Maurice had been abducted. He was never found.

M-Ryan Hoeffliger   01/11/84-7:30 a.m. • 2 • Hayden Lake, ID

This boy disappeared during the night from inside his home while everyone was sleeping. He was eventually found deceased in a lake two miles from his residence.

M-Jonathan "Myles" Robinson   12/22/09-2:50 a.m. • 23 • Switzerland

The recent university graduate was vacationing for the Christmas holidays for the fifteenth straight year with his family from Wengen, UK. He walked a friend to her room at 2:15 a.m. and left at 2:50 a.m. to return to his room, which was two hundred yards away. He disappeared for six days and was found on a slope of a cliff, dead, in an adjacent town. The train to that town had stopped operating at midnight, and there were no footpaths or roadways that were accessible during the winter season. Nobody knows how Myles got to his final location.

M-Emmett Trapp   08/02/10-8:00 p.m. • 2 • Dewey, AZ
Emmett was sleeping inside his residence with his mother. Somehow the boy disappeared. Searchers made statements showing frustration regarding the lack of tracks and other evidence. His body was found in a muddy pit.

F-Hildegard Hendrickson   06/08/13-5:00 p.m. • 79 • Wenatchee Lake, WA
Ms. Hendrickson was one of the most experienced mushroom pickers in the state of Washington. She disappeared picking mushrooms. Her purse, wallet, and valuables were left in her unlocked car. Her walking stick and mushroom bucket disappeared along with Hildegard. She was never found.

Weather Conditions

Weather plays a predominant role in many of the cases we have highlighted. The following list represents cases from all four of the Missing 411 books where inclement weather was reported by law enforcement or news articles.

Sex/Name	Date Missing • Age • State • Conditions
M-Owen Parfitt	06/1768-Unk • 70 • Shepton Mallet, England • Rain
M-George Cox	04/24/1856-a.m. • 7 • Beford County, PA • Snow
M-Joseph Cox	04/24/1856-a.m. • 5 • Bedford County, PA • Snow
M-Mrs. Farrell's Son	10/12/1875-8:00 a.m. • 4 • Australia • Thunderstorm
M-Dayton Weaver	09/16/1890-10:00 a.m. • 3 • Greenport, NY • Rain
M-Eddie Nichols	05/25/1891-10:00 a.m. • 2 • Commac, NY • Rain
M-Barofsky	07/01/1892-Unk • 6 • NJ • Thunderstorm

Weather Conditions | 327

M-Mr. Munn (son of)	02/22/1894-Unk • 2 • TX • Gale Force Wind
M-Johnny Connors	05/26/1904-p.m. • 2½ • Australia • Bitter Cold
M-J. Mitchell	01/11/1909-Unk • Unk • ID • Snowstorm
M-B. B. Bakowski	02/22/1911-Unk • 30 • Crater Lake NP, OR • Snow
F-Alice Arnold	05/22/1911-a.m. • 4 • Ickesburg, PA • Rain
F-Grace Cooper	08/08/1913-1:00 p.m. • 5 • Quebec • Rain-Cold
M-Michael Janiko	09/10/1917-2:00 p.m. • 4 • Asland, WI • Rain-Cold
M-Edward Gately	10/27/1917-10:30 a.m. • 2 • MA • Thunderstorms
M-George Dansey	10/08/1919-Unk • 30 mos. • NJ • Rain
M-Marvin Koepke	12/10/1922-5:00 p.m. • 4 • KS • Frigid Cold
M-C.G. Lee (son of)	11/29/1923-Unk • 4 • Clearwater, FL • Rain
M-Robert Cass	10/14/1925-1:00 p.m. • 3 • Ashland, NH • Rain
F-Helen Kockman	04/23/1930-6:00 p.m. • 3 • Quinney, WI • Rain
M-Julius Bakken	11/09/31-Noon • 21 • Wenatchee, WA • Snow
F-Anna Gullett	09/10/32-5:00 p.m. • 48 • NSW, Australia • Rain
M-Dailey Hamerly	05/25/33-2:00 p.m. • 2 • Moscow, ID • Thunder-Rain
M-Alden Johnson	03/27/34-3:30 p.m. • 4 • MA • Thunderstorm
F-Betty Wolfrum	05/15/34-Unk • 4 • Manitoba, Canada • Rain
F-Rita Lent	11/22/34-Noon • 3 • PA • Rain
M-John Wesley Kennon	08/31/35-5:00 p.m. • 2 • Mexico, MO • Rain
M-Steve Benson	03/15/36-10:30 a.m. • 3 • Two Buttes, CO
F-Hazel Scraba	05/23/37-Unk • 11 • Pelly, SK, Canada • Rain
F-Ludvina Machishyn	05/23/37-Unk • 10 • Pelly, SK, Canada • Rain
F-Florence Jackson	09/06/37-p.m. • 4 • AR • Heavy Rain
M-Floyd Chandler	10/11/37-4:30 p.m. • 41 • Stove Prairie, CO
M-Teddy Thompson	01/29/38-p.m. • 4 • Northern CA • Heavy Snow
M-Richard McPherson	05/26/38-Unk • 10 • Yosemite NP, CA • Rain-Snow
M-Hickle Ware	06/11/38-p.m. • 4 • Pine River, MN • Rain
F-Eliza Darnel	02/20/39-p.m. • 25 • VA • Rain-Snow
M-Billy Coleman	01/01/40-4:00 p.m. • 14 • CA • Snow
F-Helen Chenoweth	03/28-40-6:00 p.m. • 3 • IL • Rainstorm
M-Murray Upshaw Jr.	11/08/40-Noon • 2 • GA • Heavy Rains
M-Clarence Murphy Jr.	07/14/41-a.m. • 4 • CA • Rain
F-Patricia Connolly	01/29/42-Unk • 2 • Menlo Park, CA • Rain
M-Kenneth Slagle	11/26/42-p.m. • 3 • Conemaugh, PA • Freezing Temps
M-Donald Curry	04/09/44-4:35 p.m. • 4 • Belleville, PA • Rain
M-Lloyd Hokit	10/21/45-3:00 p.m. • 9 • OK • Heavy Rain

M-Dickie Tum Suden	11/01/45-9:00 a.m. • 3 • CA Sierras • Rain
M-Celestino Trujillo Jr.	04/09/47-11:30 a.m. • 3 • Ledoux, NM
M-Arnie Olson	08/11/47-5:00 p.m. • 4 • Mount Skalkaho, MT • Rain/Wind
M-Al Snider	03/05/48-5:00 p.m. • 28 • Sandy Key, FL
M-C. H. Trotter	03/05/48-5:00 p.m. • 48 • Sandy Key, FL
M-Don Frasier	03/05/48-5:00 p.m. • Unk • Sandy Key, FL
M-Gerald "Terry" Cook	04/24/48-4:00 p.m. • 3 • ME • Snow
M-Robert Carr	01/11/49-2:00 p.m. • 7 • Davis, WV • Snow
M-Eston Carr	01/11/49-2:00 p.m. • 9 • Davis, WV • Snow
M-John Helmick	01/11/49-2:00 p.m. • 15 • Davis, WV • Snow
M-David Devitt	10/09/49-Unk • 21 • Rocky Mtn NP • Snow
M-Bruce Gerling	10/09/49-Unk • 20 • Rocky Mtn NP • Snow
M-Donald McDonald	12/15/49-Unk • 17 • WA • Major Snowstorm
M-Tommy Jenkins	05/04/50-Noon • 2 • WA • Rain
F-Helen Bogen	08/07/50-10:00 a.m. • 2½ • Canada • Thunderstorm
F-Evangeline Lorimer	06/08/51-Unk • 21 • GSM NP, TN • Rain
M-Teddy Barnard	06/17/51-p.m. • 3 • Gray, ME • Rain
M-Alfred Gaspard	07/31/51-Unk • 60 • Pitt River, BC, Canada • Rain
M-Bobby Boatman	10/14/51-Unk • 14 • WA • Snow
F-Ann Bragg	12/02/51-10:00 a.m. • 76 • Birmingham, AL • Rain
M-George Bell Jr.	11/22/52-2:00 p.m. • 2 • PA • Rain
F-Catherine P. Maynard	01/19/53-Unk • 38 • WA • Snow
M-Jerry Monkman	04/25/53-5:00 p.m. • 11 • Choteau, MT
M-Kerry Smith	05/03/53-1:00 p.m. • 10 • Kaycee, WY • Rain/Wind
M-Richard Rucker	07/30/53-10:37 a.m. • 2 • WV • Rain
F-Joan Marie Treece	04/14/54-1:00 p.m. • 3 • Mountain Home, AR • Rain
F-Susan Jackson	07/07/54-5:00 p.m. • 3 • Rockville, MD • Rain
F-Ida May Curtis	07/04/55-6:00 p.m. • 2 • MT • Rain
F-Sarah Dixon	06/05/56-11:30 a.m. • 3 • CO • Thunderstorm
F-Kathy Thomas	06/05/56-11:30 a.m. • 3 • CO • Thunderstorm
F-Sandy Barcus	07/21/56-Noon • 2 • Nederland, CO • Rain
M-Jack Woods Jr.	10/29/56-p.m. • 3 • AL • Rain
F-Jill Hatch	11/02/57-11:00 a.m. • 7 • Southern CA • Snow
M-Lowell Linn	11/31/57-p.m. • 23 • Mount Rainier NP, WA • Snow
M-Dennis Wurschmidt	01/25/58-Unk • 12 • CA • Rain/Snow
M-John Wayne McKinney	03/17/58-3:00 p.m. • 5 • WV • Heavy Snow
F-Judy Peterson	04/25/58-8:30 p.m. • 3 • FL • Fog

F-Shirley Hunt	06/27/58-11:15 a.m. • Weippe, ID • Rain
F-Brenda Doud	07/06/58-p.m. • 5 • NY • Heavy Rain
F-Mary Gay Bent	07/13/58-3:00 p.m. • 5 • MT • Heavy Rain
F-Debbie Ann Greenhill	08/09/58-8:00 p.m. • 2 • KY • Multiple Storms
M-Willard Eugene Jones Jr.	01/17/59-Unk • 3 • MO • Icy Rain
F-Patricia Graham	05/31/59-10:30 a.m. • 6 • NY • Rain
M-David Raleigh	06/13/59-8:00 p.m. • 5 • NY • Rain/Wind
M-Albert Cucupa	02/16/60-Unk • 32 • NM • Snowstorm
F-Ann Marie Burr	08/31/61-5:30 a.m. • 8 • WA • Rain
M-Jerry Cooper	12/21/61-10:00 p.m. • 4 • GA • Rain
M-David Ashley Cusiter	03/04/62-3:00 p.m. • 17 • NSW, Australia • Rain
M-Stephen Papol	08/19/62-p.m. • 3 • NY • Thunderstorms
M-Edward Eskridge	02/19/63-5:00 p.m. • 16 • Green River, WY • Cold
F-Lynn Olson	06/28/63-p.m. • 16 • WY • Snow
M-Reed Jeppson	10/11/64-1:00 p.m. • 15 • Salt Lake City, UT • Rain
M-James Dwyer Bordenkircher	06/12/65-p.m. • 2 • CA • Rain
M-Kenneth Vanderleest	07/14/67-p.m. • 3 • BC, Canada • Rain
M-Clayton Ordiway	06/08/69-1:30 p.m. • 5 • Sequoia NP, CA • Hail
M-Dennis Lloyd Martin	06/14/69-4:30 p.m. • 6 • GSM NP, TN • Rain
M-Robert Winters	10/08/69-5:00 p.m. • 78 • OR • Snow
M-Geoffrey Hague	02/07/70-3:20 p.m. • 16 • GSM NP, TN • Snow
M-Adrian McNaughton	06/12/72-p.m. • 5 • Holmes Lake, ON, Canada • Rain
F-Anna Christian Waters	01/16/73-2:15 p.m. • 5 • Half Moon Bay, CA • Rain
M-Mark Hanson	03/07/75-Unk • 21 • GSM NP, TN • Snow
M-Kurt Newton	08/31/75-Unk • 4 • ME • Heavy Rain
M-Timothy Shear	11/23/75-p.m. • 22 • Little Bell Mountains, MT • Rain
M-Harold Mott	03/02/76-5:00 p.m. • 12 • PA • Torrential Rain
M-Steven Paul Thomas	04/12/76-3:30 p.m. • 19 • NY • Strong Wind
F-Trenny Lynn Gibson	10/08/76-3:00 p.m. • 16 • GSM NP, TN • Rain
M-Charles McCullar	10/14/76-Unk • 19 • Crater Lake NP, OR • Snow
M-Samuel Ipock	10/10/77-5:00 p.m. • 22 • Tumalo Falls, OR • Snow
M-Lee Littlejohn	12/23/77-1:00 p.m. • 18 mos. • CA • Rain
M-Christopher Vigil	04/30/78-6:30 p.m. • 9 • Greyrock Mountain, CO • Snow
M-Andrew Amato	09/30/78-10:30 a.m. • 4 • MA • Rain
M-Danny Hicks	12/03/80-2:00 p.m. • 2 • Raleigh, NC • Freezing Temps
M-James Beveridge	02/07/81-Unk • 9 • Southern, CA • Rain
M-Jay Charles Toney	05/25/82-1:30 p.m. • 17 • GSM NP, TN • Rain

M-Robert Baldeshwiler	06/29/82-Unk • 12 • Rocky Mountain NP, CO • Rain
M-Richard Peterson	11/05/82-3:30 p.m. • 6 • NJ • Extreme Cold
F-Debra Manial	12/12/82-3:00 p.m. • Sierras, Northern CA • Snow
M-Christopher Harvey	07/11/84-3:30 p.m. • 14 • Pagosa Springs, CO • Rain
M-Stephen Crean	08/06/85-2:40 p.m. • 37 • NSW, Australia • Rain/Snow
M-Ronald Adams	09/07/85-p.m. • 21 • High Peaks, NY • Rain
M-Cody Sheehy	04/27/86-2:30 p.m. • 6 • OR • Rain
M-Andrew Warburton	07/01/86-Unk • 9 • Canada • Rain
M-Joseph David Helt	01/16/87-4:00 a.m. • 17 • NY • Snow
M-Patrick Hildebrand	06/27/87-1:50 p.m. • 9 • Australia • Fog
M-Timothy Box	09/28/87-4:00 p.m. • 2 • Mountain View, AR • Rain
F-Tina Marie Finley	03/07/88-2:00 a.m. • 25 • WA • Rain
M-Michael Henley Jr.	04/21/88-p.m. • 9 • Zuni Mountains, NM • Snow
M-Ng Boon Heng	10/22/88-Unk • 26 • Borneo • Rain
M-Lau King Thong	10/22/88-Unk • 34 • Borneo • Rain
M-Nathan Madsen	10/22/89-2:30 p.m. • 9 • OR • Snow
M-Joshua Lewis Kern	07/13/90-6:00 p.m. • 2 • ID • Rain
F-Susan Adams	09/30/90-Unk • 42 • Selway-Bitterroot, ID • Rain/Snow
M-Casey Holliday	10/14/90-10:00 a.m. • 11 • ID • Rain/Hail
M-Corey Fay	11/23/91-6:30 p.m. • 17 • OR • Snow
M-Stefan Bissert	01/20/92-p.m. • 23 • Olympic NP, WA • Snow
M-Kenny Miller	06/24/92-Unk • 12 • Yosemite NP, CA • Wind/Rain
M-Bill McKinnon	02/14/93-p.m. • 28 • Church Mountain, WA-Snow
F-Ashley Krestianson	07/14/94-Unk • 8 • SK, Canada • Rain
M-Taylor Touchstone	08/07/96-4:00 p.m. • 10 • FL • Thunderstorms
M-John Devine	09/06/97-2:00 p.m. • 73 • Olympic NP, WA • Rain
M-David Crouch	09/07/97-Unk • 27 • WY • Heavy Rain
M-Derrick Engbretson	12/05/98-3:00 p.m. • 8 • Crater Lake NP, OR • Snow
F-Dr. Katherine Wong	02/19/99-2:00 p.m. • 47 • Bear Valley, CA • Snow
M-Joseph Wood Jr.	07/08/99-2:00 p.m. • 34 • Mount Rainier NP, WA • Rain
M-Marcus McKay	07/15/00-p.m. • 8 • Manitoba, Canada • Rain
F-Ellie James	08/16/01-Unk • 17 • Mount Kinabalu, Borneo • Rain/Fog
M-Gage Wayment	10/25/01-Noon • 2 • UT • Snow
M-Brian Douglas Faughnan	07/12/02-Unk • 35 • BC, Canada • Fog/Rain
F-Teresa Schmidt	09/06/02-3:00 p.m. • 53 • CO • Heavy Rain
M-Justin Sides	04/30/03-3:45 p.m. • 3 • Wynne, AR • Thunderstorm
M-Patric McCarthy	10/13/03-p.m. • 10 • NH • Wind & Rain

Weather Conditions | 331

M-Garrett Bardsley	08/20/04-a.m. • 12 • UT • Freezing Rain/Snow
M-Charles Huff	11/24/04-6:00 p.m. • 76 • FL • Heavy Rain
F-Michelle Vanek	09/24/05-1:30 p.m. • 35 • CO • Torrential Rain
M-George Laforest Jr.	04/21/06-Unk • 45 • NY • Rain
M-Kevin Brown	09/21/06-Unk • 2 • Alvarado, TX • Cold
M-Kory Kelly	10/16/06-7:00 p.m. • 38 • MN • "Bad Weather"
M-Daming Xu	11/04/07-p.m. • 63 • OR • Fog/Rain/Snow
M-Nicholas Garza	02/05/08-11:07 p.m. • 19 • VT • Rain
M-Michael Edwin Hearon	08/23/08-Unk • 51 • GSM, TN • Heavy Rain
M-Christopher Andrews	10/03/08-3:00 p.m. • 42 • Yosemite NP, CA • Rain
M-Fred Gillingham	10/12/08-Unk • 71 • NY • Heavy Rain
M-Robert Willis	10/31/08-Unk • 38 • Dinkey Creek, CA • Snow
M-Joshua Childers	05/04/09-11:45 a.m. • 3 • MO • Heavy Rain
M-Melvin Nadel	09/06/09-4:00 p.m. • 61 • NM • Snow
F-Madyson Jamison	10/08/09-2:00 p.m. • 5 • OK • Massive Rainstorm
F-Sherilynn Jamison	10/08/09-2:00 p.m. • 40 • OK • Massive Rainstorm
M-Bobby Jamison	10/08/09-2:00 p.m. • 44 • OK • Massive Rainstorm
F-Letisha Faust	12/09/09-Unk • 50 • Franklin CO, VA • Snow
F-Sylvia Lange	01/24/10-12:30 p.m. • 77 • Point Reyes NP, CA
M-Charles Palmer V	04/10/10-7:00 p.m. • 30 • AK • Snow
M-Eric Lewis	07/01/10 • 57 • Mount Rainier NP, WA • Snow
F-Rachael Bagnall	09/08/10-Unk • 25 • Pemberton, BC • Rain
M-Jonathan Jette	09/08/10-Unk • 34 • Pemberton, BC • Rain
F-Megumi Yamamoto	06/09/11-4:00 p.m. • 26 • Mount Baldy, NM • Snow
M-Steve Litsey	10/29/11-p.m. • 71 • OR • Snow
M-Jason Elijah Burton	12/16/11-1:30 p.m. • 21 mos. • SC • Rain
M-Paul Michael Lemaitre	07/04/12-7:00 p.m. • 66 • M • AK • Snow & Fog
M-Prabhdeep Srawn	05/13/13-Unk • 25 • NSW, Australia • Snow/Rain
F-Geraldine Largay	07/23/13-Unk • 66 • ME • Rain
M-Bryan Lee Johnston	08/28/13-Unk • 71 • Olympic NP, WA • Rain
F-Amelia Linkert	09/23/13-Unk • 69 • Craters of the Moon NP • Rain
F-Jo Elliott Blakeslee	09/23/13-Unk • 63 Craters of the Moon NP • Rain
M-Alyof Krost	10/01/13-5:45 p.m. • 62 • Lake Arrowhead, CA • Wind

Total Cases: 188
Male: 138
Female: 50

Types of weather and number of cases:
Rain: 101
Snow: 49
Thunderstorm: 9
Wind: 5
Fog: 3

Each of these types of weather can inhibit the ability of searchers to find the missing:

- Clouds obscure the sky and don't allow satellite penetration.
- Strong winds can ground search aircraft and reduce scent in the air.
- Very strong winds can reduce visibility by putting particles in the air.
- Rain and snow can hide tracks and reduce scent in the air.

As you read the books, you will notice that inclement weather of all types has reduced the ability of searchers to locate the missing. In some instances the weather arrives abruptly and lasts for long periods of time. Sometimes it happens quickly and ends quickly.

Weather Control

Local cities, counties, states, and the federal government have been "cloud seeding" for decades. The goal is to increase the amount of rainfall in specific areas. I sincerely doubt that any of the missing people have been victimized by this effort.

There have been hundreds of articles written about the control and modification of weather. If readers don't believe that weather can be modified and controlled, the United Nations once adopted a resolution that weather modification could not be used during wartime. Why would they adopt a resolution if the weather couldn't be manipulated and controlled? A search of US patents shows a wide variety of patents addressing specific weather manipulation such as "production of intense artificial clouds, fogs and mists" (#1338343).

I am in no way implying that our government is playing any role in the disappearance of these people; I am merely educating the public that all weather is not natural.

Criminal Allegations

The below cases came from all four Missing 411 books. These cases have gone through careful scrutiny, and these are the ones where someone made a criminal allegation. The most common belief was abduction or kidnapping. Either law enforcement, the family, or the news reporter believed that something may have happened criminally to the victim.

As someone who spent twenty years working for a large municipal law enforcement agency, I can guarantee that most law enforcement supervisors and detectives are very careful about making allegations public. They don't want to be embarrassed, and they usually don't want the public to know what they are thinking.

Date	Name	State	Age	Misc. Notes
6/1768	Owen Parfitt	England	70 Years	Never Found
7/1/1887	Emma Carbaugh	MD	22 Mos.	Mutilated Body Found
5/25/1891	Eddie Nichols	NY	2 Years	Missing 80 Hrs in Woods
11/8/1891	Ottie Powell	VA	4 Years	Found on Top of Mtn
4/21/1897	Mary Sholtas	PA	3 Years	Sholtas Was with Staneker
4/21/1897	Augustus Staneker	PA	4 Years	Staneker Was with Sholtas
3/4/1907	Horace Marvin	DE	4 Years	
5/22/1911	Alice Arnold	PA	4 Years	From Ranch Found 1000' Up
9/21/1912	Isabel Zandarski	OH	30 Mos.	
5/12/1915	James Glass	PA	4 Years	
5/14/1916	James Carroll	PA	4 Years	
10/27/17	Edward Gateley	MA	2 Years	
10/8/19	George Dansey	NJ	30 Mos.	
12/10/22	Marvin Koepke	KS	4 Years	Found in Area Searched 4x
10/19/23	Pearl Turner	AR	3 Years	
10/9/24	Margaret Turner	CO	20 Mos.	Found on Peak of Mtn
9/18/28	Evelyn McDermott	VT	16 Years	
10/1/29	Alfred Hotchkiss	CO	2 Years	Missing in Mtns
10/26/29	Geraldin Markline	PA	2 Years	
3/26/30	Maretha Yarborough	AR	3 Years	Traveled 8 Miles in 24 Hrs

Date	Name	Location	Age	Notes
4/23/30	Helen Kockman	WI	3 Years	
8/24/30	Kenneth Swanson	CT	2 Years	Missing with Dog
2/24/32	Else Flothmeier	PA	22 Years	
7/13/34	Bobby Connor	NY	21 Mos.	
11/22/34	Rita Lent	PA	3 Years	
9/5/35	Jack Pike	Manitoba	5 Years	Found Across River
1/15/36	Roy Rogers	AZ	4 Years	
8/16/37	Alice Baker	VT	20 Mos.	
9/6/37	Florence Jackson	AR	4 Years	
1/29/38	Teddy Thompson	CA	4 Years	
5/8/38	Marjorie West	PA	4 Years	Never Found
7/2/38	Alfred Beilhartz	CO-RMNP	4 Years	Never Found
11/10/38	Jerry Hays	AZ	5 Years	
2/20/39	Eliza Darnel	VA	25 Years	
3/23/39	Jackie Grady	CT	4 Years	
3/28/40	Helen Chenoweth	IL	3 Years	Believed Held Captive
9/15/40	Ronald Rumbaugh	PA	2 Years	Found w/Clean Clothes
11/8/40	Murray Upshaw Jr.	GA	2 Years	
5/21/41	Eldridge Albright	MD	3 Years	
7/14/41	Clarence Murphy	CA	4 Years	
2/7/42	Ronald McGee	AZ	2 Years	
9/14/44	Sylvia Sweet	NV	3 Years	Never Found
11/1/45	Dickie Tum Suden	CA	3 Years	Never Found
6/16/46	Katherine Van Alst	AR	8 Years	
7/15/46	Raymond Howe	PA	9 Years	
12/1/46	Paula Welden	VT	18 Years	Never Found
2/2/47	Irma Santos	MA	5 Years	Found after 54 Hours
4/9/47	Celestino Trujillo Jr.	NM	3 Years	Never Found
6/29/47	Greta Mary Gale	CA-Lassen NP	30 Mos.	
8/20/47	Carolyn Peterson	OH	20 Mos.	
2/18/49	Billy Abbott	PA	3 Years	
10/5/49	Eddie Grant	ID	22 Years	
5/4/50	Tommy Jenkins	WA	3 Years	
5/5/50	Anna Thorpe	PA	2 Years	Got over Barbed Wire Fence
5/20/50	Unknown Name	France	Unknown	
6/3/50	Nicole Renaud	Quebec	3 Years	

Criminal Allegations | 335

Date	Name	Location	Age	Notes
9/2/50	Lorraine Smith	Alberta	2 Years	
10/14/51	Bobby Boatman	WA	14 Years	
12/10/51	Ann Bragg	AL	76 Years	Disappeared on Mtn Trail
5/20/53	Beverly Ann Bradley	MI	2 Years	
7/30/53	Myrtle Gray	MD	3 Years	Refused to Talk
7/30/53	Richard Rucker	WV	2 Years	Diaper Found on Mtn Top
11/25/53	Barbara Sue Jones	AR	22 Mos.	Missing from Farm
4/14/54	Joan Marie Treece	AR	3 Years	Rained Heavily
6/12/54	William Sisco	AZ	32 Years	
7/7/54	Susan Jackson	MD	3 Years	After Heavy Rain Found Dry
7/20/54	Walter Gordon	CA-Yosemite	26 Years	Never Found
10/9/54	Orvar Von Laas	CA-Yosemite	30 Years	Never Found
7/18/55	Nora Moore	AL	78 Years	Broomsage in Pocket
10/11/55	Ronnie Weitkamp	IN	3 Years	Happened at Naval Depot
2/25/57	Mary Barker	NJ	3 Years	
7/13/57	David Scott	CA	2 Years	
10/8/57	Minnie Haun	TN	3 Years	
3/17/58	Johnny McKinney	WV	5 Years	
8/9/58	Debbie Greenhill	KY	2 Years	
7/14/59	Edith Wolfskill	CA	57 Years	
3/7/61	Jimmie Franck	IA	4 Years	
8/31/61	Ann Marie Burr	WA	8 Years	
12/21/61	Jerry Cooper	GA	4 Years	Brace for Foot Left Behind
3/26/62	Faye Crawford	TN	3 Years	Inside Car Handles Missing
8/19/62	Stephen Papol	NY	3 Years	
10/11/64	Reed Jeppson	UT	15 Years	Never Found
6/12/65	James Bordenkircher	CA-Sierra	2 Years	Never Found
5/12/66	Christine Woollett	WA	2 Years	
8/13/66	Amy Jackson	CA	18 Mos.	
5/3/68	David Adams	WA	8 Years	Never Found-Mtn Home
7/8/68	Karen Cooney	PA	15 Years	
1/13/69	Randy Parscale	AZ	10 Years	
6/12/72	Adrian McNaughton	Ontario	5 Years	
1/16/73	Anna Waters	CA	5 Years	Never Found-CA Coast
2/3/73	Guy Heckle	IA	11 Years	

Date	Name	Location	Age	Notes
10/19/73	Jimmy Duffy	WA	2 Years	Never Found
8/9/75	Jane Smith	Ontario	20 Years	
2/27/76	Bruce Shearin	NC	2 Years	Never Found
10/14/76	Charles McCullar	Crater Lake NP	19 Years	
7/27/78	Duane Scott	PA	31 Years	Found in Inaccessible Area
9/30/78	Andrew Amato	MA	4 Years	Never Found
3/1/79	Tina Lucas	SC	4 Years	Found without Shoes
1/13/80	Paul Fugate	AZ	41 Years	Never Found
4/30/80	Megan Ginevicz	MT	2 Years	Listed "Nonfamily Abduction"
4/29/81	Maurice Dametz	CO	75 Years	Wife Claimed Abduction
10/3/81	Stephen Oleszczuk	SC	4 Years	
8/31/82	Richard Ray Barnett	ID	2 Years	Never Found
5/3/83	Shelly Bacsu	Alberta	16 Years	Never Found
6/25/83	Nyleen Kay Marshall	MT	4 Years	Never Found
7/2/83	Michael Reel	TN	8 Years	
1/11/84	Ryan Hoeffliger	ID	2 Years	From House near Idaho
7/11/84	Christopher Harvey	CO	14 Years	Never Found-San Juan Mtns
6/3/85	David Jaramillo	UT	21 Years	Never Found
7/24/85	Jessica Azzopardi	Ontario	20 Mos.	
7/24/86	Lynn Marie Hillier	BC-Canada	2 Years	
9/16/87	Julie Ann Weflen	WA	28 Years	At Remote Electrical Station
9/28/87	Timothy Box	AR	2 Years	Missing 3 Days in Woods
3/7/88	Tina Finley	WA	25 Years	FBI on Case
4/17/89	Kathleen Pehringer	WY	41 Years	Never Found
10/22/89	Nathan Madsen	OR	9 Years	Never Found
12/1/92	Danny Hohenstein	CA	6 Years	Mtn Community
2/14/93	Bill McKinnon	WA	28 Years	Church Mtn-Never Found
5/1/94	Victor Shoemaker Jr.	WV	5 Years	Never Found
7/9/95	Jeanne Hesselschwerdt	Yosemite NP	37 Years	Body in Inaccessible Area
7/24/97	Amy Bechtel	WY	24 Years	Never Found
8/31/98	Emma Tresp	NM	71 Years	Never Found
5/7/99	Joshua Stauffer	ID	3 Years	Found 5 Miles from Home

Criminal Allegations | 337

Date	Name	Location	Age	Notes
7/15/00	Marcus McKay	Manitoba	8 Years	
10/5/00	Tristen Meyers	NC	4 Years	Never Found
10/25/01	Gage Wayment	UT	2 Years	
6/14/03	Leanna Warner	MN	5 Years	
10/13/03	Patric McCarthy	NH	10 Years	
7/31/04	David Gonzales	CA	9 Years	
9/19/04	Robert Springfield	MT	49 Years	FBI Took Body
11/24/04	Charles Huff	FL	76 Years	
9/24/05	Michelle Vanek	CO	35 Years	Never Found on 14 K Mtn
8/26/06	Stephanie Stewart	Alberta	70 Years	Never Found-Fire Lookout
9/21/06	Kevin Brown	TX	2 Years	
2/19/09	Dr. Katherine Wong	CA-Sierra	47 Years	Disappeared at Ski Resort
7/16/09	Douglas May	CA	55 Years	Found in Canyon
10/7/09	Madyson Family	OK	5, 40, 44	Two Adults, One Child
12/9/09	Letisha Faust	VA	50 Years	Missing from Car
12/22/09	Jonathan Robinson	Switzerland	23 Years	Disappeared in Wengen
5/1/10	Emma Campbell	New Zealand	29 Years	Missing from Car Accident
9/8/10	Rachael Bagnall	BC-Canada	25 Years	Missing in Wilderness
9/8/10	Jonathan Jette	BC-Canada	34 Years	Missing in Wilderness
5/28/13	Raymond Salmen	BC-Canada	65 Years	Missing in Wilderness
6/16/13	August Reiger	Ecuador	18 Years	Missing on Mtn Trail
9/23/13	Amelia Linkert	ID	69 Years	Craters of the Moon NP
9/23/13	Jo Elliott Blakeslee	ID	63 Years	Craters of the Moon NP
10/8/13	Amber Smith	MI	2 Years	Rural Residence

Chart Facts:

Total Cases: 147
Males: 77
Females: 70

Most Cases in Any Year:
1954, 2009, 2013: Five Cases in Each

Case Anomalies

5/25/1891	Eddie Nichols	NY	2 Years	Missing 80 Hrs in Woods
11/8/1891	Ottie Powell	VA	4 Years	Found on Top of Mtn

There are no cases for four years before Eddie Nichols and none for six years after Ottie Powell where a criminal allegation was made, yet these two cases occurred just six months apart.

5/12/1915	James Glass	PA	4 Years
5/14/1916	James Carroll	PA	4 Years

Glass and Carroll disappeared almost exactly one year apart. The boys were both four years old, and they both disappeared from Pennsylvania. If this wasn't enough, they had the same first name.

5/4/50	Tommy Jenkins	WA	3 Years
5/5/50	Anna Thorpe	PA	2 Years

It's an unusual set of circumstances when cases happen on back-to-back days. Both contained criminal allegations. As I've stated in past books, look at the charts and study them. It is extremely rare when disappearances happen in the same area back to back. There is almost a flip-flopping from coast to coast, so it's difficult to see a pattern.

7/20/54	Walter Gordon	CA-Yosemite	26 Years
10/9/54	Orvar Von Laas	CA-Yosemite	30 Years

Both men were in graduate programs at the University of California at Berkeley. Both went to Yosemite and disappeared at different times. They didn't know each other and weren't studying the same topics. Their families happened to meet; both believed their children had been abducted. They wrote a letter to President Eisenhower asking for Special Forces to enter the park to look for Walter and Orvar. The military never arrived, and the men were never found.

10/7/09	Madyson Family	OK	5, 40, 44	One Child, Two Adults

UPDATE: The husband, wife, and their small daughter met a man at a plot of land he owned, which they were contemplating purchasing. The man left the family and allowed them to walk his property. They disappeared, leaving their dog in the back of their truck, along with tens of thousands of dollars in the front of the truck. On November 16, 2013, deer hunters were near Kinta, Oklahoma, and discovered three partial bodies. The location of the find was 2.7 miles northwest of where the Madyson family left their truck. This area had been searched several times. The remains were scattered, and animals had eaten many of them. As of the publication of this book, there is no confirmation if this is the Madyson family or the cause of death.

In total, there are 147 cases to date where there were criminal allegations, with the most common being kidnapping or abduction.

Last in Line

The list was established after reviewing cases from the four Missing 411 books. This is an unusual statistic and one we discovered after reading thousands of cases. As unusual as it is, this list represents people who were the last in line moving through an area and disappeared. The column at the far left indicates which book the case is from:

W=*Missing 411-Western United States*
E=*Missing 411-Eastern United States*
NA=*Missing 411-North America and Beyond*
D=*Missing 411-The Devil's in the Details*

Book • Sex/Name	Date Missing • Age • State
E • M-James Glass	05/12/1915-Unk • 4 • PA
D • M-Henry Nutter	07/06/1919-Unk • 6 • Fox Lake, IL
D • F-Maretha Yarborough	03/26/30-Noon • 3 • Waldron, AR
W • F-Cecilia Mitchell	05/02/32-12:30 p.m. • 3 • CA
NA • M-Murray Walkup Miller	10/24/36-Unk • 9 • MT
E • M-Lloyd Hokit	10/21/45-3:00 p.m. • 9 • OK
W • M-Donald McDonald	12/15/49-Unk • 17 • WA

NA • F-Nancy Jean Walker	05/08/51-8:15 p.m. • 2 • MA
NA • F-Betty Joslyn	07/24/51-p.m. • 5 • Terrible Mountain, VT
E • F-Emma Bowers	07/22/53-Unk • 5 • PA
NA • M-Lowell Linn	11/31/57-p.m. • 23 • Mount Rainier NP, WA
E • M-Kenneth Scott	09/28/58-2:00 p.m. • 4 • MI
NA • M-David Raleigh	06/13/59-8:00 p.m. • 5 • NY
W • M-Bobby Panknin	08/03/63-Unk • 4 • WA
E • M-Geoffrey Hague	02/08/70-3:20 p.m. • 16 • Great Smoky Mtn NP, TN
NA • M-David Holtz	07/13/71-9:00 a.m. • 9 • Sequoia NP, CA
D • M-Donald G. Siskar	07/10/73-3:30 p.m. • 18 • Grass Mtn, WA
W • M-Jeffrey Bratcher	06/15/74-6:30 p.m. • 7 • WA
E • M-Mark Hanson	03/07/75-Unk • 21 • Great Smoky Mtns NP, TN
NA • M-Andrew Amato	09/30/78-10:30 a.m. • 4 • MA
NA • M-James Beveridge	02/07/81-Unk • 9 • Southern, CA
D • F-Kathryn Dekkers	07/24/81-3:00 p.m. • 10 • Ampersand Mtn, NY
E • M-Andrew Warburton	07/01/86-Unk • 9 • Canada
E • M-Larry Krebbs	03/30/88-Unk • 2 • Lake Texoma, OK
D • M-Ng Boon Heng	10/22/88-Unk • 26 • Mount Kinabalu, Borneo
D • M-Lau King Thong	10/22/88-Unk • 34 • Mount Kinabalu, Borneo
W • M-Kenny Miller	06/24/92-Unk • 12 • Yosemite NP, CA
W • F-Ashley Krestianson	07/14/94-Unk • 8 • SK, Canada
NA • F-Naomi Leigh Whidden	11/25/94-12:45 p.m. • 2 • GA
W • M-Bryce Herda	04/09/95-Unk • 4 • WA
D • F-Haley Zega	04/29/01-11:30 a.m. • 6 • Newton County, AR
E • M-Chris Thompkins	01/25/02-1:30 p.m. • 20 • GA
E • M-Patric McCarthy	10/13/03-p.m. • 10 • NH
W • F-Michelle Vanek	09/24/05-1:30 p.m. • 35 • CO
NA • M-Eric Lewis	07/01/10 • 57 • Mount Rainier NP, WA
D • M-George Penca	06/17/11-2:40 p.m. • 30 • Yosemite NP, CA
NA • M-Paul Lemaitre	07/04/12 • 66 • Seward, AK
NA • M-Ronald Ohm	08/09/12-p.m. • 52 • OR
D • M-Alyof Krost	10/01/13-5:45 p.m. • 62 • Lake Arrowhead, CA

Please don't make judgments on the importance of the event until you've read the total story, which is contained in the book listed to the left. You are being given just a one- or two-sentence summary of an event that in many cases was several pages long.

The list exemplifies how quickly things can happen on trails when you are alone.

E • M-James Glass   05/12/1915-Unk • 4 • Greeley, PA
James was walking to the store with his mother when he walked behind a tree and vanished. The boy's skeleton was found eight years later in a swamp.

W • F-Cecilia Mitchell   05/02/32-12:30 p.m. • 3 • CA
This young girl went with her friends to pick wildflowers and never returned. Her body was found days later. The coroner ruled death was from exposure.

NA • M-Murray Walkup Miller   10/24/36-Unk • 9 • MT
He was in the woods with his dad and brother cutting firewood. Murray made two trips to a creek to get water; on the second trip he vanished. He was found days later and stated that on the way back on the second trip, he didn't recognize the area he was in.

E • M-Lloyd Hokit   10/21/45-3:00 p.m. • 9 • OK
He was following a hunter through the woods and somehow disappeared. His body was found days later; death was from exposure.

W • M-Donald McDonald   12/15/49-Unk • 17 • WA
Donald was with a friend who was hunting elk. His friend had shot an animal, and they were tracking it when he suddenly vanished.

Donald was never found.

NA • F-Nancy Jean Walker   05/08/51-8:15 p.m. • 2 • MA
Nancy left her residence with her brothers for a flower-picking trip. The group was returning and Nancy was last in line when she somehow got lost. Twelve hours after she disappeared, the girl was found alive one mile from her residence in an area that had been searched numerous times.

NA • F-Betty Joslyn   07/24/51-p.m. • 5 • Terrible Mountain, VT

The group was hiking back from picking ferns when Betty didn't arrive at her home. The girl was found alive two days later, one half mile from her house, in an area that had been searched at least two times.

E • F-Emma Bowers   07/22/53-Unk • 5 • Mill Run, PA

Emma was a deaf mute who was following friends through the woods and disappeared. She was found alive two days later eating wild berries. What she did for two days and how she got the berries was never determined.

NA • M-Lowell Linn   11/31/57-p.m. • 23 • Mount Rainier NP, WA

Lowell and a friend used snowshoes to climb to the top of a hill. They placed their skis on for the trip back down. Lowell's friend made it down the mountain; he never arrived. The mountain has been searched several times during the summer months. Lowell and his equipment have never been found.

E • M-Kenneth Scott   09/28/58-2:00 p.m. • 4 • MI

The boy wandered away from a family gathering at a public park. His body was found fifteen miles away on a hill. He died of exposure.

NA • M-David Raleigh   06/13/59-8:00 p.m. • 5 • NY

David and his brother and father had just docked their boat after a day of fishing on the lake. Rain had just started to fall, and David was told to run from the dock to the cabin. Somehow between the dock and the cabin, the boy vanished. Four months after the disappearance, he was found nine hundred feet up a mountain, dead of exposure.

W • M-Bobby Panknin   08/03/63-Unk • 4 • WA

Bobby's mother took her kids up a rural trail to view a small waterfall. Bobby waited just fifteen feet from the group behind bushes as they viewed the falls. The group returned in minutes, and Bobby had vanished. Bobby was never found.

E • M-Geoffrey Hague   02/08/70-3:20 p.m. • 16 • Great Smoky Mtn NP, TN

Geoff was last in a line of Boy Scouts hiking back to their vehicles. The group arrived at the vehicles, and Geoff didn't. After an extensive search, he was found with his backpack in a river valley in the middle of an icy river, lying on a rock. He was found dead from exposure with his pants pulled down to his knees.

NA • F-David Holtz   07/13/71-9:00 a.m. • 9 • Sequoia NP, CA

David was hiking back from fishing with his family when he decided to take a shortcut and disappeared. David's body was found eighteen days later, 1,200 feet higher in elevation, dead from exposure.

D • M-Donald G. Siskar   07/10/73-3:30 p.m. • 18 • Grass Mtn, WA

A Neighborhood Youth Corps group was hiking back from clearing trails. Donald was in the middle of the pack until some of the boys at the back cut through a switchback, placing Donald at the rear. Once the team members reached the bus, Donald was no longer with the group.

Donald was never found.

W • M-Jeffrey Bratcher   06/15/74-6:30 p.m. • 7 • WA

Jeffery was with a group of friends walking back from an area near a rural beach toward a parking lot and vanished. It's very similar to disappearance of Bryce Herda, and they happened in close proximity to each other.

Jeffrey was never found.

E • M-Mark Hanson   03/07/75-Unk • 21 • Great Smoky Mtns NP, TN

Two hikers were working their way up a trail when bad weather hit. Mark got tired and somehow vanished. He was found days later with his boots off, dead of exposure. There are many more fascinating details to this story in the book.

NA • M-Andrew Amato   09/30/78-10:30 a.m. • 4 • MA
A group of friends were in the woods behind their home when Andrew fell and lost a toy. The group wanted to leave. Andrew refused to go. The group returned to home to get an adult; he disappeared.
Andrew was never found.

NA • M-James Beveridge   02/07/81-Unk • 9 • Southern, CA
James was hiking with family on a rural trail; he was last in line when he disappeared. He was found days later in some bushes, dead from exposure.

D • F-Kathryn Dekkers   07/24/81-3:00 p.m. • 10 • Ampersand Mtn, NY
Descending Ampersand Mountain in the New York High Peaks, Kathryn was last in line and was missing by the time the group reached the bottom. A three-day search found the girl three miles away. She refused to talk to searchers.

E • M-Andrew Warburton   07/01/86-Unk • 9 • Canada
Andrew was the last of a group of kids who were going through the woods to a lake for swimming. Andrew didn't arrive. Several days later he was found deceased in a thicket.

E • M-Larry Krebbs   03/30/88-Unk • 2 • Lake Texoma, OK
Larry and his dad were walking in a rural area on the outskirts of the lake. Somehow during that walk, Larry vanished. The lake and surrounding area were searched extensively.
Larry was never found.

W • M-Kenny Miller   06/24/92-Unk • 12 • Yosemite NP, CA
Kenny was walking with family in a line through the woods when he disappeared. He was found two and a half miles away and fourteen hundred feet higher in elevation, dead from exposure.

W • F-Ashley Krestianson   07/14/94-Unk • 8 • SK, Canada
Ashleigh was with friends on a ranch when they decided to have a race. The girl took a shortcut but never arrived at the finish line. After two months of searching, the body was found in the middle of a swamp, dead from exposure. She was missing one shoe and clothing.

NA • F-Naomi Leigh Whidden   11/25/94-12:45 p.m. • 2 • GA
Mr. Whidden was hiking through the woods with his son and two daughters. He stated that one minute Naomi was there and then suddenly she wasn't. After 25 hours of searching, the girl was found face down in mud. She lived.

W • M-Bryce Herda   04/09/95-Unk • 4 • WA
Bryce was with his family on a rural beach on the northern Olympic Peninsula. He had difficulty walking a steep trail, so he took a different route and never made it to the car. This incident happened just north of the disappearance of Jeffrey Bratcher.

Bryce was never found.

F-Haley Zega   04/29/01-11:30 a.m. • 6 • Newton County, AR
The girl was hiking with her grandparents in a wilderness area, fell behind the pair, and disappeared. Fifty-one hours later, she was found alive. She stated that she had met another girl who helped her on the journey. The girl she met was similar to a girl who had died on the same trail twenty-three years earlier.

E • M-Chris Thompkins   01/25/02-1:30 p.m. • 20 • GA
A survey crew was working on a rural road. When work was completed, Chris was the farthest member from the truck and started to walk back. Crew team members said they heard nothing; he just vanished. His coins and a thread of his pants were found on a fence next to the road, and one of his boots was found days later on the property on the other side of the fence.

Chris has never been found.

E • M-Patric McCarthy   10/13/03-p.m. • 10 • NH

Patric was vacationing with his family when he and his brothers went into the woods. They decided to race back to their house. Patric didn't make it to the house. A search found the body fourteen hundred feet up in elevation in a different direction than the residence two miles away. He died of exposure.

W • F-Michelle Vanek   09/24/05-1:30 p.m. • 35 • CO

A friend volunteered to take Michelle up Mount of the Holy Cross so she could claim the summit. Very near the top, Michelle got tired and said she'd wait behind after her friend made it. The friend returned, and Michelle wasn't there.

Michelle Vanek has never been found.

NA • M-Eric Lewis   07/01/10 • 57 • Mount Rainier NP, WA

Eric Lewis may have been the most experienced climber who was alive and still practicing the sport on Mount Rainier. He was with friends climbing and the last person in line on rope when he unlatched his carabiner. His friends went back down and could not locate him.

Eric has never been found.

NA • M-Paul Lemaitre   07/04/12 • 66 • Seward, AK

The Mount Marathon is held annually in Seward, and Paul was competing. He was the last person to top the mountain and told race officials he'd be fine. Officials went down; Paul never arrived.

Paul has never been found.

NA • M-Ronald Ohm   08/09/12-p.m. • 52 • OR

Ron was with a group that was hiking to an alpine lake. On the ridge above the group's destination, he stated he'd stop and take photos and then walk in. Ron never arrived. A massive search never found Ron or any of his equipment.

Missing from inside the Home

The column at the far left indicates in which book the story is featured:

W=*Missing 411-Western United States*
E= *Missing 411-Eastern United States*
NA=*Missing 411-North America and Beyond*
D=*Missing 411-The Devil's in the Details*

These cases were obtained after screening all four of the Missing 411 books.

BK	Date	Name	State	Age	
E	9/7/36	Harold King	WI	3 Yrs	In Swamp 3 Miles from Home
E	8/16/37	Alice Baker	VT	20 Mos	Sheriff Believed Kidnapped
W	7/5/47	Wayne Bowers	Southern CA	3 Yrs	Found 4 Miles from Cabin
D	2/25/51	Jimmy Howard	FL	2 Yrs	Found 2½ Miles from Home
NA	4/19/53	Ronald Tammen	OH	18 Yrs	Missing from Dorm Room
D	10/6/55	Brandon Beard	VA	2 Yrs	Crawled from Crib w/ Bottle
NA	8/31/61	Ann Marie Burr	WA	8 Yrs	Disappeared during Rainstorm
NA	8/13/66	Amy Jackson	Sequoia NP	18 Mos	Missing from Tent/Middle of Night
NA	7/3/69	Irene Hofke	Sequoia NP	9 Yrs	Missing from Tent while Napping
NA	12/23/77	Lee Littlejohn	CA	18 Mos	Deputy Shocked at Distance Traveled
E	9/30/82	Kevin Ayotte	MN	3 Yrs	Summer Home, Northern MN
D	1/11/84	Ryan Hoeffliger	ID	2 Yrs	Home Near ID Border
NA	7/24/85	Jessica Azzopardi	Ontario	20 Mos	Lakeshore Home
E	7/3/88	Colleen Tourtillot	WI	18 Mos	Found 1.5 Miles from Home
E	8/16/99	Frank Downey	KY	4 Yrs	Unlocked Door, Left w/Dogs
D	6/24/00	Harriet Olsen	NY	75 Yrs	Inside Home
N	10/5/00	Tristen Meyers	NC	4 Yrs	Buzzer Didn't Activate
E	8/1/04	David Tippin	GA	4 Yrs	Unlocked Door in Early a.m.
E	5/4/09	Joshua Childers	MO	3 Yrs	Unlocked Door, Found in 50 Hrs

D	8/2/10	Emmett Trapp	AZ	2 Yrs	Home in Desert
NA	12/16/11	Jason Burton	SC	21 Mos	Found on Sandbar in River
D	9/11/12	Landen Trammell	AR	3 Yrs	Left Home Watched by Grandpa
NA	9/21/12	Isabel Zandarski	OH	30 Mos	Left Home at 3:00 a.m.
NA	10/16/12	Kyle Camp	AL	10 Yrs	Left Home with Dogs

Each of these people disappeared from inside their residences.

Tristen Meyers disappeared from inside his aunt's home while she had an alarm on. She never heard the alarm/buzzer go off.

Ryan Hoeffliger was sleeping in the same bed as his sister. She had just gotten up and used the restroom, came back to bed, and went to sleep. She woke up a few hours later, never hearing her brother get up, and found he was gone. He was located days later in a lake miles away, deceased.

Jason Burton disappeared from his home and was located under extremely unusual circumstances on a sandbar in the middle of a river, alive, with no flotation device.

I find it fascinating that the only two girls who went missing from a tent on this list both involved visits to Sequoia National Park. Is it coincidental that they are back-to-back cases on this list, with both occurring in the late 1960s?

These cases will baffle your mind and challenge you for a commonsense answer.

Missing from inside a Vehicle

These six children vanished from inside vehicles. The parents who left them were baffled. They couldn't understand how they had gotten out. In one incident the police discovered there were no handles inside the car to open the doors, yet the child got out. In the Gage Wayment case, his father was tormented and never could understand how he was able to open the door. He was so tormented and guilt-ridden that he killed himself.

Date	Name	State	Age	Incident
10/16/30	Lawrence Sullivan	NV	3 Yrs	Left and found on cliff near eagles
8/15/55	Richard Hatke	ID	2 Yrs	Sleeping in car-vanished

7/21/56	Sandy Barcus	CO	2 Yrs	Left Car, hiked 7 miles thru rugged mtns
3/26/62	Faye Crawford	TN	3 Yrs	Car doors could only be opened from outside
7/14/67	Ken Vanderleest	BC	3 Yrs	Removed boots, left vehicle
10/25/01	Gage Wayment	UT	2 Yrs	Sleeping in truck, couldn't understand how doors were opened

Locations Previously Searched

This list contains incidents where the person was located in an area that had been previously searched. In one incident it was stated that searchers walked by the person at least a hundred times, if he was there.

I have consistently stated in everything I've ever written that I greatly admire and respect SAR personnel. This is in no way a jab at their abilities. This chart exemplifies an unusual condition. Somehow, some way, I don't believe these people were in the area when searchers passed through. Facts sometimes don't indicate this, but I don't believe that canines, FLIR, and ground teams can all miss a subject as often as this chart indicates.

8/19/1859	Daughter of King	OH	4 Years	
7/01/1887	Emma Carbaugh	MD	22 Mos.	Mutilated Body Found
05/25/1891	Eddie Nichols	NY	2 Years	Missing 80 Hrs in woods
4/21/1897	Mary Sholtas	PA	3 Years	Together with Staneker
4/21/1897	Augustos Staneker	PA	4 Years	Together with Sholtas
3/4/1907	Horace Marvin	DE	4 Years	Searched Dozens of Times
5/22/1911	Alice Arnold	PA	4 Years	Found on Mtn Searched 2x
5/14/16	James Carroll	PA	4 Years	
10/27/17	Edward Gateley	MA	2 Years	
7/20/21	Gregory Aubuchon	CO	18 Years	RMNP, Longs Peak-Fall
12/10/1922	Marvin Koepke	KS	4 Years	
10/14/1925	Robert Cass	NH	3 Years	
8/10/1931	Benjamin Saul	CO	3 Years	Missing 38 Hrs in Mtns
5/25/1933	Dailey Hamerly	ID	2 Years	In Plowed Field
7/13/34	Bobby Connor	NY	21 Mos.	
7/22/34	Claire Benson	CT	21 Mos.	

Date	Name	Location	Age	Notes
9/17/34	Nancy Marshall	RI	22 Mos.	Found in Marsh after 28 Hrs
11/22/34	Rita Lent	PA	3 Years	
10/11/37	Floyd Chandler	CO	41 Years	Hunter Disappeared Found
3/28/40	Helen Chenoweth	IL	3 Years	Found Clean in Pig Lot
9/5/40	Hoyt F. White	RMNP	33 Years	Missing on Mountain
9/15/40	Ronald Rumbaugh	PA	2 Years	
3/2/42	Dewey Cook	WY	25 Years	Sheepherder
6/16/46	Thomas Evans	RMNP	20 Years	Soldier Lost on Mtn
2/2/47	Irma Santos	MA	5 Years	Missing 54 Hrs near Swamps
8/20/47	Carolyn Peterson	OH	20 Mos.	Searched by 100 for 4 Days
10/11/47	Otis Mason	PA	6 Years	
8/20/49	Larry Coleman	MN	3 Years	
5/4/50	Tommy Jenkins	WA	2 Years	
8/7/50	Helen Bogen	Canada/AB	2 Years	Found in Bathtub on Farm
2/25/51	Jimmy Howard	FL	2 Years	Found 2.5 Miles from Home
5/8/51	Nancy Walker	MA	2 Years	
7/24/51	Betty Joslyn	VT	5 Years	
5/20/53	Beverly Ann Bradley	MI	2 Years	
7/7/53	Isabel Davies	NSW, Australia	75 Years	Fell off Cliff
4/18/54	Shirley Sherman	WV	3 Years	
10/29/56	Jack Woods Jr.	AL	3 Years	
12/27/57	Shirley Ramsburg	WV	3 Years	
3/17/58	Johnny McKinney	WV	5 Years	
4/25/58	Judy Peterson	FL	3 Years	
6/27/58	Shirley Hunt	ID	8 Years	Found 1 Mile from House
7/29/58	Henry Kellar	OH	16 Mos.	
8/15/58	Bobby Bizup	CO	10 Years	Found 2500' up Mountain
6/13/59	David Raleigh	NY	5 Years	
7/14/59	Edith Wolfskill	CA	57 Years	Area searched 50x
3/4/62	David Cusiter	NSW, Australia	17 Years	Fell off Cliff
5/19/62	Caroline Chamberlain	W. Australia	2 Years	Found 2 Miles from Home
9/24/64	Arthur Ivey	WA	2½ Years	Near Idaho Border
1/9/65	Bonnie Edwards	NC	9 Years	

Locations Previously Searched | 351

Date	Name	Location	Age	Notes
8/4/71	Dana Cooper	CA	13 Years	Feet Not Injured
10/10/77	Samuel Ipock	OR	22 Years	Fell off Mtn
6/29/79	Kevin Reimer	Canada	9 Years	
12/3/80	Danny Hicks	NC	2 Years	Body Found 1.5 Miles Away
10/3/81	Stephen Oleszczuk	SC	4 Years	
6/29/82	Robert Baldeshwiler	RMNP	12 Years	Flattop Mountain
7/3/82	Nicholas Dailey	WY	2½ Years	Lost in Mountains
7/2/83	Michael Reel	TN	8 Years	
9/7/85	Ronald Adams	NY	21 Years	Autistic
7/6/86	Madeline Grisdale	Canada	49 Years	Mute/Stroke Victim
9/28/87	Timothy Box	AR	2 Years	Missing 3 Days in Woods
4/21/88	Michael Henley Jr.	NM	9 Years	Body Found 6 Miles Away
7/13/88	Eric Taylor	Australia	2 Years	Found 1200' up Mtn
7/13/90	Joshua Kern	ID	2 Years	
7/3/92	Paige Adriance	WA	8 Years	
7/11/92	Sarah Wolenetz	RMNP	11 Years	
4/27/99	Corey Anderson	MA	9 Years	Found on 5th Search of Area
8/16/01	Ellie James	Borneo	17 Years	Climbing Mount Kinabalu
8/1/04	David Tippin	GA	4 Years	
7/29/05	Jeff Christensen	RMNP	31 Years	NPS Ranger
12/10/06	David Iredale	Australia	17 Years	
12/9/09	Letisha Faust	VA	50 Years	Missing from Car, 3 Mos.
5/1/10	Emma Campbell	New Zealand	29 Years	Missing from Car Accident
10/23/11	Robert Wood Jr.	VA	8 Years	Disabled
6/115/12	Patrick Amen	CA	40 Years	"We walked by him 100x"

Span of years:
1859-2012

Total Cases: 74

Most Cases in One Year (1958): 5

These incidents have occurred worldwide and are not regional. Search teams from the following countries have been victimized by this phenomenon:

- United States
- Borneo
- Canada
- Australia
- New Zealand

I've been approached by several SAR personnel over the years stating they've been involved in similar searches where the missing just "shows up." Many of these victims don't remember what happened or how they arrived at the point they did.

Scholars/Intellectuals

This list was gleaned from the four Missing 411 books. It represents individuals who have vanished whom we consider intellectuals. A large percentage of these people have never been found.

**The first letter next to the M/F designation indicates the book in which the individual case was highlighted:

W=*Missing 411-Western United States*
E=*Missing 411-Eastern United States*
NA=*Missing 411-North America and Beyond*
D=*Missing 411-The Devil's in the Details*

Book • Sex/Name   Date Missing • Age • State
W • M-William Whitehead 08/24/24-Unk • 22 • Glacier NP, MT
Student-MIT
William and his brother hiked into the park and never came out.

W • M-Joseph Halpern   08/15/33-Unk • 22 • Rocky Mtn NP, CO
Graduate student-University of Chicago
Disappeared under strange circumstances while climbing Taylor Peak.

W • M-Dr. Frederick Lumley 08/13/34-27 -Unk • Glacier NP, MT
Professor of Sociology-Ohio State University

Frederick hiked into an area near Goat Camp and disappeared somewhere in that region.

NA • M-Harley Booth   07/05/46 • 30 • Devil's Gulch, RMNP, CO
Student-Colorado A & M
Disappeared with forestry class. Found nine days into search at the bottom of cliff.

E • F-Paula Welden   12/01/46-Unk • 18 • Bennington, VT
Student-Bennington College
Disappeared on hike in the mountains.

W • M-David Devitt   10/09/49-Unk • 21 • Rocky Mtn NP
W • M-Bruce Gerling   10/09/49-Unk • 20 • Rocky Mtn NP
Students-Colorado A&M
Devitt and Gerling were climbing Flattop Mountain from Grand Lake and returning to Bear Lake. They were with a group of other students when they got separated.

NA • M-Ronald Tammen Jr. 04/19/53-9:00 p.m. • 19 • Oxford, OH
Student-Miami University, D-1 Athlete-Wrestling
Disappeared from his dormitory, leaving behind all valuables and his vehicle.

NA • M-Walter A. Gordon   07/20/54-a.m. • 26 • Yosemite NP, CA
Student-University of California, Berkeley
Left his residence in Curry Camp in the morning for a hike to Glacier Point, never came back.

NA • M-Orvar Von Laas   10/09/54-2:00 p.m. • 30 • Yosemite NP, CA
Graduate Student-University of California, Berkeley
Described by friends and family as a "genius," Orvar was vacationing with family and staying at the Ahwahnee Hotel. Told his wife he was going to take a hike and he'd be back by 4:00 p.m.; he never returned.
***The Von Laas and Gordon families found each other and determined the men didn't know each other and shared no common ground at school in which they would've met. The families wrote a letter to President Eisenhower asking for special warfare troops to respond to Yosemite and assist in the search for their sons. The letter stated, "Nothing points to voluntary disappearance in either case."

NA • M-Lowell Linn   11/31/57-p.m. • 23 • Mount Rainier NP, WA
Graduate-University of Minnesota, Engineering
Linn and a friend snowshoed partially up the mountain. They got to a point where they put on their skis and started their descent. Lowell was lost somewhere on the side of Rainier.

E • M-Lawrence E. Prange 08/14/58-Unk • 20 • Seeley Lake, MT
Student-University of Montana
Entered the region with his dog hunting for mountain goats; never came back.

D • M-Quin Charles Frizzell   6/4/66-Unk • 31 • Tenaya Canyon, Yosemite NP
Nuclear Scientist
Quinn was a nuclear scientist at Lawrence Livermore National Laboratory in Northern California. He disappeared while hiking alone. On April 8, 1971, a hiker found a skull and Frizzell's credit cards on cliffs below Mount Watkins. In September 1972 another hiker found bones, his boots, and his backpack. The park service buried everything in its place. Case closed, in their minds. No DNA testing was ever done.

NA • F-Lynne Schulze   12/10/71-p.m. • 18 • Middlebury, VT
Student-Middlebury College
Lynne was last seen walking back to her dormitory room.

NA • F-Judy Martins   05/24/78-2:00 a.m. • 22 • Kent, OH
Student-Kent State University
Judy was last seen heading back to her dormitory.

D • M-Dr. Maurice Dametz 04/29-81-3:45 p.m. • 84 • Pike National Forest, CO
Professor of Theology and Anthropology
Dr. Dametz was in the Pike National Forest digging for rocks with a friend and vanished. He was never found.

NA • F-Karen Louise Wilson   03/27/85-8:15 p.m. • 22 • Albany, NY
Student-New York University-Albany
Karen made a trip into the city and was heading back to her room when she vanished.

D • M-Stefan Bissert   01/20/92 • 23 • Olympic National Park, WA
Student-Oregon State University (Fulbright Scholar)
Stefan was a Fulbright Scholar on an exchange program from Germany studying physics. He was hiking with a fellow German student when he vanished in the park.

W • F-Amy Bechtel   07/24/97-3:00 p.m. • 24 • Lander, WY
Graduate-University of Wyoming, D-1 Athlete-Track & Field
Vanished while running on a desolate mountain road.

D • F-Dr. Katherine Wong   02/19/99-2:00 p.m. • 47 • Bear Valley, CA
Physician
Dr. Wong was skiing with her husband when she took a run alone and vanished. Searchers at the time couldn't locate any evidence she was in the area, and law enforcement thought she may have been abducted or met with foul play. Four months after she vanished, bone chips and clothing attributed to the physician were found one half mile outside the resort's boundary. She disappeared in the middle of February, and the sheriff made a statement that maybe she was killed by a bear.

NA • M-Joseph Wood Jr.   07/08/99-2:00 p.m. • 34 • Mount Rainier NP, WA
Graduate-Yale University
He was on a leisurely hike on an established trail. He engaged another hiker in conversation and then disappeared.

D • M-David Byrd Felker   07/22/02-Unk • 20 • Zamora, Ecuador
Student
Studying at a university in Ecuador during his summer. Spoke four languages and was helping children learn to read. Lost in an Ecuadorian national park.

D • M-Zachary Weston   08/10/05-Unk • 22 • Mount Rainier NP, WA
Student-MIT, Engineering and Aeronautics
Disappeared while hiking in Mount Rainier National Park. Never found.

D • M-Gilbert Gilman   06/24/06-Unk • 47 • Olympic National Park
Director of Washington State Pension Fund, two bronze stars, longtime military service, spoke five languages, ultra top-secret clearance. Never found.

NA • M-Daming Xu   11/04/07-p.m. • 63 • Three Sisters Wilderness, OR
Professor of Mathematics-University of Oregon
He told his family he was going for a day hike to Cougar Reservoir in the Three Sisters Wilderness; never came back. Never found.

D • M-Jonathan Robinson   12/22/09-2:50 a.m. • 23 • Switzerland
Graduate-Newcastle University, Math & Economics

Vacationing with family in Wengen, Switzerland. Disappeared while walking back to his hotel room at 2:50 a.m., found miles away in an area that was inaccessible at that hour.

F-Megumi Yamamoto   06/09/09-4:00 p.m. • 26 • Mount Baldy, NM
Physics Graduate Student
The Japanese-born Megumi was attending graduate school in New Mexico. She got separated from her boyfriend on a mountain trail. Eventually she was found and evacuated by a helicopter that crashed and killed her.

NA • M-Sylvia Lange   1/24/10-12:30 p.m. • 77 • Point Reyes NP, CA
Sylvia was a retired director of psychiatric nursing at the Seattle School of Nursing. She walked dogs on the beach and disappeared. Never found.

D • F-Rachael Bagnall   09/08/10-Unk • 25 • Pemberton, BC
Medical Student

D • M-Jonathan Jette   09/08/10-Unk • 34 • Pemberton, BC
Government Attaché
Bagnall was a third-year medical student, and Jette was a government attaché for Quebec. The couple went for a two- to three-day hike north of Pemberton, BC. Rain inhibited search efforts. Bloodhounds never found a scent. Not one item was ever found confirming the couple had hiked into the wilderness.

NA • M-Michael Von Gortler   06/22/11-Unk • 53 • Mount Missouri, CO
Physician
Hiking with his daughter, who was a student at University of Colorado, Boulder, majoring in evolutionary biology. Both disappeared while hiking on Mount Missouri. The pair disappeared for eight days and was later found on the side of the mountain. Both had horrific injuries. They were hiking on a perfectly clear and calm day.

D • F-Dr. Hildegard Hendrickson   06/08/13-p.m. • 79 • Chelan County, WA
Professor, Retired-Seattle University, Chairman of Economics Department
Went mushroom picking in an area near Wenatchee Lake and disappeared. She left behind her car, purse, and all valuables. Never found.

D • M-August Reiger   06/16/13-p.m. • 18 • Banos, Ecuador
Student-University of Oklahoma

August was his high school's valedictorian and described as a genius by many. Was hiking a mountain trail just ahead of his parents and disappeared. Never found.

D • M-Gene George   09/21/13-Unk • 64 • Mount Harvard, CO
Attorney
Gene was hiking in the area of Mount Harvard when he vanished. Canines found nothing of the man. Just as this book was going to print, a hiker found human remains which may be Mr. George. There are few details available and no autopsy has been completed.

D • F-Jo Elliott Blakeslee   09/23/13-Unk • 63 • Craters of the Moon NP
Physician
Jo was hiking with a friend in Craters of the Moon National Monument. Her friend was found after two days; Jo wasn't located for twenty-eight days.

D • M-Alyof Krost   10/1/13-5:45 p.m. • 62 • Lake Arrowhead, CA
Physicist
The victim was a professor of physics from Germany attending a science conference at the University of California Los Angeles Conference Center at Lake Arrowhead. He disappeared on a hike and was never found.

Total Number on List: 35

Professors/Disciplines: 5
- Sociology
- Theology/Anthropology
- Mathematics
- Economics
- Physics

Disabled or Injured

This list evolved as the research continued to reveal incidents of individuals with genetic abnormalities and physical injuries who disappeared. Many of the people would not have a condition that was readily apparent if you passed them on the trail. Some of the conditions included Down syndrome, epilepsy, early stages of Alzheimer's, diabetes, etc. Other people had injured knees, bad backs, and other conditions that may have limited their mobility but wouldn't have been visible on the trail.

Sex/Name	Date Missing • Age • State
M-Owen Parfitt	06/1768-Unk • 70 • Shepton Mallet, England
F-Anna Gullett	09/10/32-5:00 p.m. • 48 • Leura, NSW, Australia
M-Jerry Hays	11/10/38-Unk • 5 • AZ
F-Celsa Lucero	11/09/40-3:30 p.m. • 51 • NM
F-Betty McCullough	06/21/41-a.m. • 10 • OR
M-Emerson Holt	07/18/43-2:00 p.m. • 55 • Yosemite NP, CA
F-Mrs. August Nelson	07/28/43-Unk • 75 • WI
M-Joe Carter	05/21/50-3:00 p.m. • 32 • Mount St. Helens, NP, WA
F-Ann Bragg	12/02/51-10:00 a.m. • 76 • Birmingham, AL
M-Jerry Monkman	04/25/53-5:00 p.m. • 11 • Choteau, MT
F-Emma Bowers	07/22/53-Unk • 5 • PA
F-Myrtle Gray	07/30/53-Noon • 3 • Churchton, MD
F-Nora Moore	07/18/55-4:00 p.m. • 7 • AL
F-Rose Jewett	08/11/57-4:15 p.m. • 95 • ID
F-Mary Gay Bent	07/13/58-3:00 p.m. • 5 • MT
M-Bobby Bizup	08/15/58-6:00 p.m. • 10 • RMNP, CO
F-Judy Boltjes	05/02/59-2:00 p.m. • 6 • Deckers, CO
M-Jerry Cooper	12/21/61-10:00 p.m. • 4 • GA
F-Bonnie Lee Edwards	01/09/65-4:30 p.m. • 6 • Great Smoky Mtns NP, TN
M-Larry Jeffrey	05/28/66-1:30 p.m. • 6 • NV
M-Clayton Ordiway	06/08/69-1:30 p.m. • 5 • Sequoia NP, CA
M-Dennis Lloyd Martin	06/14/69-4:30 p.m. • 6 • Great Smoky Mtn NP, TN
M-David Holtz	07/13/71-9:00 a.m. • 9 • Sequoia NP, CA
M-Kevin Dye	07/18/71-3:00 p.m. • 9 • WY
M-Dana Cooper	08/04/71-Unk • 13 • CA
M-George Bombardier	11/29/71-5:00 p.m. • 55 • Brighton, NY
M-Teodoro Sibayan	01/01/72 • 13 • HI
M-Guy Heckle	02/03/73-8:00 p.m. • 11 • IA
M-Jimmy Duffy	10/19/73-2:15 p.m. • 2 • WA
M-Blake Mulligan	06/13/76-5:00 p.m. • 14 • NV
M-Duane Scott	07/27/78-Unk • 31 • PA
M-Maurice Dametz	04/29-81-3:45 p.m. • 84 • Pike National Forest, CO
M-Keith Zunke	10/24/81-Unk • 21 • OR
M-Jay Charles Toney	05/25/82-1:30 p.m. • 17 • Great Smoky Mtn NP, TN
M-Kevin Jay Ayotte	09/30/82-p.m. • 3 • MN
M-Stephen Crean	08/06/85-2:40 p.m. • 37 • NSW, Australia

M-Ronald Adams   09/07/85-p.m. • 21 • High Peaks, NY
F-Madeline Grisdale   07/06/86-Unk • 49 • MB, Canada
M-Patrick Hildebrand   06/27/87-1:50 p.m. • 9 • Australia
M-Casey Holliday   10/14/90-10:00 a.m. • 11 • ID
M-Kenny Miller   06/24/92-Unk • 12 • CA
F-Rhonda Runningbird   03/26/95-Unk • 25 • Alberta, Canada
M-Taylor Touchstone   08/07/96-4:00 p.m. • 10 • FL
M-John Devine   09/06/97-2:00 p.m. • 73 • Olympic NP, WA
F-Harriet Olsen   06/24/00-6:00 p.m. • 75 • Vermontville, NY
M-Jimmy Rambone Jr.   09/03/03-3:00 p.m. • 51 • QC, Canada
M-Robert Springfield   09/19/04-4:00 p.m. • 49 • MT
M-Christopher L. Jones 04/05/06-Unk • 37 • AR
M-Evan Thompson   05/27/06-a.m. • 8 • CO
M-Samuel Boehlke   10/14/06-4:00 p.m. • 8 • Crater Lake NP, OR
M-Douglas John May   07/16/09-5:30 p.m. • 55 • CA
M-Melvin Nadel   09/06/09-4:00 p.m. • 61 • NM
F-Katherine Truitt   01/07/10-Unk • 37 • Point Reyes NP, CA
M-Todd Hofflander   09/27/10-Unk • 39 • ID
F-Patty Krieger   10/21/10-1:00 p.m. • 65 • WA
M-Robert Wood Jr.   10/23/11-2:00 p.m. • 8 • VA
F-Patricia Wallace   07/03/12-4:00 p.m. • 74 • CO
M-Kyle Camp   10/16/12-4:30 p.m. • 10 • AL
F-Hildegard Hendrickson 06/08/13-5:00 p.m. • 79 • Wenatchee Lake, WA
M-Jerry Duran   07/24/13-4:00 p.m. • 21 • Cache County, UT
F-Amber Rose Smith   10/08/13-1:30 p.m. • 30 mos. • Paris, MI

Total Cases: 61
Males: 41
Females: 20

Most Cases in One Year (1971): 4 Cases

Oldest Person on List: 95 Years
Youngest: 2 Years

Countries Represented:
United States

Canada
Australia
England

Interesting Anomalies on List:
* There are three cases of back-to-back incidents that involved people of the same age. Each of these two-year pairings contain one national park Location:

#1:
F-Bonnie Lee Edwards   01/09/65-4:30 p.m. • 6 • Great Smoky Mtns NP, TN
M-Larry Jeffrey   05/28/66-1:30 p.m. • 6 • NV
#2
M-David Holtz   07/13/71-9:00 a.m. • 9 • Sequoia NP, CA
M-Kevin Dye   07/18/71-3:00 p.m. • 9 • WY
#3
M-Samuel Boehlke   10/14/06-4:00 p.m. • 8 • Crater Lake NP, OR
M-Douglas John May   07/16/09-5:30 p.m. • 55 • CA

You've now seen an unusual aspect of the Missing 411 cases. We have presented two extremes of the intellectual and physical spectrum of missing. We have a list of missing people who are extremely fit, smart, and overall highly intellectual. We also have a list of people who are mentally and or physically challenged.

Elevation Gain

There are stories in the four books about children who have disappeared and were found in areas much higher in elevation than when they were last seen. It's difficult to remember all of the relevant facts and heights, so we put together this chart to show the extremes we have documented. The majority of the heights covered by these kids are so far outside the norms quoted by SAR manuals, it is hard to believe. Look at some of the heights conquered by a two year old.

Are the heights and distances quoted for these children even possible?

Date	Name	State	Age	Elevation
11/2/57	Jill Hatch	CA-South	7 Yrs	3,500'
11/8/1891	Ottie Powell	VA	4 Yrs	3,372'
4/20/30	Asa Lee Lakey	CA	6 Yrs	3,000'
7/13/57	David Scott	CA-S-Sierras	2 Yrs	3,000'
8/22/63	Donald Griffen	Yosemite	4 Yrs	3,000'
11/23/91	Corey Fay	OR	17 Yrs	3,000'
6/8/67	Danny Greenwood	AZ	5 Yrs	2,580'
7/2/38	Alfred Beilhartz	RMNP-CO	4 Yrs	2,500'
8/15/58	Billy Bizup	RMNP-CO	10 Yrs	2,500'
7/14/41	Clarence Murphy	CA-Sierras	4 Yrs	2,000'
7/10/83	Gary Lee Chavoya	CA-Sierra	10 Yrs	2,000'
8/12/1910	Eddie Hamilton	Canada-SK	2 Yrs	1,800'
3/28/1993	Brad Lavies	RMNP	13 Yrs	1,600'
10/16/30	Lawrence Sullivan	NV	3 Yrs	1,400'
7/17/54	Gary Bailey	ME	3 Yrs	1,400'
6/24/92	Kenny Miller	N/O Yosemite	12 Yrs	1,400'
10/13/03	Patric McCarthy	NH	10 Yrs	1,400'
7/23/98	Trent Richardson	AZ	3 Yrs	1,350'
12/29/56	Jack Hodges	AZ	7 Yrs	1,300'
5/17/43	Doris Dean	VA	4 Yrs	1,200'
7/13/71	David Holtz	Sequoia NP	9 Yrs	1,200'**Disabled
7/13/88	Eric Taylor	Australia	2 Yrs	1,200'
5/22/1911	Alice Arnold	PA	4 Yrs	1,000'
11/10/38	Jerry Hays	AZ	5 Yrs	1,000'
8/11/47	Arnie Olson	MT	4 Yrs	1,000'
7/13/58	Mary Gay Bent	MT	5 Yrs	1,000'
5/27/51	Roger Shaddinger	CA-Sierras	9 Yrs	1,000'
7/10/83	Gary Lee Chavoya	CA-Sierras	10 Yrs	1,000'
6/13/59	David Raleigh	NY	5 Yrs	900'
9/1/57	Michael McMillan	NC	2½ Yrs	850'
1/29/42	Patricia Connolly	CA	2½ Yrs	650'

Distance Traveled

If the heights conquered by children weren't enough to startle you, the distances listed below might. These facts come directly from

SAR and law enforcement reports or news articles that were quoted in the four Missing 411 books. Think about your children when they were two years old. Could they have covered these distances?

Date	Name	State	Age	Distance
12/29/56	Jack Hodges	AZ	7 Yrs	50 Miles in 2 Days
8/31/31	Mr. I. Shields (Son)	Australia	4 Yrs	45 Miles in 5 Days
6/20/38	Timoteo Griego	NM	4 Yrs	40 Miles in 4 Days
4/26/39	Starkey's Daughter	Australia	5 Yrs	34 Miles in Less Than 36 Hours
8/5/01	William Parven	CA-South	16 Years	30-40 Miles in 4 Days
9/10/17	Michael Janiko	WI	4 Yrs	30 Miles in 3 Days
4/25/53	Jerry Monkman	MT	11 Years	30 Miles in 38 Hours
5/23/37	Ludvina Machishyn	Canada-SK	10 Years	20 Miles in 3 Days
10/16/54	Joyce Abel	WA	5 Yrs	20 Miles thru Mtns in 20 Hrs
6/23/63	Bruce Ferrin	UT	7 Yrs	20 Miles in 30 Hrs, Down Cliff
7/28/73	Christie Davis	FL	2 Yrs	20 Miles
4/11/71	Patrick Sanchez	NM	4 Yrs	20 Miles in 48 Hrs
4/27/86	Cody Sheehy	OR	6 Yrs	18 Miles
9/11/52	James Madison	ID	67 Yrs	15 Miles in Rugged Wilderness
8/17/53	Andrew Thackerson	Seq Natl Park	5 Yrs	12–18 Miles
5/10/1891	Daughter-Hammond	NE	4 Yrs	15 Miles in 4 Days
11/18/32	Bud Fisher	AZ	4 Yrs	15 Miles in 3 Days
2/13/36	Joyce Fielding	NSW, Australia	22 Mos	15 Miles in Less Than 3 Days
10/24/36	Murray Miller	MT	9 Yrs	15 Miles
10/30/45	Mike McDonald	AZ	2 Yrs	15 Miles Found in Cave
6/8/67	Danny Greenwood	AZ	5 Yrs	15 Miles Uphill 2,580' in Bldrs
9/28/58	Kenneth Scott	MI	4 Yrs	15 Miles thru Swamp
5/31/85	Tomas Cabrera	CA-South	3 Yrs	15 Miles in 30 Hours
7/24/13	Jerry Duran	UT	21 Yrs	15 Miles in 24 hrs/Brain Injury
1/11/49	Robert Carr	WV	9 Yrs	14 Miles over Mtns
10/16/06	Kory Kelly	MN	38 Yrs	14 Miles in 24 Hrs
10/14/76	Charles McCullar	OR	19 Yrs	14 Miles thru Deep Snow

8/7/96	Taylor Touchstone	FL	10 Yrs	14 Miles thru Water
7/13/12	Rhonda Cardinal	Canada-AB	42 Yrs	13½ Miles
4/20/30	Asa Lee Lakey	CA	6 Yrs	13 Miles in 3 days
11/29/23	C.G. Lee (Son of)	FL	4 Yrs	12 Miles in 24 Hours
10/1/29	Alfred Hotchkiss	CO	2 Yrs	Across Mtns in 2 Days
2/7/42	Ronald McGee	AZ	2 Yrs	12 Miles Uphill 428' in Bldrs
1/11/49	John Helmick	WV	16 Yrs	12 Miles over Mtns w/Snow
4/10/52	Keith Parkins	OR	2 Yrs	12 Miles in 19 Hrs over Mtns
8/4/55	Dennis Lloyd	WA	12 Yrs	12 Miles in 36 Hrs in Mtns
5/2/59	Judy Boltjes	CO	6 Yrs	12 Miles in 17 hrs/Heart Issue
7/13/88	Eric Taylor	Australia	2 Yrs	12 Miles and 1,200' up Mtn
5/27/06	Evan Thompson	CO	8 Yrs	11 Miles **Disabled
12/25/37	Vivienne Goldstiver	Australia	7 Yrs	11 Miles in 1–2 Days
7/24/13	Jerry Duran	UT	21 Yrs	10–15 Miles in 24 Hrs
9/29/48	Janet Federer	WY	6 Yrs	10 Miles
11/23/91	Corey Fay	OR	17 Yrs	10 Miles
10/12/1875	Mrs. Farrell's Son	Australia	4 Yrs	9 Miles thru Mtns in 80 Hrs
5/26/1904	Johnny Connors	Australia	2½ Yrs	9 Miles in 3 Days
8/30/59	Richard Herman	OR	6 Yrs	9 Miles in 29 Hrs
3/2/76	Harold Mott	PA	12 Yrs	9 Miles
8/5/64	Richard Spyglass	Canada-ON	4 Yrs	8½ Miles
6/15/1907	Lawrence Marsh (Son)	ID	19 Mos	8 Miles in 2 Days
3/26/1930	Maretha Yarborough	AR	3 Yrs	8 Miles in 24 Hrs
1/2/1941	Jackie Helman	WA	6 Yrs	8 Miles in 9 Hrs
6/27/48	Bobby Brown	TX	2 Yrs	8 Miles in 24 Hrs
3/13/16	Kenneth Crandall	MT	2½ Yrs	8 Miles
7/4/53	Patty Ann McLean	MT	3 Yrs	8 Miles up Cliff-Saw Small Cows
5/25/82	Jay Toney	RMNP	17 Yrs	8 Miles in Creekbed Unconscious
4/24/1856	George Cox	PA	6 Yrs	7 Miles
4/24/1856	Joseph Cox	PA	5 Yrs	7 Miles
10/16/30	Lawrence Sullivan	NV	3 Yrs	7 Miles Uphill 1400'
9/6/37	Florence Jackson	AR	4 Yrs	7 Miles
4/9/44	Donald Curry	PA	4 Yrs	7 Miles thru Rugged Mtns/23 hrs
7/21/56	Sandy Barcus	CO	2½ Yrs	7 Miles thru Rugged Mtns

5/31/59	Patricia Graham	NY	3 Yrs	7 Miles into Swamp-48 hrs	
4/4/64	Kenneth Edwards	CA-South	2 Yrs	7 Miles-2 Days up Cliff	
6/16/46	Katherine Van Alst	AR	8 Yrs	7 Miles	
6/13/76	Blake Mulligan	NV	14 Yrs	7 Miles	
6/5/26	Marlon Robb	UT	17 Yrs	6 Miles	
3/15/36	Steve Benson	CO	3 Yrs	6 Miles in a Dust Storm	
9/4/48	Lawrence Fustini	PA	30 Mos	6 Miles	
4/17/53	Anna Woodruff	CA-South	3 Yrs	6 Miles	
4/21/88	Michael Henley Jr.	NM	9 Yrs	6 Miles	
4/17/54	Joe Davis	TX	4 Yrs	6 Miles	
5/8/55	Jess Davis	OR	2 Yrs	6 Miles and 2 Mtns in 24 Hrs	
8/22/63	Donald Griffen	Yosemite	4 Yrs	6 Miles Uphill 3,000', Bldr Field	
4/21/88	Michael Henley Jr	NM	9 Yrs	6 Miles	
10/9/24	Margaret Turner	CO	20 Mos	5 Miles-Found on Barren Peak	
12/5/39	Jackie Landreth	OK	3 Yrs	5 Miles in 48 Hrs in Mtns	
5/17/43	Doris Dean	VA	4 Yrs	5 Miles and Uphill 1,200'	
8/27/45	Red Cramer	CA	30 Mos	5 Miles in 18 Hours	
9/25/49	Terry Lindholm	MI	8 Yrs	5 Miles in 12 Hours	
8/6/50	Gunnar Peterson	WA	65 Yrs	5 Miles, 10 Days on Berries	
1/30/52	Stephen Parker	NY	3 Yrs	5 Miles in 4½ Hrs	
7/30/53	Richard Rucker	WV	2 Yrs	5 Miles	
6/22/55	Johnny Johnson	England	3 Yrs	5 Miles in 3 Days	
11/2/57	Jill Hatch	CA	7 Yrs	5 Miles Uphill 3,500'	
8/15/57	Rickey Craig	WA	5 Yrs	5 Miles	
6/28/58	Anthony Martini	MA	11 Yrs	5 Miles in 8 Hrs	
5/31/59	Patricia Graham	NY	3 Yrs	5 Miles in Swamp	
6/28/59	Carol Van Hulla	MI	3 Yrs	5 Miles	
7/10/62	Lisa Shackelford	IL	3 Yrs	5 Miles	
11/1/91	Brian Sines	ID	29 Yrs	5 Miles Uphill	
5/7/99	Joshua Stauffer	ID	3 Yrs	5 Miles Found on Top of Hill	
6/17/05	Brennan Hawkins	UT	11 Yrs	5 Miles	
5/27/06	Evan Thompson	CO	8 Yrs	5 Miles Found in Cave	
7/14/94	Ashley Krestiansen	Canada-ON	5 Yrs	4½ Miles	
11/10/38	Jerry Hays	AZ	5 Yrs	4½ Miles up 1,000' Bldr Field	
8/22/1874	Eddie Prigley	KY	3 Yrs	4 Miles	
8/20/1883	James Vaughan	ID	18 Mos	4 Miles	

Date	Name	State	Age	Distance/Condition
6/3/1893	Earl Gilliam	OR	3 Yrs	4 Miles
6/2/1897	Harry Bakers Dhtr	NY	2 Yrs	4 Miles in Bear Cave
4/4/1906	Minnie Parsons	NY	7 Yrs	4 Miles
12/20/35	Charles Warren	AR	2 Yrs	4 Miles
5/11/38	David Baumgarten	CA-South	2 Yrs	4 Miles Uphill
5/2/44	Ronald Boggs	OH	3 Yrs	4 Miles-Found in Cave
10/21/45	Lloyd Hokit	OK	9 Yrs	4 Miles-On Ridge
10/20/46	Eugene Shue	PA	3 Yrs	4 Miles
7/5/47	Wayne Bowers	CA	3 Yrs	4 Miles
8/11/47	Arnie Olson	MT	4 Yrs	4 Miles
2/16/49	Rickey Tankersley	AL	2 Yrs	4 Miles in 16 Hrs
2/1/46	Donald Sell	PA	2 Yrs	4 Miles in 4 Hrs
10/6/55	Brandon Beard	VA	2 Yrs	4 Miles in 7 Hrs in Mountains
7/16/58	Robert Haughney	PA	6 Yrs	20 Miles in 12 Hrs in Mtns
9/28/87	Timothy Box	AR	2 Yrs	4 Miles in 3 Days
8/2/10	Emmett Trapp	AZ	2 Yrs	4 Miles thru Desert
8/20/10	Paige Wilson	WA	8 Yrs	4 Miles
7/24/86	Lynn Marie Hillier	Canada-BC	2 Yrs	3½ Miles

Aircraft Associated with Missing Person Cases

Below is a list of aircraft crashes associated with cases in our book. Each of these crashes occurred when the aircraft was directly involved in a SAR effort.

The person named is the victim rescuers were attempting to save.

Sex/Name	Date of Crash • Age • State • Conditions
M-Al Snider	03/05/48-5:00 p.m. • 28 • Everglades NP, FL • Helicopter
M-Keith Reinhhard	08/12/88-Unk • 49 • Silver Plume, CO • Cessna 182R
M-John Devine	09/12/97-3:45 p.m. • 73 • Olympic NP, WA • Helicopter
M-Jaryd Atadero	10/3/99-3:30 p.m. • 3 • Poudre Canyon, CO • Helicopter
F-Megumi Yamamoto	06/09/11-4:00 p.m. • 26 • Mount Baldy, NM • Helicopter

These five cases represent the crash of an aircraft that occurred while searching for a victim. For details on the incidents, refer to the section on the missing person. I was surprised that there were this many cases of aircraft crashes associated with cases we have researched.

Missing Aircraft

A reader in Finland sent us an interesting correlation between missing airplanes in the Bermuda Triangle and missing people we have documented in the Missing 411 books. According to the website www.bermuda-triangle.org, 129 aircraft disappeared from December 5, 1945, through December 15, 2008. What is fascinating is that four people documented in our books vanished on the same day as four of the aircraft. Here is the list:

July 8, 1968
Karen Cooney, missing from Corry, Pennsylvania
Source: *Missing 411-Eastern United States*, pages 205–206
Cessna 180, missing between Grand Bahama and West Palm Beach
N944MH
Two people on board

April 30, 1978
Chris Vigil, disappears from the mountains in northern Colorado
Source: *Missing 411-The Devil's in the Details*
Cessna 172, missing in Dillon, South Carolina
NIGH

September 6, 2002
Theresa Schmidt, missing from the mountains outside of Deckers, Colorado
Source: *Missing 411-Western United States*, pages 229–231
Piper Pawnee-1977, missing southeast of Nassau, the Bahamas
N59684
Pilot only on board

November 5, 1982
Richard Peterson, missing from Delmont, New Jersey
Source: *Missing 411-Eastern United States*, pages 281–282

Beechcraft 65-B80, flying from Fort Lauderdale to Eleuthera Island, Bahamas.
NIHQ
Three persons on board

It seems like an extraordinary coincidence that a person disappears in North America on the same date as an airplane in the Bermuda Triangle.

List of Missing from this Book

Book • Sex-Name	Date Missing • Age • State
M-Owen Parfitt	06/1768-Unk • 70 • Shepton Mallet, England
M-George Cox	04/24/1856-a.m. • 7 • Beford County, PA
M-Joseph Cox	04/24/1856-a.m. • 5 • Bedford County, PA
M-Mrs. Farrell's Son	10/12/1875-8:00 a.m. • 4 • Tenterfield, Australia
F-Emma Grace Carbaugh	07/01/1887-10:00 a.m. • 22 mos. • Sabiliasville, MD
M-Dayton Weaver	09/16/1890-10:00 a.m. • 3 • Greenport, NY
M-Eddie Nichols	05/25/1891-10:00 a.m. • 2 • Commac, NY
M-Earl Gilliam	06/03/1893-p.m. • 3 • Heppner, OR
F-Lillian Carney	08/08/1897-Noon • 6 • Masardis, ME
M-Johnny Connors	5/26/1904-p.m. • 2 • Packsaddle Bore, Australia
F-Minnie Parsons	04/04/1906-5:00 p.m. • 7 • Jamestown, NY
M-Lawrence Marsh (Son of)	06/15/1907-6:00 p.m. • 19 mos. • ID
F-Alice Arnold	05/22/1911-a.m. • 4 • Ickesburg, PA
F-Grace Cooper	08/08/1913-1:00 p.m. • 5 • QC, Canada
M-Michael Janiko	09/10/1917-2:00 p.m. • 4 • Asland, WI
M-Henry Nutter	07/06/1919-Unk • 6 • Fox Lake, IL
M-Gregory Aubuchon	07/20/21-Unk • 18 • RMNP, CO
M-Marvin Koepke	12/10/1922-5:00 p.m. • 4 • Junction City, KS
M-C.G. Lee (Son of)	11/29/23-Unk • 4 • Clearwater, FL
M-Robert Cass	10/14/25-1:00 p.m. • 3 • Ashland, NH
F-Glenis M. Gilbert	04/09/28-4:00 p.m. • Unk • NSW, Australia
M-Alfred Hotchkiss	10/01/29-a.m. • 2 • Ridgeway, CO
M-Vernon Daniel	12/15/29-2:00 p.m. • 2 • Bayfield, CO
F-Maretha Yarborough	03/26/30-Noon • 3 • Waldron, AR

M-Asa Lee Lakey	04/20/30-Unk • 6 • Mount Burney, CA
F-Helen Kockman	04/23/1930-6:00 p.m. • 3 • Quinney, WI
M-Benjamin Saul	08/10/31-6:00 p.m. • 3 • Jarre Canyon, CO
M-I. Shields (Son)	08/31/31-Unk • 4 • Mossgiel, NSW
M-Julius Bakken	11/09/31-Noon • 21 • Wenatchee, WA
F-Anna Gullett	09/10/32-5:00 p.m. • 48 • NSW, Australia
M-Bud Fisher	11/18/32-p.m. • 4 • Gila Bend, AZ
M-Dailey Hamerly	05/25/33-2:00 p.m. • 2 • Moscow, ID
M-John Kennon	08/31/35-5:00 p.m. • 2 • Mexico, MO
F-Joyce Fielding	02/03/36-Unk • 22 mos. • NSW, Australia
M-Steve Benson	03/15/36-10:30 a.m. • 3 • Two Buttes, CO
F-Hazel Scraba	05/23/37-Unk • 11 • Pelly, SK, Canada
F-Ludvina Machishyn	05/23/37-Unk • 10 • Pelly, SK, Canada
M-Floyd Chandler	10/11/37-4:30 p.m. • 41 • Stove Prairie, CO
F-Vivienne Goldstiver	12/25/37-Unk • 7 • Toonpan, Australia
M-Hickle Ware	06/11/38-p.m. • 4 • Pine River, MN
M-Timoteo Griego	06/20/38-p.m. • 4 • Leyba, NM
F-Daughter of Mrs. Starkey	04/26/39-a.m. • 5 • South Australia
M-Jackie Landreth	12/03/39-p.m. • 3 • Cloudy, OK
M-Hoyt F. White	09/05/40-Unk • 33 • RMNP, CO
M-Jackie Helman	01/02/41-3:00 p.m. • 6 • Badger Pocket, WA
F-Patricia Connolly	01/29/42-Unk • 2 • Menlo Park, CA
M-Kenneth Slagle	11/26/42-p.m. • 3 • Conemaugh, PA
F-Doris Dean	05/17/43-p.m. • 4 • Shenandoah NP, VA
M-Donald Curry	04/09/44-4:35 p.m. • 4 • Belleville, PA
F-Red Cramer	08/27/45-7:00 p.m. • 2 • Los Gatos, CA
M-Thomas Evans	06/16/46-a.m. • 20 • RMNP, CO
M-Harley Booth	07/05/46-Unk • 30 • RMNP, CO
M-Raymond Howe Jr.	07/15/46-5:00 p.m. • 9 • Pittsburgh, PA
F-Irma Santos	02/02/47-2:00 p.m. • 5 • Carver, MA
M-Celestino Trujillo Jr.	04/09/47-11:30 a.m. • 3 • Ledoux, NM
M-Arnie Olson	08/11/47-5:00 p.m. • 4 • Mount Skalkaho, MT
M-Al Snider	03/05/48-5:00 p.m. • 28 • Sandy Key, FL
M-C. H. Trotter	03/05/48-5:00 p.m. • 48 • Sandy Key, FL
M-Don Frasier	03/05/48-5:00 p.m. • Unk • Sandy Key, FL
M-Robert Carr	01/11/49-2:00 p.m. • 7 • Davis, WV
M-Eston Carr	01/11/49-2:00 p.m. • 9 • Davis, WV

List of Missing from this Book | 369

M-John Helmick	01/11/49-2:00 p.m. • 15 • Davis, WV
M-Joe Carter	05/21/50-3:00 p.m. • 32 • Mount St. Helens, WA
F-Helen Bogen	08/07/50-10:00 am • 2 • Monitor, AB, Canada
M-Jimmy Howard	02/25/51-11:30 a.m. • 2 • FL
M-Leo Gaspard	07/31/51-Unk • 60 • Pitt Lake, BC, Canada
F-Ann Bragg	12/02/51-10:00 a.m. • 76 • Birmingham, AL
M-Stephen Parker	01/30/52-4:30 p.m. • 3 • Rome, NY
M-James Madison	09/11/52-6:00 p.m. • 67 • Nez Perce Natl Forest, ID
F-Silvia Green	03/24/53-7:00 p.m. • 26 • NSW, Australia
M-Jerry Monkman	04/25/53-5:00 p.m. • 11 • Choteau, MT
M-Kerry Smith	05/03/53-1:00 p.m. • 10 • Middle Fork Powder River, WY
F-Mary Lewis	06/16/53-Unk • 83 • NSW, Australia
F-Isabel Davies	07/07/53-5:00 p.m. • 75 • NSW, Australia
F-Myrtle Gray	07/30/53-Noon • 3 • Churchton, MD
F-Barbara Sue Jones	11/25/53-Unk • 22 mos. • Marianna, AR
F-Joan Marie Treece	04/14/54-1:00 p.m. • 3 • Mountain Home, AR
M-Timothy Farmer	05/05/54-11:00 am • 2½ • NSW, Australia
F-Susan Jackson	07/07/54-5:00 p.m. • 3 • Rockville, MD
F-Joyce Abel	10/16/54-1:00 p.m. • 5 • Okanogan, WA
M-Howard Newell	01/22/55-Noon • 6 • Little River Harbour, NS, Canada
M-Brandon Beard	10/06/55-9:00 a.m. • 2 • Craigsville, VA
F-Sandy Barcus	07/21/56-Noon • 2 • Nederland, CO
M-Jack Hodges	12/29/56-a.m. • 7 • Seligman, AZ
M-Jack Ostrom	05/29/57-Unk • 74 • Jawbone Lake, ON, Canada
M-Henry Yarbrough	05/21/58-Noon • 2 • Jasper, TN
M-Robert Haughney	07/16/58-a.m. • 6 • Strabane, PA
M-Bobby Bizup	08/15/58-6:00 p.m. • 10 • RMNP, CO
F-Shirley Hunt	06/27/58-11:15 a.m. • 8 • Weippe, ID
F-Judy Boltjes	05/02/59-2:00 p.m. • 6 • Deckers, CO
M-David Ashley Cusiter	03/04/62-3:00 p.m. • 17 • NSW, Australia
F-Caroline Chamberlain	05/19/62-4:30 p.m. • 2 • Kojonup, Western Australia
M-Edward Eskridge	02/19/63-5:00 p.m. • 16 • Green River, WY
M-Arthur Leo Ivey	09/24/64-7:30 p.m. • 2 • Spokane, WA
M-Reed Jeppson	10/11/64-1:00 p.m. • 15 • Salt Lake City, UT
M-John Nezza	07/17/65-Unk • 80 • Mount Shasta, CA
M-Billy Hoag	05/10/67-4:30 p.m. • 11 • Hannibal, MO
M-Joey Hoag	05/10/67-4:30 p.m. • 13 • Hannibal, MO

M-Craig Dowell	05/10/67-4:30 p.m. • 14 • Hannibal, MO
M-David Adams	05/03/68-5:00 p.m. • 8 • Tiger Mountain, Issaquah, WA
M-Patrick Sanchez	04/11/71-2:30 p.m. • 4 • Chilili, NM
M-Kenny Robinson	04/11/71-2:30 p.m. • 5 • Chilili, NM
M-George Bombardier	11/29/71-5:00 p.m. • 55 • Brighton, NY
F-Anna Christian Waters	01/16/73-2:15 p.m. • 5 • Half Moon Bay, CA
M-Donald G. Siskar	07/10/73-3:30 p.m. • 18 • Grass Mountain, WA
M-Timothy Shear	11/23/75-p.m. • 22 • Little Bell Mountains, MT
M-Samuel Ipock	10/10/77-5:00 p.m. • 22 • Tumalo Falls, OR
M-Christopher Vigil	04/30/78-6:30 p.m. • 9 • Greyrock Mountain, CO
F-Tina Lucas	03/01/79-11:30 a.m. • 4 • Sumter, SC
M-Danny Hicks	12/03/80-2:00 p.m. • 2 • Raleigh, NC
M-Maurice Dametz	04/29-81-3:45 p.m. • 84 • Pike National Forest, CO
F-Kathryn Dekkers	07/24/81-3:00 p.m. • 10 • Ampersand Mtn, NY
M-Stephen Oleszczuk	10/03/81-3:55 p.m. • 4 • North Charleston, SC
M-Nicholas Dailey	07/03/82-a.m. • 2½ • Muddy Mountain, WY
M-Ryan Hoeffliger	01/11/84-7:30 a.m. • 2 • Hayden Lake, ID
M-Christopher Harvey	07/11/84-3:30 p.m. • 14 • Pagosa Springs, CO
M-Tomas Cabrera	05/31/85-a.m. • 3 • Tecate, Mexico
M-Stephen Crean	08/06/85-2:40 p.m. • 37 • NSW, Australia
M-Ronald Adams	09/07/85-p.m. • 21 • High Peaks, NY
F-Madeline Grisdale	07/06/86-Unk • 49 • MB, Canada
M-Joseph Stallman	01/19/87-5:00 p.m. • 2 • Washington, WI
M-Patrick Hildebrand	06/27/87-1:50 p.m. • 9 • Australia
M-Timothy Box	09/28/87-4:00 p.m. • 2 • Mountain View, AR
M-Michael Henley Jr.	04/21/88-p.m. • 9 • Zuni Mountains, NM
M-Eric Taylor	07/13/88-4:30 p.m. • 2 • Cooktown, Australia
M-Keith Reinhard	08/07/88-4:00 p.m. • 49 • Silver Plume, CO
M-Ng Boon Heng	10/22/88-Unk • 26 • Mount Kinabalu, Borneo
M-Lau King Thong	10/22/88-Unk • 34 • Mount Kinabalu, Borneo
F-Susan Adams	09/30/90-Unk • 42 • Selway-Bitterroot Wilderness, ID
M-Stefan Bissert	01/20/92-p.m. • 23 • Olympic NP, WA
F-Paige Adriance	07/03/92-3:00 p.m. • 8 • Boardman Lake, WA
F-Sarah Wolenetz	07/11/92-3:00 p.m. • 11 • Bear Lake, RMNP, CO
M-Danny Hohenstein	12/01/92-5:00 p.m. • 6 • Paradise Pines, CA
M-Bill McKinnon	02/14/93-p.m. • 28 • Church Mountain, WA
F-Masami Somaki	02/12/94-1:00 p.m. • 32 • Mount Cook, NZ

List of Missing from this Book | 371

M-John Devine	09/06/97-2:00 p.m. • 73 • Olympic NP, WA
M-David Miller	05/19/98-Unk • 22 • Red Rock Wilderness, AZ
F-Dr. Katherine Wong	02/19/99-2:00 p.m. • 47 • Bear Valley, CA
M-Joshua Stauffer	05/07/99-4:00 p.m. • 3 • Downey ID
F-Harriet Olsen	06/24/00-6:00 p.m. • 75 • Vermontville, NY
F-Haley Zega	04/29/01-11:30 a.m. • 6 • Newton County, AR
M-David Byrd Felker	07/22/02-Unk • 20 • Zamora, Ecuador
M-Justin Sides	04/30/03-3:45 p.m. • 3 • Wynne, AR
M-Helmut Simon	10/15/04-5:00 p.m. • 67 • Salzburg, Austria
M-Jeff Christenson	07/29/05-Unk • 31 • RMNP, CO
M-Zachary Weston	08/10/05-Unk • 22 • Mount Rainier NP
M-Gilbert Mark Gilman	06/24/06-Unk • 47 • Olympic NP, WA
M-Kevin Brown	09/21/06-Unk • 2 • Alvarado, TX
M-Robert Willis	10/31/08-Unk • 38 • Dinkey Creek, CA
F-Megumi Yamamoto	06/09/09-4:00 p.m. • 26 • Mount Baldy, NM
F-Letisha Faust	12/09/09-Unk • 50 • Franklin CO, VA
M-Jonathan Robinson	12/22/09-2:30 a.m. • 23 • Switzerland
F-Emma Campbell	05/01/10-5:45 a.m. • 29 • Port Hills, NZ
M-Emmett Trapp	08/02/10-8:00 p.m. • 2 • Dewey, AZ
M-Ben McDaniel	08/18/10-7:30 p.m. • 30 • Vortex Springs, FL
F-Rachael Bagnall	09/08/10-Unk • 25 • Pemberton, BC, Canada
M-Jonathan Jette	09/08/10-Unk • 34 • Pemberton, BC, Canada
M-George Penca	06/17/11-2:40 p.m. • 30 • Yosemite NP, CA
M-Landen Trammell	09/11/12-8:00 am • 3 • Onia, AR
M-Prabhdeep Srawn	05/13/13-Unk • 25 • Charlotte Pass, Australia
M-Raymond Salmen	05/28/13-Unk • 65 • Harrison Lake, Canada
F-Hildegard Hendrickson	06/08/13-5:00 p.m. • 79 • Wenatchee Lake, WA
M-Mitchell Dale Stehling	06/09/13-4:08 p.m. • 51 • Mesa Verde NP, CO
M-August Reiger	06/16/13-Unk • 18 • Banos, Ecuador
M-Gary Tweddle	07/16/13-Unk • 23 • NSW, Australia
F-Geraldine Largay	07/23/13-Unk • 66 • Sugarloaf Mountain, ME
M-Jerry Duran	07/24/13-4:00 p.m. • 21 • Hardware Ranch, UT
M-Bryan Lee Johnston	08/28/13-Unk • 71 • Olympic NP, WA
M-Gene George	09/21/13-Unk • 64 • Mount Harvard, CO
F-Amelia Linkert	09/23/13-Unk • 69 • Craters of the Moon NP
F-Jo Elliott Blakeslee	09/23/13-Unk • 63 Craters of the Moon NP
M-Cullen Finnerty	09/26/13-9:27 p.m. • 30 • Webber Township, MI

M-Alyof Krost   10/01/13-5:45 p.m. • 62 • Lake Arrowhead, CA
F-Amber Rose Smith   10/08/13-1:30 p.m. • 30 mos. • Paris, MI

Span of Years: 1768-2013

Total Names on List: 174
Males: 122
Females: 52

Year with Most Disappearances: 2013 (15 Cases)
Second Most Disappearances: 1988 (5 Cases)
Countries with Incidents in 2013:
    Australia   5/13/13, 7/16/13
    Canada   5/28/13
    Ecuador   6/16/13
    United States   Numerous

The year 2013 had more scholars/intellects disappear than any other year:

F-Dr. Hildegard Hendrickson   06/08/13-p.m. • 79 • Chelan County, WA
M-August Reiger   06/16/13-p.m. • 18 • Banos, Ecuador
M-Gene George   09/21/13-Unk • 64 • Mount Harvard, CO
F-Jo Elliott Blakeslee   09/23/13-Unk • 63 • Craters of the Moon NP
M-Alyof Krost   10/1/13-5:45 p.m. • 62 • Lake Arrowhead, CA

Something very unusual is happening throughout the world in regard to missing people. I don't believe that the fact that we are more aware of missing person cases played a significant role in the acquisition of additional cases. I believe that a spike in missing cases actually occurred.

Missing 411 List of Victims from Three Books:
W=*Missing 411-Western United States*
E=*Missing 411-Eastern United States*
NA=*Missing 411-North America and Beyond*
**Column at the far left indicates in which book the case was highlighted

List of Missing from this Book | 373

Book • Sex/Name	Date Missing • Age • State
NA • M-Henderson, John (Son of)	11/15/1826-Unk • 4 • NS, Canada
NA • F-King, Unknown	08/19/1859-Unk • 6 • OH
NA • F-Belliveau, Daughter of	1865 • 5 • QC, Canada
E • F-Katie Flynn	06/1868 • 3 • MI
E • M-Eddie Prigley	08/22/1874 • 3 • IN
E • M-Stephen Ford	08/05/1880 • 9 • PA
NA • M-Unknown	12/25/1880 • Unk • WI
E • M-Wolfe	07/08/1882 • 10 • PA
E • M-Bachman	06/10/1883 • 4 mos. • PA
W • M-James Vaughan	08/20/1883 • 18 mos. • ID
NA • F-Mrs. John McClaren	04/24/1886-Unk • Unk • CT
E • F-Davis	05/09/1888 • Unk • 30 mos. • PA
NA • F-John Hammonds (Daughter of)	05/10/1891-Unk • 4 • NE
NA • F-John Hammonds (Daughter of)	05/10/1891-Unk • 8 • NE
NA • M-Emmet Cline Powell	11/09/1891 • p.m. • 4 • VA
E • M-Barofsky	07/01/1892-Unk • 6 • NJ
NA • M-Reynolds, Mack, Brown, Doniher	10/15/1893 • Unk • CO
NA • M-Mr. Munn (Son of)	02/22/1894-Unk • 2 • TX
NA • M-Unknown	09/07/1895-Unk • Unk • ME
W • F-Alexis Bork	11/07/1896-p.m. • Unk • MT
E • M-Frank Floyd	01/07/1897-Unk • Unk • IA
E • F-Mary Sholtas	04/21/1897-Unk • 3 • PA
E • M-Augustus Staneker	04/21/1897-Unk • 4 • PA
NA • F-Harry Baker (Daughter of)	06/02/1897 • 2 • NY
NA • M-Roy Craw	11/06/1899 • 4 • WI
E • F-Simpson	05/27/1901-Unk • 3 • PA
E • M-Jack Wells	11/05/1901-Unk • Unk • MT
E • M-Riley Amsbaugh	07/25/1902-Unk • 55 • OH
NA • F-William Dunphy (Daughter of)	09/02/1903-Unk • Infant • MT
E • M-E. C. Jones	11/12/1903-Unk • Unk • OH
E • M-Horace Marvin Jr.	05/04/1907-Unk • 4 • DE
E • M-J. Mitchell	01/11/1909-Unk • Unk • ID
NA • U-Unknown Name	08/04/1909 • 18 mos. • MI
E • M-Johnie Lembke	08/12/1910-Unk • 15 • OH
E • M-Roy Bilgrien	10/21/1910-Unk • 2 • WI
W • M-B.B. Bakowski	02/22/1911-Unk • 30 • Crater Lake NP, OR

E • F-Elsie M. Davis	07/30/1911-Noon • 24 • ME
NA • F-Isabel Zandarski	09/21/1912-3:00 a.m. • 30 mos. • OH
E • M-James Glass	05/12/1915-Unk • 4 • PA
NA • M-Kenneth Crandall	03/13/1916-6:00 p.m. • 3 • MT
NA • M-James Carroll	04/15/1916-7:15 p.m. • 4 • PA
E • M-Edward Gately	10/27/1917-10:30 a.m. • 2 • MA
E • M-Edward Gerke	06/11/1918-Unk • Unk • WI
E • M-Abe Ramsay	03/11/1919-3:15 p.m. • 3 • Great Smoky Mtns, TN
E • M-George Dansey	10/08/1919-Unk • 30 mos. • NJ
E • M-David Brown	11/18/22-Unk • 51 • ME
E • M-Mertley Johnson	11/18/22-Unk • 24 • ME
E • F-Bernice Price	03/22/23-Unk • Unk • CA
NA • F-Pearl Turner	10/19/23-Noon • 3 • OK/AR
W • M-Joseph Whitehead	08/24/24-Unk • 29 • MT
W • M-William Whitehead	08/24/24-Unk • 22 • MT
NA • M-Marion or Marlon Robb	06/05/26-Unk • 17 • UT
E • M-Alfred J. Bishop	11/03/26-Unk • Unk • VT
E • M-Eddie Hamilton	07/06/28-Unk • 2 • SK, Canada
NA • F-Evelyn McDermott	09/18/28-11:30 a.m. • 16 • VT
E • F-Geraldine Markline	10/26/29-Unk • 2 • PA
E • M-Kenneth Swanson	08/24/30-Noon • 2 • CT
NA • M-Lawrence Sullivan	10/16/30-11:00 a.m. • 3 • NV
W • M-Emmett Mitchell	07/10/31-Unk • 50 • ID
E • M-William Pitsenbarger	08/07/31-Unk • 61 • ID
E • F-Else Flothmeier	02/24/32-p.m. • 22 • PA
W • F-Cecilia Mitchell	05/02/32-12:30 p.m. • 3 • CA
E • M-Wesley Piatote	08/04/32-p.m. • 7 • WA
NA • F-Eva Hall	08/15/32-p.m. • 13 • ON, Canada
E • M-Clarence Clark	10/17/32-Unk • 62 • NY
W • M-Godfrey Wondrosek	04/26/33-Unk • 26 • Yosemite NP
W • M-Frank Lobears	06/25/33-Unk • 7 • WA
W • M-Joseph Halpern	08/15/33-Unk • 22 • CO
E • M-Alden Johnson	03/27/34-3:30 p.m. • 4 • MA
W • F-Betty Wolfrum	05/15/34-Unk • 4 • MB, Canada
E • M-Bobby Connor	07/13/34-6:00 p.m. • 21 mos. • NY
NA • F-Evelyn Rauch	07/15/34-9:00 a.m. • 2 • AB, Canada
E • F-Claire Bensen	07/24/34-p.m. • 21 mos. • CT

List of Missing from this Book | 375

W • M-Dr. Frederick Lumley   08/13/34-27 • Unk • MT
NA • F-Nancy Marshall   09/17/34-3:00 p.m. • 22 mos. • RI
E • F-Rita Lent   11/22/34-Noon • 3 • PA
W • M-Herbert Brown   1935-Unk • Unk • OR
E • F-Thelma Ann Wilke   05/03/35-p.m. • 21 mos. • WI
E • M-George Wanke   07/27/35-Unk • 58 • MB, Canada
E • M-Jack Pike   09/05/35-Unk • 5 • MB, Canada
E • M-Charles Warren   12/20/35-p.m. • 2 • AR
NA • M-Roy Rogers   01/15/36-Unk • 4 • AZ
E • M-Raymond Maki   01/27/36-Unk • 18 • MI
E • M-Mr. Bell   08/31/36-Unk • 62 • MB, Canada
E • M-Harold King   09/07/36-Unk • 3 • WI
NA • M-Murray Walkup Miller   10/24/36-Unk • 9 • MT
NA • M-Jerome Coonan Jr.   04/29/37-5:00 p.m. • 2 • PA
E • F-Alice Baker   08/16/37-p.m. • 20 mos. • VT
NA • M-Edward Schnaknacht   09/01/37-p.m. • 4 • AB, Canada
E • F-Florence Jackson   09/06/37-p.m. • 4 • AR
W • M-Teddy Thompson   01/29/38-p.m. • 4 • Northern CA
E • F-Marjorie West   05/08/38-Unk • 4 • PA
W • M-David Baumgarten   05/11/38-Noon • 2 • CA
W • M-Richard McPherson   05/26/38-Unk • 10 • Yosemite NP, CA
W • M-Alfred Beilhartz   07/02/38-8:30 a.m. • 4 • Rocky Mtn NP
E • M-Donald Farrington   09/11/38-8:00 a.m. • 3 • NY
W • M-Jerry Hays   11/10/38-Unk • 5 • AZ
NA • F-Eliza Darnel   02/20/39-p.m. • 25 • VA
NA • F-Jackie Grady   03/23/39-p.m. • 4 • CT
NA • M-Harold Hixon   06/14/39-p.m. • 6 • WY
NA • M-Charles Hixon   06/14/39-p.m. • 4 • WY
E • F-Emma Steffy   07/16/39-Unk • 75 • PA
W • M-Billy Coleman   01/01/40-4:00 p.m. • 14 • CA
E • F-Helen Chenoweth   03/28-40-6:00 p.m. • 3 • IL
NA • M-Larry Lewis   06/09/40-10:00 a.m. • 5 • CA
NA • M-Jim McGrath   06/10/40-Noon • 80 • MN
E • M-Simon Skogan   07/02/40-Unk • 9 • MB, Canada
E • M-Ronald Rumbaugh   09/15/40-2:00 p.m. • 2 • PA
E • M-Rudy Kunchick   10/21/40-Unk • 4 • PA
E • M-Murray Upshaw Jr.   11/08/40-Noon • 2 • GA

NA • F-Celsa Lucero	11/09/40-3:30 p.m. • 51 • NM
E • M-Eldridge Albright	05/21/41-2:00 p.m. • 3 • PA
W • F-Betty McCullough	06/21/41-a.m. • 10 • OR
E • F-Betty Bossier	06/25/41-10:30 a.m. • 3 • PA
NA • M-Clarence Murphy Jr.	07/14/41-a.m. • 4 • CA
E • M-Joseph Prato	10/25/41-Unk • 19 mos. • PA
W • M-Ronald McGee	02/07/42-a.m. • 2 • AZ
E • M-Dewey Cook	03/02/42-Unk • 25 • WY
E • M-Alvan Diggan	05/30/42-Unk • 3 • PA
W•M-Emerson Holt	07/18/43-2:00 p.m. • 55 • Yosemite NP
W • M-Ernest Polley	07/23/43-Unk • 22 • CO
E • F-Mrs. August Nelson	07/28/43-Unk • 75 • WI
E • M-Carl Herrick	11/23/43-Unk • 37 • VT
NA • M-Ronald Arthur Boggs	05/02/44-11:00 a.m. • 3 • OH
E • M-C.H. Bordwell	08/01/44-Unk • Unk • MN
NA • F-Sylvia Sweet	09/14/44-p.m. • 3 • NV
NA • M-David Faust	09/05/45-p.m. • 4 • WI
E • M-Lloyd Hokit	10/21/45-3:00 p.m. • 9 • OK
W • M-Mike McDonald	10/30/45-a.m. • 2 • AZ
W • M-Dickie Tum Suden	11/01/45-9:00 a.m. • 3 • CA Sierras
E • M-Al Owens	11/07/45-Unk • 71 • MT
E • M-Middie Rivers	11/12/45-3:00 p.m. • 75 • VT
NA • M-Donald Eugene Sell	02/01/46-12:30 p.m. • 2 • PA
E • F-Katherine Van Alst	06/16/46-2:30 p.m. • 8 • AR
E • M-Edward Woelfle	10/06/46-a.m. • 15 • MI
E • M-Eugene Shue	10/20/46-2:00 p.m. • 3 • PA
E • F-Paula Welden	12/01/46-Unk • 18 • VT
E • M-Jimmy Senser	04/06/47-5:00 p.m. • 4 • PA
W • F-Greta Mary Gale	06/29/47-10:00 a.m. • 30 mos. • Northern CA
W • M-Wayne Bowers	07/05/47-Unk • 3 • CA
E • F-Carolyn Peterson	08/20/47-11:00 a.m. • 20 mos. • OH
E • M-Louis Dunton	10/07/47-6:00 p.m. • 3 • NH
NA • M-Gerald "Terry" Cook	04/24/48-4:00 p.m. • 3 • ME
NA • M-Bobby Brown	06/27/48-Noon • 2 • TX
E • M-Donald Collier	07/02/48-4:00 p.m. • 23 mos. • PA
E • M-Jerry Lee Hoffman	08/05/48-6:00 p.m. • 3 • OH
NA • F-Madeline Sowers	09/03/48-Noon • 2 • Virginia

List of Missing from this Book | 377

NA • M-Lawrence Fustini   09/04/48-6:00 p.m. • 30 mos. • PA
NA • M-Judd McWilliams   09/15/48-Unk • 82 • ID
NA • F-Jewell Hinrickson   09/23/48-Unk • 33 • ID
NA • F-Marilyn Murphy   09/28/48-5:30 p.m. • 2 • Australia
W • F-Janet Federer   09/29/48-1:00 p.m. • 6 • WY
NA • M-H. B. Davis   10/08/48-p.m. • 72 • MT
NA • M-Mickey O'Connor   10/09/48-p.m. • 3 • WY
E • M-Rickey Tankersley   02/16/49-4:30 p.m. • 2 • AL
E • M-Billy Abbott   02/18/49-4:30 p.m. • 3 • PA
NA • F-Jacqueline Simons   04/19/49-4:00 p.m. • 3 • MI
E • M-Billy Clever   04/26/49-p.m. • 3 • PA
W • M-Daryl Webley   04/30/49-4:00 p.m. • 2 • WA
E • M-Michael Fontaine   05/30/49-Unk • 6 • ME
E • M-Larry Coleman   08/20/49-Unk • 3 • MN
W • M-Frank Norris   09/21/49-Unk • 46 • WY
NA • M-Douglas Stofer   09/28/49-6:00 p.m. • 2 • MI
NA • M-Eddie Grant   10/05/49-p.m. • 22 • ID
W • M-David Devitt   10/09/49-Unk • 21 • Rocky Mtn NP
W • M-Bruce Gerling   10/09/49-Unk • 20 • Rocky Mtn NP
E • M-Otis T. Mason   10/11/49-5:00 p.m. • 6 • MD
W • M-Donald McDonald   12/15/49-Unk • 17 • WA
E • M-John Koza   04/26/50-Unk • 50-60 • MT
NA • M-Tommy Jenkins   05/04/50-Noon • 2 • WA
E • F-Anna Thorp   05/05/50-Unk • 2 • PA
E • M-Jackie Copeland   05/14/50-1:00 p.m. • 2 • PA
NA • F-Unknown   05/20/50-4:00 p.m. • Unk • France
E • F-Nicole Renaud   06/03/50-3:00 p.m. • 3 • ME
NA • F-Marcella Ramiskey   07/01/50-5:00 p.m. • 4 • Mount Rainier NP, WA
NA • M-Gunnar Peterson   08/06/50-p.m. • 65 • WA
E • F-Susan Sweely   08/09/50-7:00 p.m. • 2 • IL
W • F-Lorraine Smith   09/02/50-5:00 p.m. • 2 • AB, Canada
NA • F-Irene Rempel   10/10/50-2:00 p.m. • 3 • SK, Canada
E • M-Paul Jepson   10/12/50-3:30 p.m. • 8 • VT
E • F-Freida Langer   10/28/50-4:00 p.m. • 53 • VT
E • M-Leroy Williams   03/16/51-Unk • 64 • IA
NA • F-Nancy Jean Walker   05/08/51-8:15 p.m. • 2 • MA
NA • M-Roger Shaddinger   05/27/51-Noon • 9 • CA

W • M-Larry McGee	06/07/51-3:00 p.m. • 7 • NM
W • F-Janet McGee	06/07/51-3:00 p.m. • 5 • NM
W • M-Steven Cross	06/07/51-3:00 p.m. • 3 • NM
E • F-Evangeline Lorimer	06/08/51-Unk • 21 • Great Smoky Mtn NP, TN
W • F-Alma Hall	06/09/51-Unk • 28 • BC, Canada
W • M-Raymond Hall	06/09/51-Unk • 6 • BC, Canada
NA • M-Teddy Barnard	06/17/51-p.m. • 3 • Gray, ME
NA • F-Betty Joslyn	07/24/51-p.m. • 5 • Terrible Mountain, VT
W • M-Bobby Boatman	10/14/51-Unk • 14 • WA
W • M-Keith Parkins	04/10/52-Noon • 2 • OR
E • M-David Feif	07/06/52-Unk • 85 • MA
E • M-Ralph Stutzman	08/17/52-Unk • 46 • IN
NA • M-George Bell Jr.	11/22/52-2:00 p.m. • 2 • PA
W • F-Catherine P. Maynard	01/19/53-Unk • 38 • WA
W • M-Joey Barkley	03/11/53-1:00 p.m. • 2 • CA
NA • F-Anna Maria Woodruff	04/17/53-6:00 p.m. • 3 • Southern, CA
NA • M-Ronald Tammen Jr.	04/19/53-9:00 p.m. • 19 • OH
NA • F-Beverly Ann Bradley	05/20/53-Noon • 2 • MI
W • F-Patty Ann McLean	07/04/53-2:30 p.m. • 3 • MT
W•F-Geraldine Huggan	07/05/53-10:00 a.m. • 5 • ON, Canada
E • F-Emma Bowers	07/22/53-Unk • 5 • PA
NA • M-Richard Rucker	07/30/53-10:37 a.m. • 2 • WV
NA • M-Andrew Thackerson	08/17/53-a.m. • 5 • Sequoia NP, CA
E • M-John Sweet	10/26/53-Unk • Unk • IL
NA • M-Lemar Pepmuller	11/21/53-Unk • 22 • ID
NA • M-Charles Warner	11/21/53-Unk • 40 • WA
NA • M-Joe Davis	04/17/54-a.m.-• 4 • TX
E • F-Shirley Sherman	04/18/54-1:00 p.m. • 3 • WV
E • M-Gary Bailey	07/17/54-Unk • 3 • ME
NA • M-Walter A. Gordon	07/20/54-a.m. • 26 • Yosemite NP, CA
NA • M-Orvar Von Laas	10/09/54-2:00 p.m. • 30 • Yosemite NP, CA
W • M-Jess Davis	05/08/55-a.m. • 2 • OR
E • M-Fred Holmes	05/25/55-9:00 a.m. • 23 mos. • PA
NA • M-Johnny Johnson	06/22/55-Unk • 3 • Salisbury, England
W • F-Ida May Curtis	07/04/55-6:00 p.m. • 2 • MT
E • F-Nora Moore	07/18/55-4:00 p.m. • 7 • AL
NA • M-Richard Hatke	08/15/55-4:00 p.m. • 2 • ID

List of Missing from this Book | 379

E • M-Ronnie Weitkamp	10/11/55-Noon • 3 • IN
NA • F-Sarah Dixon	06/05/56-11:30 a.m. • 3 • CO
NA • F-Kathy Thomas	06/05/56-11:30 a.m. • 3 • CO
NA • F-Vilate Kerren Young	07/04/56-p.m. • 15 mos. • UT
E • F-Dianne Abbott	07/06/56-2:00 p.m. • 2 • ME
E • M-Louis Blair	08/05/56-Unk • 26 • AB, Canada
E • M-Jerry Garcia	08/12/56-Unk • Unk • AZ
E • M-John Davis	08/26/56-Unk • 72 • WA
NA • M-Jack Woods Jr.	10/29/56-p.m. • 3 • AL
E • F-Judy Rodencal	10/30/56-7:30 a.m. • 16 • WI
NA • F-Mary Jane Barker	02/25/57-a.m. • 3 • NJ
W • M-Thomas Bowman	03/23/57-7:00 p.m. • 8 • Southern CA
W • M-David Allen Scott	07/13/57-1:00 p.m. • 2 • Yosemite NP, CA
E • F-Rose Jewett	08/11/57-4:15 p.m. • 95 • ID
E • M-Richard Craig	08/15/57-10:00 a.m. • 5 • WA
M-Tommy Bowman	08/23/57-7:00 p.m. • 8 • Southern CA
NA • M-Michael Douglas McMillan	09/01/57-4:00 p.m. • 2 • NC
E • F-Candida Streeter	10/03/57-5:30 p.m. • 2 • PA
E • F-Minnie Haun	10/08/57-1:00 p.m. • 3 • Great Smoky Mtn NP, TN
W • F-Jill Hatch	11/02/57-11:00 a.m. • 7 • Southern CA
E • M-Earl Somerville	11/05/57-Unk • 48 • MN
NA • M-Lowell Linn	11/31/57-p.m. • 23 • Mount Rainier NP, WA
E • F-Shirley Ann Ramsburg	12/27/57-5:00 p.m. • 3 • WV
NA • M-Dennis Wurschmidt	01/25/58-Unk • 12 • CA
E • M-John Wayne McKinney	03/17/58-3:00 p.m. • 5 • WV
NA • F-Judy Peterson	04/25/58-8:30 p.m. • 3 • FL
NA • M-Anthony Martini	06/28/58-2:30 p.m. • 11 • MA
NA • F-Denise Rowe	06/28/58-4:00 p.m. • 3 • NY
NA • F-Brenda Doud	07/06/58-p.m. • 5 • NY
W • F-Mary Gay Bent	07/13/58-3:00 p.m. • 5 • MT
NA • M-Henry Kellar	07/29/58-7:00 p.m. • 16 mos. • OH
E • F-Debbie Ann Greenhill	08/09/58-8:00 p.m. • 2 • KY
E • M-Lawrence E. Prange	08/14/58-Unk • 20 • MT
E • F-Cindy Lou Maclane	09/09/58-9:00 a.m. • 2 • BC, Canada
NA • M-Tony R. Beauchamp	09/16/58-3:00 p.m. • 2 • BC, Canada
E • M-Kenneth Scott	09/28/58-2:00 p.m. • 4 • MI
NA • M-Alex Thorne	10/04/58-Unk • 44 • MB, Canada

NA • M-Sam Adams	10/27/58-Unk • 39 • MT
NA • M-Russell Dunham	11/25/58-4:00 p.m. • 3 • MD
E • M-Willard Eugene Jones Jr.	01/17/59-Unk • 3 • MO
NA • F-Patricia Graham	05/31/59-10:30 a.m. • 6 • NY
NA • M-David Raleigh	06/13/59-8:00 p.m. • 5 • NY
E • F-Carol Van Hulla	06/28/59-6:00 p.m. • 3 • MI
NA • F-Edith Irene Wolfskill	07/14/59-Unk • 57 • CA
W • M-William Carmack	07/22/59-Unk • 55 • MT
W • M-Richard Herman	08/30/59-Noon • 6 • WA
NA • M-Fred Nalman	09/07/59-Unk • 14 • ID
E • M-Meryl Newcombe	10/29/59-Unk • 50 • ON, Canada
E • M-George Weeden	10/29/59-Unk • 63 • ON, Canada
W • M-Arthur Jordan	11/08/59-Unk • 59 • MT
E • M-Randy Moy	01/08/60-3:30 p.m. • 3 • OH
W • F-Fran Weaver	02/01/60-Unk • 56 • WY
W • M-Albert Cucupa	02/16/60-Unk • 32 • NM
W • M-Martin Ryan	06/30/60-p.m. • 8 • OR
W • M-Bruce Kremen	07/13/60-Unk • 8 • Southern CA
W • M-Sander Lingman	11/01/60-Unk • 35 • ON, Canada
W • M-Fritz Frey	11/14/60-Unk • 65 • MT
NA • M-Jimmie Franck	03/07/61-2:00 p.m. • 4 • IA
W • F-Vanita Crook	05/03/61-Unk • 25 • WY
NA • F-Ann Marie Burr	08/31/61-5:30 a.m. • 8 • WA
W • M-James McCormick	12/05/61-Unk • 16 • OR
NA • M-Jerry Cooper	12/21/61-10:00 p.m. • 4 • GA
NA • F-Faye Crawford	03/26/62-10:00 p.m. • 3 • TN
E • F-Lisa Shackelford	07/10-62-11:00 a.m. • 3 • IL
NA • M-Stephen Papol	08/19/62-p.m. • 3 • NY
NA • F-Gloria Estela	01/09/63-p.m. • 2 • TX
E • M-John Long	04/10/63-a.m. • 58 • MN
W • M-Claude Goodwin	06/16/63-Unk • 8 • WA
NA • M-Bruce Ferrin	06/23/63-10:00 a.m. • 7 • UT
W • F-Lynn Olson	06/28/63-p.m. • 16 • WY
W • M-Bobby Panknin	08/03/63-Unk • 4 • WA
W • M-Donald R. Griffen	08/22/63-8:30 a.m. • 4 • Yosemite NP, CA
NA • M-Kenneth Edwards	04/04/64-2:00 p.m. • 2 • Southern CA
W • M-Fernand Martin	04/24/64-Unk • 36 • ON, Canada

List of Missing from this Book | 381

W • M-Richard Spyglass	08/05/64-7:00 p.m. • 5 • SK, Canada
E • F-Bonnie Lee Edwards	01/09/65-4:30 p.m. • 6 • Great Smoky Mtns NP, TN
NA • M-James Dwyer Bordenkircher	06/12/65-p.m. • 2 • CA
W • M-Tom Garafalo	11/25/65-Unk • 28 • WY
E • M-Frank Mean	04/21/66-Unk • 55 • WY
W • F-Christine Woollett	05/12/66-8:00 p.m. • 2 • WA
NA • M-Larry Jeffrey	05/28/66-1:30 p.m. • 6 • NV
NA • M-Wilson Mann	05/31/66-Unk • 3 • OR
W • M-Dennis Johnson	07/12/66-1:30 p.m. • 8 • Yellowstone NP, WY
E • F-Mabel Moffitt	08/10/66-Unk • 55 • AK
NA • F-Amy Jackson	08/13/66-p.m. • 18 mos. • Sequoia NP, CA
W • F-Diane Prevost	09/17/66-Unk • 2 • ON, Canada
W • F-Annie Puglas	04/19/67-Unk • 43 • BC, Canada
W • M-Kenneth Coon	04/28/67-Unk • 5 • BC, Canada
W • M-Danny Greenwood	06/08/67-1:00 p.m. • 5 • AZ
NA • M-Kenneth Vanderleest	07/14/67-p.m. • 3 • BC, Canada
W • M-John Gunn	07/28/67-Unk • 19 • Yosemite NP, CA
W • M-Kenneth Klein	07/28/67-Unk • 23 • Yosemite NP, CA
W • M-Tom Opperman	08/08/67-Unk • 21 • Yosemite NP, CA
E • F-Karen Cooney	07/08/68-Unk • 15 • PA
W • M-Lowell Smith	10/05/68-Unk • 60 • WA
W • F-Evelyn Rosemann	10/19/68-Unk • Unk • Yosemite NP, CA
W • M-Randy Parscale	01/13/69-Unk • 10 • AZ
W • F-Laura Flink	02/21/69-Unk • 21 • WA
NA • M-Clayton Ordiway	06/08/69-1:30 p.m. • 5 • Sequoia NP, CA
E • M-Dennis Lloyd Martin	06/14/69-4:30 p.m. • 6 • Great Smoky Mtn NP, TN
NA • F-Irene Hofke	07/03/69-1:00 p.m. • 9 • Sequoia NP, CA
E • F-Marcelene Cummungs	07/14/69-Unk • 54 • WA
NA • M-Thomas McClintock	08/05/69-Unk • 12 • Sequoia NP, CA
W • M-Raymond Ewer	08/09/69-Noon • 19 • UT
E • M-Louis Sandoval	09/06/69-Unk • 66 • ID
W • M-Robert Winters	10/08/69-5:00 p.m. • 78 • OR
E • M-Geoffrey Hague	02/08/70-3:20 p.m. • 16 • Great Smoky Mtn NP, TN
E • M-Douglas Chapman	06/02/71-10:30 a.m. • 3 • ME
E • M-Douglass Legg	07/10-71-Unk • 8 • NY
NA • M-David Holtz	07/13/71-9:00 a.m. • 9 • Sequoia NP, CA
NA • M-Kevin Dye	07/18/71-3:00 p.m. • 9 • WY

W • M-Dana Cooper	08/04/71-Unk • 13 • CA
NA • F-Lynne Schulze	12/10/71-p.m. • 18 • VT
NA • M-Teodoro Sibayan	01/01/72 • 13 • HI
NA • M-Adrian McNaughton	06/12/72-p.m. • 5 • Holmes Lake, ON, Canada
E • F-Elizabeth Kant	10/16/72-Unk • 45 • ON, Canada
NA • M-Guy Heckle	02/03/73-8:00 p.m. • 11 • IA
W • F-Joanne Burmer	02/25/73-Unk • 38 • CA
W • F-Leah Good	04/30/73-Unk • 49 • Yosemite NP, CA
E • M-Vital Vachon	05/01/73-Unk • 56 • ON, Canada
NA • F-Christie Davis	07/28/73-Unk • 2 • FL
E • M-Greg Lewellen	08/03/73-Unk • 66 • UT
W • F-Elizabeth Cardwell	09/16/73-Unk • 31 • AB, Canada
W • M-Jimmy Duffy	10/19/73-Unk • 2 • WA
W • M-Brian Henry	05/05/74-Unk • 21 • ON, Canada
W • F-Jennifer Klein	05/25/74-Unk • 3 • UT
W • M-Jeffrey Bratcher	06/15/74-6:30 p.m. • 7 • WA
W • M-Yehudi Prior	09/23/74-Unk • 2 • BC, Canada
E • M-Mark Hanson	03/07/75-Unk • 21 • Great Smoky Mtns NP, TN
W • M-Edward Arcand	06/08/75-Unk • 27 • AB, Canada
E • F-Milda Mcquillan	06/17/75-Unk • 71 • MN
W • F-Jane Smith	08/09/75-Unk • 20 • ON, Canada
W • M-Steve Martin	08/16/75-Noon • 15 • WA
E • M-Kurt Newton	08/31/75-Unk • 4 • ME
W • M-Raymond Juarnitich	10/08/75-Unk • 48 • ON, Canada
NA • M-Bruce Shearin	02/27/76-a.m. • 2 • NC
E • M-Harold Mott	03/02/76-5:00 p.m. • 12 • PA
NA • M-Steven Paul Thomas	04/12/76-3:30 p.m. • 19 • NY
W • M-Jeff Estes	05/24/76-Unk • 25 • Yosemite NP, CA
NA • M-Blake Mulligan	06/13/76-5:00 p.m. • 14 • NV
E • F-Trenny Lynn Gibson	10/08/76-3:00 p.m. • 16 • Great Smoky Mtn NP, TN
W • M-Charles McCullar	10/14/76-Unk • 19 • Crater Lake NP, OR
W • M-Howard Booth	07/17/77-Unk • 49 • AB, Canada
NA • M-Lee Littlejohn	12/23/77-1:00 p.m. • 18 mos. • CA
NA • F-Judy Martins	05/24/78-2:00 a.m. • 22 • OH
W • M-Edward Nye	06/22/78-p.m. • 14 • OR
E • M-Duane Scott	07/27/78-Unk • 31 • PA
NA • M-Andrew Amato	09/30/78-10:30 a.m. • 4 • MA

List of Missing from this Book | 383

NA • M-Kevin Reimer	06/29/79-Noon • 9 • AB, Canada
W • F-Gayla Schaper	06/29/79-7:15 p.m. • 28 • WA
W • M-James Caraley	07/18/79-Unk • 22 • AB, Canada
W • F-Carol Laughlin	09/09/79-Unk • 19 • Yosemite NP, CA
W • M-Paul Fugate	01/03/80-2:00 p.m. • 41 • Chiricahua NM, AZ
W • F-Megan Ginevicz	04/30/80-Unk • 2 • MT
W • M-Larry Krebbs	05/30/80-5:30 p.m. • 2 • OK
E • M-Foster Bezanson	10/25/80-Unk • 64 • ON, Canada
NA • M-James Beveridge	02/07/81-Unk • 9 • Southern CA
W • M-Steve Maclaren	06/30/81-Unk • 25 • AB, Canada
W • F-Stacy Arras	07/17/81-4:00 p.m. • 14 • Yosemite NP, CA
NA • M-Justin Stahly	09/03/81-Noon • 2 • IA
E • F-Thelma Pauline Melton	09/25/81-4:15 p.m. • 58 • Great Smoky Mtn NP, TN
NA • M-Keith Zunke	10/24/81-Unk • 21 • OR
E • M-Jon Dabkowski	01/14/82-5:30 p.m. • 11 • PA
E • M-Greg Minarcin	01/14/82-5:30 p.m. • 10 • PA
E • M-Jay Charles Toney	05/25/82-1:30 p.m. • 17 • Great Smoky Mtn NP, TN
W • M-Robert Baldeshwiler	06/29/82-Unk • 12 • Rocky Mountain NP, CO
W • M-Richard Ray Barnett	08/31/82-7:00 a.m. • 2 • WA
W • F-Ann Riffin	09/13/82-Unk • 33 • NM
E • M-Kevin Jay Ayotte	09/30/82-p.m. • 3 • MN
E • M-Richard Peterson	11/05/82-3:30 p.m. • 6 • NJ
W • F-Debra Manial	12/12/82-3:00 p.m. • 29 • Sierras, Northern CA
W • M-Tyler Inman	12/21/82-Unk • 3 • WA
W • F-Shelly Bacsu	05/03/83-Unk • 16 • AB, Canada
W • F-Nyleen Kay Marshall	06/25/83-4:00 p.m. • 4 • MT
E • M-Michael Reel	07/02/83-9:30 a.m. • 8 • Great Smoky Mtns, TN
E • M-Larry Davenport	07/17/83-p.m. • 20 • Great Smoky Mtns NP, TN
W • M-Gary Lee Chavoya	07/30/83-Noon • 10 • CA
W • M-Sharel Haresym	09/04/84-Unk • 35 • AB, Canada
W • M-Toivo Reinikanen	09/26/84-Unk • 36 • ON, Canada
W • M-Daniel Hilkey	01/22/85-Unk • 29 • OR
NA • F-Karen Louise Wilson	03/27/85-8:15 p.m. • 22 • NY
W • M-David Jaramillo	06/13/85-Unk • 21 • UT
W • M-Lloyd Reese	06/13/85-Unk • 13 • UT
NA • F-Jessica Azzopardi	07/24/85-3:30 p.m. • 20 mos. • ON, Canada
NA • M-Kevin Robert O'Keefe	10/08/85-Unk • 36 • AK

E • M-Emerson Carbaugh	11/11/85-6:00 p.m. • 64 • PA
W • M-David Huckins	02/04/86-Unk • 21 • Yosemite NP, CA
NA • M-Cody Sheehy	04/27/86-2:30 p.m. • 6 • OR
W • M-Edward Ludwig	05/30/86-Unk • 27 • AB, Canada
E • M-Andrew Warburton	07/01/86-Unk • 9 • Canada
W • F-Lynn Hillier	07/24/86-Unk • 2 • BC, Canada
E • M-Clayton McFaul	08/15/86-Unk • 59 • ON, Canada
W • M-Tom Klein	09/08/86-Unk • 28 • WA
NA • M-Joseph David Helt	01/16/87-4:00 a.m. • 17 • NY
NA • M-Jesse Rinker	05/04/87-4:30 p.m. • 2 • AB, Canada
W • F-Theresa Bier	06/01/87-Unk • 16 • Sierras, CA
W • F-Julie Ann Weflen	09/16/87-3:30 p.m. • 28 • WA
E • M-John Clifford	10/10/87-Unk • 65 • ON, Canada
W • F-Tina Marie Finley	03/07/88-2:00 a.m. • 25 • WA
E • M-Larry Krebbs	03/30/88-Unk • 2 • Lake Texoma, OK
E • F-Colleen Tourtillott	07/03/88-6:00 p.m. • 18 mos. • WI
W • M-Timothy Barnes	07/05/88-Unk • 24 • Yosemite NP, CA
W • M-Nicolas Hibbert	07/08/88-Unk • 66 • ON, Canada
W • F-Kathleen Pehringer	04/17/89-Unk • 41 • WY
W • F-Ruth Jacobus	06/07/89-Noon • 76 • Sierras, CA
W • M-Nathan Madsen	10/22/89-2:30 p.m. • 9 • OR
E • F-Eloise Lindsay	11/04/89-Unk • 22 • Great Smoky Mtns, SC
NA • M-Joshua Lewis Kern	07/13/90-6:00 p.m. • 2 • ID
NA • M-Casey Holliday	10/14/90-10:00 a.m. • 11 • ID
W • F-Elizabeth Bartholomew	01/08/91-Unk • 80 • Sierras, CA
W • F-Lillian Owens	06/28/91-Unk • 46 • AB, Canada
E • M-Dustin Rhodes	07/06/91-Unk • 64 • ON, Canada
W • M-William Caswell	07/21/91-Unk • 52 • ON, Canada
W • M-Brian Sines	11/22/91-Unk • 29 • ID
W • M-Corey Fay	11/23/91-6:30 p.m. • 17 • OR
W • M-Kenny Miller	06/24/92-Unk • 12 • Yosemite NP, CA
NA • M-George Woltjen	10/24/92-Unk • 60 • NY
W • M-Travis Zweig	03/10/93-10:30 a.m. • 2 • CA
E • M-Brad Lavies	03/28/93-Unk • 13 • Great Smoky Mtn NP, TN
NA • M-Thomas Carleton	10/09/93-Unk • 44 • NY
W • M-Michael McIntyre	04/07/94-Unk • 37 • ON, Canada
E • M-Victor Shoemaker	05/01/94-Noon • 4 • WV

List of Missing from this Book | 385

W • M-William Sisco — 06/12/94-p.m. • 32 • AZ
W • M-Wayne Powell — 06/18/94-Unk • 39 • OR
W • M-Donald Shelenberger — 07/03/94-Unk • 35 • AZ
W • F-Ashley Krestianson — 07/14/94-Unk • 8 • SK, Canada
NA • F-Naomi Leigh Whidden — 11/25/94-12:45 p.m. • 2 • GA
W • M-Donald Belliveau — 01/27-95-Unk • 28 • AB, Canada
W • F-Rhonda Runningbird — 03/26/95-Unk • 25 • AB, Canada
W • M-Bryce Herda — 04/09/95-Unk • 4 • WA
W • F-Jeanne Hesselschwerdt — 07/09/95-Unk • 37 • Yosemite NP, CA
W • M-William Reed — 08/01/95-Unk • 69 • ON, Canada
W • M-Knut Thielemann — 08/04/95-Unk • 22 • AB, Canada
W • M-Daniel Edmonds — 08/22/95-Unk • 22 • UT
W • M-Abraham Kalaf — 07/24/96-Unk • 79 • AZ
NA • M-Taylor Touchstone — 08/07/96-4:00 p.m. • 10 • FL
W • M-Michael Madden — 08/10/96-Unk • 20 • Sierras, CA
E • M • Frank Szpak — 09/23/96-Unk • 69 • ON, Canada
E • M-Michael Malinoski — 10/24/96-Unk • 37 • PA
W • F-Karen Mero — 02/15/97-Unk • 27 • Northern CA
W • M-Ruben David Felix — 02/23/97-Unk • 2 • ID
W • M-Melvin Hoel — 03/12/97-Unk • 64 • AB, Canada
W • M-Kenneth Churney — 03/15/97-Unk • 36 • ON, Canada
W • F-Hannah Zaccaglini — 06/04/97-Unk • 15 • Northern CA
E • M-Bernard Champagne — 07/10/97-Unk • 80 • ON, Canada
W • F-Amy Bechtel — 07/24/97-3:00 p.m. • 24 • WY
W • M-David Crouch — 09/07/97-Unk • 27 • WY
W • M-Jonathan Aujay — 06/11/98-Unk • 38 • Southern CA
NA • M-Trent Richardson — 07/23/98-4:30 p.m. • 3 • AZ
W • M-Raymond Matlock — 09/07/98-Unk • 28 • WA
W • F-Emma Tresp — 09/08/98-Unk • 71 • NM
W • F-Joan Lawrence — 09/23/98-Unk • 77 • ON, Canada
W • M-Robert Bobo — 10/02/98-Unk • 36 • OR
W • M-Derrick Engbretson — 12/05/98-3:00 p.m. • 8 • Crater Lake NP, OR
E • M-Ernest Matthew Cook — 04/22/99-10:30 p.m. • 27 • OK
W • M-Carl Landers — 05/25/99-10:00 a.m. • 69 • Northern CA
W • M-Todd Lucchesi — 05/31/99-Unk • 28 • Northern CA
NA • M-Michael Palmer — 06/04/99-4:00 a.m. • 15 • AK
NA • M-Joseph Wood Jr. — 07/08/99-2:00 p.m. • 34 • Mount Rainier NP, WA

E • M-Frank Downey	08/16/99-8:30 p.m. • 4 • KY
W • M-Jaryd Atadero	10/02/99-Unk • 3 • CO
E • M-Joseph Moore	03/11/00-Unk • 22 • WV
W • M-Kieran Burke	04/05/00-Unk • 45 • Yosemite NP, CA
NA • M-Marcus McKay	07/15/00-p.m. • 8 • MB, Canada
W • F-Rosemary Kunst	08/18/00-4:00 p.m. • 70 • Northern CA
NA • M-Tristen Myers	10/05/00-p.m. • 4 • NC
W • M-Patrick Whalen	11/02/00-Unk • 33 • Glacier NP, MT
W • M-Zbigniew Gajda	01/04/01-Unk • 42 • ON, Canada
E • F-Gloria McDonald	01/26/01-2:00 p.m. • 68 • AR
W • M-Michael Walsh	03/01/01-Unk • 56 • Yosemite NP, CA
W • M-Corwin Osborn	06/17/01-Unk • 45 • OR
W • M-Jason Franks	08/09/01-Unk • 21 • OR
NA • M-Gage Wayment	10/25/01-Noon • 2 • UT
E • M-Chris Thompkins	01/25/02-1:30 p.m. • 20 • GA
NA • M-Brian Douglas Faughnan	07/12/02-Unk • 35 • BC, Canada
E • M-Raymond Tunnicliffe	08/26/02-Unk • 79 • SK, Canada
W • F-Cecilia Barnes	09/01/02-Unk • 53 • OR
W • F-Teresa Schmidt	09/06/02-3:00 p.m. • 53 • CO
W • M-Walter Reinhard	09/20/02-Unk • 66 • Yosemite NP, CA
W • M-Jerry McKoen	09/21/02-Unk • 48 • Northern CA
W • F-Angela Fullmer	12/05/02-4:00 p.m. • 34 • Northern CA
E • F-Leeanna Warner	06/14/03-4:30 p.m. • 5 • MN
E • M-Michael Linklater	07/13/03-Unk • 44 • ON, Canada
W • M-Fred Claasen	08/01/03-Unk • 46 • Yosemite NP, CA
NA • M-Jimmy Rambone Jr.	09/03/03-3:00 p.m. • 51 • QC, Canada
E • M-Patric McCarthy	10/13/03-p.m. • 10 • NH
NA • M-Raymond Walter Wiggs III	10/24/03-a.m. • 19 • CO
W • M-Austin Sparks	01/04/04-a.m. • 15 • Northern CA
W • F-Joan Shelton	02/07/04-Unk • 65 • AZ
E • M-Christopher Hallaxs	03/17/04-Unk • 30 • MI
W • M-David Gonzales	07/31/04-8:00 a.m. • 9 • Southern CA
E • M-David Tippen	08/01/04-a.m. • 4 • GA
W • M-Garrett Bardsley	08/20/04-a.m. • 12 • UT
NA • M-Richard Lee	09/11/04-Unk • 47 • WA
W • M-Bart Schleyer	09/14/04-Unk • 49 • YT, Canada
W • M-Robert Springfield	09/19/04-4:00 p.m. • 49 • MT

List of Missing from this Book | 387

NA • M-Charles Huff	11/24/04-6:00 p.m. • 76 • FL
W • M-Doug Pierce	04/21/05-Unk • 86 • Sierras, CA
E • M-Charles Beltz	06/07/05-Unk • 56 • PA
W•M-Michael Ficery	06/15/05-Unk • 51 • Yosemite NP, CA
W • M-Brennan Hawkins	06/17/05-5:30 p.m. • 11 • UT
W • M-Gregory Brown	07/05/05-a.m. • 49 • WA
W • F-Nita Mayo	08/08/05-3:00 p.m. • 64 • Sierras, CA
W • M-Tom Howell	09/12/05-Unk • 46 • AB, Canada
W • F-Michelle Vanek	09/24/05-1:30 p.m. • 35 • CO
W • M-Wai Fan	09/28/05-Unk • 43 • AB, Canada
W • M-Kenneth Schneider	10/03/05-Unk • 78 • UT
NA • M-Tristan Owens	10/04/05-5:30 p.m. • 2 • MO
W • M-Roy Stephens	11/16/05-p.m. • 48 • OR
E • M-Christopher L. Jones	04/05/06-Unk • 37 • AR
NA • M-George Laforest Jr.	04/21/06-Unk • 45 • NY
W • M-Evan Thompson	05/27/06-a.m. • 8 • CO
NA • M-Jack Coloney	06/02/06-10:15 a.m. • 46 • NY
W • M-David Knowles	08/17/06-5:00 p.m. • 43 • Northern CA
W • F-Stephanie Stewart	08/26/06-Unk • 70 • AB, Canada
W • M-Samuel Boehlke	10/14/06-4:00 p.m. • 8 • Crater Lake NP, OR
E • M-Kory Kelly	10/16/06-7:00 p.m. • 38 • MN
W • M-Jonathan Betts	10/20/06-4:00 p.m. • 32 • AZ
NA • M-David Iredale	12/10/06-Unk • 17 • Australia
E • M-Jeremy Thomas	02/16/07-2:20 p.m. • 22 • GA
E • M-Michael Auberry	03/17/07-1:00 p.m. • 12 • Great Smoky Mtns, TN
W • M-Michael Bailey	04/20/07-Unk • 38 • ON, Canada
W • M-Robert Neale	05/02/07-Unk • 77 • AB, Canada
E • F-Hannah Klamecki	06/13/07-Unk • 5 • IL
E • M-Luciano Trinaistich	07/24/07-Unk • 69 • ON, Canada
NA • F-Ottorina "Trina" Bonaventura	07/30/07-Unk • 80 • Yosemite NP, CA
W • F-Christine Calayca	08/06/07-Unk • 20 • ON, Canada
NA • M-Daming Xu	11/04/07-p.m. • 63 • OR
NA • M-Nicholas Garza	02/05/08-11:07 p.m. • 19 • VT
W • M-William Pilkenton	02/15/08-Unk • 7 • BC, Canada
E • M-Joe Clewley	07/13/08-Unk • 73 • MI
W • M-James Arthur	07/28/08-Unk • 67 • Sierras, CA
E • M-Derrick Hennegan	08/04/08-4:30 p.m. • 35 • MI

W • M-Yi-Jien Hwa	08/11/08-Unk • 27 • Glacier NP, MT
E • M-Michael Edwin Hearon	08/23/08-Unk • 51 • Great Smoky Mtns, TN
W • M-Ronald Gray	09/19/08-Unk • 62 • ID
NA • M-Earl Funk	09/29/08-p.m. • 49 • VA
W • M-Christopher Andrews	10/03/08-3:00 p.m. • 42 • Yosemite NP, CA
NA • M-Fred Gillingham	10/12/08-Unk • 71 • NY
W • M-Wyatt Little Light	12/23/08-Unk • 2 • MT
W • M-Dwight Riggs	01/21/09-Unk • 61 • AZ
NA • M-Owen Castle	02/03/09-5:00 p.m. • 2 • TX
W • F-Nancy Moyer	03/06/09-7:00 p.m. • 36 • WA
W • M-Avery Blakeley	03/26/09-1:30 p.m. • 2 • ID
E • M-Joshua Childers	05/04/09-11:45 a.m. • 3 • MO
W • F-Lindsay Baum	06/22/09-9:15 p.m. • 10 • WA
NA • M-Douglas John May	07/16/09-5:30 p.m. • 55 • CA
W • M-Melvin Nadel	09/06/09-4:00 p.m. • 61 • NM
E • F-Madyson Jamison	10/08/09-2:00 p.m. • 5 • OK
E • F-Sherilynn Jamison	10/08/09-2:00 p.m. • 40 • OK
E • M-Bobby Jamison	10/08/09-2:00 p.m. • 44 • OK
W • M-Clinton Daines	10/16/09-Unk • 35 • UT
W • M-Anthony Green Jr.	11/06/09-Unk • 31 • Yosemite NP, CA
NA • F-Katherine Truitt	01/07/10-Unk • 37 • Point Reyes NP, CA
NA • F-Sylvia Lange	01/24/10-12:30 p.m. • 77 • Point Reyes NP, CA
NA • M-Charles Palmer V	04/10/10-7:00 p.m. • 30 • AK
W • M-Michael Hinsperger	05/13/10-Unk • 57 • ON, Canada
NA • M-Eric Lewis	07/01/10 • 57 • Mount Rainier NP, WA
NA • M-Tyler Wright	08/10/10-Unk • 35 • BC, Canada
NA • F-Paige Wilson	08/20/10-4:00 p.m. • 8 • WA
NA • M-Todd Hofflander	09/27/10-Unk • 39 • ID
NA • M-John Doe	10/01/10-7:30 p.m. • 3 • CA
NA • F-Patty Krieger	10/21/10-1:00 p.m. • 65 • WA
NA • F-Margaret Kohler	02/20/11-p.m. • 53 • OR
NA • M-Darcy Brian Turner	06/20/11-Unk • 55 • BC, Canada
NA • M-Michael Von Gortler	06/22/11-Unk • 53 • CO
NA • F-Makana Von Gortler	06/22/11-Unk • 20 • CO
NA • M-Scott Lilly	07/31/11 • 30 • VA
NA • M-Eric Robinson	08/07/11-Unk • 63 • UT
NA • M-Kevin Kennedy	08/21/11-Unk • 59 • AB, Canada

List of Missing from this Book | 389

NA • M-Gerald Deberry   10/10/11-6:45 p.m. • 53 • AK
NA • M-Robert Wood Jr.   10/23/11-2:00 p.m. • 8 • VA
NA • M-Steve Litsey   10/29/11-p.m. • 71 • OR
NA • M-Daniel Trask   11/03/11-Unk • 28 • ON, Canada
NA • M-Jason Elijah Burton   12/16/11-1:30 p.m. • 21 mos. • SC
NA • M-Colin Gillis   03/11/12-1:45 a.m. • 18 • NY
NA • M-Patrick Amen   06/15/12-p.m. • 40 • CA
NA • M-James "Jake" Dutton   06/15/12-Unk • 32 • OR
NA • F-Patricia Wallace   07/03/12-4:00 p.m. • 74 • CO
NA • M-Paul Michael Lemaitre   07/04/12-7:00 p.m. • 66 • M • AK
NA • F-Rhonda Cardinal   07/13/12-Unk • 42 • AB, Canada
NA • M-Robert Perry Bissell   07/24/12-Unk • 57 • OR
NA • M-Ronald Ohm   08/09/12-p.m. • 52 • OR
NA • F-Linda Arteaga   09/22/12-Unk • 53 • AR
NA • M-Kyle Camp   10/16/12-4:30 p.m. • 10 • AL

**When you study this list, you'll notice that many cases are separated by three to seven days. The second case will sometimes be on the opposite end of the continent. It almost appears as though there a distinct effort is being made to not raise awareness that there may be a pattern.

Total Cases on This List: 606
Total Cases from Previous List: 174
Total Cases: 780

Monthly Breakdown of Cases from Both Lists:
January   39
February   33
March   39
April   56
May   70
June   89
July   117 (High)
August   91
September   80
October   91

November	47
December	26 (Low)
Unknown	2
Total	780

Times of abduction were compiled from both lists.
**If the incident happened before fifteen minutes or forty-five minutes after the hour, it was placed at the previous half hour. If it happened after those times, it was rolled over to the next half hour.

Time	# of Cases	Time	# of Cases
Midnight	0	12:30 p.m.	3
12:30 a.m.	0	1:00 p.m.	19
1:00 a.m.	0	1:30 p.m.	9
1:30 a.m.	0	2:00 p.m.	31(Tied for 2nd)
2:00 a.m.	2	2:30 p.m.	11
2:30 a.m.	1	3:00 p.m.	25
3:00 a.m.	1	3:30 p.m.	12
3:30 a.m.	0	4:00 p.m.	33(High)
4:00 a.m.	2	4:30 p.m.	19
4:30 a.m.	0	5:00 p.m.	31(Tied for 2nd)
5:00 a.m.	0	5:30 p.m.	11
5:30 a.m.	1	6:00 p.m.	21
6:00 a.m.	1	6:30 p.m.	3
6:30 a.m.	0	7:00 p.m.	12
7:00 a.m.	1	7:30 p.m.	5
7:30 a.m.	2	8:00 p.m.	5
8:00 a.m.	4	8:30 p.m.	4
8:30 a.m.	2	9:00 p.m.	1
9:00 a.m.	6	9:30 p.m.	2
9:30 a.m.	1	10:00 p.m.	2
10:00 a.m.	12	10:30 p.m.	1
10:30 a.m.	9	11:00 p.m.	1
11:00 a.m.	8	11:30 p.m.	0
11:30 a.m.	6		
Noon	31		

List of Missing from this Book | 391

Unknown Times: 334
A.M.-Only Times: 27
P.M.-Only Times: 69

<u>Most Incidents in any Year</u>:
1958: 16
2013: 15
1949: 14
1953: 13
1957: 13
1951: 12

List Anomalies
<u>Back-to-Back Cases</u>:

NA • M-Larry Lewis   06/09/40-10:00 a.m. • 5 • CA
NA • M-Jim McGrath   06/10/40-Noon • 80 • MN

E • M-Murray Upshaw Jr.   11/08/40-Noon • 2 • GA
NA • F-Celsa Lucero   11/09/40-3:30 p.m. • 51 • NM

NA • F-Madeline Sowers   09/03/48-Noon • 2 • Virginia
NA • M-Lawrence Fustini   09/04/48-6:00 p.m. • 30 mos. • PA

NA • F-Marilyn Murphy   09/28/48-5:30 p.m. • 2 • Australia
W • F-Janet Federer   09/29/48-1:00 p.m. • 6 • WY

NA • M-H. B. Davis   10/08/48-p.m. • 72 • MT
NA • M-Mickey O'Connor   10/09/48-p.m. • 3 • WY

NA • M-Tommy Jenkins   05/04/50-Noon • 2 • WA
E • F-Anna Thorp   05/05/50-Unk • 2 • PA

NA • M-Jack Woods Jr.   10/29/56-p.m. • 3 • AL
E • F-Judy Rodencal   10/30/56-7:30 a.m. • 16 • WI

W • M-Walter Reinhard   09/20/02-Unk • 66 • Yosemite NP, CA

W • M-Jerry McKoen   09/21/02-Unk • 48 • Northern CA

NA • F-Patricia Wallace   07/03/12-4:00 p.m. • 74 • CO
NA • M-Paul Michael Lemaitre   07/04/12-7:00 p.m. • 66 • M • AK

<u>Disappearances on the Same Day in Different Locations</u>:

NA • M-Anthony Martini   06/28/58-2:30 p.m. • 11 • MA
NA • F-Denise Rowe   06/28/58-4:00 p.m. • 3 • NY

NA • M-Kevin Reimer   06/29/79-Noon • 9 • AB, Canada
W • F-Gayla Schaper   06/29/79-7:15 p.m. • 28 • WA

NA • M-Patrick Amen   06/15/12-p.m. • 40 • CA
NA • M-James "Jake" Dutton 06/15/12-Unk • 32 • OR

Victim Ages (Combination of Both Lists)

Age	M	F
4 Mos.	1	0
18 Mos.	4	3
2	69	34
3	53	37
4	43	10
5	13	15
6	17	6
7	9	4
8	15	7
9	16	2
10	15	4
11	7	2
12	7	0
13	4	1
14	7	1
15	7	2
16	4	6
17	7	0
18	5	2
19	7	1
20	7	3
21	11	2
22	14	4
23	6	0
24	2	2
25	4	5
26	4	2
27	6	1

28	8	3
29	3	2
30	9	0
31	4	1
32	4	1
33	2	2
34	3	1
35	7	1
36	5	1
37	5	2
38	3	2
39	3	0
40	2	1
41	2	1
42	3	1
43	2	1
44	4	0
45	3	1
46	5	1
47	1	1
48	5	1
49	6	2
50	2	1
51	4	1
52	2	0
53	2	5
54	0	1
55	8	0
56	2	2
57	3	1
58	2	1

List of Missing from this Book

59	3	0
60	3	0
61	3	0
62	4	0
63	3	1
64	6	1
65	4	2
66	5	1
67	3	0
68	0	1
69	4	1
70	3	2
71	2	2
72	2	0
73	2	0
74	1	1
75	1	4
76	1	2
77	1	2
78	2	0
79	2	1
80	4	2
81	0	0
82	1	0
83	0	1
84	1	0
85	1	0
86	1	0
95	0	1
Totals	539	219
Unknown	22	

National Parks

"A Lack of Integrity"
That's the quote I heard from a retired special agent from the park service when I asked him why his organization doesn't track and document missing people. His words, not mine.

Here is a list of national parks and monuments throughout the world where I have documented missing people.

<u>Australia</u>
Black Rock
Blue Mountains
Wilson's Promontory

<u>Borneo</u>
Mount Kinabalu

<u>Canada</u>
Jasper
Elk Island

<u>Ecuador</u>
Podocarpus

<u>United States</u>
Chiracahua
Crater Lake
Craters of the Moon
Glacier
Glacier Bay
Great Smoky Mountains
Lassen
Mesa Verde
Mount Rainier
Mount St. Helens
Olympic

Point Reyes
Saguaro
Sequoia/Kings Canyon
Shenandoah
Yellowstone
Yosemite

This list represents twenty-four locations of missing person cases where many individuals were never found. Yet, the US National Park Service doesn't believe it's important to track missing people and understand where, when, and how they disappeared. They told me that they rely on the "institutional memory" of their employees when they need background information on missing cases. In the twenty-first century, this is completely irrational and unnecessary.

I do find it interesting that many of the cases that qualified for inclusion in this book occurred at national parks in other parts of the world.

NAMUS

NAMUS: National Missing and Unidentified Persons System

The following excerpt describing this unique organization, which is sponsored by the National Institute of Justice (NIJ), comes directly from the NAMUS website:

> Although the problem of missing persons and unidentified human remains in this country has existed for a long time, significant progress has been made in recent years. In 2003, the DNA Initiative was launched. The Office of Justice Program's (OJP) National Institute of Justice (NIJ) began funding major efforts to maximize the use of DNA technology in our criminal justice system. Much of NIJ's work has focused on developing tools to investigate and solve the cases of missing persons and unidentified decedents.

The NamUs databases are just one element of a broader program to improve the Nation's capacity to address these cases. For example, NIJ also funds free testing of unidentified human remains and provides family reference-sample kits, at no charge, to any jurisdiction in the country. Other efforts include training law enforcement officers, medical examiners, judges, and attorneys on forensic DNA evidence.

In the spring of 2005, NIJ assembled Federal, State, and local law enforcement officials, medical examiners and coroners, forensic scientists, key policymakers, and victim advocates and families from around the country for a national strategy meeting in Philadelphia. The meeting, called the "Identifying the Missing Summit," defined major challenges in investigating and solving missing persons and unidentified decedent cases. As a result of that summit, the Deputy Attorney General created the National Missing Persons Task Force and charged the U.S. Department of Justice with identifying every available tool—and creating others—to solve these cases. The National Missing Persons Task Force identified the need to improve access to database information by people who can help solve missing persons and unidentified decedent cases. NamUs was created to meet that need.

The NamUs reporting and searching system will improve the quantity and quality of—and access to—data on missing persons and unidentified human remains. Through NamUs, a diverse community of criminal justice professionals, medical examiners and coroners, victim advocates, families of missing persons, and the general public now can contribute to solving these cases.

In December 2013, I was contacted by NAMUS's regional system administrator, Janet Franson. She introduced herself as a retired homicide investigator from Florida now working for NAMUS. She said that a colleague had introduced her to our Missing 411 books and research and wanted to know how we could work together to put some of our research on the NAMUS site.

NAMUS requires a police report to validate the missing person case, then a verbal confirmation from the law enforcement agency that the case can be indexed on the NAMUS site.

Because we have been able to obtain law enforcement reports for many of the cases we've researched, we were able to supply Ms. Franson and NAMUS with the following missing person cases for inclusion in the database:

Date of Incident/Name/Location
07/12/66-Dennis Johnson-Yellowstone NP, WY
10/19/73-Jimmy Duffy-Wenatchee, WA
04/29/81-Maurice Dametz-Douglas County, CO
10/08/85-Kevin Robert O'Keefe-Glacier Bay NP, Alaska
11/11/97-Chet Hanson-Mount Rainier NP, WA
07/14/99-Joseph Wood-Mount Rainier NP, WA
08/12/05-Zachary Weston-Mount Rainier NP, WA
06/17/11-George Penca-Yosemite NP, CA
06/08/13-Hildegard Hendrickson-Chelan CO, WA

While the list may look small, other NAMUS investigators have heard of our books and ordered reports for others to be included on the database. These are the actual cases where we supplied the reports to NAMUS. It is good to know that we are contributing our research to a national goal of documenting the missing on a searchable national site.

It's important to understand that there are medical examiners across the country who have rooms filled with unidentified bones—sometimes full skeletons. Once NAMUS has the names of missing people, they send out investigators to get DNA samples from relatives. DNA is taken from the unidentified bones, and those results will be compared to known DNA samples. It is hoped that unidentified remains will be given a name, be reunited with family, and be given a proper burial. To not know the fate of a missing loved one can devastate and forever change a person's life. Let's hope that we can continue to build onto NAMUS's site.

I sincerely hope that I have opened your eyes and changed your paradigm about people who disappear in the wild lands of the world. The addition of cases from ocean and air disappearances and reports associated with aerial crashes exemplifies the fact that there is still more to learn about these phenomena. Whatever is happening, it is a worldwide issue and not restricted to North America. I know this journey has been lengthy, but I believe we are getting closer to a full understanding of the facts surrounding the missing.

You and I have walked this path together. I know that with your assistance, we can have a substantial impact on the missing people of this world and bring resolution to many of the families who have been ignored by government agencies. Let's keep the pressure applied and keep these names in the public spectrum.

I always appreciate constructive feedback and new information. Please feel comfortable contacting me at Missing411@yahoo.com.

Keep up with our research at www.canammissing.com.

INDEX

A-
Abel, Joyce 211-212,
Abqjournal.com 162,
Accidents in Mountain Rescue
    Operations 84,
Ada Weekly 174,
Adam, Kevin 125,
Adams, David 212-217 (Photo),
Adams, Ronald 169-170,
Adams, Susan 106, 112-113
    (Photo),
Adriance, Paige 220-221,
Africa 308,
Afro American 126,
Agar, Carl 253,
Aiken Standard 62,
Alabama 1-2,
    Alabama Anniston Star 2,
    Birmingham 1-2,
    Double Oak Mountains 1-2,
    Shelby County 1-2,
Albany Herald 293-294,
Albuquerque Tribune 159,
Alford, Bob 197,
Amen, Patrick 23,
Apache Indians 3,
Apes, Bill 312,
Appalachian Trail 124-125, 184,
Arcaro, Eddie 100,
Aricayos, Roy 104,
Arizona 2-11,
    Beaver Creek Ranger
        Station 7,
    Dewey 8,
    Gila Bend 2-4,
    Maricopa County 3,
    Mount Floyd 5,
    Phoenix 3, 9,
    Red Rock Wilderness 6-8,
    Sedona 9-11,
        Oak Creek Canyon 11,
    Seligman 4-6,
    Vultee Arch Trailhead 7,
    Yavapai County 7, 9,
Arkansas 11-22, 174,
    Buffalo Wilderness 18,
    Iron Mountain 15,
    Lake Norfork 14,
    Little Rock 20,
    Marianna 12-14,
    Mountain Home 14-15,
    Mountain View 15-16, 21,
    Newton County 17-18,
    Onia 21,
    Pilot Mountain 12,
    Saint Joe 189,
    Village Creek State Park
        20,
    Waldron 11-12,
    White River National
        Wildlife Refuge 12,
    Wynne 20-21,
Arnold, Alice 184-185,
Arrow on Ground 86,
Arteaga, Linda 189,
Associated Press 88,

Atadero, Jaryd 47, 75,
Attorney 57, 80, 94,
Aubuchon, Gregory 69-70,
Aujay, Jonathan 46,
Australia 270-299,
    New South Wales 270-289,
        Blackheath 278-279,
            Golf Course 278,
        Blue Mountains
            National Park 270,
        Charlotte Pass 282-286,
        Collaroy 278,
        Goondiblule Station
            276-277,
        Hillston 274,
        Katoomba 270, 277,
            279, 281-282,
        Kosciusko National
            Park 282-283,
        Leura 270, 273-276,
        286-290,
            Elysian Rock 281,
        Linden 279-281,
        Mingindl 276,
        Mossgiel 274-275,
        Mount Kosciusko 285,
        Rose Bay 275,
        Tenterfield 271-273,
        Wentworth Falls 270-
            271, 277-279,
        Willandra National
            park 274,
    Queensland 290-294,
        Black Mountain
            National Park 293,
        Bowling Green
            National park 292,
        Broken Hill 291,
        Cocktown 293-294,
        Packsaddle Bore
            290-292,
        Ross River Dam 292,
        Toonpan 292-293,
    South Australia 294-296,
        Andamooka Station
            294-295,
    Victoria 296-298,
        Wilsons Promontory
            National park
            296-297,
    Western Australia 298-299,
        Cranbrook 298,
        Kojonup 298-299,
        Lake Magenta Nature
            Reserve 298,
        Stirling Range National
            park 298,
Austria 320-322,
    Autz Valley 320-321,
    Gamskarkogel Peak 320,
    Salzburg 320-321,

B-

Bagnall, Rachael 254-257,
Bakken, Julius 206-207,
Baltimore Afro American
    128-129,
Baltimore American 181,
Baltimore Ravens 134,
Barcus, Sandy 61-63,
Barger, Ray 60,
Barnum, Dave 16,
Beard, Brandon 202-203,
Beckett, ERd 96,

Beilhartz, Alfred 47, 55, 61, 74,
Belfast Telegraph 317,
Beloit College 303,
Benedict, Michaele 33,
Benson, Steve 53-55,
Bentzeil, David 181,
Berries xvii-xix, 17, 119-120,
123, 185, 265,
    Blackberries 34,
    Blueberries 259,
    Huckleberries 185,
Bigfoot xiii
Big Spring Herald 5,
Billings Gazette 52, 62, 65, 67, 246-247,
Bissert, Stefan 219-220,
    Fullbright Scholar 220,
Bittersweet Farms 169,
Bizup, Bobby 63-67, 199,
Black Blizzard 54,
Blakeslee, Jo Elliott 106, 115-119 (Photo),
Blimp 42,
Bloodhounds xx, 3, 5, 8-9, 15, 18, 21, 23, 27, 30, 37-38, 40, 42, 45, 53, 65, 76, 68, 77, 86, 88, 99, 107-108, 110, 114, 121-123, 129, 131, 141, 148-149-150, 158, 169, 170-171, 214, 218, 227, 248, 256,
Blount, Catherine 126,
Boeing 209,
    Radio Club 218,
Bogen, Helen 250-252,
Blue Ridge Parkway xxii,
Blytheville Courier 20,
Boltjes, Judy 67-68,

Bombardier, George 167-168,
Bone Disease 6,
Boogers 121,
Booth, Harley 60-61,
Borneo 300-302,
    Kuching 300,
    Mount Kinabalu 300-302,
    Sabah Parks 300,
Boston Daily Globe 151,
Boston News 152,
Boy Scout 62, 121, 148, 174, 190,
Boyd, Brian 132,
Box, George 17,
Box, Timothy 15-16, 21,
Bragg, Ann 1-2,
Brambles 129,
Brassaw, Ernest 119,
Brink, Matthew 135,
Brown, Karla 197,
Brown, Kevin 196-197,
Bryce, Kevin 213,
Buckley, Dan 114, 118,
Buffalo, Claude 109,
Bulletin 177,
Burdine, Tony 26,
Burns, Mack 3,
Burr, Ann Marie 41, 238,
Burton, C.H. 266,
Byrd, Mike 303-304,

C-

Cabrera, Thomas 42-44,
Calgary Daily Herald 268,
California 22,
    Alpine County 31,
    Bear Valley 30-32,

SAR Team 31,
Ski Resort 30-31,
Burney 23,
Butte County 26,
Butte Creek 25,
Caruthers 29,
Central Coast 32-39,
Central Sierra 27-32,
Crystal Springs Reservoir 334,
Dinkey Creek 29-30,
Fresno County 30,
Half Moon Bay 32-34,
Hall's Meadow 30,
Hatch Elementary 35,
Lake Arrowhead 44-46,
Lake Tahoe 30,
Los Angeles 3,
Los Angeles County 46,
Los Gatos 41-42,
Magalia Reservoir 25,
Menlo Park 39-40,
Milpitas 30,
Police 31,
Mount Burney 22-23,
Mount Shasta 24-25,
Paradise Pines 25-26,
Sacramento 25,
San Bernardino County 45,
San Diego 43,
San Francisco 33,
San Francisco Bay Area 39-42,
General Hospital 35,
San Mateo County 35,
Santa Clara County 42,
Santa Cruz Mountains 41,
Sequoia-Kings Canyon NP 30,
Shaver Lake 29,
Sierra Nevada Mountains 25-26,
Southern 42-46,
Stanford University 39,
State University-Long Beach 161,
University of California, Los Angeles 44,
University of San Francisco Medical Center 35,
Yosemite 27-29,
Callender, Sam 201,
Camden News 13,
Camp Carson 59,
Campbell, Emma 203, 205, 313-315,
Canada 250-269,
Alberta 250-252,
Gooseberry Lake Provincial Park 250-251,
Monitor 250-252,
Westlock 250,
British Columbia 252-259,
Harrison Lake 257,
Mount Currie 255,
Pemberton 254-257,
Pitt Lake 252-254,
Prince George 254,
Saxifrage Mountains 255,
University of 154,
Valentine Lake 255, 257,

Vancouver Island 256,
Whistler 256,
Manitoba 259-260,
    Fort Alexander Indian Reservation 259-260,
    Lake Winnipeg 259,
    Winnipeg 259,
Newfoundland xvii,
Nova Scotia 260-264,
    Little River Harbour 260-262,
    Melbourne 263,
    Shag Harbour 261,
    Yarmouth County 261,
Ontario 264-265,
    Brampton 285,
    Jawbone Lake 264-265,
    McKee Rivers 265,
    Porcupine 264,
    Timmins 264,
Quebec 265,
    Burnt Island 265-267,
    Lake Timiskaming 265-267,
Saskatchewan 267-269,
    Pelly 267-269,
    Swan River 268,
Canines xx, 21, 25, 68, 79, 93, 124, 137, 171,
Carbaugh, Emma 181-182,
Carbaugh, William 181,
Carney, Charles 123,
Carney, Lillian 123-124,
Carr, Eston 239-241,
Carr, Robert 239-241,
Carter, Joe 209-211,

Cascades xxi, 177,
Cass, Robert 151-152,
Cassidy, Ray 313,
Castellano, Elvirez 155,
Cave 144-145, 280,
    Diving 102-104,
Caviness, William 172,
CCC 54, 58, 154, 174,
Cell Phone 124-125, 135-139,
    Triangulation 136,
    Voicemail 93,
Chamberlain, Caroline 298-299,
Chandler, Floyd 55-57,
Charleston Gazette 159,
Chicago Daily Herald 82,
Chong, Ng 302,
Christensen, Jeff xv, 87-91,
Chronicle Telegram 194,
Citation (Horse) 100,
Civil Air Patrol 60-62, 79, 84, 117, 160,
    Crash 84,
Clarke's Beach xviii-xix,
Clothing
    Removed xx,
Clovis News 154,
Clusters xvi,
CNN 9, 306,
Cochrell, Leo 111,
Cocker Spaniel 25,
Coleman, Billy 23,
Colorado 46-96,
    Agnes Caille Falls 95,
    Animas River 47,
    Arapahoe County 76,
    Arapahoe National Forest 61,
    Archuleta County 79-82,

Bayfield 51,
Boulder 62,
Buena Vista 94,
Bureau of Investigation 80,
Cache La Poudre River 55, 57, 71, 75,
Chaffee County 95,
Cheesman Reservoir 76,
Clear Creek County 82-84,
Colorado A & M 60,
Colorado Springs 53,
Cottonwood Creek 95,
Deckers 67-68,
Denver University 75,
Douglas County 76,
Drake 61,
Durango 47-51,
Eldora 61,
Estes Park 58,
Fort Collins 55,
Georgetown 83,
Goat Rock 71,
Greeley 157,
Greyrock Mountain 71-73 (Photos),
Hinsdale County 78-82,
Jarre Canyon 52,
La Plata County 49,
La Porte 71,
Larimer County 73, 89,
Little South Poudre River 57,
Mount Chiquita 87-88,
Mount Columbia 95,
Mount Harvard 94-95,
Mount Missouri 94,
Mount Pendleton 83,
Mount Princeton 95,
Mount Ypsilon 88,
Ouray 47,
Pagosa Springs 50-51, 78-82,
Rampart Range 68,
Ridgeway 50-51,
San Juan National Forest 78-82,
Sedalia 68,
Silver Plume 82-84,
Stove Prairie 55-57,
Two Buttes 53-54,
University of Colorado-Boulder 94,
Winter Park 87,
Connolly, Patricia 39-41,
Connors, Johnny 290-292,
Cox, Wesley 162,
Cooper, Grace 265-267,
Courier News 16,
Courtney, Mike 66,
Cox, George 178-180,
Cox, Joseph 178-180,
Cramer, Red 41-42,
Craters of the Moon National Monument 115-119,
Crean, Stephen 282-284,
CTV.com 258, 286,
Cumberland Times 240,
Curry, Donald 187-189,
Cusack, Jerry 66,
Cusiter, David 281-282,

D-
Dailey, Nicholas 248-249,
Daily Ardmoreite 54,
Daily Interlaker 147,

Daily News 188,
Dailycamera.com 88,
Daily Signal 165,
Dametz, Maurice 52, 67, 75-78.
Daniel, Jewel 51,
Daniel, Vernon 51-52,
Dateline NBC 17-18,
Davies, Isabel 278-279,
Davis, Blair 190,
Davis, Perry 83,
Davy, Burton 60,
Dawson, Percy 48,
Dean Doris 201-202,
Death, Despair and Second Chances 65-66, 70,
Defense Intelligence Agency 226,
Dekkers, Kathryn 168-169,
De Rivera, Juan Maria 47,
Dehydration 6, 202,
Denton, Louis 152,
Denver Broncos 134,
Denver Post 79,
Department of Interior xvi, xxi, 8,
Deputy Sheriff 46,
Deseret News 114, 199,
Detroit Free Press 309,
D'Evlyn, Dwight 9,
Devil 310,
    Devil's Bridge Trail 7,
    Devil's Den 152,
    Devil's Gulch 60,
    Devil's Head Lookout 67,
    Devil's Head Mountain 67,
    Devil's Head Peak 52, 75,
    Devil's Nest 61,
    Devil's Orchard Nature Trail 117,
    Devil's Punchbowl 46,
    Devil's Slide 33,
    Devil's Thumb Lake 62,
    Hells Gate State Park 108,
Dilbert, Jacob 179,
Disability 126, 131, 309,
    Alzheimers 171,
    Autism 169-170,
    Asthma 149,
    Blood Condition 168,
    Brain Injury 200,
    Hearing 65-66,
    Lennox Gastaut Syndrome 296,
    Mental 131,
    Rheumatic Fever 68,
    Stroke 259-260,
Discovery Channel 103,
DNA 8, 74,
Dongo, Tom 7,
Dowell, Craig 144-145,
Drobney, Dan 84,
Duran, Jerry 125, 200,
Dutton, James xxi,

E-

Earl, Frank 177,
Easton Free Press 185,
Eau Claire Leader 242,
Eberhart, O.R., 55,
Ecuador 303-306,
    Banos 305-306,
    Podocarpus National Park 304,

Pontificia Universidad
    Catolica del Ecuador
    304,
Quito 306,
Zamora 303-305,
Edmonton Journal 251,
Ellensburg Daily Record
    208,
Elvander, Herbert 36,
Emporia Gazette 122,
Emsworld.com 153,
England-See "United
    Kingdom"
Erickson, George 120,
Eskridge, Edward 247-248,
Eskridge, Richard 247,
Eugene Register 197,
Evans, Joseph 65,
Evans, Thomas 59-61,
Evening Independent 96,

F

Fairies xvii-xix,
Fairmont Resort 287,
Farmer, Timothy 279-281,
Faust, Letisha Marie 203-205
    (Photo),
FBI xi, 27, 114, 139, 304,
Felker David Byrd 303-305,
Ferris, William 57,
Fetters, Dewey 54,
Fever xx,
Fielding, Joyce 276-277,
Finnerty, Cullen 130, 132-140,
    133 (Photo),
Fisher, Bud 2-4,
Flamingo Stakes 98,

FLIR 9, 18, 58, 114, 118, 169,
    171, 214, 312, 314-315, 317,
Florida 96-106,
    Chatham River 99,
    Clearwater 96-98,
    Collier County 100,
    Everglades City 99,
    Miami 100,
    Pasco County 96,
    Pensacola, 101,
    Rabbit Key 98,
    Sandy Key 97,
    Tamiami Trail 100,
    Vortex Springs 101-104,
Flying Saucer 313,
Flynn, Katie 133,
FOIA-Freedom of Information
    Act xv-xvi, 8, 28, 89, 118,
    233,
Forstmann, Gerd 220,
Forsythe, Stephen James 284,
Fort Worth Star Telegram 197,
Franklin News 205,
Frasier, Don 97, 99,
Free Lance Star 43, 201,
Fritz, Kurt 321,
Fugate, Paul xvi, 90,
Fullbright Scholar 220,

G

Galveston Daily 48,
Gaspard, Leo 252-254,
George, Gene 94-96,
Germans 42, 44-46, 219-220,
    228,
Germany 44-46,
    Magdeburg 44,

Otto Von Guericke
 University 44,
University of Stuttgart 219,
Ghost 18-19,
Gilbert, Glenis 273-274,
Gilliam, Earl 175-176,
Gillman, Gilbert Mark 226-227,
Glasgow Herald 293,
Goldstiver, Vivienne 292-293,
Govetts Leap 279,
Grand Canyon national park xxii,
Grand Valley State 134, 138,
Granite 29,
Grape Belt 183,
Gray, Myrtle 125-127,
Great Smoky Mountain National Park, TN xxii, 216,
Greeley Tribune 54, 56-57, 66,
Green, Silvia 277,
Gregg, Mike 43,
Griego, Timoteo 154-156,
Griffin, Katie 152-153,
Griffin, Stephen Rowan 152-153,
Grisdale, Madeline 259-260,
Guetz, Dale 62,
Gullett, Anna 275-276,
Gunn, Matt 255,

H

Haggitt, H.D. 40,
Hale, Joyce 17,
Half Moon Bay Review 36,
Hals, Eric 221-222,
Hamerly, Dailey 106, 108-109,
Harrington, Paul 161-163,
Harvey, Chris 78-82,
Haughney, Robert 191-192,
Hawaii 104-106,
 Kaanapali 106,
 Kapalua 105,
 Lahaina Mountains 105,
 Maui 104,
 Night Marchers 105,
Hayward Daily Review 25,
Helman, Jackie 207-209,
Helmick, Charles 192,
Helmick, John 239-241,
Hendrickson, Hildegard 94, 119, 228-232 (Photo),
Heng Ng Boon 300-302,
Henley, Michael 159-160,
Henn, Rainer 321,
Herald Journal 148, 172-173,
Hewitt, Neil 66,
Hialeah Park 98,
Hicks, Danny 172-173,
Hiester, Richard 65,
High Country News 92,
Hightower, Al 6,
Hildebrand, Patrick 296-298,
Hoag, Billy 144-145,
Hoag, Joey 144-145,
Hodges, Jack 4-6,
Hodges, Lloyd 4-5,
Hoeffliger, Ryan 41, 236-239,
Hohenstein, Danny 25-26,
Holz, Rainer 321,
Hoosier Democrat 69,
Hope Star 12,
Hotchkiss, Alfred 50-51,
Howard, Jimmy 100-101,
Howe Jr., Raymond 189-191,

Hoyt, Avery 183,
Hudson, Mike 16,
Huffington Post Xi, 21,
Hunt, Shirley 106, 111-112,
Hutchinson News 122,
Hutterite Colony 148,
Hypothermia xx, 6, 74,

I

Idaho 106-119,
    Bannock County 114,
    Battle Lake 113,
    Boise 107,
    Butte County 115,
    Caldwell 107,
    Coeur d' Alene 108, 236,
    Craters of the Moon National park 106, 115-119,
        Devil's Orchard Nature Trail 117,
        Tree Molds Trailhead 114,
    Downey 106, 113-115,
    Elk River 309,
    Hamilton 113,
    Hayden Lake 41, 236-239,
    Kootenai County 238,
    Lolo Creek 111,
    Moscow 106, 108-109,
    Nez Perce National Forest 106, 109-110,
    Payette River 107,
    Pocatello 114,
    Red River Ranger Station 109,
    Selway-Bitteroot Wilderness 106, 112-113,
    Snake River 107,
    Weippe 106, 111-112,
Idaho/Washington Border 234-239,
Illinois 119-121,
    Fox Lake 119-121,
    Grand Lake 120,
Indiana 69
    Michigantown 69,
Indiana Gazette 187,
Iola Register 58,
Ipock, Samuel 176-177,
Issaquah Press 214,
Ivey, Arthur Leo 234-236,

J

Jablonski, John 242,
Jackson, Susan 127-129,
James, Ellie 301-302,
James, John 145,
Jensen, Tom 218,
Jeppson, Reed Taylor 198-199,
Jette, Jonathan 254-257,
Jewett, Rose 309,
Johnson, Dennis 216,
Johnson, Roy 120,
Johnston, Bryan Lee 232-234,
Jones, Barbara Sue 12-14,
Jones, Jimmy 13,
Joplin Globe 15,
Jsonlinenew.com 304,

K

Kansas 54, 57, 121-123,
    Junction City 121-122,
    Smoky Hill River 121,
    Woodson County 57,

Yates Center Law
  Institute 57,
Kansas City Star 119,
Kelly, Kory 140,
Kennebec Journal 124,
Kennon, John Wesley 143-144,
Kentucky
  Derby 98,
Kibbey, Dave 137,
Killian, H.B. 196,
Kimball, Dan 227,
King Kamehameha 105,
KIRO.com 227,
KIVI.com 118,
Kleinbaum, James xxi,
Knapman, Paul 318,
Knights of Pithius 82,
Knoxville News Sentinel 34, 38,
Knoxville Sun xxii,
KOAT.com 161,
Kockman, Helen 243-244,
Koepke, Marvin 121-123,
Koester, Robert xxii, 4, 24, 42, 44, 63, 97, 107, 149, 159, 167, 192, 208, 212, 273, 275, 295,
KPHO 9,
Krost, Alyof 44-46,
KTHV 21,

L

Lake Superior 241,
Lakey, Asa Lee 22-24,
Lakota Sioux Tribe 7,
Lamm, Richard 76,
Lamy, Jimmy 169,
Landers, Carl 24-25, 301,

Landreth, Jackie 174-175,
Lang, Thomas 10-11,
Langston C.S., 13,
Largay, George 124,
Largay, Geraldine 124-125,
Larson, Anton 111,
Las Vegas Daily 157,
Leadens, Terry 84,
Leader Post 260,
LeClair Steve 256,
Lee, C.G. (Son of) 96-98,
Lee, Dave 26,
Legg, Douglas 169,
Lemurians xii
Lethbridge Herald 251,
Lewis, Mary 277-278,
Lewiston Daily News 129,
Lewiston Evening Tribune 124,
Lewiston Morning Tribune 108, 110, 111, 114, 116,
Linkert, Amelia 106, 115-119 (Photo),
Lists
  Aircraft Crashes 365,
  Aircraft Missing Same Day as People 366-367,
  Disabled or Injured 357-359,
  Cornerstone Cases 323-324,
  Criminal Allegations 333-337,
  Distance Traveled 361-365,
  Elevation Gain 360-361,
  Last in Line 339-346,
  List of Missing-This Book 367-372,
  List of Missing from Three Books 372-389,

Location Previously
    Searched 349-351,
Missing By Month 389-390,
Missing By Time of Day
    390-391,
Missing from Inside Home
    347-348,
Missing from Inside a
    Vehicle 348-349,
Missing Scholars/
    Intellectuals 352-357,
National Parks 396-397,
Victims Age 393-395,
Weather Conditions
    326-332,
Littlejohn, Lee 23,
Lock Haven Express 184,
Longview Washington Times
    210,
Lost Children of the Allegheny
    179,
Lost Person Behavior xxii, 4,
    24, 42, 44, 63, 97, 107, 149,
    159, 167, 192, 208, 212, 273,
    275, 295,
Lowell Sun 100, 129,
Lucas, Olga 193,
Lucas, Tina 192-194,
Luick, Bruce 249,
Lustig, Sonny 226,

M

Machado, Charlene 36,
Machishyn, Ludvina 267-269,
Madison, James 106, 109-111,
Magicvalley.com 118,
Maine 123-125,
    Acadia National Park 261,
    Appalachian Trail 124-125,
    Bates College 7,
    Baxter Park 124,
    Lone Mountains 125,
    Masardis 123,
    Mount Abraham 125,
    Mount Katahdin 124,
    Sugarloaf Mountain 124,
    Warden Service 124,
Manning, John 246,
Marathon Runner 24,
Mark Twain Rescue Squad 145,
Marsh, Lawrence (Son of)
    106-107,
Marsh, Roger xi
Martin, Dennis 216,
Maryland 125-129,
    Anne Arundel County 126,
    Baltimore 202,
    Bethesda 6,
    Chesapeake Bay 126,
    Chevy Chase 128,
    Churchton 125-127,
    Fort Meade 126,
    Hagerstown 181,
    Rockville 127-129,
    Sabiliasville 181-182,
    Seneca Creek 128,
Massachusetts 129-130,
    Carver 129-130,
    Institute of Technology 225,
McCarthy, Charles 179,
McClennan John 266,
McCullar, Charles 32,
McDaniel, Ben 101-104,
McFadden, J, 3,

McKinnon, Bill 221-223,
McMeans, J.D., 191,
McSherry, David 75,
Mesa Verde National Park 91-93,
    Cliff Palace 91,
    Petroglyph Trail 92,
    Spruce Canyon 92,
    Spruce Tree Trailhead 92,
Mexico 42-44,
    Tecate 42-44,
    Tijuana 43,
Miami News 196,
Michigan 130-140,
    Baldwin River 135,
    Colfax 133,
    Howell 134,
    Kent County 139,
    Lake County 135-139,
    Little Star Lake 138,
    Newaygo County 131-132,
    Paris 130-132,
    University of 94,
    Walhalla 133,
    Webber Township 132-140,
Microsoft xvi,
Miller, George 60,
Minnesota 140-143,
    Brainerd 140-143,
    Leech Lake Indian Reservation 140,
    Minnesota Hockey Camp 140-143,
    Pine River 140-143,
    Red Lakes Wilderness 140,
Miller, David Barclay 6-8,
    Photo 7,

Milwaukee Journal 49, 120, 241, 242-243,
Milwaukee Sentinel 68, 244, 253,
Missouri 143-146,
    Hannibal 143-145,
    Mexico 143-144,
    Murphy Cave 144-145,
    Whetstone Creek 144,
Missing Presumed Dead xx,
Mississippi
    River 12,
Moberly Monitor 61,
Monkman, Jerry 147-149,
Montana 27, 146-151,
    Bozeman 150,
    Choteau 147-149,
    Fuse Creek 147,
    Granite County 146,
    Hamilton 148,
    Judith Basin County 150,
    Little Bell Mountains 150,
    Meagher County 150,
    Mount Hughes 146,
    Mount Skalkaho 146-147,
    Mud Lake 146,
    Teton Canyon 148,
    Sapphire Mountains 146-147,
Montana Standard 146,
Montreal Gazette 268,
Morgenson, Randy 90,
Morning Herald 191,
Morning Sentinel 125,
Moscow Pullman Daily 221,
Mrs. Farrell's Son 271-273,
Mushrooms
    Morel 229,

Myers, Tristen 9-10,
Mysterious Sedona 7,
Mysteries Solved and Unsolved 307,

N
Nadel, Mel 161,
Nambe Mills 112,
NAMUS 397-400,
National Guard 13, 18, 108, 145, 218,
    Idaho 115,
National Park Service xiv-xvii, xxii, 27-29, 47-48, 73, 87-91, 219, 396-397,
    Craters of the Moon National Monument 115-119,
    Critical Incident Management Team 90,
    Mount Rainier National park 224-226,
        Comet Falls Trailhead 225,
        Van Trump Park 225,
    North Cascades National Park, WA 221,
    Olympic National Park 219, 224, 226-227, 232,
        Staircase Ranger Station 226,
    Wilson, Charis 89,
National Ski Patrol 209,
Nelson, Scott 47,
New Hampshire 151-154,
    Ashland 151-152,
    Bridgewater Mountain 151,
    Richmond 152-153,
Newell, Harold 263,
Newell, Howard 260-264 (Photo),
Newfoundland xvii,
New Mexico 154-163,
    Albuquerque 158,
    Baldy Peak 162-163,
    Chilili 158-159,
    Cibola County 160,
    Grants 159-160,
    Ledoux 156-159, 161,
    Leyba
    Manzano Mountains 158,
    Mount Baldy 160-162,
    Oso Ridge 159-160,
    Pecos Wilderness 161-162,
    San Miguel County 154,
    Sangre De Cristo Mountains 156, 161,
    Santa Rosa 156,
    Sky Line Trail 161,
    Villanueva State Park 154,
    Zuni Mountains 159-160,
New York 163-172,
    Adirondack Mountains 170,
    Ampersand Mountain 168-169,
    Brighton 167-168,
    Commac 165-166,
    Greenport 164,
    High Peaks 168-170,
    Indian Pass 169,
    Jamestown 182-184,
    Lake Placid 169, 171,
    Long Island 165-166,
    New London 167,
    Paul Smiths 167-168,

Plattsburgh 171,
Rocky Falls 169,
Rome 166-167,
Rouse Point 167,
Syracuse 166-167,
Tannery Creek 167,
Vermontville 167-168, 170-171
New York Times 10, 137, 165,
New Zealand 311-315,
   Air Force 312,
   Aoraki/Mt. Cook National Park 311-312,
   Canterbury 313,
   Christchurch 203, 313,
   Defense Forces 314,
   Lake Tekapo 312,
   Mount Cook 311-313,
      Mueller Hut 312,
   Mount Grey 313,
   Port Hills 313-315,
New Zealand Herald 314,
Nezza, John 24-25,
Nichols, Eddie 165-166,
Nielsen, Loren 114,
Night Marchers 105,
North Carolina 174-175,
   Falls Lake 172,
   Raleigh 172-173,
   Roseboro 9,
   University of 203,
   Wake County 172-173,
   Wake Forest 172,
North Cascades National Park, WA 221,
Norwood, A.E. 1-2,
Novanewsnow 262,
Nurse 92
   Pediatric 92,
Nutter, Henry 119-121,

O

O'Brien, Amy 316,
Ocala Star Banner 16,
Ohio, Akron 59,
   Bay Village 94,
   Toledo 169,
Okanagan Air Services 253,
Oklahoma 54, 175-178,
   Classen School of Advanced Studies 305,
   Cloudy 174-175,
   Highway Patrol 174,
   Kiamichi Mountains 174-175,
   University of 305,
Oleszczuk, Stephen 194-195,
Olsen, Harriet 167, 170-171,
Olson, Arnie 146-147,
Olson, Elmer 146,
Oracle Corporation 287,
Orange County Register 26,
Oregon 175-178,
   Bend 176,
   Heppner 175-176,
   Pendleton 175,
   State University 219,
   Tumalo Falls 176-177,
Oregonian 176,
Oregonlive.com xx,
Ostrom, Jack 264-265,
Otzi 320-321,
Owens, Richard 167,
Owosso Argus Press 122,

P

Pangelinan, Steve 31,
Pannich Oscar 5,
Parfitt, Owen 308-310,
Parker Stephen 166-167,
Parker, Ted 84,
Parkins, Keith 175,
Parnell, I. Byrd 193,
Parsons, Minnie 182-184,
Perron, Edith 48,
Peck, Gregory 98,
Penca, George 27-29,
    Photo 28,
Peninsula Daily News 234,
Pennsylvania 178-192,
    Allegheny National Forest 183,
    Bedford County 178, 186,
    Belleville 178, 187-189
    Blue Knob State Park 179,
    Conemaugh 178, 186-187,
    Fire Department 188,
    Gallittzin State Forest 179,
    Greenwood Furnace State Park 187-188,
    Highland Park 189,
    Ickesburg 178, 184-185,
    Lone Pine 192,
    Penn Township 190,
    Pittsburgh 178, 189-191,
    Sand Mountain 188,
    Somerset 186,
    Spruce Hollow 178-180,
    Strabane 178, 191-192,
    Washington County 192,
Perryopolis Junction 191,
Peterson, Jodi 92,
Philadelphia Record 164,
Phillips Lookout 279,
Photographers 210-211,
Physician 30-31, 94,
Physics 220,
Physician 255,
Pine River Journal 142,
Pittsburgh Post Gazette 24,
Pittsburgh Press 23, 52,
Pollard, Burt 123,
Pope John Paul II 64,
Post Standard 167,
Powers, Glen 62,
Press Republican 168, 171,
Professor 44-46, 228, 303,
Pueblo Indians 91,
Pullman Daily 221,

Q

Qombo, George 276,
Quintana, Ceferino 154,

R

Raleigh Register 239,
Rambone, Jimmy 150,
RCMP 253, 256, 258, 260, 263, 267-268,
Reading Eagle 212,
Record Journal 225,
Reiger, August 305-306 (Photo),
Reiger, Chris 306,
Reinhard, Keith 82-85,
Religion 8, 29,
    Latter Day Saints 213,
    Pontificia Universidad Catolica del Ecuador 304,

Pope John Paul II 64,
Saint Catherine of Siena, CO, 63,
Saint Malo Catholic Retreat, CO 63,
Saint Mary's Hospital, WI 303,
Saint Mary of Wasatch 199,
Theology (Phd) 75,
Rheumatic Fever 68,
Robinson, Jonathan 316-319,
Robinson, Kenny 158-159,
Rocky Mountain National Park xv, 47-48, 55, 57-61, 63-67, 69-70, 74, 85-86
    Bear Lake 85,
    Bear Lake Lodge 60,
    Chasm Lake 47-48, 69-70, 85,
    Devil's Gulch, 61,
    Devil's Nest 61,
    Fern Lake Trail 85,
    Flat Top Mountain 59-61,
    Glacier Basin Campground 69,
    Gunshots 88,
    Lawn Lake Trailhead 87,
    Long's Peak 69,
    Long's Peak Inn 47,
    Mount Chiquita 87,
    Mount Meeker 63 (Photo),
    Mount Ypsilon 88,
    Twin Peaks 58,
    Twin Sisters Peak Trail 58,
Rocky Mountain News 157,
Roosevelt, Theodore 91,
Roseville Girls College 278,
Roswell Daily Record 160,

S

Saint Catherine of Siena 63,
Salmen, Daniela 258,
Salmen, Raymond 257-259,
Salt Lake Tribune 51,
San Antonio Light 61, 121, 155,
San Jose Mercury 42,
San Jose News 40,
San Mateo Times 40,
Sanchez, Patrick 158-159,
Santa Fe New Mexican 113,
Santos, Irma 129-130,
Santos, Robert 129-130,
Sarasota Herald Tribune 68,
Saul, Benjamin 52-53, 67,
Schmidt, Theresa 67, 76,
Schoupan, Allen 72-73,
Schweitzer, W.C., 55,
Scott, Glen 188,
Scraba, Hazel 267-269,
Scuba Diver 101-104,
Seattle Times 225, 232,
Semiconscious 112, 130, 143, 281, 308,
Shear, Timothy 150,
Shields, Son 274-275,
Shimanski, Charlie 84,
Shooting
    At Cars 259,
Sierra Alpine Lodge 24,
Simon, Erika 320,
Simon, Helmut 320-321,
Simons, Jacqueline 133,
Siskar, Albert 218-219,
Siskar, Donald 217-219 (Photo),
Sisso, Kent 232,
Skull 48,

Slagle Jr., Kenneth 186-187,
Slater, Brad 200
Slumack 252,
Smith, Amber Rose 130-132,
Smith, Burt 79,
Smith, H, 13,
Smith, Frank 298,
Smith, Kerry 245-247,
Smith, Warren 155,
Smoke Jumpers 146,
Snelling, Bruce 84,
Snider, Al 97,
Snook, Susannah 309,
Somaki, Masami 311-313,
Somalia 226,
Sorensen, Eric 103,
Sorrel 34,
South America 255,
South Carolina 192-195,
    Dorchester County 194,
    North Charleston 194-195,
    Sumter 192-194,
Sparks, Austin 23,
Spencer, Cliff 92,
Spindler, Konrad 321,
Spokane Daily Chronicle 148, 235,
Spokesman Review 107, 148, 225, 237,
Spivey, Jim xviii,
Springfield, Robert 27,
Srawn, Prabheep 284-286,
St. Petersburg Times 98-99,
Stafford, Rob 18,
Stallman, Joseph 244-245,
Stark, Lee 210,
Stauffer, Joshua 106, 113-115,
Stauffer, Melanie 114,
Stauffer, Rodney 114,
Stehling, Dale 91-94 (Photo),
Strehling, Denean 92,
Stephens, James 235,
Strieber, Whitley xii
Strube, Lynn 145,
Sumter Daily 193,
Sun Sentinel 98,
Sunday Times Signal 202,
Swamps 141, 152, 297,
Switzerland 316-319,
    Eiger 316,
    Lauterbrunnen 316-319,
    Wengen 316-319,
        Blue Monkey Bar 316,
        Eiger Hotel 316,
Sydney Mall 272,
Sydney Morning Herald 273-274, 277, 279-281, 283, 291,
Sydney University 278,

T

Tampabay.com 102,
Targett, H. F., 47-48,
Taylor, Bradley 22,
Taylor, Eric 293-294,
Telegraph UK 318,
Tennessee 195-196,
    Great Smoky Mountains 34,
    Jasper 195-196,
    Knoxville 34,
    Marion County 196,
Terry, Scott 190,
Texas 196-198,
    Alvarado 196-197,
    Andrew 78,

Fort Worth 196,
San Antonio 3,
The Age 271, 292, 295, 297-298,
The Bulletin 176,
The Coloradoan 86,
The Item 301,
The Province 258,
The Telegraph 288,
Thomasville Times 241,
Thompson, Sam 174,
Thong, Lau King 300-301,
Times Herald 59,
Tingwall, Andy 162,
Thompson, Bill 42,
Thoru, L. J. 100,
Thunderstorm 20, 197,
Tienhaara, Tara 223,
Timmins Times 265,
Toledo Blade 170,
Toronto World 266,
Trammell, Landen 21-22,
Trapp, Emmett 8-11,
Treece, Joan Marie 14-15,
Tribe
    Midgets 116,
Trott, Otto 210,
Trotter, C.H. 97,
Trujillo, Celestino 156-158,161,
Turner, Margaret 48-50,
Turner, Pearl 11,
TVNZ 314,
Tweddle, Gary 270, 282, 286-290 (Photo), 318,

U
UFO 234,
Ukiah Daily 17,

Ultra Top Secret Clearance 227,
Unconscious 166, 183,
Union Democrat 31,
United Kingdom
    Cornwall 301,
    Cremorne 286,
    Gloucester 307,
    Midland Railway 307,
    Newcastle University 316,
    Shepton Mallet 308-310,
United Nations 34, 226,
United States Army
    Air Corps 60,
    Cavalry 121,
    Fort Carson 79, 85,
    Fort Meade 126,
    Helicopter Crash 99,
United States Navy
    Moffitt Field 42,
United States Air Force 5, 59, 110, 159,
    Griffith Air Force Base 167,
    Lowry Field 59, 62-67,
    Luke Air Force Base 5,
    Malmstrom Air Force Base 150,
    Mather Field 23,
    McChord Air Force Base 213,
    Shaw Air Force Base 193,
    Tinker Air Force Base 214,
United States Coast Guard 98,
United States Forest Service 7-8, 22, 217,
United States Postal Service 150,
University of Oregon xxi,

University of Toledo 134,
USS Pueblo 213,
Utah 198-201,
    Cache County 200,
    Emigration Canyon 198,
    Hardware Ranch 125,
    Logan 200,
    Salt Lake City 198-199,
    Salt Lake Tribune 3,
    St. Mary of Wasatch 199,
    Uinta-Wasatch-Cache
        National Forest 200,
    Wasatch Mountains 199,

V

Valedictorian 225, 305,
Van Brunt, Stockton 165,
Veatch, Skip 31,
Vermont
    Bennington 152,
Victoria Advocate 79, 93,
Vigil, Chris 47, 55, 71-74
    (Photos)
Virginia 201-206,
    Blue Mountains 202,
    Craigsville 202-203,
    Floyd County 204,
    Franklin County 203-205,
    George Washington
        National Forest 202,
    Patrick County 203,
    Shenandoah National Park
        201-202,
Von Gortler, Michael 94,

W

Wagner, Alvin 5,

Waldner, David 148,
Ware, Hickle Harley 140-143,
Washington 206-234,
    Ape Canyon 210,
    Badger Pocket 206-209,
    Bellingham 221,
    Boardman Lake 206,
        220-221,
        Boardman Lake Trail
        220,
    Chelan County 231,
    Church Mountain 206,
        221-222,
    Coleville Indian
        Reservation 211,
    Ellensburg 207,
    Fish Lake 207
    Granite Falls 220, ,
    Grass Mountain 206,
        217-219,
    Howard Hanson Reservoir
        217,
    Issaquah 212-217,
    King County 214, 218,
    Meadow Creek 207,
    Milwaukee Bowl Ski
        Resort 209,
    Moses Lake 233,
    Mount Baker 221,
    Mount Rainier National
        Park 206,
    Mount St. Helens 206,
        209-211,
        Spirit Lake Lodge 209,
    Okanogan 206, 211-212,
    Olympic National Park 206,
        219-220,

Deer Lake 220,
Hoh River Valley 220,
Soleduck 220,
Snoqualmie National Forest 217,
Spokane 108, 234-236,
Squaw Creek 208,
Tacoma 41, 213, 238,
Tiger Mountain 206, 212-217,
University of Washington Medical School 116,
Wenatchee 94, 119, 206-207,
Wenatchee Lake 206-207, 212, 228-232,
Western Washington University 221,
Whatcom County 222-223, Letter
Yakima 207,
Washington/Idaho Border 234-239
Washington Post 6,
Waters, Anna Christian 32-39, Photo 33,
Waters, George 34-35,
Way, L.C. 69,
Weather xii,
Control 332,
Weaver, Dayton 164,
Weaver, George 164,
West Virginia 124, 239-241, Davis, 239-241,
Weston, Zachary 224-226,
White, Hoyt 57-59,

White River 12,
Wilkins, Harold 307,
Willis, Robert 29-30,
Wilson, Charis 89,
Wilson, R.R. 147,
Winters, Robert 32,
Wisconsin 119, 241-245,
Ashland 241-243,
Collins Marsh State Wildlife Area 243,
Killsnake State Wildlife Area 2432,
La Crosse County 244,
Lake Superior 241,
Porcupine Mountains State Park 241,
Quinney 241, 243-244,
University of 303,
Washington 241, 244-245,
Wolenetz, Sarah 875-87,
Wong, Katherine 30-32,
Wood, E.O. 42,
WMUR 152,
Wyoming 245-249,
Casper 246, 248,
Cheyenne 69,
Great Falls 248,
Green River 247-248,
Kaycee 246,
Muddy Mountain 248-249,
Natrona County 248-249,
Outlaw Canyon, 246,
Powder River 245-246,

X

Xu, Daming xxi,

Y

Yamamoto, Megumi 160-162,
Yarborough, Maretha 11-12,
Yarbrough, Henry 195-196,
Yellowstone xxii,
Young, Tom 83-84,
Young, Vincent 292,
Youngstown Vindicator 248-249,
Yosemite xvii, xxii, 27-29,

Z

Zega, Haley 17-18,
Zook, Ellis 188,